Visual Research Methods in Architecture

by Igea Troiani
(University of Plymouth)
and Suzanne Ewing
(University of Edinburgh)

Bristol, UK / Chicago, USA

First published in the UK in 2021 by
Intellect, The Mill, Parnall Road, Fishponds, Bristol, BS16 3JG, UK

First published in the USA in 2021 by
Intellect, The University of Chicago Press, 1427 E. 60th Street,
Chicago, IL 60637, USA

Copyright © 2021 Intellect Ltd

All rights reserved. No part of this publication may be reproduced,
stored in a retrieval system, or transmitted, in any form or by
any means, electronic, mechanical, photocopying, recording, or
otherwise, without written permission.

A catalogue record for this book is available from
the British Library.

Cover designer: Aleksandra Szumlas
Copy-editor: MPS Ltd
Production editor: Helen Gannon
Typesetting: Contentra Technologies

Hardback ISBN: 978-1-78938-186-3
ePDF ISBN: 978-1-78938-187-0
ePub ISBN: 978-1-78938-188-7

Printed and bound by Hobbs the Printers

To find out about all our publications, please visit
www.intellectbooks.com.
There, you can subscribe to our e-newsletter,
browse or download our current catalogue,
and buy any titles that are in print.

This is a peer-reviewed publication.

Visual Research Methods in Architecture

Contents

Introduction: Visual research methods and 'critical visuality'   1
Igea Troiani and Suzanne Ewing

PART I – DRAWINGS AND DIAGRAMS: DISCIPLINARY SEEING AND KNOWING   33

1. Is the plan dying?   35
   Peter Blundell Jones
2. Analogical Images: Aldo Rossi's *Autobiografia Scientifica*   43
   Susanna Pisciella
3. How to draw a line when the world is moving: Architectural   58
   education in times of urgent imagination
   Tariq Toffa
4. Drawing as being: Moving beyond ways of knowing,   76
   modes of attention and *habitus*
   Ray Lucas
5. Learning to see: Otto Neurath's *Visual* Autobiography   95
   Valeria Guzmán-Verri
6. Duration and anexactitude: What is at stake with data-based   112
   urban drawing in research?
   Miguel Paredes Maldonado

PART II – PHOTOGRAPHY: PRESENCE AND POSITIONING AS A RESEARCHER   125

7. Looking at photographs: Thinking about architecture   127
   Hugh Campbell
8. Architecture's discursive space: Photography   141
   Marc Goodwin
9. Desert Cities   158
   Aglaia Konrad
10. Visual methodology on display: Taking photographs of *Separation*   176
    Shelly Cohen and Haim Yacobi

11. Visaginas: Looking at the town through photography 188
Povilas Marozas

12. Writing with pictures: Reconsidering Aby Warburg's *Bilderatlas* 201
in the context of architectural scholarship, education and Google Images
Willem de Bruijn

PART III – FILM: AFFINITIES AND APPROPRIATIONS FOR RESEARCHING 215
CONTEMPORARY CULTURE

13. Next to nothing: Psychogeography and the 'film essay' 217
Gavin Keeney and David Jones

14. Ciné-Cento: Eisenstein's visual methodology and the space of film 231
Niek Turner

15. Constructing an architectural phenomenography through film 247
Ruxandra Kyriazopoulos-Berinde

16. An animated portrait of Casa Malaparte: Filmic practice as design 260
research in architecture
Popi Iacovou

17. Exploring, explaining and speaking in tongues: Visual scholarship 276
and architectural education
Lesley Lokko

18. The plasmatic image: Experimental practices between film and architecture 287
Morten Meldgaard

PART IV – MISCELLANEOUS MIXED MODES AND NEW MEDIA 297

19. Visual agency: Participatory painting as a method for spatial negotiation 300
Agnieszka Mlicka

20. 'just painting': Performative painting as visual discourse 317
Tonia Carless

21. Visual heuristics for colour design 335
Fiona McLachlan

22. Digitally stitching stereoscopic vision 353
George Themistokleous

23. Audio-visual instruments and multi-dimensional architecture 370
Mathew Emmett

24. Kaleidoscopic drawings: Sights and sites in the drawing of the city 387
Sophia Banou

Notes on Contributors 403
Index 411

Introduction: Visual research methods and 'critical visuality'

Igea Troiani and Suzanne Ewing

Architecture is a visual, textual and corporeal discipline as well as a spatial and material one. However, unlike geography or ethnography, both of which have evolved methods of visual research in their fields, visual research methods in architecture are poorly defined. In this book we take lead from cultural geographer, Gillian Rose ([2001] 2012: xix) who defines 'critical visual methodology' as, 'an approach that thinks about the visual in terms of the cultural significance, social practices and power relations that produce, are articulated through and can be challenged by, ways of seeing and imagining'. In *Visual Methodologies*, Rose ([2001] 2012) offers a series of qualitative methodological strategies that focus around different types of imagery to aid visual interpretation in cultural geography research. Qualitative interpretation of the visual can address questions of cultural meaning and power differently, sometimes more appropriately, than quantitative methods (Rose [2001] 2012: 3). Acknowledging the rise and consolidation of visual research methods across the social sciences in the past 20 years, such as visual ethnography, image-elicitation interviews and visual participatory research, Rose (2015) observes that the value of visual research methods has emerged as the capacity to: generate evidence that other methods cannot; invite different registers of affect; reveal the 'taken-for-granted' and enrich participatory and action research. These methods have a particular strength in qualitative, people-centred research projects. She argues that beyond making sociological and ethnographic work 'visible', there is a potential performative approach to the making of images as well as their examination (Rose [2001] 2012: 10). Visual research methods may extend possibilities beyond just interpretation of visual material – and use of the visual in communication of research findings – to critique and perform practice-based 'critical visuality'.

Like cultural geography, architecture is a discipline that uses practice-based methods where representation is a valid, productive and interpretative domain. *Visual Research Methods in Architecture* reviews research practice that traverses humanities and creative practice-based research. In addition to the fact that there is no consolidated literature on visual research methods in architecture, this book's originality is in setting out ground for how visual research methodologies may be explicitly and distinctively activated in architectural research and interdisciplinary scholarship, following leads in visual culture studies. It does not attempt to engage with de-contextualized quantitative and descriptive dimensions of data visualization or mapping as research, but instead emphasizes the generative, analytical and culturally situated practices of visual research methods. Contributing authors demonstrate and extend the practice knowledge of architectural research by responding to what is distinctive or specific about the architect's gaze, what might be made visible and how 'visuality' is understood and used as a method by research practitioners from a range of disciplinary positions, traditions and experiences. From established to emerging researchers, researcher-practitioners to media-specific practitioners, with backgrounds and topics traversing Europe, the United States, Australia and Africa, and from different disciplinary backgrounds, contributors to the book explore and use 'critical visualizations'. They represent a variety of voices, writing styles and nationalities, showcasing important variations in immediacy and relevance of modes of writing and subject, some being more artistic, experimental or open-ended than others. Most of the essays are testimonial. Oral or written testimonies – accounts of and for practice – are deeply personal, experiential, rare and embedded in methodological approaches that are not easy to corroborate or verify with other sources. The contributions in this book have been selected and edited to bring to the fore the varied and often implicit visual practices of architectural researchers, whether emergent, experimental or consolidated and expertly practised. This is a new and negotiated territory that employs positive interdisciplinary risk-taking. Authors observe and provide critique through the creation of visual texts including drawings, diagrams, photography, film, paintings, visual devices and their hybrid forms. Particularly where observation is combined with sociocultural critique, the contributors cumulatively probe how use of visual methods for qualitative research creates more eloquent and effective visual literacy and agency so as to inform our understanding of occupied space and architecture.

The book intends to appeal to historians and theorists of design, as well as to architectural educators and practitioners. The outset of this volume (and our editorial position) is an observation that research practice in architectural humanities currently slips between two main modes: history/theory text-based discourses, and the visual production of architectural design. By exploring 'critical visuality' and explicitly promoting visual literacy and agency, the book aims to examine this research space 'slippage' in order to foreground inter-related knowledge generation. A 'balanced diet' approach to the book's content, operating between and combining representation styles and modes, is at the core of our study of visual research methods in architecture. Valuing 'critical visuality' and 'critical visual practice' anchors the book's purpose and argument.

The key findings from the assembled material make conclusions about the condition of 'critical visuality' as a kind of practice; what 'critical gaze' means in relation to the architect or architectural researcher; visual reciprocity; and dimensions of visual labour and capital – as aspects of 'critical visualization'. 'Critical visuality' is defined here as a way of using vision to intellectually and intuitively critique architecture and space. Aesthetic appreciation and aesthetic interpretation are deeply embedded in our sociocultural constructs of beauty and ugliness that determine our design morals, practice approaches and environments. Philosopher Donna Haraway (1988: 581) has argued for reclaiming a metaphorical reliance on vision to avoid limiting binary oppositions and to deepen nuanced understanding of situated knowledge. Time-based drawings, diagrams and videos allow for space and time to be included in the research and for 'critical visual' analysis to become an actively open process. The combining of different visual media can facilitate exchanges that were previously not possible. Vital though, is that 'critical visuality' when applied by an architectural researcher-practitioner allows for a deeper, socioculturally positioned response to space that might otherwise be neglected. Visual research methods in architecture are shown in particular to expose and inform understandings of the complexities and constructions of social life situated in culture and space, and how it is transformed. The assembled research in the book's chapters demonstrates how working with varied visual media can positively inform architectural research as not only didactic description but as a means to structure disciplinary thought.

The book is arranged in four parts, each foregrounded by an 'Orientation' and structured by the primary visual media in which the research manifests: Part 1 Drawing and Diagrams, Part 2 Photography, Part 3 Film and Part 4 Miscellaneous Mixed Modes and New Media. Sometimes chapters feature one or more visual media. The flow is from well-established or naturalized representation techniques in architecture (Drawing, Photography, Film) to a final section that encompasses emergent, innovative and hybrid research methodologies which explore and expose 'critical visual' practices as disciplinary and interdisciplinary.

Each of the four 'Orientations' of the book are purposely opened with a 'grounding' extract from a key architect or theorist practising in the field of visual studies – Perry Kulper, Sigfried Giedion, Denise Scott Brown and Mike Webb – to set a tone for the media being examined in each part. They also indicate the need to further explore questions of 'critical visuality' in histories and cultures of particular disciplinary formations and traditions. The subsequent series of chapters in each part are then broadly ordered into three sections that traverse: Techniques and Tools of Thinking Architecture and Visual Culture; Practising Architecture and Visual Culture Research and Teaching Architectural Research and Visual Culture.

Part 1 – *Drawing and diagrams: Disciplinary seeing and knowing*

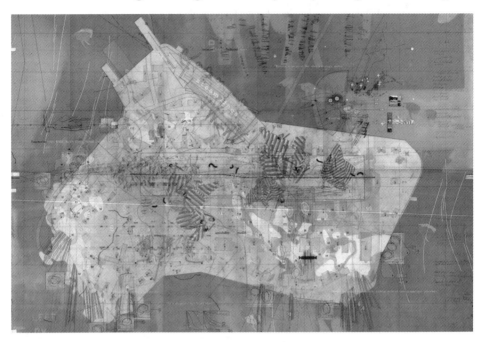

Figure 1: David's Island Strategic Plot Drawing made: 1996–97 Drawing size: 24" x 36" Materials: Mylar, graphite, ink, tape, found imagery, x-rays, foil, photographs, transfer letters and transfer film, cut paper. © Perry Kulper.

The book aims to present a range of interdisciplinary approaches that open up territory for new forms of visual architectural scholarship.

> Partially, as a result of allowing uncertainties to enter drawings I have enjoyed freedom of many kinds. A more relaxed and accommodating approach has allowed me to work 'creatively' (always a dangerous word) in broadened ways by supporting expanded relational capacities in the drawings to discuss things that might not otherwise be in play. I try to visualize and support ideas long enough to see if they might be relevant to a project in the long run. Increasingly, I am less judgmental about possible ideas for a project, especially in the early phases of a project – about whether everything in play is suitable for the piece of work. Depending on what I am working on I often make drawings, or parts of drawings that are not targeted at a synthetic building proposal, but are specific in their intent – studying erasure as a possible representational and spatial activity, for example.
>
> (Kulper 2012)

INTRODUCTION

The medium of drawing is a 'key disciplinary ally for architecture' (Kulper 2013: 59). It is a technique of thinking and actioning architecture. Contemporary architectural practitioner, researcher and educator, Perry Kulper (2013: 59) speaks of his drawing research as constructing 'an emerging visual field of study' and of approaching his work through 'modes of visualization' where 'visualization and thinking are fused as a relational and synthetic practice'. He describes his drawings as 'visual constructions', 'visual formulations', 'visualized species' or 'visual curiosity cabinets' that offer 'embroidered relationships and abstractions, known and discovered' that aspire to 'a new species of spatial vision with ethical and participatory ambitions' (Kulper 2013: 59–63; 2014: 20–22). This rich, saturated graphic field resists definition as either pure design or pure research practice. Yet it is a uniquely architectural field of precise inquiry, substantiation and conclusive definition, a place to discover, expose and realize, as in his 1996–97 'David's Island' drawing (Figure 1). 'David's Island' is explicitly set up as a representation to ask questions, to 'formulate', to literally give form to a question. It is a space of enquiry of material and spatial conditions for action that sets the tone for a critical drawing practice in architecture. Kulper demonstrates a way of constructing a different mode of [design] practice that has traction 'to discover', re-discover, inform, synthesize and be understood as a method of research *through* practice.

Kulper researches through his own drawing practice. This is perhaps partially recognizable as a model of artistic practice – the artist-researcher-author with auto-ethnographic tendencies. Kulper (2014: 30) acknowledges the need for conceptual artistic risk, but also 'practised restraint'. As an individual practitioner, modes and methods of production are self-conscious, 'tailored' and traverse a balanced tension between conceptual risk-taking and daring to draw (Kulper 2014: 22). In his graphic drawing practice, Kulper knowingly borrows from composited, typographic printing technologies and techniques, two-dimensional descriptive geometry and three-dimensional rendering, activating both the analogue and digital. However, his drawing work is not solely graphic. He sees visualization as directly connected to spatial and programmatic thinking specific to architecture. This is drawn from deep disciplinary knowledge of the ways that architectural drawing has consciously operated in relation to the construction of architectural space (Perez-Gomez and Pelletier 1997).

An example of drawing operating in relation to architectural space is the medieval Saint Gall monastery, drawn as a plan by Eugène Viollet-le-Duc, and the protagonist of Chapter 1 in the book, entitled 'Is the plan dying?' by the British architectural historian, **Peter Blundell Jones**. Blundell Jones contends that Viollet-le-Duc's drawing is a literal *grounding* of a project, working 'from the plan up' in detail. The plan is both a drawing and a diagram, consolidating what a building and a community are about. In contrast to Viollet-le-Duc's monastery plan, Blundell Jones observes the visual demise of the architectural plan drawing in printed architectural media today and interprets this as part of a waning in cultural and social discourse in western architecture. Perspectival views offer instantaneous visual spatial gratification with little work required on the part of the viewer. Having established the plan's embodiment of idealized and actualized 'social life', Blundell Jones notes the influence of Michel Foucault's examination of plans as instruments of power, and Henri Lefebvre's attention to socially produced space. If the plan's role in relation to social and spatial organization and order has been diminished in current architectural renderings, then an inability to 'order' the world, and to navigate social life – in both design process and in critical reception and production – is at stake.

Built works that can be visited and recorded and archives and publications of original drawings and models are primary sites of disciplinary architectural knowledge. How does an architect draw from these in their research practice and imaginative invention? Chapter 2 responds to this question in the example of architect Aldo Rossi's *A Scientific Autobiography* published in 1981, following a 1976 exhibition of Rossi drawings. Rossi's practice is situated in a particular international moment of critiquing the modern movement, foregrounding questions of memory and the city. Italian academic **Susanna Pisciella's** research on this treatise re-constructs an image archive based on Rossi's textual references in the chapter, 'Analogical images: Aldo Rossi's *Autobiografia Scientifica*'. Pisciella questions how an architect constructs and uses a visual archive, 'building his own memory archive into "a universe of analogies"'. Following René Daumal and others, analogy is shown to be the particular methodology that Rossi uses to produce new visual and drawing knowledge. Analogy allows Rossi to tell tales, to build stories – though not exactly visual arguments – to set up architectural drawings and designs. Rather than work on impressions, Pisciella systematically selects 'chains' of Rossi's images to demonstrate Rossi's deeply 'critical visual' practice. The treatise by Rossi has the quality of a drama, script or public performance more than the intimacy of a novel and single author-reader experience. Therefore, the reader-viewer's imagination is an active participant in making their own interpretations through Rossi's visual findings and associations.

What is or should architecture and architectural research concern itself with in a globalized, contested twenty-first century? This question drives **Tariq Toffa's** architectural pedagogical practice at the University of Johannesburg. Chapter 3, entitled 'How to draw a line when the world is moving: Architectural education in times of urgent imagination' by Toffa, argues that architecture's contemporary purpose is to produce agency rather than products. Arguing that globalization neglects the social, Toffa contends that an ethical imagination in drawing is needed to generate new visions and voices. Drawing from Arif Dirlik's argument about the inseparability of the aesthetic and the social, Toffa exposes the power relations inherent in Euro-American-centric 'visibility' as having a significant influence on architectural design pedagogy and spatial designers. Through speculative, mixed-media drawing work, promoting a dialectic method and working explicitly *with* difference, Toffa's studios explore research inquiries and conditions informed by methodological tactics of 'voicing', 'multi-modality', 'siting (surfacing)', 'spaces of publics', 'territory', 'perspective' and 'reflexivity'. Noting the recent shifts in sociology and art history, where 'sociological reflexivity' is used as a research tool (d'Oliveira-Martins 2014: 193), the aim of Toffa's and his students' pedagogic work is to refocus an ethical imaginary that transcends and re-writes disciplinary and racial conventions through site-specific actions. Drawing can make social power relations visually tangible and Toffa's essay makes an original contribution by presenting new drawing practices for research that decolonizes and emancipates space and architectural education.

The practice of making and working with drawings, diagrams and notations is demonstrated as a distinct visual research method for architecture by British-based academic **Ray Lucas** in Chapter 4, 'Drawing as being: Moving beyond ways of knowing, modes of attention and *habitus*'. Theoretically extending Pierre Bourdieu's (1992) concept of *habitus* to Martin Heidegger's philosophy, and drawing on the work of anthropologist Tim Ingold, Lucas posits drawing as a way of operating in the world. He sees the exchange as a contextual entanglement. Lucas asks whether drawing can be considered as a mode of being and orientates an approach to the ways that the drawings have been acculturated in the specific and socially enacted practices that define everyday life. Through his own drawing practice, traversing architecture and anthropology, Lucas shows drawing as part of research, as a form of theoretical inquiry and field/work: a 'graphic' anthropology. Like Blundell Jones, Lucas notices a 'death of [hand] drawing' in architecture. Lucas calls for a changing role and potential of hand drawing in relation to understanding who drawings are for. Against a reading of Georges Bataille's asymmetrical power relations embodied in gift giving, Lucas sees the exchange of drawings as a practice of distributing selfhood. He concludes that not all drawings are, or should be, shared because drawing operates as an aspect of self-development, and this exploration is fundamental to developing an evolving critical drawing practice.

The political and communicative project of visual language offering discursive statements in relation to opening a new reality is explored in Chapter 5, 'Learning to see: Otto Neurath's *Visual Autobiography*' by **Valeria Guzmán-Verri**. Austrian philosopher of science and sociologist, Otto Neurath aims to understand and assemble informative wholes to drive modernism and the modern movement. His 1937 text, 'Visual representation of architectural problems', led to the project

From Hieroglyphics to Isotype: A Visual Autobiography. This developed Neurath's (2010) interest in the experience of learning to see, of visual education and the democratization of knowledge, in visual experience and in drawing as play. Guzmán-Verri traces Neurath's argument that a visual consciousness, understood as 'knowing how to see well' (Didi-Huberman 2009: 198) is deeply experiential, contextual and playful. Following Georges Didi-Huberman and Walter Benjamin, Guzmán-Verri researches Neurath's work and influence on artists such as Harun Farocki. From her findings, Guzmán-Verri contends that a decisive difference in positioning, when attending to info-scapes, can shape new visual consciousness. She argues that there is an urgency to address and understand the agency of visual data in contemporary discourse and world making, namely, what is made visible, what is overlooked or not seen, where agency lies. In so doing, info-society as info-scape is understood as a dissolved, distributed, desiccated condition, brought out through the critical visual examination of material.

How the architect might use their gaze as part of their research practice for the purpose of visual literacy in navigating and constructing this world is discussed in Chapter 6 'Duration and Anexactitude: What is at stake with data-based Urban Drawing in Research?' by Spanish architect and academic **Miguel Paredes Maldonado**. Digital data spatial intelligence in urban research and design is prevalent in contemporary drawing representation. However, the smart city paradigm is shown to be problematic because it is generated through top-down, assembled 'wholes' (de Landa 2016). Paredes Maldonado asks whether it is possible to articulate a data-based infrastructural counter-project that subverts these urban narratives of optimization, efficiency, atomization and top-down 'smartness'. This chapter offers data-based urban drawing research practice from architectural design studios run by Paredes Maldonado in Cagliari, Sardinia in April 2017 and subsequently posits the 'anexact' drawing research methodology that is used in the studios, which embeds durational data with as much status as the gleaned quantitative information. The combination of data and generation of the data visualizations is reflected on by Paredes Maldonado as a visual research method that follows Bernard Cache's approach to defying existing productive paradigms, looking for 'other means' to philosophize. Gilbert Simondon's concepts of technical ensemble and transferences form a theoretical framework for the re-positioning of this visual research.

Ways of seeing, imagining, drawing and diagramming can be both general and specific. Architectural drawing always presses on the 'imagined'. Kulper (2013: 63) shows that drawing tools are not singular, and if several are employed simultaneously or accumulatively, it is their relational aspects that then also need to be attended to. Drawing codes and conventions in disciplinary architectural 'seeing' have inbuilt significance, inflected by expertise of the reader-interpreter

INTRODUCTION

(Blundell Jones), standpoint (Toffa), *habitus* (Lucas) and ways in which seeing has been learnt (Guzmán-Verri), accumulated and used analogically (Pisciella), or practised through critical data visualization (Paredes Maldonado). When extending critical visual methods into qualitative architectural research, it is in the area of articulating and challenging social practices that critical visual research methods of drawing seem to offer the most relevant and precise tools. Architecture already knows that conventional drawing methods of research and representation are not innocent in design practice. The disciplinary history of architecture has accumulated different modes and methods of drawing as tools of spatial practice. They are entangled with power and control when actively utilized in critical formulating, mapping and spatial planning practices.

Part 2 – Photography: Presence and positioning as a researcher

Figure 2: Sigfried Giedion's formatting of his own photographs of the Pont Transbordeur in Marseille (taken in January, 1927) when designing pp. 62f of *Bauen in Frankreich* as published in Harbusch (2015) (copyright: gta Archives/ ETH Zurich) + *Journal of Architecture*/ Harbusch.

> I have found it preferable, in order to arrive at a true and complete understanding of the growth of the new tradition, to select from the vast body of available historical material only relatively few facts. *History is not a compilation of facts, but an insight into a moving process of life.* Moreover, such insight is obtained not by the exclusive use of the panoramic survey, the bird's eye view, but by isolating and examining certain specific events intensively, penetrating and exploring them in the manner of the close-up.
>
> (Giedion [1946] 1967: vi, Foreword to the first edition; italics in original text)

As Gregor Harbusch (2015: 609) has shown, social architectural historian, Siegfried Giedion's ([1946] 1967) seminal work, *Space, Time and Architecture*, was an ongoing process of architectural research through close looking and photography during site visits, 'a pivotal moment of insight' informed by his individual viewpoint. Following his teacher, art historian, Heinrich Wölfflin, and against the expectations of his publisher, Giedion fought for the necessity of more images in his publications, which were significantly augmented in reprinted editions. There are 321 photographs in the 500 pages of the 1946 fifth edition. This was driven by an ambition – shared by Harvard University Press who published the book – to open the work to a wider public. The project was therefore one of both conventional scholarship and interpretation for a non-specialist audience, which relied on the original visual images as an important means to engage both audiences. The project's roots are in the communicative domain of a lecture series. Giedion's book-directing role, with Herbert Bayer and László Moholy-Nagy, in the production of the synthesized printed publication, demonstrates his attentiveness to the reader, with carefully directed instructions for use highlighting the role of text, images and comment as all crucial to the reader's experience. As Harbusch (2015) demonstrates, Giedion's overarching explicit intention was to promote modernism as the 'new tradition' through his scrupulous visual research. This is achieved through techniques and methods of photographic 'correspondences' – the often juxtaposed photographic images on page spreads – as a conceptual backbone to his research. The inter-relations between text and images were of primary concern to Giedion's framing and substantiating of his argument about modern architecture.

Space, Time and Architecture is unusual in its encounter with the historian's deliberate presence through his notes, comment-captions and photographs, which demonstrate the author's particular experience of travelling to the site or project: argued as architecture's constituent, rather than transitory, facts (Figure 2). Giedion ([1946] 1967: 11–17) further offers readers an insight into his personal research position, discussing 'The Identity of Methods'. He argues for a renewed conjunction of thinking and feeling through history as an active way of living, and the historian as being the agent bringing rigorous constituent facts to attention through direct engagement and affective experience. This argument is founded in a desire to work across sciences and arts, including sociology and psychology, with the primary aim to 'observe seriously' (Giedion [1946] 1967: 4). His project is deliberately visual and transdisciplinary, juxtaposing photographs of contemporary architecture, often fragmented views, with archival drawings, paintings, sculpture and scientific devices. A close-up photograph of a soaring iron structure is placed adjacent to one of Edgar Degas's stage-lit ballet dancers; a time lapse photograph of a golf swing motion is juxtaposed with a collage of a variety of angled views of the Rockefeller building, New York; images by Francesco Borromini are next to Vladimir Tatlin's work etc. This montage method of 'comparative reading of artistic expressions from different epochs' (Harbusch 2015: 598) offers a breadth of visual references that condense and reduce the nuances of the main research argument to a plea for modernization. The balancing of the visual, textual and commentary aspects of *Space, Time and Architecture* is dynamic but is a carefully considered, structured choreography of a broad range of photographic evidence.

The chapters in the 'Photography' section of the book explore the use of photographs both in terms of a researcher's repertoire and choreography, and also as research which is a positioned practice. The oversimplified view of architecture being 'served' by photography, or as just a subject matter for photography, is addressed by Irish academic **Hugh Campbell** in Chapter 7 'Looking at photographs: Thinking about architecture'. In it, Campbell questions the shared impulses and modes of the two disciplines. Both architecture and photography frame the world and human behaviour. How is space then shaped, framed and inhabited? Campbell identifies two tendencies as the shared ground – fleeting moments of wonder, and depictions of the larger social scene – which he discusses through the work of photographers Rinko Kawauchi and Alec Soth. Scholarship on the relationship between architecture and photography often sets one practice up as more dominant, and therefore research methods and paradigms unquestionably follow the prevailing discipline. However, the possibilities of an augmented capacity for alertness and attentiveness, following Pierre Bourdieu's (1992) *habitus*, are argued by Campbell to recognize making and meaning considered equally. Campbell contends that the history, theory and practice of photography is *always* at play with architectural design and research practice in the photographs of John Szarkowski and Stephen Shore.

The act and scope of seeing and reading photography is probed by London born, Helsinki-based architectural photographer **Marc Goodwin** in the analysis of his own, and other contemporary, commercial photography in Chapter 8 'Architecture's discursive space: Photography'. Goodwin's comparative visual analysis of the practice-based research finds that the acceptable norms of visualizing development in the global economy are for clear blue skies, uninterrupted interiors and symmetrical shots. Corporate clichés create and perpetuate significant visual capital flowing through the catalogues and advertisements of real estate agents worldwide. Commercial photographic image-making displays architectural design as white buildings, wooden floors, neat theatre interiors. The commodification (or commons) of visual data varies from open source to prescriptively copyrighted. However, production value is not simply economic, with the photographer working with a significant surplus of images and skilled judgement and invention. Goodwin's visual research method responds to the corporate landscape in which he practices. Employing superficially similar modes of search categorizations on platforms such as Google images, and with reference to the everyday photographic practice of contact sheets, Goodwin extends his research practice to the assembly of alternative sets of images drawn from the surplus visible material only usually available to the photographer rather than the public. Goodwin argues, much as Lucas does, for a self-driven generous production of visual material through which to focus a 'critical (commercial) gaze'.

Austrian photographer and educator, **Aglaia Konrad,** searches in her photographic praxis for the decision making on a political and economic level that has led to the built phenomena of rapid urbanization. She aims to uncover and translate these phenomena into an artistic vocabulary presented to the public for their critique. As an artist, she describes the encounter with the unexpected as entailing 'more than noticing', requiring active engagement with found conditions. Konrad's Chapter 9 entitled 'Desert cities' shows a contextualized practice of photography, recalling Giedion's foregrounding of the constituent facts of architecture through site visits. The research subject is vast in scope – sixteen cities in Egypt, located in an inhospitable, arid context. Konrad's chapter in this volume notes that she does not want 'to be an artist who also acts as an anthropologist, or a geographer, or a *journaliste*'. The perspective and positioning of her *Desert Cities* project is based on her evolved, iterative artistic photographic practice, a project of primarily making the invisibility of the decision making have some sort of visibility. The constructed images of Konrad's visual essay are positioned in careful relation with each other, on image sheets that create a space and ground for reading and interpreting according to similarity, difference, scale and proximity. Konrad's exposure constitutes what it means to live in the harsh conditions of the desert in these particular configurations of distinctly urban forms and embodies her own subjective gaze as an artist-photographer.

The capacity of photography to critique the ordering of society is evident in the exhibition 'Separation' that includes both interior and exterior subjects. Israel/

Palestine-based urban researchers and curators of 'Separation', **Shelly Cohen** and **Haim Yacobi,** explain in Chapter 10 'Visual methodology on display: Taking photographs of *Separation*' how the exhibition of commissioned photographs is reorienting Israeli architectural discourse from the aesthetic to political and social dimensions. As an indexical series of twelve large images of the separation wall in Jerusalem, the photographs show the materiality of the wall and question what spatial demarcation and boundary mean. Is spatial separation also social separation or are there slippages, reinforcements and resistances between these? Does the focus on the apparent material definitiveness of the spatial separation actually expose tactical possibilities for transgressions and unforeseen social relations? Through their attentiveness to the empirical, the evidence on the ground, and as Toffa explored in Chapter 3, Cohen and Yacobi engage in a form of critical visual decolonization and deterritorialization. What their visual research uncovers are different viewpoints, a sense of transcendence of the situation with hope, encounters with 'the other', yet a sense of fear. In the exhibition project, the photographers and curators work together, allowing space for varied practices and visual interpretations.

With a sensitivity towards the specificities of the production, dissemination and reception of architectural imagery and as an advocate for the abandonment of the role of the aesthetic connoisseur-interpreter of architecture, Lithuanian landscape architect **Povilas Marozas** pleads for reflection on different, and sometimes differing, 'contextual' visual positions. In Chapter 11 entitled 'Visaginas: Looking at the town through photography', Marozas reviews four different photographic interpretations of the twentieth-century Lithuanian town: as heroic communal efforts (by Vasilij Chiupachenko); everyday use of place (by Vitaly Bogdanovich); nostalgic documentation and disengagement in decline (by Gintaras Čésonis) and empty atmosphere (by Nicolas Grospierre). Marozas does not simply read the photographs taken by the photographers as an archival source for research but sees that they have potential to be read as practice signifiers of place definition. With an architect-photographer's gaze, he positions interpretation and situated research as a practice of performed photography, where his own photography is formulated as an active visual research method for reading place. Marozas' theoretical apparatus is built from Victor Burgin's materialist analysis of photography where practices of signification, explored through semiology, psychoanalysis and use-value involve the viewing subject. Donna Haraway's (1988) embodied knowledge production, and particularly her approach to embodiment of vision informs Marozas' visual research practice, alongside Irit Rogoff's (2006) performative mode of production that activates situated knowledge and a wider community of knowing the self in relation to place.

Conventional art history scholarship positions the photographic image in the service of the written word. In Chapter 12, 'Writing with pictures: Reconsidering

Aby Warburg's Bilderatlas in the context of architectural scholarship, education and Google images', UK-based artist and academic, **Willem de Bruijn** exposes an alternative visual research method – Warburg's 'pictorial argumentation' in his 'reading' room, where images are part of a visual and spatial performance in the Bilderatlas. The pictorial motifs construct a mental thought-space, a mnemonic experience that becomes a history with its own pivot points and movement. De Bruijn offers an example of this by discussing the dancing maenad in Warburg's Alberti Panel. As a visual research method, the Bilderatlas is an immersive, dynamic textual and visual script. De Bruijn scrutinizes the contemporary work of images through the Google search engine, as a source of such digital online atlases. He finds that there are similar possibilities for composition, narration and performance in Warburg's and Google Image Search's approaches. However, the algorithmic functions are shown to be limiting. Critical insertion or disruption of the linked search results are restricted, in contrast with the way that the dancing maenad acts in Warburg's visual research. De Bruijn argues that writing with pictures will have to become *common* practice as much as a *critical* practice because it allows for exploring and developing new forms of architectural inquiry.

Photography has been the focus of much work in social science and cultural geography on visual research methods (Pink 2001, 2007; Rose [2001] 2012: 297–327). The visual construction of social life in the twentieth century, and of western cities in particular, has been entwined with histories of photography, the emergence of the photographer-author and the photographic image (Rose [2001] 2012: 11–15). Giedion's lengthy re-working of his book, of the correspondences between text and images and between different visual elements in the space of the page, shows the complexity of visually editing and communicating an argument about contemporary architecture and cities. While the exchanges between architecture and photography are long-standing, there are shared impulses and modes (Campbell) that can be distilled and that may activate an external audience's move from aesthetic to political concerns (Cohen and Yacobi). The photographic practitioners included here (Goodwin, Konrad, Marozas) use their honed skills to inform and inflect their research practice and the questions that address underlying decision-making frameworks and implicit expectations of the commissioned (or not) series. The revisiting of Warburg's innovative, immersive, dynamic, situated work and the photographic images in his collection (De Bruijn) is positioned as an overlooked form of pictorial argumentation. It has much resonance with our need to navigate the saturated online visual landscape skilfully and with stamina, as well as to construct new critical practices of 'writing' with pictures as a more inclusive, explicitly authored and interpreted approach in an algorithmic search era.

INTRODUCTION

Part 3 – Film: Affinities and appropriations for researching contemporary culture

Figure 3: Preparation for Las Vegas deadpan film shoot, Las Vegas, 1968. Photo by LLVRS. Copyright Princeton University, School of Architecture.

'You don't think, you shoot', she [Scott Brown] says. 'Because by the time you've worked out with yourself why you want that thing, it's gone'.
(Scott Brown cited in Anna Fixsen 2016)

The idea of an affinity between architecture and film is implicit in both *The View from the Road* and *Learning from Las Vegas*. The potentially distracted – cinematic – gaze of the car driver confronts the roadway engineer with the task of framing and directing the automobilized observer's perception of the city: 'The cinema tells its story with dramatic changes in the separation between camera and actor, from close-up to long shot depending on what is being said. So it is on the city highway: the designer can decide what he wants to emphasize – a total skyline, a distinct character, a single landmark – and adjust the viewing distance accordingly. As in the cinema, contrasting distances will keep his sequences legible and eventful' (Appleyard et al. 1964: 11). Engineer and architect become directors of the gaze. The films produced by Venturi and Scott Brown and their students in the Learning from Las Vegas Research

Studio attest to this attitude, which makes the visual survey of the existing city a prerequisite for architectural design.

(Stierli 2013: 184)

Another seminal book from the architectural canon in which the role of the visual is a practised, generative scholarship rather than illustrative of the written argument is Robert Venturi, Denise Scott Brown and Steven Izenour's (1989) *Learning from Las Vegas*, first published in 1972. It was the result of the interdisciplinary Learning from Las Vegas (LLV) studio run in 1968 by the three architects at Yale. It involved spending 'three weeks in the library, four days in Los Angeles, and ten days in Las Vegas' with thirteen students – 'nine students of architecture, and two planning and two graphics students' (Venturi et al. [1972] 1989: xi). According to Stadler and Stierli (2015: 15), 'The central goal was to obtain an understanding of the automobile-oriented city and to find an adequate image for it'. The design research method used by Venturi, Scott Brown and Izenour involves the architect changing their tools of representation from photography and analytical drawing to filmmaking (Figure 3). Instead of only sketching the urban landscape, they 'picked up cameras and treated architecture from the perspective of appearance and phenomenon' (Stadler and Stierli 2015: 9). Scott Brown et al. identify new techniques of film and video recording and analysis as vital to their research project on architectural signage experienced sequentially along the street. Some 40 years after *Learning from Las Vegas* was published, art and design theorists Hilar Stadler and Martino Stierli in collaboration with the artist Peter Fischli (2015) re-read the iconic photographs and films from the LLV studio. Beyond the more well-known influence of artist Ed Ruscha's 'deadpanning' methodology of recording everyday life and landscapes, they locate the origins in a broader field of popular visual culture practice, such as movie-making. For instance, the video *Las Vegas Electric* (1968) – a four-minute car journey focused on the Las Vegas strip signage at night time, was structured sequentially so as to follow George Sidney's opening sequence in his 1964 movie, *Viva Las Vegas*, starring Elvis Presley as racing car driver, Lucky Jackson.

Other researchers at the time, such as Reyner Banham in the film *Reyner Banham Loves Los Angeles* (1972), experimented with newly available media and technologies of the time to engage with American culture. Making some 125 short films from 1950 to 1982 – of which arguably the best known is their cinematic representation of the relative size of things in the universe, *Powers of Ten* (Eames and Eames 1977) – Charles and Ray Eames (2012) employed creative, sometimes advertising driven, filmmaking to explore architectural design, history, theory and narrative in interdisciplinary ways. Visuality was heightened through close looking and transference to the printed page and through large-scale multi-screen projection, which broadened spectatorship and the dissemination of their research findings.

INTRODUCTION

In Chapter 13 'Next to nothing: Psychogeography and the 'film essay'', landscape researchers, **Gavin Keeney** and **David Jones** advocate observing nature and the world in their pedagogic practice that might inform more nuanced and less interventionist urban landscape making, such as the 'Third Landscapes' of Gilles Clément (2009). Critical of contemporary modern landscape design practice in Australia that they read as complicit with constructing a world denying nature, their proposition is for a more radical mode of filmic landscape design practice to be found in the artistically grounded 'film essay'. When applied to environmental design disciplines, the 'film essay' acts as a critique of the usual rules and biases of project design development and presentation methodologies. Keeney and Jones argue that the 'film essay' can uncover new theoretical paradigms in the realization of built projects. Video investigations in design education studios examine post-industrial conditions and appropriate the methodological practice of the 'film essay' as counter to the conventional site master plan. The authors outline the origins of the 'film essay' as practised by Alexandre Astruc, Jean-Luc Godard, Chris Marker, Tacita Dean and Harun Farocki. In their chapter in this book, Keeney and Jones advocate filmic narrativity and playfully excessive, experimental storyboarding in landscape architecture pedagogy as a means to unsettle programmatic and methodological biases, where the landscape architecture image is not singular but 'endlessly returns to the *mélange*'.

Film, as intimately tied to the experience of modernity, underpins Chapter 14 'Ciné-Cento: Eisenstein's visual methodology and the space of film'. Irish-based academic, **Niek Turner** examines the Soviet revolutionary filmmakers, who used montage in film and film theory as a new way of seeing the world. He focuses on Sergei Eisenstein's theoretical essays that explicitly employ visual research. Informed by Walter Benjamin and contemporary computer scientist Lev Manovich, Turner examines the role that space plays in Eisenstein's (1925) most famous film, *Bronenosets Potemkin* (*Battleship Potemkin*) through a series of new visual methods, made possible by ongoing development in computing and software. The software allows the visual researcher to study film as one would study text and to explore spatial and architectural qualities. An observed lack of engagement in recent architectural history and theory research with new visual technologies may be limiting the capacity of knowledge generation and insight, in the way that Eisenstein's own research methods clearly impacted on filmic and spatial practice and thinking. The capacity of computers to manipulate and analyse vast amounts of visual data including film sequences and individual shots opens up new ways of analytical and visual critique previously not possible.

Chapter 15, 'Constructing an architectural phenomenography through film' by Romanian and British educated researcher **Ruxandra Kyriazopoulos-Berinde,** focuses on how meaning and memory of home are communicated through selected films by the Russian filmmaker, Andrei Tarkovsky. The phenomenographic methodology used in this research covers diverse textual and visual material. Phenomenography emerged in the 1970s as a qualitative research method focused on describing the various ways in which a phenomenon is experienced by a certain number of people (Bowden 1996: 49–66). Kyriazopoulos-Berinde's chapter in this book contends that 'In phenomenographic research, the products are a flux of descriptions that grasp into more depth the plurality of modes inscribed in the experience itself'. Ulrich Sonnemann's (1954) term, phenomenography, was coined to differentiate from phenomenology and encompasses a description of experience that extends from the hermetic to the communicative and inter-subjective. As an empirical research method, phenomenography can address the qualitatively diverse ways that one phenomenon may be experienced by a number of people, seeking to establish thematic patterns, parallels and differences. While usually limited to textual and discursive media, Kyriazopoulos-Berinde re-reads and reclaims the term in her research to include audio-visual communication of experience and explains the steps of the phenomenographic method she uses to visually analyse the films. This leads to constructing categories of cinematic architectural experience.

Chapter 16, 'Building an audio-visual portrait of Casa Malaparte: Performative research between site analysis and architectural and interior design' by architectural researcher and performance artist, **Popi Iacovou,** works with an iconic building that has also featured in a number of films including Jean-Luc Godard's (1963) *Le Mépris*. While the exterior view is well known, its private ownership means that the interior view is rarely accessible. Iacovou's research acknowledges an embedded position, including her living in the house and filming her experience of it, which leads her to argue that her audio-visual research outputs should be understood as an ongoing 'building script'. Her approach to research is to develop a strategy for 'performing' this ongoing project, using film, stills, archive material and mixed media animation in order to research the experience of living in Casa Malaparte. She conceives this as a hybrid visual method of occupational portraiture. As performative research, it aims to embody the past, present and potential life of Malaparte's idiosyncratically designed house, analogous to the individually painted, drawn or photographed portrait of a person. Iacovou proposes that the unique role of the 'architect-performer' is that they are able to address the limits of architectural representation to include lived experiential and atmospheric dimensions of designed space, deliberately working with points of cinematic view, episodes and composed sound through collages of 'found' material.

Being outside the established set pieces of the architectural canon is the context of Chapter 17 'Exploring, explaining and speaking in tongues: Visual scholarship and architectural education' by South African-based architecture academic and writer, **Lesley Lokko**. It responds to the earlier question of what should architecture and architectural research concern itself with in a globalized, contested twenty-first century. In the context of post-2015 South Africa, this question is integral to the values embedded and transmitted in architectural education and is a vital part of the decolonizing of knowledge taking place across South African cities, institutions and young African students. Lokko works in the space of constructed tension between conventional ways of understanding architecture and more speculative means of investigation that respond and are directly generated from what is actually 'on the ground' in African cities. Particularly important is acknowledgement of the lack of written word in the majority of African cultures, where intimacy and performance (oral storytelling and community building) are more significant. 'How to see' what is going on in African cities is a fundamental and necessary, although complex, foundation for any research project that aims to re-think education curricula. Modes of exploring rather than explaining are paramount. It is in this gap that the visual research method uses – in, for instance, Lokko's *Eclectic Atlases* films of Spintex Road in Accra – can have most effective visual, social and political agency.

Chapter 18 'The plasmatic image: Experimental practices between film and architecture' by Danish academic **Morten Meldgaard** reflects on the term 'transvisuality' (Kristensen et al. 2015a) and explores 'how' contemporary film operates as part of post-industrial mediascapes and within fluxes of image production. With the advent of the digital revolution, architectural drawing has moved further away from its origin as a medium for reflective invention or formulation, and towards a higher degree of nondescript processing of information. This development has been lamented. But criticism tends to forget that it is exactly the present state of digital technology that allows us to invent new practices of cinematic architectural drawing, while aligning it with similar practices in cinema and beyond, that are able to grasp what Scott Lash (2010) has labelled 'intensive culture'. As part of the Programme for Architecture, Space and Time at The Royal Danish Academy of Fine Arts School of Architecture, Meldgaard's collaborative workshop, involving architects and filmmakers in the 'Out of Field' projects, attempts to disrupt established hierarchies between architectural drawing, moving image and written word. Deriving from artistic practice rooted in Theodor Adorno's (1998: 107) approach to writing text as a 'carpet of thought operations which create its own critical density', Meldgaard's pedagogic methodology foregrounds audio-visual drawing research practice rather than scientific method in search of new mixed media drawing practices.

Since its invention, film has been utilized as an appropriate method to represent and critique the modern condition. From *Learning from Las Vegas*'s filmic research used to explore the controversially new condition of 'The Strip' (Figure 3), to Banham's film essay tour that rewrites an architectural history of the everyday American city, to the Eames's close scrutiny of zooming in and out of the earth and the things on its surface, the visuality of the medium constructs a contemporary gaze of modern life. The array of alternative uses of film as visual research methods, each devised for different research aims, show how the 'taken-for-granted' can be disturbed (Rose 2015). This continues with Lokko's scrutiny of Accra and Iacovou's inhabiting reality check of Casa Malaparte. Critiquing not just the visual image of modernity but its experience, filmic research methods can offer original analysis of films by reputable filmmakers (Turner on Eisenstein, Kyriazopoulos-Berinde on Tarkovsky). Learning film techniques as part of a hybrid design and research education can be an effective means of re-focusing the architect's gaze on what might really matter now and what is truly contemporary 'intensive culture', not only what is inherited as disciplinary praxis and representation (Keeney/Jones and Meldgaard).

Part 4 – Miscellaneous mixed modes and new media

Figure 4: *Jelloslice* Oil on prepared board. © Michael Webb © Archigram Archive.

INTRODUCTION

You are looking at part of a solidified cone of vision enclosing the landscape of the Henley regatta. Most of the left hand part of the image has been obliterated by cropping; furthermore the cone is truncated horizontally yielding a hyperbolic top surface. I was the beholder representing what I saw, but I moved my easel as it were; it matters not where. And as I did so voids began opening up behind the objects comprising the landscape.

The conic truncation means that these voids will erupt through the hyperbolic top surface. For example, the void created by the large weeping willow tree (centre right) near to the beholder, when it erupts through the surface, will reproduce at larger scale the outline of the tree's hanging tendrils. A second willow further from the beholder will reproduce an outline where the increase in scale is less.

(Webb 2018, unpublished)

The vapid technological developments of new visual media, including computer software that enables the exchange between analogue and digital to affect other forms of conventional media, and the use of new technologies such as Virtual Reality (VR) or Artificial Intelligence (AI) and GIS/ space data, are leading to mixed media techniques of 'critical visuality'. From the most traditionally embodied means of architectural representation, fixed in place (such as painting) – to network distributed VR and AI, the potential combinations, inter-relations and dimensions of visual research practice are expanding exponentially. Archigram member, Michael Webb, experimented in the 1950s with technologies of the time-drawing, painting, photocopy, collage. Now Webb's paintings and drawings are the result of a conversation informed by digital technologies. They also evidence a repertoire of previous visual methods, that are practised daily and in a disciplined manner, recalling Kulper's 'practised restraint'.

Concerned with matters of space and architecture, Webb's paintings and drawings have become a project and an iterative practice in themselves. With his Archigram collaborators, Webb shared a curiosity in and experimentation with new techniques such as air-brush work – a conceptual precursor to flattened computer rendering – and in re-thinking the limits of the normalized rules of drawings in projects such as 'Rent-A-Wall' and 'Drive-In House'. In the oil painting for the 'Cushicle' project, Webb did not use a paintbrush but instead used an exacto knife handle with a sponge taped on to it. His technique of consistent sponged dabs builds up tones and smooth gradients as he explores the condition of the pressure of air in the proposition. In his more recent work, such as his *Jelloslice* painting (Figure 4) – started in 1987 but still ongoing – Webb has developed a formalized technique of conceptual pixilation where the whole surface is composed of a series of micro-discs of individual colour hues, rearranged and correlated through an interpretation of Albert H. Munsell's colour system (Munsell 1905). There is a deliberate relationship with the concerns of the drawing and the technique utilized to expose those concerns. The chapters in this section of the book evidence an interest in performative practices (Rose [2001] 2012: 10) of miscellaneous mixed modes and new media as generative of visual research methods. The formulations of work become hybridized, and to some extent are more open-ended and speculative than those of more historically tested methods such as drawing, photography and film.

Architecture's relationship with hand and digital painting and client patronage of painterly artistry has been entwined in the western tradition since the Renaissance and this has transformed in recent times through engagement with rising neoliberal consumption, the digital 'experience economy' and the iconic building market. Originally associated with nineteenth-century visionary creators such as Joseph Gandy, John Soane and Augustus Pugin and as a medium of promised commission, painting delivered symbolic and cultural capital for architectural designers working mostly in nation states. Drawing and painting with ink, watercolour and brushed or washed surfaces continued through the Beaux-Arts tradition to measured drawing exercises and colour-coded production drawings. While painting has become a more marginalized practice in architecture, architects have become more global, wanting to reach wider markets, served by virtual and digital visual communication. Recent painters or painter-practitioners such as Madelon Vriesendorp, Will Alsop, Zaha Hadid, Steven Holl and Stan Allen actively use (hand or digital) painting through which to think and design. For Vriesendorp, Hadid and Alsop their paintings are visionary, generative explorations. For Holl and Allen, the paintings establish closer atmospheric and experiential imaginaries of projected architectural space. While 'starchitects' have used the media for the purposes of seducing clients to win projects, following traditions of earlier patronage relationships, architectural researchers explore hand and digital painting or other new digital technologies to formulate critical perspectives on architectural production and culture today. This critical work has shifted attention to a growing need for agency and activism; metaphysical visual expansion; and post-humanist explorations where the visual device augments or displaces the human body, to act as an enhanced version of visual architectural researcher – accomplishing things the human eye cannot, for instance at the microscopic or cosmological scale.

Chapter 19 'Visual agency: Participatory painting as a method for spatial negotiation' explores how painting can engage stakeholders in the architectural process. In the pedagogical practice-led project by Polish/Dutch artist, **Agnieszka Mlicka,** the medium of painting enables groups, including architects, to work with the complexity and contingency of the social, economic and political dimensions of

INTRODUCTION

urban space, through layering paint and colour. The aim of Mlicka's pedagogical visual research is to move beyond representation of the site in order to negotiate space as a socially constructed environment of exchange. Arguing in her chapter for 'a shift from the conventional view of painting as a vertical window on the world [...] to a horizontal field of connections and encounters', Mlicka, following on from the work of her mentor Jeremy Till, promotes and tests open-ended, participatory painting (rather than verbal discourse) through a series of research workshops. Unfamiliarity, plasticity and ambiguity are concepts that emerge. Willingness to establish a shared visual language that is unfamiliar to some of the workshop participants becomes significant in maximizing genuine participation. Several individuals painting on a large sheet also enables a plasticity of multiple style and tone. The open, ambiguous nature of the painterly group practice encourages affirmation of experience, deeper conversation and self-awareness of the participants' own and others' preconceptions or implicit intentions.

Mlicka's participatory visual research practice has influenced the work of British researcher and architect, **Tonia Carless,** who practises performative painting and explores this as collaborative spatial research beyond the bounds of the architectural studio to critique gentrification. In Chapter 20, 'just painting: Performative painting as visual discourse', Carless identifies public space at the point of change as the space of 'regeneration projects' for capital investment. The research, which is both visual and spatial, examines local spatial politics and Henri Lefebvre's (1974, 1991) notion of confrontation between abstract space and the space of use values. Fundamental to Carless's position and explicitly activist practice is the notion that the aesthetic of the painterly practice is also social and economic. Through constructing counter-images to the developer's, the temporally specific and *en plein-air* mode of painting – fluid in both practice and medium – challenges the rendered visualizations (also criticized by Blundell Jones in Chapter 1) that enable the space to be capitalized upon. The collaborative, interdisciplinary nature of the work aims to interrupt and challenge flows of image-economic capital to build alternative archives to the stores of consumerist accumulation, and to re-construct the value of public space. The observational, ethnographic and discursive aspects of painting (which Carless also mixes with digital panoramic experiments) can be utilized as critical architectural and urban research practices that build alternative qualitative material of cultural and social imagination and memory.

Paint as a material has been intertwined with colour theory in the nineteenth and twentieth centuries, often being the medium to constitute colour charts and other illustrative spectrum devices. Scottish architect **Fiona McLachlan**'s research in Chapter 21, 'Visual heuristics for colour design', notes the limits of colour charts as visual representations that do not capture metaphysical sensations or physiological and psychological experiences. McLachlan therefore establishes three distinctive types of abstracted painted images that act as a visual heuristic device in research on the use of colour in architectural design practice. McLachlan examines visual indexing, two-dimensional building portraits and three-dimensional visualizations. Research collaboration with the Haus der Farbe in Zurich captures external façade colours of thousands of building facades in the city through observation and comparison. These are then constructed as a data-set of large colour swatches of hand-mixed paint. The two-dimensional building portraits simultaneously present original data and are a constructed interpretation of the findings. Recalling Rose's caution to resist formalizing or objectifying visual images in constructive interpretation, attention to the 'constructed codes of recognition' (Bryson cited in Rose [2001] 2012: 57) and expectations of artistic production through viewing and dissemination is crucial. Painting's transparently subjective character offers appropriate approaches to analyse and interpret the experiential qualities of designed space.

Investigating bodily vision in time and space, Chapter 22 'Digitally stitching stereoscopic vision' by **George Themistokleous** focuses on the interaction between new digital technologies and an older device, Charles Wheatstone's 1830s stereoscope. Through experimental design practice and interdisciplinary theoretical investigation Themistokleous asks questions about visual perception. A custom-made optical device, *Diplorasis*, appropriates and combines readings on embodied and disembodied vision. It enables an engagement with both the corporeal and virtual body. Themistokleous' own visual misalignment, keratoconus, generates divergent images in his eyes and has triggered his research into the relationship between vision and normalized forms of visual representation, with conditions such as overlap of images, split vision, doublings and correctives. The interval between the body and its image is explored with reference to Maurice Merleau Ponty's theories of phenomenology and Jonathan Crary's history of optics, informed by the nineteenth-century scientific understanding of the physiology of human eyes. The research exploits the disjunction between experience and its cause. As a visual research method, the *Diplorasis* dismantles, divides, subdivides and reconfigures views for and by the body seeing the display and offers a new, assembled visuality.

What are the affective triggers or phenomena that shape experience, and how might tools that record multi-sensorial perceptual data be developed? British-based artist and academic, **Mathew Emmett** explores this in Chapter 23 'Audio-visual instruments and multi-dimensional architecture'. A 'fused' interpretation of visual, audio, haptic and kinaesthetic characteristics emerges as a complex process requiring mappings between communication medium and content. Emmett focuses on the audio-visual and the medium-content exchange that produces computational abilities derived from a site-specific condition. Instruments act as highly vigilant multi-modal sensors that can increase understanding of human-environment

INTRODUCTION

cogency, situated cognition, spatio-sensory amplification and spatial intelligence. Emmett's visual research methodology operates between cognitive science and art practice. The graphic Cognitive Tope map, with a range of metrical layers and fields, was developed to collate combined physical and psychological recordings, drawing from theories and practices of situational analysis. Emmett creates a specific audio-visual and corporeal fieldwork tool with the researcher incorporated into the map as a research instrument, to pursue sophisticated site analysis and experimental design practice. Multi-dimensional architecture transforms the architects' role to that of a progenitor of causal affect, and by an original enhanced language and research instrument set, the perceptual, cognitive and psychoactive dimension becomes the centre of architectural discourse.

Chapter 24 'Kaleidoscopic drawings: Sights and sites in the drawing of the city' by Greek-trained academic **Sophia Banou** draws attention to collective and individual, conventional and impulsive, visual or scopic 'regimes' that construct the image and perception of the city. Our current condition of an increasingly saturated visuality has been shaped by many modalities of visual perception that have emerged since modernity. Banou shows that the encounter with the city relies on the malleability of visual perception as a process of knowledge through acts of representation, where the city emerges as the terrain of innumerable gazes. Visuality, described by Hal Foster as 'sight as a social fact' (1988: ix), is distinct from the singularity of subjective vision, and the scopic involves modalities of both looking and representing. The kinetic condition of the modern city is the starting point of Banou's research. She asks how conventionally static architectural representation might accord with this by carrying the capacity not just to represent but also to look. Interplay and fusion between perception and representation is explored in the design research of the *Kaleidoscopic City,* an installation drawing, expanding notions of site-specificity into visual-specificity. The scientific device of the kaleidoscope transfigures by decomposing and composing (Didi-Huberman 2000), transcribing different attributes of the sites onto the installed three-dimensional drawing.

The miscellaneous visual modes, media and devices used as embodied research methods in Part 4 of this book address architecture's role in the delivery of symbolic, cultural, political or economic capital. There is an observable shift in the context of architectural production and culture from models of singular patronage and power to concerns with everyday culture and its appropriation of, or gleaning from, this capital. Rather than models of studio artistry and mastery, the contingent outdoor, the participatory and the collaborative can be directly responsive to the conditions and concerns of the marketization of space and architecture (Mlicka, Carless). Both Mlicka's and Carless's practice work towards heightened empathy, positing the potential for these to be relevant methodologies and practices for pedagogical and non-specialist activity through performance. Webb's focus on technique,

25

conceptual pixellation and chromaticity is understood as visually performative. The limits of representation, the apparatuses of vision and visual techniques are also fertile grounds for nuanced research methods to depict, interpret, mediate and analyse the world (McLachlan on colour design and indices, Themistokleous on bodily vision). With trajectory towards experimental design practice and new insights in working with site, Emmett (between cognitive science and art practice) and Banou (between representation theory and urban studies) show the productive potential of trans-visual research practices.

Conclusion: Visual research methods in architecture

The emergence of studies in visual culture (elite and popular) has changed the research methodologies practised by many humanities disciplines. When visual culture studies emerged, it was met with both contestation and delight by different disciplines. For Art History, Rosalind Krauss (1997) presented the argument that any engagement with visual culture would only be to the detriment of a discipline because the notion of learning a discipline is 'bound to knowing how to do something, certain skills' through close reading of 'works of art or works of literature'. For Krauss, engaging with visual culture would lead to de-skilling and should be resisted at all costs. Other social science disciplines are more optimistic about how engaging with visual culture can benefit their fields. Sarah Pink's (2007, 2009) *Doing Visual Ethnography* and *Doing Sensory Ethnography* etc. stake out important ground in the field of anthropology and firmly situate visual research practice as a valid contribution to the expansion of ethnographic disciplinary knowledge through attentiveness to methodological and reflexive practices. In studies of Cultural Geography, Gillian Rose's ([2001] 2012) *Visual Methodologies*, the key influence on our reading of visual research methods in architecture, focuses on the interpretation of visual materials to inform research. Rose and Divya Tolia-Kelly ed. (2012) illuminate the important relationship between the practice of critical visuality and materiality, done by humans with objects for media representation, or new media technologies or devices for drawing, painting, photographing or filming. Visual culture has to some extent been co-opted into architectural scholarship with positive and negative outcomes. If we consider visuality as a valid practice mode of/for humanities research, this book endeavours to set out some of the ways that design research might use visuality, with and without words or other media, as a tool and as a more explicit and precise method through which to undertake and disseminate research.

Our argument acknowledges that the architect's gaze and hand differ from the artist's, ethnographer's or the cultural geographer's gaze and hand because of the politics of subject focus, modes of production and outputs within each discipline. The architectural researcher or designer's use of hand and digital tools or devices for drawing, photographing, filming or more experimental visual modes and media seeks out explicit and emergent architectural knowledge. This may take place through: drawing as an open site of inquiry; photography's potential to generate new evidence in the visual construction of social, spatial, cultural and material life; film's original methods of analysis of the dynamic contemporary condition; and painting and other digital media and device-based modes for performative practice. The range of mixed media-specific research practices assembled in this book resonate with, but expand in different ways, the evidenced value of visual research methods in other disciplines (Rose 2015).

Interdisciplinary exchanges and potentially new means of interdisciplinary research scholarship – between these visual media – can be beneficial to the architect's design research practice if the architect uses them with specific purpose, either on their own or with written commentary. In *Travelling Concepts in the Humanities*, Mieke Bal (2002: 37) argues that 'the concept of focalization [… which is] *not* identical to that of the "gaze" or the "look" […] can help to clarify a vexed issue in the relationship between looking and language'. Bal sees the exchange to be *inter* disciplinary where focalization is used in relation to the visual domain, not narratology – that is, it allows travel from what is visually focused upon to the narrative and back again. This movement allows for a distancing from location and from the subject of the picture itself: 'What becomes visible in the *movement* of the look' (Bal 2002: 39).

W. J. T. Mitchell (1995) published *Picture Theory* to analyse the 'pictorial turn' in contemporary culture, the widely shared notion that visual images have replaced words as the dominant mode of expression of our time. *Picture Theory* tried to analyse the pictorial, or […] 'visual' turn, rather than to simply accept it at face value. It was designed to resist received ideas about 'images replacing words' and to not 'put all the eggs in one disciplinary basket, whether art history, literary criticism, media studies, philosophy, or anthropology' (Mitchell 2005: 2) and to which we add architecture. Mitchell (2005: 47) argues poignantly:

> The most far-reaching shift signalled by the search for an adequate concept in visual culture is its emphasis on the social field of the visual, the everyday processes of looking at others and being looked at. This complex field of visual reciprocity is not merely a by-product of social reality but actively constitutive of it. Vision is as important as language in mediating social relations, and it is not reducible to language, to the 'sign,' or to discourse. Pictures want equal rights with languages, not to be turned into language. They want […] to be seen as complex individuals occupying multiple subject positions and identities.

The making of visual research is inherently politically motivated and supports Mitchell's (2005: 2) contention that 'Images are not everything' but 'they manage to convince us that they are'. Images take on their own lives because they not only represent the world but go beyond even that which we experience. Roland Barthes (1977: 32) argues in 'The rhetoric of the image', in *Image Music Text*, that images are resistant to meaning, leaving their status as a 'vague conception'. As 'vague conception', Juhani Pallasmaa (2005: 13) argues that 'the preconscious perceptual realm, which is experienced outside the sphere of focused vision, seems to be just as important existentially as the focused image'. Pallasmaa (2005: 44) writes; 'Images of one sensory realm feed further imagery in another modality. Images of presence give rise to images of memory, imagination and dream'. Images are open to individual and unique readings depending on the reader. This complex full-body relationship between writing, orality, aurality, making and looking at images, and experiencing visual knowledge in the world, affects not only the production and tools of architecture but also the production of architectural scholarship.

In 'The power of images' Mitchell (2005: 33) suggests that images are not powerless. The issue is to determine where their politics lie and how they operate. Politics surrounds the image-maker/researcher's motives, their gender, race, class and age and how each has constructed their gaze. The object and purpose of visual research and their audience are key issues for architectural researchers to be attentive to, in order to understand position, limitations and agency, to validate marginal and overlooked positions. Architectural design research takes place every day in many practices but is often only legitimized within the university as scholarship. As G. James Daichendt (2012: 21) suggests, 'The artist [and architect] outside the university is not necessarily concerned with the previous discussion regarding research'. Although the architectural design researcher working within higher education, whose audience is academic, is less free than the architectural design researcher working outside academic confines, working within the university can command more authority because of institutional affiliation and validation through recognized forms of academic scholarship.

The practice of architectural visual culture, with its range of visual literacy, is less valued by the academic community at present but this need not remain the case. It is argued here that no matter what medium or combination of media is used, 'critical visuality' allows space, its occupation, the body, and the temporal and social inter-relations to be given attention for architectural purposes. For this reason, visual research methods in architecture will, by their very nature, allow architecture to overlap with anthropology, ethnography, phenomenological philosophy, fine arts, photography, filmmaking, digital drawing, computation and mapping etc. Shared disciplinary preoccupations and methods of research allow architecture to create new interdisciplinary research. Knowing reflexivity

INTRODUCTION

embedded in these practices might also lead to new and increasingly rigorous ways of 'doing architectural scholarship'.

The precise ways in which visuality can be used in architectural research seem multifarious. By curating adjacencies in each part of the book across thematic threads of Techniques and Tools of Thinking, Practicing and Teaching Architecture and Visual Culture Research, we aim to expose the rich territory of knowledge production and agency of architectural research that traverses individual scholarship and design research practice, commission-based architectural production, studio pedagogies and formally framed funded research projects or studies. Creative visual research in architecture is intertwined with the tools and techniques used by different modes of visual representation. Shifting from using a drawing or a diagram to photography to filmmaking or to a performative painting or a digital visual device presents the design research architect or architectural scholar with modes of practice and effective research capacity specific to each medium. When chosen purposely and with care, these media can enhance the research and scholarship they contribute to in architecture and the rigorous design of spaces and places for our contemporary society. Just as architects began to use photography and film for research when they became more publicly accessible, it is envisaged that as VR and AI evolve and become more accessible they too will be experimented with as research tools. *Visual Research Methods in Architecture* exposes both how media appropriated by a discipline can be used with depth, originality and rigour, and also how emerging new technologies can initiate new modes of critical visual research practice.

Acknowledgements

This book began as a series of lectures in a Research Methods for Design module that Troiani devised in 2011; then with the session call to the annual AIARG (All-Ireland Architecture Research Group) conference in Dublin (2015) and was followed by our keynote address at the Architecture Humanities Research Association (AHRA) Ph.D. symposium at the University of Sheffield on 5 April 2016 on the kind invitation of Dr Stephen Walker.

REFERENCES

Adorno, T. (1998), 'Essayet som form' (orig. German 'Der Essay als Form' [1958], in *Noten zur Literatur*, Gesammelte Schriften, Band 11, Frankfurt/M: Suhrkamp, 2003, pp. 9–33), in T. Adorno, *Passage*, vol. 28-29/1, Århus: Århus Universitet, pp. 100–14.

Appleyard, D., Lynch, K. and Meyer, J. R. (1964), *The View from the Road*, Cambridge, MA: The MIT Press.

Bal, M. (2002), *Travelling Concepts in the Humanities: A Rough Guide*, Toronto, Buffalo and London: University of Toronto Press.

Barthes, R. (1977), *Image Music Text* (trans. Stephen Heath), New York: Hill & Wang.

Bourdieu, P. ([1980] 1992), *The Logic of Practice*, Oxford: Polity Press.

Bowden, J. (1996), 'Phenomenographic research: Some methodological issues', in G. Dall'Alba and B. Hasselgren (eds), *Reflections on Phenomenography: Towards a Methodology?*, Göteborg: Acta Universitatis Gothoburgensis, pp. 49–66.

Clément, G. (2009), *L'homme symbiotique, commentaire de six dessins*, http://www.gillesclement.com/cat-lhommesymbiotique-tit-L-Homme-symbiotique. Accessed 19 June 2018.

Cooper, J. (dir.) (1972), *Reyner Banham Loves Los Angeles (One Pair of Eyes)*, motion picture, London: BBC.

Crary, J. (1990), *Techniques of the Observer: On Vision and Modernity in the Nineteenth Century*, Cambridge, MA: The MIT Press.

Daichendt, J. G. (2012), *Artist Scholar: Reflections on Writing and Research,* Bristol: Intellect Books.

Didi-Huberman, G. (2000), 'Connaissance par le Kaléidoscope: Morale du joujou et dialectique de l'image selon Walter Benjamin'/Knowledge through the Kaleidoscope: The philosophy of toys and the dialectical image according to Walter Benjamin', *Etudes Photographiques* 7, https://etudesphotographiques.revues.org/204?lang=en. Accessed 10 October 2013.

——— (2009), *Quand les images prennent position. L'œil de l' histoire*, Paris: Minuit.

D'Oliveira-Martins, M. (2014), 'Sociological reflexivity and the sociology of emotions', *Sociology and Anthropology* 2:5, pp. 190–95, http://www.hrpub.org. Accessed March 2018.

Eames, C. and Eames, R. (dir.) (1977), *Powers of Ten: A Film Dealing with the Relative Size of Things in the Universe and the Effect of Adding Another Zero*, motion picture, United States: Public Broadcasting Service.

——— (2012), *The Films of Charles and Ray Eames: Box Set,* motion picture box set, United States: Eames Office.

Eisenstein, S. (dir.) (1925), *Bronenosets Potemkin/Battleship Potemkin*, motion picture, Russia: Mosfilm.

Ellis, J. (1992), *Visible Fictions: Cinema, Television, Video*, London: Routledge.

Fixsen, A. (2016), 'Exhibition: The photography of Denise Scott Brown', *Architectural Record*, September, pp. 53–54.

Foster, H. (1988), *Vision and Visuality*, Seattle: Bay Press.

Giedion, S. (1928), *Bauen in Frankreich. Bauen in Eisen. Bauen in Eisenbeton*, Leipzig/Berlin: Kinkhardt & Biermann.

——— ([1946] 1967), *Space, Time and Architecture: The Growth of a New Tradition*, Cambridge, MA: Harvard University Press.

Godard, J-L. (dir.) (1963), *Le Mépris (Contempt)*, motion picture, France: Cocinor.

Haraway, D. (1988), 'Situated knowledges: The science question in feminism and the priviledge of partial perspective', *Feminist Studies*, 14:3, pp. 575–99.

INTRODUCTION

Harbusch, G. (2015), 'Work in text and images: Sigfried Giedion's *Space, Time and Architecture*, 1941–1967', *The Journal of Architecture*, 20:4, pp. 596–620.

Krauss, R. (1997), 'Krauss and the art of cultural controversy', interviewed by Scott Rothkopf, *The Harvard Crimson*, 16 May, http://www.thecrimson.com/article/1997/5/16/krauss-and-the-art-of-cultural/. Accessed 28 January 2015.

Kristensen, T., Michelsen, A. and Wiegand, F. (2015b), 'Introduction', in T. Kristensen, A. Michelsen and F. Wiegand. (eds), *Transvisuality: The Cultural Dimension of Visuality, Volume II: Visual Organizations*, Liverpool: Liverpool University Press, pp. 12–52.

Kulper, P. (2012), 'Drawing architecture: Conversation with Perry Kulper', interviewed by WAI Architecture Think Tank, *Archinect*, 5 August, https://archinect.com/news/article/54767042/drawing-architecture-conversation-with-perry-kulper. Accessed 12 June 2018.

—— (2013), 'A world below', in N. Spiller, *AD: Architectural Drawing*, London: John Wiley and Sons, pp. 56–63.

—— (2014), 'Instinctual marks, relational fields, sies of wonder', in P. Kulper and N. Chard, *Fathoming the Unfathomable: Archival Ghosts and Paradoxical Shadows*, Pamphlet Architecture 34, Princeton: Princeton Architectural Press, pp. 8–33.

Landa, M. de (2016), *Assemblage Theory*, Edinburgh: Edinburgh University Press.

Lash, S. (2010), *Intensive Culture: Social Theory, Religion and Contemporary Capitalism*, Los Angeles and London: SAGE Publications.

Lefebvre, H. (1969), *Explosions: Marxism and the French Revolution*, New York: Monthly Review Press.

—— (1991), *The Production of Space*, trans. Donald Nicholson-Smith, Oxford: Wiley-Blackwell. Originally published 1974, *La production de l'espace*, Paris: Anthropos.

Merleau Ponty, M. (1962), *Phenomenology of Perception* (trans. Colin Smith), New York: Humanities Press, and London: Routledge & Kegan Paul; trans. revised by Forrest Williams (1981; reprinted, 2002); new trans. by Donald A. Landes (2012), New York: Routledge.

Mitchell, W. J. T. (1995), *Picture Theory: Essays on Verbal and Visual Representation*, Chicago and London: The University of Chicago Press.

—— (2005), *What Do Pictures Want? The Lives and Loves of Images*, Chicago and London: The University of Chicago Press.

Munsell, A. H. (1905), *A Colour Notation*, Boston, MA: G.H. Ellis Company.

Neurath, O. (1937), 'Visual representation of architectural problems', *Architectural Record*, July, pp. 56–61.

Neurath, O. (eds Eve, M. and Burke, C.) (2010), *From Hieroglyphics to Isotype: A Visual Autobiography*, London: Hyphen Press.

Pallasmaa, J. (2005), *The Eyes of the Skin: Architecture and the Senses*, Chichester: Wiley-Academy.

Perez-Gomez, A. and Pelletier, L. (1997), *Architectural Representation and the Perspective Hinge*, Cambridge, MA: The MIT Press.

Pink, S. (2001), 'More visualizing, more methodologies: On video, reflexivity and qualitative research', *The Sociological Review*, 49:4, pp. 586–99.

—— (2007), *Doing Visual Ethnography*, London: SAGE Publications.

—— (2009), *Doing Sensory Ethnography*, London: SAGE Publications.

Rogoff, I. (2006), 'Academy as potentiality', in A. Nollert et al. (eds), *A.C.A.D.E.M.Y.*, Berlin: Revolver, pp. 1–9.

Rose, G. (2000), 'Practising photography: An archive, a study, some photographs and a researcher', *Journal of Historical Geography*, 26:4, pp. 555–71.

—— ([2001] 2012), *Visual Methodologies: An Introduction to Researching with Visual Materials*, 3rd ed., London and Los Angeles: SAGE Publications.

—— (2014), 'On the relation between "visual research methods" and contemporary visual culture', *Sociological Review,* 62, pp. 24–46.

—— (2015), 'Visual research methods in an expanded field: What next for Visual Research methods?' *Visual/Method/Culture*, 25 September, https://visualmethodculture.wordpress.com/2015/09/25/visual-research-methods-in-an-expanded-field-what-next-for-visual-research-methods/. Accessed 11 June 2018.

Rose, G. and Tolia-Kelly, D. P. (eds) (2012), *Visuality/Materiality: Images, Objects and Practices,* Farnham, Surrey: Ashgate.

Rossi, A. (1981), *A Scientific Autobiography,* trans. L. Venuti, Cambridge, MA: The MIT Press.

Scott Brown, D. (1971), 'Learning from pop', in R. Venturi and D. Scott Brown (eds), *The View from the Campidoglio: Selected Essays, 1953-1984*, New York: Harper & Row, pp. 26–33.

Sidney, G. (dir.) (1964), *Viva Las Vegas*, motion picture, United States: Jack Cummings Productions.

Sonnemann, U. (1954), *Existence and Therapy: An Introduction to Phenomenological Psychology and Existential Analysis,* New York: Grune and Stratum.

Stadler, H. and Stierli, M. (eds) (2015), *Las Vegas Studio: Images from the Archive of Robert Venturi and Denise Scott Brown*, Zurich: Verlag Scheidegger & Spiess.

Stierli, M. (2013), *Las Vegas in the Rearview Mirror: The City in Theory, Photography, and Film*, Los Angeles: Getty Research Institute.

Venturi, R., Scott Brown, D. and Izenour, S. ([1972] 1989), *Learning from Las Vegas: The Forgotten Symbolism of Architectural Form*, Cambridge, MA: The MIT Press.

Vogt, A. M. (2006), 'Interpretation im 20. Jahrhundert, Siegfried Giedion: Inszenierung der Avantgarde', in A. M. Vogt, *Adolf Max Vogt. Schriften. Die Hunde bellen, die Karawane zieht weiter*, Zurich: gta Verlag, pp. 268–72.

Webb, M. (2011), 'Interview: Michael Webb', interviewed by Tim Abrahams, *Cosmopolitan Scum*, 28 October, https://cosmopolitanscum.com/2011/10/28/interview-michael-webb/. Accessed 13 June 2018.

Webb, M. (2018), Unpublished correspondence with author.

PART I

DRAWINGS AND DIAGRAMS: DISCIPLINARY SEEING AND KNOWING

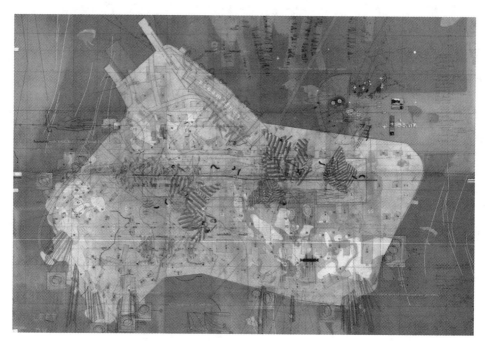

Figure 1 (from Introduction): David's Island Strategic Plot Drawing made: 1996–97 Drawing size: 24" x 36" Materials: Mylar, graphite, ink, tape, found imagery, x-rays, foil, photographs, transfer letters and transfer film, cut paper. © Perry Kulper.

> Partially, as a result of allowing uncertainties to enter drawings I have enjoyed freedom of many kinds. A more relaxed and accommodating approach has allowed me to work 'creatively' (always a dangerous word) in broadened ways by supporting expanded relational capacities in the drawings to discuss things that might not otherwise be in play. I try to visualize and support ideas long enough to see if they might be relevant to a project in the long run. Increasingly, I am less judgmental about possible ideas for a project, especially in the early phases of a project – about whether everything in play is suitable for the piece of work. Depending on what I am working on I often make drawings, or parts of drawings that are not targeted at a synthetic building proposal, but are specific in their intent – studying erasure as a possible representational and spatial activity, for example.
>
> (Kulper 2012)

1

Is the plan dying?

Peter Blundell Jones, University of Sheffield

When did you last see a building design presented that was exciting mainly for its handling of plan? When James Stirling was still alive and his latest project appeared in *Building Design*, it was often the plan that one looked at first to understand the general proposition of the building, and this was also often where the innovations were made. Famously, he used axonometric or isometric projections of various kinds to throw it into three dimensions, but the plan was still there, for plan and section were primary in his thinking. But nowadays nearly all we see is perspectival or photo-like images, and whether a project is published in a newspaper or as a web image, we are compelled to judge and admire it on this basis. Of course we are no longer restricted to line drawings, and colour has become ubiquitous while the most exciting perspective angle can quickly be selected by computer. There are algorithms to add sun and shade, the weather, people walking about, trees, flowers, water and whatever else promises maximum attraction. Legions of experts sit before screens coaxing maximum excitement out of such images, often not the building's designers. So realistic are these images that it can be difficult to be sure whether or not the building has actually been built, and as a corollary, whether it is worth building at all, since a full enough presentation on page or screen has already completed the cycle of dissemination. But it actually leaves less to the imagination, for although lazy onlookers are saved the work of projecting themselves into the putative space, they are also prevented from doing so because most of the information is simply not there.

It was not always so. Le Corbusier famously declared that 'the plan is the generator' (cited by Conrads 1971: 60). Augustus Pugin (1853: 52) complained that the degraded architecture of his time was due to concentration on the elevations at the expense of the plan. And it is the plan we need to look at to understand social complexes like the medieval monastery, reflected in the famous 'Plan of St Gall', which was discovered by accident on the back of a parchment reused as a legal document (Figure 1). Dating from around 820 AD, it is of interest for revealing 'the plan of an abbey of that period', as Eugène Emmanuel Viollet-le-duc remarks in his *Dictionnaire Raisonné de l'architecture Française du XI au XVI Siècle* (*Rational Dictionary of French Architecture from the XI to the XVI Century*) (1878: 241), which features a whole page of description beginning with the church and its various altars, going on through the cloister, refectory, dormitory and monks' quarters, the cellars, baths and latrines, then the novitiate, infirmary and the house of the physician, and all the quarters of lay brothers engaged in farming and production, including workshops for shoe-makers and coopers. It was possible to deduce from this plan the full hierarchical complexity of the monastic way of life with all its social relationships, and the drawing seems to have been made for this purpose and sent to spread the word for the building of new monasteries.

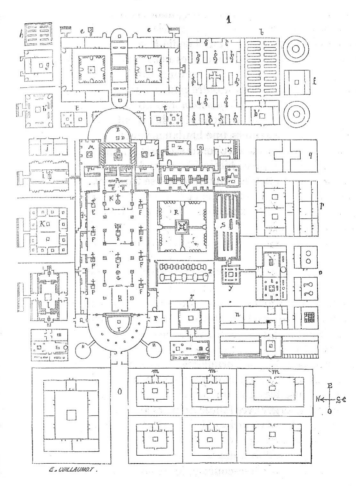

Figure 1: Plan of St Gall, ca. 820 AD.

In the late twentieth century, Walter Horn and Ernest Born (1979) wrote a huge monograph based on the St Gall plan, and constructed a scale model detailing all its various elements, labelling it up with all 26 letters of the alphabet as well as 40 numbers. With all this detail it was possible to deduce from the plan the purposes, sizes, shapes of rooms and the relationships between them, for example the progressive linearity of the church or the centrality of the cloister. The plan was recognized as essential for defining a type, and we know from surviving monastic buildings how impossible it would be to sum them up in a photograph of one side: books usually resort to a bird's eye view, essentially an upward projection of the plan. St Gall provides a clear example of the plan as key figure, but it is far from singular in architectural history. Andrea Palladio's work is attractive in elevation, but his *I Quattro Libri dell' Architettura* (*The Four Books of Architecture*) ([1570] 1965) would never have made its international impact without the plan, spaces and relationships depicted. Much of the discussion at the Beaux-Arts was about the plan, about the choice of *parti* and the experience of the *marche* of a building: i.e. how you moved through it (Drexler 1977: 163, 185). To add a non-western example, Chinese complexes like the Forbidden City are even more plan-dependent for understanding, as their carpet-like organization makes them more space than object, leaving little to be seen in external elevations. And during the early modern movement work on the ground plan reached a kind of extreme, as part of the effort to redefine dwelling and to discover what the new kind of building should be like. In 1928 the Berlin critic Adolf Behne wrote:

> Architecture is most richly concentrated in the creation of the ground plan, where the architect is led most decisively beyond the limits of personal work to the development of the created object. Each ground plan requires its own type of solution, for when it is developed in full seriousness, it is part of the task of the ground plan to order our life on the ground, on this earth.[1]

Perhaps there really is less to look at in the plans of most contemporary buildings. In the case of offices, for example, general purpose structures with open plans and deep floors have taken over, and the developer wants maximum lettable floor area for the sake of profit while the shared parts of the plan used for circulation and services are driven by regulations that prescribe a minimum dimension, which for the sake of economy soon also becomes a maximum. One square metre of floor space is supposedly as good as the next, and people working in the building have little or no say in the procurement process. With no voice, they lose interest, just putting up with an environment already fully prescribed, some even obliged to hot-desk, finding a fresh workplace each day. Designing such offices can be a boring process for architects also, caught within this technical and economic web and obliged to work fast, adapting generic solutions by computer. In the days of drawing by hand, it necessarily took more time and effort, but it also took far longer, allowing time for contemplation and development. This is not to say that we now altogether lack buildings that are interesting in three dimensions, or that they cannot therefore also look dramatic in plan and section, but the ordering of plan seems mostly subordinate to the pursuit of an image, and tends not to articulate social significance like St Gall. Most such modern examples are not plan-driven.

Reluctance to grapple with the plan may also reflect a growing suspicion about plans ever since Foucault ([1975] 1979: 195–228) revealed that they could be representations and even instruments of power. Then Henri Lefebvre ([1974] 1991: 361) accused architects of making their own worlds of imagined space while forgetting real socially produced space: a criticism certainly applicable with large developments of the 1960s like London's Barbican Centre.[2] Thirdly there was a kind of shock-horror reaction when it was revealed that maps were not objective, but bent to particular purposes by their makers: originally military strategy, or a national mapping agency in the case of the UK's Ordnance Survey (OS).[3] Academics and students started instead to make their own amateur maps, and soon any kind of investigation yielding a graphic product was called a map, but most were lamentably thin, with nothing like the detail and range of concerns recorded by the OS. It seems surprising now that we ever took the OS as 'objective', for one need go no further than examining the graphic conventions of the key to see how a strict classification was shared by the drafts-persons, whose work had to be consistent and depersonalized. If they lacked a convention for something, it simply could not be depicted, and mavericks could scarcely start extending the conventions on their own. But for all their limitations, OS maps do record a rich mixture of readable information, and their biases and limitations can be taken into account. The historic ones often allow of no alternative. This scepticism about maps and plans may account to some extent for a retreat from 'the plan as generator' and indeed from anything that looks like master-planning or social engineering, but we can hardly stop classifying and dividing physical space and imposing meanings upon it. Thresholds and rules of use are everyday with us, while patterns of power and possession loom more strongly than ever, for example, at times even throwing the whole nature of public space into question (Sennett 1977).

Neglect of the plan may result from competition with other media. Many lay people claim to be poor at reading maps and plans, and complain that such images are not what we see. Well, photographs are not what we see either, for the frame and angle are highly selective, and the colour and light values are drastically altered. Photos give no information to the other senses, and are deprived of the depth cues of binocular vision. The effect of linear perspective tends to be exaggerated because it wins over other perceptual cues, and as with early Renaissance paintings, the chequerboard floor adds a tempting depth. Although we may be able to read spaces through photographs, especially with the help of plans and sections to put different views together, they are still appreciated through perceptual conventions we learn early in life, then take completely for granted. Video can add movement and sound to bring architecture more to life, but the continuous filmic walk-through a building generally turns out to be disappointing. On the one hand it makes the viewer feel blinkered, unable to direct what seems too narrow a gaze, while on the other there is a lack of haptic information, about how the body is moving through the space. This is a reminder of the degree to which a real body in real space encourages controlled interaction. One can start and stop, look this way and that, switch interest instantly from peripheral vision to detail, or turn around knowing from one's semi-circular canals how far one has turned – in contrast, when watching a video, the 360° pan is totally confusing.

Since the running video shot does not work, the projected architectural space of most movies is highly contrived: not a real space at all, but a virtual one made by the montage of consecutive takes. If there is a constructed set, often only half of it is there, and there is often advantage in dishonestly pairing up the interior of one building with the exterior of another. A good film editor can link the eye movement of one shot to that of the next, and use continuity of music or sound to carry the experience across the change of scene. We respond by assembling the story in our perception, often much as the director and editor intended. Architecture can provide the backdrop, but not for what it truly is. In *Der Himmel über Berlin* (*Wings of Desire*) (1987) for example, film director Wim Wenders paid homage to Hans Scharoun's State Library in Berlin with tracking shots across its impressively unfolding spaces, but he did not follow the architecturally crucial main routes through the building in true sequence. In *A Touch of Evil* (1958), Orson Welles created an impressive opening shot with a continuous take of about three minutes, involving a single set and a cast of hundreds. The camera, on a crane, starts inside a building, then moves out of a window and down the street, rising then dropping as it goes. This extraordinary shot certainly achieves the intention of grabbing the audience's attention, even if few actually notice the lack of cuts on first viewing, merely sensing the smooth continuity. But the camera does not present the possible eye view of a real person in the space. In sum, architectural and cinematic space are very different, and we should not confuse the two (Keiller and Blundell Jones 2015: 244–50). This explains some of the trouble with flying computer projections: impressive in their way but failing to reproduce a sense of experience, and giving the odd feeling that one's feet are not on the ground. Viewing virtual reconstructions of archaeological sites, one is frustrated also by inability to control the movement: it seems too fast to be able to stop and look, too slow to wait for the entire repeat.

The fate of the plan as drawing or diagram depends on the way we experience it, and that is now changing. Line drawings lent themselves to reproduction on paper even before photographs could be effectively reproduced, so there were already effectively reproduced plans in the journal *The Builder* (1846–1966) in the nineteenth century, and early editions of Banister Fletcher's *A History of Architecture on the Comparative Method* (1896) made their mark with enticingly clear line drawings re-engraved for reproduction. By around 1930, with black-and-white photographs printable and a higher resolution on drawings, the high-quality book could permit so convincing an architectural experience that a work like Le Corbusier's Villa Savoye could be very widely disseminated by it – few actually visited. By mid-century, journals like *The Architectural Review* had found reliable and appealing ways to bring a substantial architectural experience to the reader, so we could feel confident in our knowledge of buildings we had never seen. It was necessary to possess the journal in order to pore over the drawings, with a magnifying glass if necessary, and to be able to shift one's gaze from one drawing to another to understand the interaction of plan and section, or to place the photographs. Getting six or eight pages in the *Review* was about as much coverage as most buildings ever received, for general histories tended to rely on one image and even single architect monographs could not usually dedicate so much space to a single work. The journal was a pleasure to own, to look back over and to compile. In the absence of other specific information about buildings, its monthly arrival was a treat. Published details could be cribbed, as architects remained generous, and seldom attempted to patent their ideas.

Now the journals are dying, or at least moving onto the web. *Building Design* is only available electronically and the closure of print versions of *The Architectural Review* and *The Architects' Journal* (AJ) has been announced.[4] This is a gradual transition intended to ease us from one medium to the other, but it is already clear from Internet institutions like *World Architecture News* that superficial news stories and photo-like images are the new norm, while fashionable architects are lining up to give each other awards with a flattering *bon mot*: in short, there is little real criticism or depth in presenting what a building is about. It is already a problem that we have become used to judging products through skilfully concocted images by succumbing to advertising and buying online, then too quickly pressing 'like'. By appraising architecture in the same kind of way we risk making it into the same kind of thing, to be judged similarly, and in the absence of better information our appreciation cannot proceed beyond a superficial level. An online subscription service should be able to afford more detail, but already re-drawings of plans and sections are being simplified, probably to allow people to read them on phone or tablet, inevitably at lower resolution, and possibly at the wrong aspect ratio, which should horrify those brought up to respect proportion. With the basic online non-subscribed version of AJ, for example, news stories about buildings have a rolling sequence of images including plans, but they are at low resolution and you cannot stop them to get a good look. Subscribers can obtain images from AJ's Building Library at higher resolution and even printed out, though probably only a tiny section of the audience will ever bother to do that. Architecture online is therefore developing as a very different experience from turning over the pages of the journal at one's leisure. There is also the problem of comparing drawings: even with two screens it is more difficult to juggle them, and certainly more difficult to trace the inter-relation of a plan with multiple photographs. One no longer feels one has the representation of a building in one's possession: indeed, ownership becomes a rather slippery affair. The Internet has brought extraordinary riches, with Wikipedia now valuable as a first port of call for preliminary investigation, and Google allowing pursuit of even rather arcane things while its satellite map service allows one to check a building's siting from one's desk. Yet, if electronic versions are altogether to replace the architectural journal, we must consider the potential losses besides capitalizing on the potential gains. Possessing the means to understand a building from the plan up is essential if intelligent discourse on architecture is to continue.

Acknowledgements

The editors would like to thank Christine Poulson for permission to print this chapter posthumously, and take this opportunity to recognize Peter's scholarship, enthusiasm and engagement in his important contribution to this edited volume.
Peter Blundell Jones (1949–2016)

REFERENCES

Behne, A. (1984), 'Von der Sachlichkeit', *Eine Stunde Architektur Architextbooks 5*, Berlin: Archibook Verlag.

Conrads, U. (ed.) (1971), *Programmes and Manifestoes of Twentieth Century Architecture*, Cambridge, MA: The MIT Press.

Drexler, A. (1977), *The Architecture of the Beaux Arts*, New York: Museum of Modern Art.

Fletcher, B. (1896), *A History of Architecture on the Comparative Method*, London: Athlone Press.

Foucault, M. ([1975] 1979), *Discipline and Punish: The Birth of the Prison*, Harmondsworth: Peregrine Books.

Frearson, A. (2015), 'Architects' Journal and Architectural Review to end print editions after 120 years', https://www.dezeen.com/2015/10/05/architects-journal-architectural-review-emap-end-print-editions-digital-only/. Accessed 3 December 2015.

Hobley, A. (dir.) (2010), *Maps: Power, Plunder and Possession*, UK: BBC Four.

Horn, W. and Born, E. (1979), *The Plan of St Gall: A Study of the Architecture and Economy of, and Life in, a Paradigmatic Carolingian Monastery*, Oakland, CA: University of California Press.

Keiller, P. and Blundell Jones, P. (2015), 'Filmic space: An encounter with Patrick Keiller', in P. Blundell Jones and M. Meagher (eds), *Architecture and Movement: The Dynamic Experience of Buildings and Landscapes*, London and New York: Routledge, pp. 244–50.

Lefebvre, H. ([1974] 1991), *The Production of Space* (trans. D. Nicholson-Smith), Oxford: Blackwell.

Magnificent Maps: Power, Propaganda and Art (2010), The British Library, London, 30 April–19 September.

Palladio, A. ([1570] 1965), *The Four Books of Architecture*, New York: Dover Publications.

Pugin, A. W. N. (1853), *The True Principles of Pointed or Christian Architecture*, London: Henry G. Bohn.

Sennett, R. (1977), *The Fall of Public Man*, New York: Knopf.

Viollet-le-duc, E. E. (1878), *Dictionnaire Raisonné de l'Architecture Française du XI au XVI Siècle 1*, Paris: A. Morel, fol. 'Architecture Monastique'.

Welles, O. (dir.) (1958), *A Touch of Evil*, USA: Universal Pictures.

Wenders, W. (dir.) (1987), *Der Himmel über Berlin* (*Wings of Desire*), West Germany and France: Road Movies Filmproduktion and Westdeutscher Rundfunk.

NOTES

1. Translation by the author.
2. The plan has its own logic from the view of the God-like architect, but way-finding on the raised decks is so poor that a yellow line had to be painted to guide people through.
3. Examples of this have been presented in the television series *Maps: Power, Plunder and Possession*, 2010, BBC Four (presented by J. Brotton), as well as the exhibition *Magnificent Maps: Power, Propaganda and Art*, 30 April–19 September 2010, London: The British Library.
4. The intended closure of AR and AJ print editions was announced on 5 October 2015 (Frearson, 2015). Editors' note: this decision has since been reversed.

2

Analogical Images: Aldo Rossi's *Autobiografia Scientifica*

Susanna Pisciella, IUAV, University of Venice

In 1976, the Institute for Architecture and Urban Studies in New York (IAUS) organized the first international exhibition of architect Aldo Rossi's (1937–97) work titled *Aldo Rossi: An Exhibition of Drawing*, where no architectural projects were described, instead drawings were displayed as autonomous projects in themselves, hovering between history and the memory of the city (Rispoli 2012: 144). Peter Eisenman, in *Houses of Memory: The Texts of Analogy*, comments,

> For Aldo Rossi the European city has become the house of dead. Its history, its function has ended; it has erased the specific memories of the houses of individual childhood to become a locus of collective memory. As a giant or collective house of memory it has a psychological reality which arises from its being a place of fantasy and illusion, an analogy of both life and death as transitional states. For Rossi writings and drawings are an attempt to explore this giant house of memory.
>
> (Eisenman 2007: 133)

Aldo Rossi's architectural drawings contain the scale of the city, such as the Cemetery of Modena, a city devoted to the dead, and the School of Broni, an urban fortress, the Theatre of the World (Rossi 1982). He was also conversely attracted to the future structure of the city as complete architecture itself, the city at its essential beginning, such as Diocletian's Palace in Split. His attention is on urban persistences, collective constructions like the Palazzo della Ragione of northern Italian cities, the Alhambra in Granada, the Cà Granda in Milan: buildings capable of producing civic and spiritual sense at the same time, which are at the base of the community, of the city. For Aldo Rossi, the main issue in architecture is to be aware of what the city is, which for him is the combination of both the civil dimension of public architectural institutions (Enlightenment imprint) and the need for a shared symbolic system as the soul of the city (Christian/liturgical identity). If the *Scientific Autobiography* comes from the pressure of a confession, its destiny was to become a treatise. How does an architect 'know' the city? Built works that can be visited and recorded, ranges of archives and publications of drawings and models, have made disciplinary architectural knowledge. How does Rossi draw from these in his research practice and imaginative invention, alongside personal experience, interpretation and evaluation?

At the end of the 1960s, after the experience of the vast destruction of war, a new sensibility against the myth of anthropocentrism and technology began to arise in the field of architectural theory. In the cultural context of New York with many European refugees, Europe was an interesting subject of observation from the other side of the Atlantic sea. The new sensibility was about the necessity of overcoming the functionalist and mechanistic heritage of the Modern Movement and its refusal of any symbolism. Aldo Rossi's work was situated in this context, concerned with the re-awakening of the interiority of the individual and the city, its latent singularity and imagery. This is why his *Autobiography* was published first in the United States and then in Italy. His contribution comes more from drawings and writings than from built architecture. While his drawings are widely circulated, the images from where they come are less known, and are the subject of this chapter's analysis.

Figure 1: Aldo Rossi, *Autobiografia Scientifica*, Il Saggiatore, 2009 (image produced by author).

Rossi's most significant writings are those introducing single projects and also his *Autobiografia Scientifica* (*A Scientific Autobiography*) published in 1981. In this publication, Rossi structures his theory and methodology in the form of a ritual, metamorphic journey through the imagery of his memory, of the Bible, of science. Rossi confesses that his initial intention was just to analyse the projects, but then, in doing so, he composed an additional autonomous project. I propose that he did address the original goal as the book focuses on the inside of his particular architectural process: an invisible tale standing below and giving life to the deepest reasons for form. Rossi in fact uses an image-based way to reach his projects. Images are linked to one another by analogies that generate chains of metamorphic compositions. *A Scientific Autobiography* contains almost two hundred precise images embedded in the written text, which, except for almost a dozen, are not visible illustrations, but evocations. As part of my research I have sourced many of them, in order to re-read this thin booklet and its visual work, to permit the latent text between the lines to emerge.

Figure 2: A postcard from the 1950s showing San Carlone, 'The most colossal statue in the world' (image produced by author).

Figure 3: Trojan Horse, *The World Displayed by the Rev Royal Robbins*, W.W. Reed & Co., New York, 1830 (image produced by author).

> This interior-exterior aspect of architecture was certainly first suggested to me by the San Carlone at Arona, a work which I have drawn so many times that it is now difficult to relate it to the visual education of my childhood. I subsequently understood that it pleased me because here the limits that distinguish the domains of architecture, the machines and instruments were dissolved in marvellous invention.
>
> (Rossi 1981: 2)

> As with the Homeric Horse, the pilgrims enter the body of the Saint as he would be a tower or a wagon steered by a knowing technician. After he mounts the exterior stair of the pedestal, the steep ascent through the interior of the body reveals the structure of the work and the welded seams of the huge pieces of sheet metal. Finally he arrives to the interior-exterior of the head; from the eyes of the saint, the view of the lake acquires infinite contours, as if one were gazing from a celestial observatory.
>
> (Rossi 1981: 2)

Rossi deposits the entire system of his theory, much more than in any other apparently more structured and scientific publication, to reach what 'theory' literally means: from the Greek *theao*, the full visualization of his cultural system – the duplicity of Christianity and Enlightenment – through these images. Analogy is the device that permits and shapes relations between distant events, for instance a table for supper and the same table for death (Figures 2 and 3). He awakes in the reader a sort of demiurgic *Chora* from where shapes spring out, accumulatively materializing into projects, which, in turn, transform into new projects referring to one another. The result is a fascination kidnapping the reader-viewer, who is softly seduced into a shifted world, where hierarchies are overturned and tales are more powerful than chronology, convenience, use and profit. The reader-viewer enters a circularity, recalling systems such as the anatomical theatre or the game of goose, Dante's Hell structure or Monte Carmelo. A circularity made of more than a hundred places – Ferrara, Izmir, Lisbon, Bursa, Colmar etc. – and more than a hundred authors – M. H. B. Stendhal, E. L. Boullée, H. Melville, P. Klee, W. A. Mozart etc.

> I have always thought that the term 'teatrino' was more complex than 'teatro': it refers not just to the size of the building but also to the private, specific, repetitive character of all that is fiction in the theatre. Others have considered 'teatrino' to be an ironic or diminutive word. My terming of the 1979 project 'scientific' has its source in a number of ideas: it is certainly a mixture of the anatomical theatre in Padua and the *teatrino scientifico* in Mantua, an allusion both to the scientific function and to those puppet theatres where Goethe loved to spend time in his youth.
>
> (Rossi 1981: 29)

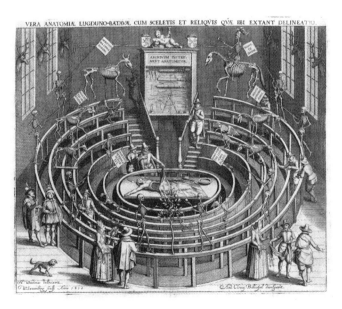

Figure 4: *Anatomical Theatre*, Leiden. Print from Engraving dated 1610 (image produced by author).

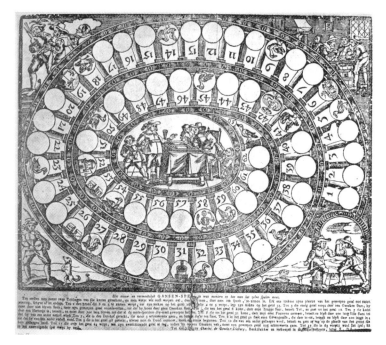

Figure 5: The game of the goose. Engraving by J. F. Pifferer, printed in Barcelona, eighteenth century (image produced by author).

> The labyrinth amused us because we found the goose game in it, thinking to make the design simulating a children's game. But how could we not have recalled that the sinister element of this game, especially for children, is represented by the square of death? The subject of death was something that had automatically found its way into the process of design.
>
> (Rossi 1981: 11)

A Scientific Autobiography joins urban tradition with the needs of the contemporary urban landscape, regaining elements belonging to the romantic imagery of the historical city, internal memory, stages for human life. The visualization of the imaginary journey that Rossi builds is important, not only to better understand his architectural methodology, but also in order to re-awaken the imaginary of the architectural culture of the 1960–80s when modernist heritage was strong and mainly based on functionalism. Peter Eisenman promotes the book in the *Oppositions* Series that stood against the diffuse architectural culture of that time. *Oppositions* was part of the activity carried out by IAUS, founded by Peter Eisenman in New York, gathering American and European intellectuals, including Manfredo Tafuri, Rafael Moneo, John Hejduk, Kenneth Frampton and Aldo Rossi, around the necessity of understanding a more complex approach to architecture and the city.

The geographical foreground of *A Scientific Autobiography* is the Po Valley, with a constellation of cities in the background drawn from the long trips he made from Seville to Lisbon to Nantucket to Bursa. The Po Valley is the particular district that acts as the native landscape of his imagery: city profiles emerging from constant fog, the internal warm lights of small local theatres in the night, ploughed fields at sunset, filtered photographic shoots by Luigi Ghirri (Ghirri 1989) that belong to the same landscape, and become the soul landscape. In Rossi's drawings he tops urban lighthouses with the small metal flag that he declares derive from Hölderlin *Hälfte des Lebens*, but which remind the viewer of medieval towers of the North of Italy, Pianura Padana, or the fifteenth-century communes of northern Italy and the Adriatic lighthouses of his childhood. The rhythm of the text is marked by the chains of analogies that cross between memory and observation.

Many of the image references in the *Autobiography* are from Mantua, Milan, Parma, Ferrara. These cities belong to a particular historical geography, the so-called Età dei Comuni e delle Signorie, which over three centuries was part of a race to become the most beautiful city. While the central part of Italy belonged to the Pontificate and the south was Impero delle due Sicilie, with Naples and Palermo as capital cities, the northern cities belonged to particular families. For instance: Ferrara to the Este, Parma to the Farnese, Mantua to the Gonzaga. The families invested in the best architects to build the most beautiful and innovative theatres, public feasts and infrastructures. The territorial unit was no longer a vast region, but the city itself, projecting itself onto the surrounding country. This competitive city-state system grew from a combined tradition of Catholic canons promoting the language of art and protestant infiltrations permitting freedom in scientific development. This led to an equilibrium characterizing the cultural and city context of Milan, where Rossi grew up, where Christian sensibility coexisted with the more recent sensibility of Enlightenment.

Aldo Rossi perfectly understood and represented this duality. I argue that one reason that post-war international debate was attracted to his drawings was due to the natural gentleness he used in re-proposing a model fascinated by this European golden age that was, at the same time, a timely interpretation of the post-war need for a complete regeneration of the place of human dwelling. His softness of approach is evidenced by the watercolour technique he used and the continuous attempt to include the city in the oneiric atmosphere of the dream, with similar pastel colours to De Chirico's paintings. No people are present in his drawings, despite his repeated claim in *A Scientific Autobiography* that the city is the theatre stage of humanity. However, the definition of the city given in Diderot and D'Alembert's *Encyclopédie* (Diderot and D'Alembert 1751: XVII vol, pp. 277–82) is solely the 'assembly of several houses, streets, walls [...] a closed enclosure of walls which contains several neighborhoods, streets, squares', an easier definition than that of Aristoteles in the *Etica Nicomachea* (Aristoteles 2000, Libro X, 7:15), which requires the city (polis) to guarantee human happiness. The 'Illuminists' have been defined as 'terrible simplifiers' (Berlin 2013: XLVI) with a tendency to exclude what does not respond to universal standards, for instance human happiness. Their main preoccupation was to find the scientific, universal rules valid for any system and any of its singular elements, including the biological dimension of man but not his interiority. The Illuminist heritage led to architectural organization of typologies and automatic construction technology epitomised by J. N. L. Durand (Durand 2000: 89–119).

Born in Milan in 1931, Rossi's family abandoned the city at the beginning of the war for the less dangerous Lake Como, where he attended both secondary and high school at the Archiepiscopal College of the Somaschi Fathers. The Catholic college, 'Alessandro Volta', was not dedicated to a Saint, but to a scientist, the inventor of the battery (volts). This autobiographic detail indicates the vivid doubled tradition of Enlightenment Rationalism and the Catholic, combining in Milan as 'moral capital' (Bonghi 1881). This coexistence is further emphasized by proximity to Calvinist Switzerland –Rossi married a Swiss actress and taught at ETH School. The cultural polycentrism of Rossi's family and educational background led to an *ars combinatoria* that is never a passive pastiche of shapes induced by nostalgia or pleasure for the allegory. But rather this approach is an attempt to reveal affinities and connections that are normally hidden, together with awareness of the impossibility of pursuing the unitary systems characterized by the modern movement. He was aware of the crisis of architectural language and captured a pluralism, similar to his near-contemporary, Italo Calvino, also a dreamer and a graceful traverser of scriptures, but continuously exploring structural principles, such as in the *Six Memos for the Next Millennium*. A kind of analogy and visual resonance exists between the *Invisible Cities* tales of Calvino and the stories that Aldo Rossi creates to nurture each of his projects. The images included in this chapter are selected from nearly two hundred references of books, places, myths that Rossi traverses in *A Scientific Autobiography*. They are arranged as chains of images in the book to perform as a very intensive trip through his imagery, always in balance between the scientific – cataloguing – and the apparition – ritual.

What gives continuity to the narration is the mythopoeic approach to the architectural/city project, the continuous necessity to find the supporting tale to develop the shape of architecture. Along the metamorphic steps, the Japanese sliding *yatai* becomes the mobile puppet theatre for Pinocchio, in turn, generating the Teatro del Mondo floating from Venice to Dubrovnik, a mobile point of reference in the fluvial plains, like the Maine lighthouses so much loved by Rossi. Filaret's column for the never completed Palazzo del Duca in Venice produces the Berlin IBA dwelling blocks, while the osteological-archaeological studies and the

Depositions by Rosso Fiorentino, Antonello da Messina and Grünewald transform into the cemetery for Modena. The chains of analogies go on with oneiric images intertwined with biographical ones. The connections are analogical, which means that the images are always double, as they need an image as a mirror to reflect themselves. Repetition of elements is seen in the series of flying buttresses of Milan's Duomo, then fades in the Lisbon cemetery chapels, later in the monks' houses in Pavia, into the continuity of the arches of the Segovia-Cordoba Aqueduct leading to the Berlin facades projects. The volumetric qualities of the San Carlone statue, the Troy Horse, the confessionals in the churches, lead to the projects for the Carlo Felice Theatre in Genova and the Bonnefanten Museum in Maastricht. Places able to host tens of people in everyday life or just a solitary visitor, like the Pio Albergo Trivulzio, lead to projects like the Pertini Monument in Milan or to the Lighthouse Theatre in Toronto.

> Below I quote a brief description of the Duomo in Milan taken from my blue notebooks. The description is from 1971, and it often seems to me to resemble one of my projects. In effect it shows how any work we experience becomes our own. 'Noteworthy experience of the architecture of the Duomo in Milan: I have not climbed to the top for some time now. It relates to the problem of the

Figure 6: The Duomo Roof, Milan (photograph by author).

alignment of elements and, naturally, to verticality. Having gone up the stair, one walks down along open-air passageway. The passageway cuts through the flying buttresses by means of narrow rectangular doorways which follow one another with the rhythm of the buttresses. (...)' The Duomo is the *fabrica del dôm*, and hence the architecture, like the *cà granda*, is above all the house which is constructed for everyone. Therefore it cannot be finished. This structure affords the possibility of moving inside and over the city; the walk on the roof of the Duomo in fact constitutes an important experience of urban architecture. For my own part, I have long been impressed with those equal volumes on the side of the building; they reappear in the central streets of my projects for Modena and for Fagnano Olona.

(Rossi 1981: 57)

In Lisbon there is a cemetery which is curiously called 'the cemetery of pleasure' but no one has never explained to me the origin of this name; in America there are cemeteries as large as parks or suburbs. There are different customs and forms for the places of death as for those of life, but often we hardly grasp the boundary between the two conditions.

(Rossi 1981: 15)

Figure 7: The Cemetery of Pleasures, Lisbon (photograph by author).

Figure 8: Certosa of Pavia, houses of monks (photograph by author).

> I realize that in discussing Antonioni's film I was alluding to the drawing *The cabins of Elba*, but this later became the project for student housing in Chieti, while in other drawings I have called it *Impressions d'Afrique* (not only as an homage to Raymond Roussel). Thus I believe that a project may be a conclusion to a chain of associations, or else may be forgotten and left to other people or situation. My youthful observation of long workers' scaffolds, of courtyards full of voices and meetings which I spied on with a sort of fear in my bourgeois childhood, had the same fascination as the cabins or, better, as the small houses which came to mind in other situations and places, like the monks' houses at the Certosa in Pavia or those endless American suburbs.
>
> (Rossi 1981: 41)

Analogies permit Rossi to connect fiction (interiority) and reality (contingency): two dimensions otherwise often irreconcilable. The deep meaning he attributes to analogy is not just a visual issue, but has more to do with invisibility and its power. Rossi quotes *Le Mont Analogue* (*Mount Analogue*) by René Daumal from 1952, 'the intermixing of time and space has approached me to the idea of analogy; definitions that approximate things by referring to one another' (Rossi 2009: 115).

> Perhaps Daumal's concept of analogy particularly struck me because of his comment about 'the astounding speed of the already seen' which I connected with the Ryle's definition of analogy as the end of a process. This book, in its ability to sum up my other readings and personal experiences, brought me to a more complex vision of reality, especially insofar as the conception of geometry and space was concerned. I encountered something similar to this in Juan

Figure 9: San Juan de la Cruz, *Climb of Mount Carmelo*. From Giovanni della Croce, *Salita al Monte Carmelo*, Rome: OCD, 2010 (image produced by author).

> de la Cruz's ascent of Mount Carmel: the representation of the mountain in his magnificent drawing/ writing brought me back to my initial perception of the Monti Sacri.
>
> (Rossi 1981: 81)

In the very first page of *A Scientific Autobiography* Rossi reveals the two main structuring references: Dante Alighieri and Max Planck. Both use analogical methods, both are involved in the issue of invisibility and its effect on what we see, of finding the hidden constant between the relative and the absolute. Planck, in *Planck Constant*, explored the symmetry of what is invisible for its excessive magnitude or for its smallness. Dante explores the invisibility of what transcends physical life, seeking the rules regulating the peaks and abysses of interiority, namely Heaven and Hell. He visualizes through a complex system of images what is normally inaccessible to biological eyes. Dante builds an extremely rigorous and repetitive structure of tercets to gain freedom for the flow of images to move through rigid bonds. Each tercet is a clear image, developing into a following one and creating periodicity, like geology. So *A Scientific Autobiography* is continuously hovering between life and death, the predictable and unpredictable, what had been long forgotten by post–Modern movement architecture. Rossi traces symmetries between cities of life and cities of death, the very similar structures of, for instance the Lisbon Cemetery of Pleasures and Milan Duomo's roof. From this duplicitous (or dual) perspective, an architect has to plan everything to host the repetitions of daily life, which constantly risks to be run over by death. So that a set table could also remain so, as a still life (Rossi 1992: 25). Repetitiveness can be transformed into ritual, where maximum attention is devoted to every gesture, each time as different from the others.

> It is impossible to create anything fantastic without a rigid, incontrovertible and precisely, repetitive basement [...] If I were to speak today of architecture, I would better say it is a matter of ritual than creativity.
>
> (Rossi 1992: 60)

From Max Planck, Aldo Rossi even borrows the title from the book where Planck reconstructs the order of his research's guiding principles, where science is not just a question of physical observation, but requires theoretical capacity to see what is invisible. They both position science as conscious of its limits, not opposed to theology but complementary to it. But Rossi chose another fragment by Planck to start his *Autobiography* with, recalling the role of memory, the lifelong accumulation of images to be stored for the construction of one's own interiority, a universe of analogies that underlies the projects, which Mandel'stam has called 'the conservation of the background is the law of energy conservation of art works' (Mandel'stam 2015: 74).

> my mind absorbed avidly, like a revelation, the first law I knew to possess absolute, universal validity, independently from all human agency: the principle of the conservation of energy. I shall never forget the graphic story Müller (prof. of Maths) told us, at his raconteur's best, of the bricklayer lifting with great effort a heavy block of stone to the roof of a house. The work he thus performs does not get lost; it remains stored up, perhaps for many years, undiminished and latent in the block of stone, until one day the block is perhaps loosened and drops on the head of some passerby.
>
> (Rossi 1992: 17)

In the short text *Le distanze invisibili*, Rossi recalls the story of the Japanese temple of Ise, where the architecture of the temple is a fact of pure rituality itself.

> There are two equal, nearby and ancient temples. Their antiquity exists solely in the continuous reconstruction of one of the two. Every twenty-five years,

the previous temple is completely destroyed, while the one nearby is being completed. And the new temple has only a piece of wood from the other temple. Its recognition is no longer in the material, old or new, or in the object itself, but purely in the image, in an event that, once recognized, reproduces itself almost without asking the reason. In the Western world this may correspond in part to the ritual.

Ritual in Rossi's *A Scientific Autobiography* is the ritual of preparation. The fascination for what modern architectural practice often excludes, the preparation not only for what has been planned, but for the unplanned too, like death, is the hidden protagonist. The book *Apparecchio alla morte* (*Apparatus for Death*) by Saint'Alfonso de Liguori (1758) prepared for death through 36 spiritual exercises. The attention paid to precise proportioning of architecture given by fifteenth-century architectural treatises tells the importance of full regulation in order to permit unexpected marvels to take place in the project, in order to gain freedom. Ritual becomes the circular methodology of the flowing of images in *A Scientific Autobiography*, the character regulating the analogies and the evocative visual references through the constant activity of observation and description. Obsession with the smallest of daily and ongoing rituals is evident in Rossi's attraction to the monastic brotherhoods and lives of Saints (Pavia Certosa, the Santiago de Compostela, *Historia Lausiaca*) as the prefiguration for the construction of a community. The construction of a parallel dimension of mystical landscape, recalled by the apparition of Elijah, from which the community of Monte Carmelo derives, shows desert theology combined with a very strong contemplative and cognitive tension. Each architectural project has the task to awaken relevant rituals and to connect all their associated images, their universe of analogies with its community. The city is an intensification of architecture and requires renewal of its imagery.

REFERENCES

Alighieri, D. (1991), *La Divina Commedia*, Milan: Hoepli.

Aristoteles (2000 edition), *Ethika Nikomacheia* (*Etica Nicomachea*), Milan: Bompiani.

Berlin, I. (2013), *Against the Current* (*Controcorrente*), Milan: Adelphi.

Bonghi, R. (1881), in *La Perseveranza* newspaper, in the occasion of Milan 1881 Expo.

Calvino, I. (1972), *Le città invisibili*, Turin: Einaudi.

——— (1974), *Invisible Cities*, San Diego, CA: Harcourt.

——— (1993), Lezioni Americane (*Six Memos for the Next Millennium*), Milan: Mondadori.

Daumal, R. (2012), *Le Mont Analogue* (*Mount Analogue*), Milan: Adelphi.

De Liguori, S. Alfonso (1995), *Apparecchio alla morte* (*Apparatus for Death*), Milan: Gribaudi.

Diderot and D'Alambert (1751), *Encyclopédie ou dictionnaire raisonné des sciences, des arts et des metiers,* 1st ed., vol. XVII, Paris: Imprimeur du Roy, voice 'ville' by L. de Jaucourt.

Durand, J. N. L. (2000), *Précis of the Lectures on Architecture,* Los Angeles: Getty Research Institute.

Eisenman, P. (2007), 'Houses of memory: the Texts of Analogy', in *Eisenman Inside Out: Selected Writings 1963–1988,* New Haven, CT: Yale University Press.

Ghirri, L. (1989), *Italian Landscape,* Quaderni di Lotus no.11, Milan: Lotus (for Elemond Division).

Hejduk, J. (1998), 'Sentences on a house and other sentences', in *Such Places as Memory,* Cambridge, MA: The MIT Press.

Mandel'stam, O. (2015), *Conversazione su Dante,* Genoa: Il Melangolo.

VV.AA. Opposition Books Series (1973–1984), IAUS Institute for Architecture and Urban Studies, Cambridge, MA: The MIT Press.

Planck, M. (1968), *Wissenschaftliche Selbstbiographie (Scientific Autobiography),* Westport, CT: Greenwood.

Rispoli, E. R. (2012), *Ponti sull'Atlantico: L'Institute for Architecture and Urban Studies e le relazioni Italia-America 1967–1985,* Macerata: Quodlibet.

Rossi, A. (1981), A *Scientific Autobiography,* Opposition Books Series, Cambridge, MA: The MIT Press.

—— (1980), *Aldo Rossi: an exhibition of Drawing,* IAUS New York exhibition, in E.R. Rispoli, *Ponti sull'Atlantico: L'Institute for Architecture and Urban Studies e le relazioni Italia-America 1967–1985,* p. 144.

—— (1982), *The Architecture of the City,* Cambridge, MA: The MIT Press.

—— (1989), *Le distanze invisibili,* in A. Ferlenga (curated by), *Aldo Rossi. Architetture 1988–1992,* Electa, Milano 1992.

—— (1992), 'Un'educazione realista' ('A realistic education'), in *Opera Completa 1988–1992,* Milan: Electa.

—— (2009), *Autobiografia Scientifica,* Milan: Il Saggiatore.

3

How to draw a line when the world is moving: Architectural education in times of urgent imagination

Tariq Toffa, University of Johannesburg

'An international university of choice, anchored in Africa ...'

– Vision slogan of the University of Johannesburg
(Rensburg 2016: 4)

'Where would it go if it lifted its anchor?'

– Brenden Gray, Department of Graphic Design, Faculty of Art,
Design and Architecture (FADA), University of Johannesburg,
FADA Decolonisation Conversation, 9 June 2016

When local is global

In March 2015 Chumani Maxwele, a student at the University of Cape Town, South Africa, hurled a bucket of human waste onto the bronze statue of the nineteenth-century British arch-imperialist Cecil John Rhodes at the heart of the campus. The statue, occupying pride of place at one of the continent's top-rated universities in one of its most beautiful and tourist-friendly cities, was brought crashing back to reality by this son of a mineworker from one of the country's poorest regions. The student, shirtless and donning a mineworker's hardhat (the iconic image of a mineworker), brought the faeces and urine contents from a portable flush toilet container used in one of the city's poverty-affected peripheral 'black' townships to the proverbial gatekeepers of education and privilege. Unknown at the time, this performative symbolism would be the spark that would catalyse into motion nationwide student/worker protests over the following two years (see Figures 1 and 2).

Examples of campus unrest are in many respects symptomatic of the tensions between 'global' competitiveness and 'local' relevance. Arif Dirlik argues insightfully 'that esthetic choices are ultimately social choices as well. The problem with the architecture of globalisation ultimately is that it is a negation of the social …' (Dirlik 2007: 46). Thus, as Mosquera and Fisher (2004: 8) observe, what 'has been reintroduced into artistic and critical discourse by the "locals" of the world […] is a renewed concern with ethical and political agency […]'. Building critical pedagogies in this context over a few years of intensive experimentation, myself and colleagues at the University of Johannesburg developed approaches and a body of work to engage with such conditions. This chapter describes some of our experiments in the making of 'discursive spaces', and in particular in how a series of design-research methodologies have been employed in order to offer an architectural education relevant to times of urgent imagination.

In the context of the spatial-related disciplines (architecture, planning, landscape, urban design, etc.), my work involves the relationship between *spatial*

Figure 1: The removal of the bronze statue of Cecil John Rhodes at the University of Cape Town (UCT) on 9 April 2015 (photo by Sadiq Toffa, 2015).

Figure 2: Protests at/against the UCT School of Architecture, Planning & Geomatics, October 2015. The sign reads: 'COLONIAL CITY DESIGN LIVES HERE' (photo by Tim Geschwindt, 2015).

discourses (i.e. discourses about how spatial-related disciplines are implicated in historical, social and cultural structures) and *discursive spaces* (i.e. discursively engaged and contextually appropriate technique, drawing, representational and design methods, as well as physical spaces).[1] Experimentations in the latter are also the means and tools that may enable cultivation of the former to act in the real social world and its built environment, participating in and potentially contributing towards constructing larger political, societal, global or national discourses.

Some of these emergent techniques of discursive spaces – named 'voicing', 'multi-modality', 'siting / surfacing', 'spaces of publics', 'territory', 'perspective' and 'self-reflexivity' – are discussed below.[2] They point to the need to historicize, contextualize and interrogate the knowledge areas and technique of the design disciplines, so that within this rigorous dialogue new discursive technique can begin to take shape.

Voicing

In a powerful critique of universally applied 'canonical' social theory, de-colonial scholar Ramón Grosfoguel argued that this in fact was largely confined to 'social theories based on the social-historical experience of men of five countries' (Italy, France, England, Germany and the United States), which constituted 'the foundation of the Social Sciences and the Humanities in the Westernized universities today'. And thus,

> [t]he other side of this epistemic privilege is epistemic inferiority. Epistemic privilege and epistemic inferiority are two sides of the same coin. [...] The knowledge produced from the social/historical experiences and world views of the Global South, also known as 'non-Western', are considered inferior and not part of the canon of thought.
>
> (Grosfoguel 2013: 72, 73)

These unequal global structures of knowledge can also be reflected and exacerbated by many factors on a regional scale. Not unlike the modern sociospatial histories of rural–urban tensions in many regions of the African continent, these relations of knowledge find echoes today for example in the educational space in 'arrival cities' like Johannesburg, where a large contingent of students arrive from outside the metropolis for their studies and whose frames of knowledge, skills and lived experience can often be similarly 'outside'.[3] Arguably, and in more general and abstract terms, implicitly inferior knowledges can also be further estranged from the academy by an 'atomization' of modern life and thinking, 'by the collapse of an integrated experience of life, and by the irreversible emergence of autonomy in various domains that are incapable of regaining their common foundation' (Heynen 1999: 14).

The primary innovation in the methodological approach of 'voicing' is therefore to bring normative disciplinary discourses into a dialogue with students' own value bases and ethical foundations from their own views, position and lived experiences (which have limited spaces for authentic expression within the current academic context). The topicality emerging from such 'marginal' and 'fragmented' lived experiences was extensive and varied: issues ranged from governance, the school system, homelessness, race, feminism, class, 'black tax' (the obligation for new graduates to support their families financially), domestic violence, xenophobia, abortion, bullying, 'black' hair, spirituality and environmental concerns (Figures 3 and 4).

The searching for new voice as well as a suitable visual and verbal language with which it can speak can be a daunting task. The explorations need to be necessarily

Figure 3: Voicing: Exploring spirituality and Christianity in Africa (images by Mvuleni Mnisi, 2017).

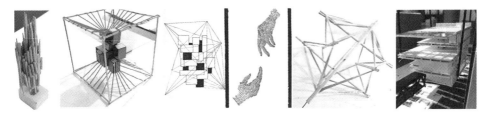

Figure 4: Voicing: Exploring the African concept of *ubuntu* ('humanity'), often translated as 'I am because we are' (images by Phiko Tshainca, 2017).

multi-modal, but the challenges are many. Since the various knowledge areas of disciplines typically reinforce – and hence reproduce – each other, likewise the project needs to be supported and supplemented by other approaches and interventions, for one of the biggest challenges is to resist falling back upon default design, aesthetic and representational formula and techniques as well as conventional assessment criteria.

Multi-modality

In the design studios, voicing was tied to operating with 'multi-modality'. Apart from general individual preferences that may exist towards oral, textual or graphic communication, student strengths and weaknesses in contexts of deep inequalities like South Africa are also inseparable from structural realities. For example, English is not a first language for most in South Africa (it is largely confined to the larger cities and may even be a fifth language in some cases) and so many students are disadvantaged by English-only tertiary instruction, especially in the early years of study. Disparate levels of pre-tertiary education and lack of academic 'preparedness' between well-resourced and under-resourced schools is another factor. Thus, within such conditions, placing multiple modes (image, text, model, listening, speech etc.)

on 'equal' footing in higher education (in both instruction and output) attempts to soften the extensions of structural bias and disadvantage in order to build a common platform that facilitates inclusive, reflective and critical thinking.

More than simply a case of expecting students to 'do the work' of bringing alterity to the established academic project, voicing and multi-modality as operating modes in the making of discursive space asks of the 'expert' educator to be willing to move beyond comfortable certainties. In order to ground and nurture other knowledges into the academy through purposeful and methodical experimentation, to an extent educators need to be willing to become students themselves.

Siting/surfacing

Parallel and complementary to voicing is 'siting', employed as a catalytic element in a process of surfacing and developing lived realities, values, voices, questions and world-views that are 'true to life'. Here we aim not to remain confined by the reproductive zone of disciplinary questions and practices in researching and building project context (site analysis, climatic analysis, design informants etc.). Rather, this 'siting' entails selecting places for project work that allow for the development of alterity in discourse, technique and design, and – as it often turned out – even a lexicon with which to be able to articulate it. Often physical sites were preferred whose sheer critical mass of density and complexity enabled a level of epistemic diversity, such as inner-city contexts, or they could be selected to provoke or surface dissonances, such as popular but elite/classist urban areas.

Other roles of 'siting' lay in scrutinizing their place in the epistemic timeline of the design-research process. Sites for architecture are usually introduced at the beginning of a design project and thus occupy discursive/epistemic primacy of place, but this need not necessarily be taken for granted as it often reproduces other taken-for-granted conventions. 'Siting' introduced at a later stage of a research process in certain cases may encourage a broader developing dialogue as opposed to dominating the setting out or scope of a discourse.

Spaces of publics

The notion of a common 'public' that qualifies a space or social category is generally used but little interrogated in architectural design-research discourse. My work has preferred the use of the term 'spaces of publics' over the more ubiquitous and often idealized and bourgeois conception of 'public spaces'. 'Public spaces' typically reference European and North American examples through which the type is known and substantiated. Conversely, 'spaces of publics' prioritize a social context to which thought and design must respond, the particularities of habitat and needs to which such spaces must serve, and the structures that frustrate them. This inversion exposes a limitation of readily available imagery and appropriate visual techniques. Martin Murray expands on some of the problems embedded in conventional notions of 'public':

> [...] the overall design of urban space is not simply a matter of context and aesthetics, it is also a complex sociospatial process that encodes power relations, value orientations, and symbolic meanings into the routine practices of everyday life. [...] The organization and management of urban space selects and restricts what activities, behaviours, and practices can take place, authorizing some while delegitimating and condemning others.
>
> (Murray 2011: 8–9)

Inherited Eurocentric architectural presumptions and conventions, together with city spatial dynamics dominated by real estate capitalism, produce and deepen urban landscapes of polar extremes of wealth and poverty, which are sometimes also racialized (such as in South Africa). These are manifest between as well as within territories, such as affluent islands serviced by workers from beyond their boundaries. New public spaces – ostensibly 'public', but surveilled, securitized, socially sterilized and stigmatizing 'otherness', are neither fully public nor private and are frequently 'post-public' (Murray 2011: 20). These spatial forms not only exacerbate social tensions but also produce inequitable and inefficient urban landscapes.

The question of how to understand and include 'publics' in the design of their spaces can be complex. To generate more transformative conditions, at the macro level Edgar Pieterse (2013, 2015), director of the African Centre for Cities, for example has emphasized the need for 'trade-offs' and 'deal-making' by informed citizens and publics, fostered through explicit political discourses alongside governmental and governance changes. Within this macro context, design/research projects in the spatial-related disciplines can help to cultivate a sensibility towards a more humane assembly of differences. Many student design-research projects have therefore been located at the intersections of such 'colliding worlds' (Bremner 2004). One project explored the University of Johannesburg campus itself with its surrounding and nearby neighbourhoods, bringing the relatively wealthy but introverted campus and its design departments into engagement and negotiation with the lives and spaces of its surrounding publics (see Figure 5).[4] Another project explored the iconic Johannesburg suburbs of Sandton and Alexandra.[5] Separated only by a thin strip of highway and industry, nowhere else in southern Africa

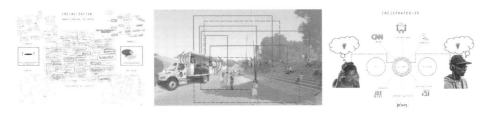

Figure 5: 'Spaces of publics' between the University of Johannesburg (UJ) and the adjacent Fietas neighbourhood, explored through a radio station as a roaming catalyst to facilitate sites of architectural intervention for longer-term strategies (images by Sibusiso Lwandle, 2015).

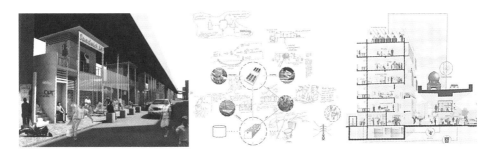

Figure 6: 'Spaces of publics' in the work of 'UJ_Unit2: Architecture and Agency' explored the spaces of relationships between people, systems and infrastructure, and the individual and collective needs of diverse publics (images by Sibusiso Lwandle, 2015).

has extreme prosperity and poverty in such close proximity. These all surface juxtapositions and dissonances, and seek to develop appropriate cognitive, design and lexical tools with which to be able to engage them.

Spaces of publics does not only include the social dimensions of publics and the organization of social space, but also how these are mediated through space/built form and their related tangible and intangible systems and infrastructures. An experimental design-research studio 'UJ_Unit2: Architecture and Agency'[6] was built on the concept of 'Open Building' first articulated by John Habraken (1972). UJ_Unit2 attempted to study, manage and design for diverse decision-making within the built environment (Figure 6). Students were encouraged to engage with the relationships between people, systems and infrastructure, and to consider the individual and collective needs of diverse publics through visual diagrams and mappings (UJ_Unit2). Often collapsing disciplinary boundaries and scales, these frames also assist design-researchers to develop knowledge and skills to be better-equipped to engage and influence higher-level policies and to offer these into lower level project interventions (Toffa et al. 2015: 297).

Territory

'Space' rather than 'building' is considered here a primary organizing and analytical tool of architecture that connects with other spatial-related disciplines such as urban planning and landscape design. Following the 'spatial turn' (Warf and Arias 2009), considerations of space have become commonplace across a wide variety of fields, allowing 'space' to be engaged with from a variety of disciplinary and theoretical perspectives. However, this has also made the term increasingly ambiguous. 'Territory', or the 'territorialization of space', as one spatial lens, has therefore become more useful in UJ design/research studios for reading, rendering and reshaping spaces. Territory implies both belonging and repelling,[7] both inclusion and exclusion, and entails working with the political, social and spatial structures through which they are constituted.

These potential 'surfacings' are particularly relevant within contexts of neo-liberal patterns of urbanization or urban regeneration, which is the condition of most city centres in contemporary South Africa. These forms of urbanization must find balance between the for-profit investments of big business and the relatively clean and purportedly safer environments that they bring, with the marginalization of residents and communities such as those who cannot afford the associated higher rentals.

From elite Sandton to Hillbrow, Johannesburg's most densely populated and stressed 'infamous' inner-city neighbourhood, and from the internalized artificial worlds of shopping malls to gated housing estates, 'territory' can manifest in a variety of ways and often with significant impacts on the urban condition (Figure 7). Across such diverse urban and typological conditions, the lens of territory attempts to foreground the intentions and mechanisms through which territorialization occurs.

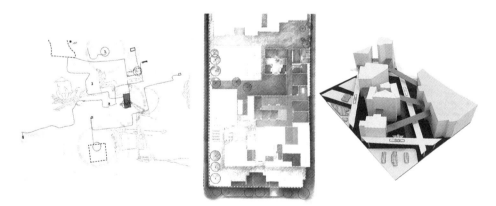

Figure 7: Explorations of 'territory' in Johannesburg (images by Julian Almond and Kirsty Fick, 2014; model by Tumelo Legote, 2018).

In Hillbrow, a voluntary 'City Improvement District' made up largely of property owners, architecture students undertook to understand and engage various 'political' dimensions of territory and the related hierarchies that they produce.[8] Hillbrow functions in physical space through a variety of mechanisms of management and control (security guards, cameras, fences, buffers, level changes etc.). At a second level of reading territory, higher-level institutional structures and their constituencies were identified as important stakeholders (schools, organizations, collectives etc.), and at a third level students engaged in more informal networks through conducting semi-structured interviews on the ground and obtaining participant mind-map sketches.

Working with multiple readings of territory also allows a study of the spatialization of class, not solely in economic terms, but also as bound with constellations of interests, tastes, prejudices, priorities and fears. Sociological categories and distinctions prove particularly useful, such as conceptions of 'social structure' and the relationships between groups that it entails, or 'social networks' and 'social groups'. For example, tightly knit or 'primary' versus larger and more impersonal 'secondary' groups, heterogeneous versus more homogenous groups, 'category' groups with shared characteristics versus 'aggregate' groupings that are more accidental/spontaneous, can be explored, alongside 'social statuses' and their related hierarchies (implied by age, race, gender, skill etc.).

Working with territory as a research technique frames the political, social and hierarchal elements of place, and frames the design/research act as one that can serve to consolidate its sociospatial structures, or alternatively, as one that can allow for the possibility of reshaping the interaction within or between groupings and their spatializations. Ultimately, these engagements seek to *constructively* (as opposed to purely obsequiously or judgmentally) engage the built environment and its social structures, and to locate where, and how much, lee-way exists between tensions, to support strategies that may provide a broader basis for negotiated, collaborative action and the most humane assembly of differences.

Perspective

German art historian and media theorist Hans Belting (2011) studied how optical or visual theory (*'ilm al-manazir'*, or 'the science of what appears') in classical Islamic culture became part of Renaissance math and science and eventually stood behind the development of linear perspective and pictorial theory in the European Renaissance. The differences in application were cultural, not scientific, each making different use of the same knowledge (Belting 2011: 12). The story of perspective transforms again in more recent times: in Cézanne's struggle against

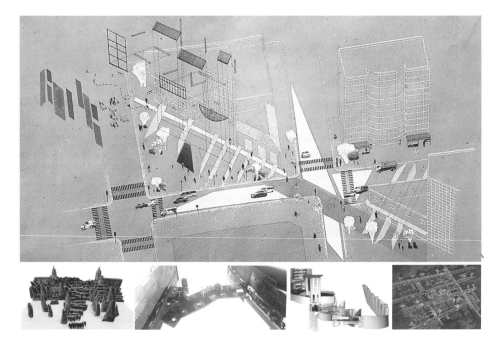

Figure 8: Explorations of the social functions of perspective (images by Cornel Hugo, Portia Mabudisa, Chantelle van Tonder, Ntokozo Nhlapo and Wade Hassett, 2015–2018).

perspective, towards primitivism and cubism, modern art in many ways rebelled against perspective pictures as banal, clichéd and an impediment to 'progress' (Belting 2011: 19–21).

While landscape architect and theorist James Corner describes perspective as one of 'the tools of thought passed down from Enlightenment and modernist paradigms' and as 'technical instruments that enable the utopian renovation of huge tracts of urban fabric' (Corner 1999: 224),[9] Belting allows us to see perspective, not born and essentialized in 'the west' with inevitable outcomes of measurement and control, but rather as culturally nuanced and contingent. This allows the possibility of a repurposing. Thus another discursive technique being explored in the design studio is a social function of perspective, employed as a powerful imaginative act towards empowering the most vulnerable, augmented with other techniques of discursive space that speak to wider communities and publics (Figure 8).

Reflexivity

Sociology in the last 50 years has increasingly undergone something of an 'inward turn', towards 'sociological reflexivity as a methodological element and research tool' for social analysis (d'Oliveira-Martins 2014: 193). A comparable process has also unfolded in other disciplines in various ways. Art historian Charles Harrison argued for critical thinking in 'the relationship of the notional spectator to that which the picture shows', implying greater responsibility in the ways that 'self' and 'other' are represented (Harrison 1994: 217). In architectural practice, reflexivity can tend to be confined to notions of 'sensitivity'. While this notion is often employed when western-centric discourse finds itself in unfamiliar and uncomfortable territory, such as in impoverished or ghettoized environments or in contexts like 'informal' or slum settlements,[10] reflexivity is applicable generally to architecture as an elite practice, and in virtually all contexts and not merely those deemed 'other'.

Reflexivity is more than a question of sensitivity because it acknowledges that the author-designer in any context is always 'written' into the design 'text', whether this fact is acknowledged or not. Reflexivity in architecture therefore involves critical re-evaluations of the architectural process in order to draw attention to its terms of reference and the ways in which meaning and value is made. This re-evaluation occurs on at least two fronts. Many sociologists distinguish between 'methodological' reflexivity (within a discipline) and 'substantive' reflexivity (within the self or individual subject) (d'Oliveira-Martins 2014: 192). In other words, reflexivity can be facilitated either by methodology or by the individual. My work has considered these two processes as inter-related, one facilitating the other. This inter-related reflexive process involves a de-centering of power and power-knowledge of the author-architect (without forgoing genuine expertise, which can enrich and contribute rather than overwrite). It also involves a collapsing of the distance and softening of the relation between 'designer' as subject (even if anonymous) and 'user' as object (even if foregrounded). Rather, both are participants and partners in the making of meaning and value and its crystallizations into space. If unseated as a distanced and hidden writer of other places, as a participant and co-author the designer becomes him/herself 'written' into the design 'text'. Reflexivity in methodology, representation and design can therefore be critical when engaging and representing conditions of difference, if not in architecture generally (for is not architecture always for others?).

Reflexive frameworks have been employed in the student design-research projects in various ways, often over-layered with other techniques depending on their contexts. A project in Denver, an informal settlement located 5 km outside of Johannesburg CBD, is one example.[11] The process was cyclical, whereby students continuously revisited the area in order to expand / adapt / update / supplement conventional architectural lenses and disciplinary questions, where these (or they) were too limited or ill-equipped to suitably speak to existing conditions. The project was structured not according to a steady course of disciplinary outputs (i.e.

a progression from conceptual to technical drawings, or macro to micro scales) but these were synthesized into an overarching framework that took its cues from an unfolding of a methodological reflexivity.

The design process methodology unfolded in three distinct parts, named 'introduction', 'structures' and 'corporeality'. First students were asked to self-reflexively (i.e. 'substantively') look at the vulnerable and introverted settlement from the outward in, attempting to document their fears, presuppositions and prejudices but also the unfolding and deepening of their access, knowledge, and familiarizations or dissonances. Secondly, students attempted to do the reverse, attempting to understand social / spatial / physical 'structures' operating within and through their interactions with community representatives. In the third part of the process, students brought together and recorded inter- and intra-patterns and tensions (between students and community representatives / structures) of a 'corporeality'. This corporeality was not a normative modelling of an existing physical site but rather 'siting' was understood here as a progressive projection of one's own recordings and interactions, built up through the course of the research (Figure 9).

Through intending to broaden conceptual, thematic and spatial categories at each stage of the project, projects such as these, which are located in informal settlements, also sought to contribute to building a sufficiently complex understanding of the conditions that have been named as 'informality', beyond discourses that may position informal settlements only within conditions of lack (i.e. economic poverty as a poverty of imagination). We found that reflexive processes like these all require time, and particularly a concept of time that is structured according to value placed in the meaning made through process

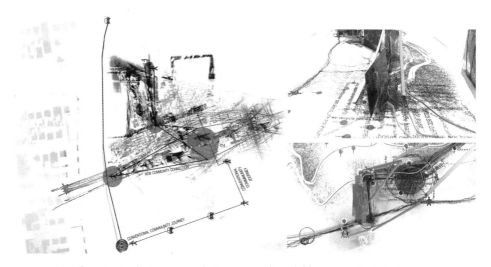

Figure 9: Reflexivity in design-research (images and model by Lance Ho Hip, 2014).

(embodied in both the design and designer) rather than value determined solely by the architecture as an output / object / product. Such structures and valuations of time run counter to conventional disciplinary processes and hence are likely to represent a challenge in any architectural project.

The architectural design-research process: Testing techniques of urgent imagination

Disciplinary thought and practice are not neutral knowledges, and typically these are further crystallized into disciplinary technique, which determines operations often regardless of new operators. Shaped in complex conditions of power and politics, such disciplinarity tends to the reproduction of these relations and technique, and can become detached from reality and humanity.

In the context of the spatial-related disciplines, a focus on technique (drawing and representational conventions, lenses, approaches etc.) can therefore mean the 'papering over' of social, economic or other contradictions in order to (re)produce measurable and recognizable disciplinary outputs. The result is a sort of 'cognitive dissonance', a term from social psychology that refers to the attempt to reduce or avoid the mental discomfort or psychological stress that results from holding 'conflicting frames of meaning' or belief (Sennett 1998: 90). These may arise from particular kinds of social situations or from being confronted with information that contradicts declared ideas, beliefs, ideals and values. Both individuals and groups experience cognitive dissonances in one way or another (for example, with regard to class, race, gender, power, privilege etc.), and the disciplines, too, embody and reproduce these conditions in their own ways.

A counterpoint to conditions of cognitive dissonance is 'localizing' or 'focal attention', where 'human beings focus on the difficulties and contradictions' (Sennett 2008a: 278). Yet a 'probing craftsman' (Sennett 2008b) also did more than simply stumble upon problems and then 'learning from mistakes'. Rather, conditions of 'resistance' were created precisely in order to know them. This could allow opportunities for growth or 'instructive experiences' (Sennett 2008a: 10), developed through facing and engaging a condition of difficulty or strangeness that one's experience, knowledge or skill had not adequately prepared one for. Similarly, discursive spaces in the spatial-related disciplines entail adaptive techniques of focal attention to surface tensions embedded in the status quo, so that an engaged, discursive design culture and tools can be developed. All of the discursive techniques described in this chapter have in part sought to do this. As Theodor W. Adorno once put it: 'A work must cut through the contradictions and overcome them, not by covering them up, but by pursuing them' (1965, cited in Heynen 1999: 1).

Some of the techniques should not be regarded as necessarily 'universal' disciplinary tools (which in any case is only cautionary in contexts that wield epistemic privilege), but relational to social, physical and especially their discursive contexts, and in constant dialogue with them. Such dialectic methods may be more valuable within – although not limited to – contexts that despite their ubiquity may be unfamiliar, uncertain or unknown within a disciplinary status quo, such as what some have called 'the Other 90%' (i.e. 'the percentage of the world's population not traditionally served by professional designers') (Smith [sa], 'Design with the Other 90%').

At the same time that dialectic methods may be contextually engaged, educational sociologists Young and Muller (2010: 14) discern that such forms of knowledge must also be regarded as *emergent from* and not *reducible to* the contexts in which they are produced and acquired'. Rather, the constant in dialectic approaches between the discursive and the material is neither 'theory', 'technique', nor even 'context', but an expansive ethical imaginary that drives it and in the crucible of dialogue gives it form. In the words of Teddy Cruz, architecture must bring an ethical and 'urgent imagination' (Catling 2014). This mode of purposeful creativity marks a key difference with, on the one hand, the location of agency in disciplinary technique that can remain vague on its ends or, on the other hand, with theoretical framings of space that remain divorced from a design culture or pragmatic delivery.

Despite the urgency in global and local crises – whether social, political, urban, ecological, economic or epistemic – these emergent forms remain 'alternative'. An unsustainable mainstream remains 'normality'. Yet if it is the relevance and humane ethic of a 'new normal' (Buhlungu 2016) rather than disciplinarity that the academy seeks to cultivate, experimenting and developing such approaches is crucial.

The student protests that emerged in South Africa in 2015 were but one signal of a global call to break from these patterns. Often these are inspired by the most fundamental of concerns rather than global brands or commodified knowledge: on going a second day without a meal, or having the responsibility of lifting brothers and sisters out of poverty, or being taught in a fourth or fifth language (Kalla 2015). And yet, it is a discourse that is *not* one of lack, but one of profound depth and breadth, which demands from all of us a new, urgent and ethical imagination.

REFERENCES

Belting, H. (2011), *Florence & Baghdad: Renaissance art and Arab science* (trans. D. L. Schneider), Cambridge, MA: Belknap.

Bremner, L. (2004), *Johannesburg: One City Colliding Worlds*, Johannesburg: STE Publishers.

Buhlungu, S. (2016), 'Resolution taken by the Extended Dean's Advisory Committee of The Faculty of Humanities, University of Cape Town at a meeting held on Friday 30th September 2016', http://www.humanities.uct.ac.za/sites/default/files/image_tool/images/2/Humanities%20DAC%20Resolution%20Sept%202016.pdf. Accessed January 2018.

Catling, C. (2014), 'Damned if you do, damned if you don't: What is the moral duty of the architect?' *The Architectural Review*, https://www.architectural-review.com/rethink/viewpoints/damned-if-you-do-damned-if-you-dont-what-is-the-moral-duty-of-the-architect/8669956.article. Accessed January 2018.

Corner, J. (1999), 'The agency of mapping: Speculation, critique and invention', in D. Cosgrove (ed.), *Mappings*, 1st ed., London: Reaktion Books, pp. 213–52.

Dirlik, A. (2007), 'Architecture of global modernity, colonialism and places', in S. Lee and R. Baumeister (eds), *The Domestic and the Foreign in Architecture*, Rotterdam: 010 Publishers, pp. 37–46.

D'Oliveira-Martins, M. (2014), 'Sociological reflexivity and the sociology of emotions', *Sociology and Anthropology*, 2:5, pp. 190–95, http://www.hrpub.org. Accessed March 2018.

Grey, B. (2015), 'Design for and with local communities', project brief and outline.

Grosfoguel, R. (2013), 'The structure of knowledge in Westernized Universities: epistemic racism/sexism and the four genocides/epistemicides of the long 16th century', *Human Architecture: Journal of the Sociology of Self-Knowledge*, 11:1, Article 8 (Fall), pp. 73–90, http://scholarworks.umb.edu/humanarchitecture/vol11/iss1/8. Accessed 5 January 2017.

Habraken, J. N. (1972), *Supports: An Alternative to Mass Housing*, New York: Praeger.

Harrison, C. (1994), 'The effects of landscape', in W. J. T. Mitchell (ed.), *Landscape and Power*, Chicago: The University of Chicago Press, pp. 203–340.

Heynen, H. (1999), *Architecture and Modernity: A Critique*, Cambridge, MA and London: The MIT Press.

Kalla, S. (2015), '#FeesMustFall: A tale of two Witses – one for the rich, another for the poor', http://www.thedailyvox.co.za/feesmustfall-a-tale-of-two-witses-one-for-the-rich-another-for-the-poor/. Accessed 20 November 2015.

Mamdani, M. (2015), 'Settler Colonialism: Then and now', *Critical Inquiry*, 41:3 (Spring), pp. 596–614, https://www.jstor.org/stable/10.1086/680088. Accessed 1 August 2019.

—— (2019), 'Why South Africa can't avoid land reforms', https://www.nytimes.com/2019/06/17/opinion/south-africa-land-reform.html. Accessed 1 August 2019.

Mosquera, G. and Fisher, J. (2004), 'Introduction', in G. Mosquera and J. Fisher (eds), *Over Here: International Perspectives on Art and Culture*, Cambridge, MA: The MIT Press, pp. 2–9.

Murray, M. J. (2011), *City of Extremes: The Spatial Politics of Johannesburg*, Durham, NC and London: Duke University Press.

Opper, A., Morgado, C. and Wright, E. (2014), 'studio AT DENVER: General Course Outline', unpublished.

Pieterse, E. (2013), 'Can regeneration save the city?', Public lecture delivered at The Faculty of Art, Design and Architecture (FADA), University of Johannesburg, 5 November.

———— (2015), Keynote address delivered at the 'All Change!: New Architectural and Urban Narratives on the African Continent' Symposium, delivered at the Goethe-Institut Johannesburg, 26 May.

Rensburg, I. (2016), *Vice-Chancellor's Report 2016*, University of Johannesburg.

Sennett, R. (1998), *The Corrosion of Character: The Personal Consequences of Work in the New Capitalism*, London: W. W. Norton.

———— (2008a), *The Craftsman*, New Haven, CT and London: Yale University Press.

———— (2008b), 'Labours of love', *The Guardian*, https://www.theguardian.com/books/2008/feb/02/featuresreviews.guardianreview14. Accessed November 2017.

Smith, C. E. (Curator) [Sa], DESIGN WITH THE OTHER 90%, https://www.designother90.org/about/. Accessed January 2018.

Toffa, T., Osman, A. and Bennett, J. (2015), 'Architecture and agency: Ethics and accountability in teaching through the application of Open Building principles', in DEFSA (Design Education Forum South Africa), *Design Education Conference 2015: Ethics and Accountability in Design: Do They Matter?*, Johannesburg, South Africa, 2–4 September, Midrand Graduate Institute, http://www.defsa.org.za/papers/architecture-and-agency-ethics. Accessed 25 January 2018.

UJ_Unit2 (2015), UJ_Unit2: Architecture and Agency (Design \ Make \ Transform), http://uj-unit2.co.za/. Accessed 20 November 2015.

Wakefield, A. (2014), 'A bird's-eye view of the battlefield: Aerial photography', http://www.telegraph.co.uk/history/world-war-one/inside-first-world-war/part-eight/10742060/aerial-photography-world-war-one.html. Accessed 20 November 2015.

Warf, B. and Arias, S. (eds) (2009), *The Spatial Turn: Interdisciplinary Perspectives*, Oxon and New York: Routledge.

Young, M. and Muller, J. (2010), 'Three educational scenarios for the future: Lessons from the sociology of knowledge', *European Journal of Education*, 45:1, Part I, pp. 11–27.

NOTES

1. In both academic and professional practice and process, architecture always entails or is 'related' to much more than end outputs/products (whether a building or drawing). Narrower definitions mask that the tendency toward professional/vocational bias and outputs typically ignores and reproduces a wide range of conditions of power and politics.

2. These were explored at the architecture school in the Faculty of Art, Design and Architecture (FADA) at the University of Johannesburg (UJ) between 2014 and 2018.

3. In the context of southern Africa, 'rural' and 'urban' are not simply descriptive terms denoting generic aspects of urbanization, but are also markers of a wide range of factors. In the twentieth century, ideas of the 'rural' in southern Africa became an engineered part of the modern institutional apparatus of colonialism and apartheid, which drew directly from North American 'Indian' reserves/reservations as pioneering settler colonial models (in 1910 the settler government of South Africa sent a delegation to North America to

study how to set up tribal homelands). Initially known likewise as 'reserves' and later as 'Bantustans', 'homelands' or 'states', these would become a cornerstone of apartheid colonialism that would see millions of Africans forcibly removed from 'White South Africa' into these impoverished areas. In 'post'-apartheid South Africa as much as one third of the population still lives in these predominantly rural regions (with another third increasingly in informal shanties on the peripheries of the 'urban') (Mamdani 2019; 2015: 608).

4. Led by Brenden Grey, the interdisciplinary project vision is described thus: 'Between 2015 and 2020 the departments of Architecture ..., Multimedia ..., Industrial ... and Communication Design ... are partnering with CERT (Center for Education Rights and Transformation) and a variety of community organisations to collaborate on the project, "Design for and with Local Communities." The project investigates how, by adopting democratic and participatory approaches to community-based research and design, a lasting change can be made on the quality of life of the UJ community and nearby communities' (Grey 2015).

5. Called 'Arrival City', the project was launched in 2018 and coordinated by myself and Jabu Makhubu.

6. 'UJ_Unit2: Architecture and Agency' was launched in 2015 and led by Professor Amira Osman, with the author and Jhono Bennett as joint coordinators, assisted by Tuliza Sindi and in partnership with Professor Stephen Kendall and Phil Astley (RIBA). See www.uj-unit2.co.za.

7. The meaning of territory as 'belonging' is derived from the Latin root *territorium*, and as 'repelling' derived from an alternative Latin root *terrere*.

8. Called 'Public space | Spaces of publics', this was a research project which I coordinated in 2014.

9. Notions of perspective are also bound up with power. Belting (2011: 45) argued that 'perspective functioned as an instrument of colonialism' and as 'a demonstration of the progress'. Aerial photography would also bring new ramifications, as demonstrated for example by the development of aerial reconnaissance during the First World War (Wakefield 2014).

10. 'Informal settlement' is a both humanizing and euphemizing term used especially in South Africa for what otherwise might be called shantytowns, squatter settlements or slums.

11. This research project, coordinated by the author, was undertaken as a component of a larger seven-week research and planning studio programme, 'studio AT DENVER', with coordinators Alex Opper, Claudia Morgado and Eric Wright. The larger project was a focused engagement with the community of Denver, Johannesburg, towards a collection of 'community action plans' (Opper et al. 2014).

4

Drawing as being: Moving beyond ways of knowing, modes of attention and *habitus*

Ray Lucas, Manchester Metropolitan University

Introduction

This chapter considers the possibilities inherent in inscriptive practices such as drawing, diagrams and notations understood as ways of dwelling within or sustaining a moment. This is an alternative to discussions of drawing as a mode of knowledge production, a debate that is as popular as it is contentious. Drawings represent an alternative way of *knowing*, which affords distinctive understandings to academic texts. Whilst maintaining this position as a powerful line of enquiry, it does not go far enough, and it is more accurate to describe the practice of drawing as an alternative *mode of being in the world* akin to Martin Heidegger (1978, 1993). Beyond being a *habitus* (Bourdieu 1992) extended to other areas of life, drawing is a way of operating within the world. The temporality of the creative practice, explored in the philosophy of Henri Bergson, informs the theoretical framework for the chapter based on inscriptive practices implicating time and intuition. Does drawing constitute an alternative mode of *being*?

This contextual entanglement within the world and place within a context finds expression in the works of environmental psychologist James Gibson (1968) and recently revived by anthropologist Tim Ingold (2000, 2007). The notion of perception in the environment is transcribed in both a practical and figurative sense in the act of drawing: be that an abstract piece that engages with aleatory practices, materiality or bodily engagement; or figurative drawings that interpret a perspectival scene or are re-ordered instrumentally according to orthographic conventions. Ingold's contention is that creativity constitutes a fundamental human activity largely ignored by theoretical queries that tend to focus on material, economic or social aspects of creative practice as in *Art and Agency* (Gell 1998).

In order to demonstrate this concept of drawing as being, I shall discuss my own drawing practice as an academic researching across the fields of architecture and anthropology. Whilst there is undeniable value in looking at the works produced by artists and architects, we often omit to draw as part of our own research. The implication is that whilst drawings and other creative practices are valid fields or objects of study, we do not afford them the same status as text, i.e. as an instrument for producing intellectual work. In this chapter, I shall describe one case study: A Graphic Anthropology of Namdaemun Market, which establishes a method for drawing as a form of theoretical inquiry.

Inscription as practice

Practice has recently been the focus of a great deal of attention in the social sciences, and practice-based approaches to research are on the rise across a range of disciplines. Other terminology is often used, such as discussions of skills (Marchand) or techniques (Ingold 2000: 403). Notably, Ingold develops an idea of inscription as central to his discussions. For Ingold, inscription is in opposition to the assumption that drawing and other practices are transcriptive or simply taking down what is observed in the world. Inscription as practice involves an act of intellect in the transfer of gestures to marks to surface.

This has relevance to architecture – as both an academic and a professional design discipline – because it allows the asking of a series of questions about the means by which knowledge is produced. Recent anthropologies of creativity focus not on the outputs of artists or architects, but rather on the practices by which such works are created. This shift in focus is of fundamental importance, as it enlarges the possibilities for research in architecture, moving away from either the history of architecture or architectural theory and posits that there can simply be research in architecture: a research that retains its theoretical implications and historical context, but which also engages more fully with the disciplinary knowledge base in form, space, dwelling and materials. Such knowledge is produced through practices that include drawing and model making. Written works are no longer the sole mode of knowledge production.

Pierre Bourdieu (1992) seeks to establish the foundations for a theory of practice with a focus on anthropological, lived space of the everyday and ordinary. Central to this is Bourdieu's notion of *habitus*. Practices take time to engage in; they are activities placed within a context of a time as well as a place. *Habitus* can be understood, as a theory of inhabitation: all those practices that make up our daily existence and that go by unobserved, unnoticed, unchallenged or that are rarely thought about. One inhabits this set of practices through belief systems contained within everyday life. Whilst it is difficult to argue that drawing goes unnoticed within architectural discourse, assumption and commonly received opinion does predominate, leaving opportunities for exploring deeper understandings of drawing practice. According to Bourdieu (1992: 53), *habitus* are:

> systems of durable, transposable dispositions, structured structures predisposed to function as structuring structures, that is, as principles which generate and organise practices and representations that can be objectively adapted to their outcomes without presupposing a conscious aiming at ends or an express mastery of the operations necessary in order to attain them.

Habitus can therefore be understood as being a meta-practice: an organizing principle for a set of practices. Bourdieu calls these principles structuring structures, which can be used to transfer practices from one circumstance to another. This transferability lies at the heart of an approach that renders the activity in one sphere as applicable to another.

One example can be found in the study of the Papua New Guinea Malanggan discussed in the work of anthropologist Suzanne Küchler. In certain Malanggan, there is a representation of knotting and pleating used as an organizing principle on the surface of carved wooden sculptures. The *habitus* of knotting is applicable both to the literal tying of ropes and to the carving of a sculpture. More than a motif, the knot is a form of practice and understanding that can be transferred from one circumstance to another. The durability of the practice is also notable, in that a practice is remembered and not specific to a particular activity or event.

Habitus complicates the everyday, which might at first appear as completely familiar and unworthy of study. The reverse is true, however. Because practices are so fundamental and basic to our being, they are understood as a temporal and engaged state rather than an abstract and eternal one. The ways in which an understanding from one circumstance or one practice can influence another is the key to *habitus*. *Habitus* and practices are the constituent parts of our multiple ways of being human and nothing less than this. Bourdieu notes importantly that such approaches to *habitus* and practice are not a process of obedience. These are not social rules but instead exemplify the ways in which we have been enculturated. This is another important distinction for there are other terms for the social norms and constraints that are artificially imposed, say by religious belief, social class or other larger structures. *Habitus* are collections of culturally specific and socially enacted practices that define everyday life.

> The habitus, a product of history, produces individual and collective practices [...] It ensures the active presence of past experiences, which, deposited in each

organism in the form of schemes of perception, thought and action, tend to guarantee the 'correctness' of practices and their norm constancy over time, more reliably than all formal rules and explicit norms.

(Bourdieu 1990: 54)

Habitus is rooted in memory, and enforces a set of practices in a manner much more powerful than social constraints and laws. The term 'dispositions' is key to understanding this, i.e. *habitus* is a set of attitudes and ways of being, moving and interacting with the world. *Habitus* is implicit rather than explicit. We reinforce our pasts by re-enacting and developing past practices, framed within this overall structuring structure of *habitus*.

While Bourdieu discusses examples of *habitus* and practice that fall into the category of ritual, he contrasts these activities with exchanges and gift-giving. The manner of this distinction is expressed in terms of the temporality of the practice. Where rituals can be understood to have an a-temporal quality, set outside of the everyday lived existence of people and presented as an eternal present, there is another quality to the time explored in commonplace exchange practices.

Drawing is often critiqued and researched in the ritual mode: an unchanging totality, complete and finished – where it is more usefully understood as an exchange, as a gift with temporality, direction of travel and implications of reciprocity. Exchange practices can refer to economic exchanges, gender-based exchanges such as marriages, and also to gift-giving and other status-based movements of goods and wealth. Gifts are one of the most theorized exchanges in anthropology, seen as a fundamental category from which we can learn a great deal about other forms of exchange.

This lies in a distinction between categories of reversibility or irreversibility in practices (Lucas 2006: 181). Exchanges are cyclical and move in a given direction rather than being reflected back and forward. Gift-giving continues as a self-perpetuating cycle where the gift given in return is of equal value, but different goods are given. The implications of returning a gift to the giver are deep, containing elements of causing offence, of a lack of acceptance; and it would be difficult for a friendship or other relationship to survive the return or refusal of a gift. Gifts are reciprocated and not returned. Bourdieu (1990: 110) writes: 'Gift exchange is the paradigm of all the operations through with symbolic alchemy produces the reality-denying reality that the collective unconsciousness aims at as a collectively produced, sustained and maintained misrecognition of the "objective" truth'.

Bourdieu discusses the implications of a practice-based theory of gift-giving, which he presents as a collective denial of objective reality. In other words, gift exchanges are an example of *habitus* that establishes an alternative basis for being. Gifts are given to establish, maintain and represent social relationships: as a way of forming or strengthening the bonds between individuals or groups of people. We subscribe to this alternative reality when engaging in gift-giving practices, one in which people often assume it to be a selfless act, one with no motivation other than an expression of love, friendship or solidarity. This sounds very cynical of course, but it is the role of social theorists to question and understand such processes by which we construct our social identities.

The relationship between the theory of the gift within artworks is discussed in greater detail by Roger Sansi (2015). Whilst discussing artworks in general, and with a focus on contemporary art practice and its interest in anthropological themes and theories, there are some further connections to be established between the practices of drawing as research and those of the giving and receiving of gifts. Sansi takes this position regarding art practices that rely on collaboration and settings outside of the art market, but the argument can be extended further to inform an understanding of the production and reception as practices of reaching a common understanding. The aim here is not to conceptualize drawing[1] as a gift exchange but rather to understand its nature as practices of distributing selfhood (Sansi 2015: 11). As Mauss (2003: 227, in Sansi 2015: 11) notes: 'one gives oneself when giving'. This can be further extended to: One draws oneself when drawing.

Drawing as perception

To add further nuance, it is through one's own perception that one draws. Drawing represents how we observe the world and then translate that reading into a mark into a surface. Drawn from readings of Maurice Merleau-Ponty and James Gibson (Lucas 2012), perception is at the root of anthropologist Tim Ingold's discussion of lines. Ingold (2015: 86) writes:

> [...] The archaeologist does not just touch the stone but touches with it – with hands that already know the hardness and softness, roughness and smoothness. Tree and stone, in other words, are at once on both the hither and the far side of vision and touch, respectively. My bodily seeing the tree is the way the tree sees through me, and my bodily touching the stone is the way the stone touches through me.

Ingold suggests here an intertwining in perception, a manner in which the senses allow for an exchange with the world. Drawing relies upon perception – most obviously the action of the visual system as Gibson (1983) would describe it – not as a passive reception of an external world but as an active sensing of it. The sensory-motor system interacts with a series of manual gestures in the case of drawing observationally, transforming the observed phenomena into kinetic, tactile and haptic responses. As Ingold (2015: 86) notes, natural features are not in themselves sentient but are 'immersed' in our sentience producing a unity between the perceiver and the perceived.

This notion that perceivers become one with what they perceive is crucial, and further elaborated by the precise mode of that perception: a drawing is a perception before it is a thing or an image.

> The visible is what is seized upon with the eyes, the sensible is what is seized on by the senses.
>
> (Merleau-Ponty 2002: 7)

In his extended study of the phenomenology of perception, Maurice Merleau-Ponty underlines the distinction between the physiological processes in how the various sense organs act and the manner in which perception is constructed. This positions perception as a cognitive process, not the basis for thinking, but a form of thinking in itself. We often discuss situations where the senses are educated for a particular purpose: the auditory acuity of a concert pianist for example, or the celebrated olfactory sense of a sommelier. A growing body of literature discusses the idea of embodiment in intelligence (Farnell 2014; Sudnow 2001), i.e. cognitive processes reside throughout the body rather than solely in the brain. The scene seized upon by the eyes is made sensible by drawing it.

In his discussion of *The Pleasure of Drawing*, Jean-Luc Nancy (2013) discusses mimetic drawing and its relation to perception in a useful manner, repeating comments from Degas and a number of others in his 'sketchbook' sections. Nancy (2013: 12) writes: 'this is what Degas means when he is reported to have said: "Drawing is not the form, it is the manner of seeing the form"'. This ties drawing to perception as one mode or possibility of seeing, a way of focusing attention. Drawing, then, is a particular method for perceiving. It has certain rules and affordances: excludes some things whilst including others. It can result in an enduring trace of gestures that allows that perception be shared with others.

Perception as being

Returning to Ingold and his readings of Gibson's work on the senses, beings are understood always as in-the-world. After all there is no point in attempting to abstract people from their environment. We must always think about ourselves not only as being in our environment, but in terms of that environment being in us. All too often, the distractions of context are abstracted from attempts at understanding, the classic neutral laboratory setting so opposed by Gibson for example. This has implications for the discussion of drawing.

German art historian and theorist, Hans Belting, connects perception with identity, noting that viewers risk losing their sense of self when presented with images. Belting concludes that there is a resonance between the viewer and the image. I would contend that this relationship is deeper and more fundamental in the case of one who produces a drawing.[2] As Belting (2011: 57) notes:

> Time and again, viewers have lost their identity, or feared losing it, when they were forced to adopt new forms of perception. Confronted with images of a kind that they had never seen before, they felt that they were turning into beings of a different kind, and proclaimed – either joyfully or regretfully – that humanity was at an end.

If the risk of losing identity through merely viewing an image is possible, what are the identity implications for producing an actual drawing? Clearly there is a discussion of new forms of image here, a later example of virtual reality given of this technology of enchantment (to borrow from Gell 1999: 159), but the direction of travel in drawing is notably different: more of an exchange and dialogue than the mono-directional process described here. As Ingold (2013: 127) clarifies, 'It is doubtful whether the intention of the artist is to plant anything in the viewers' mind, save perhaps the seed from which the work grew, so that viewers can follow it through for themselves, looking with rather than at it'.

One aim of sharing a drawing is to communicate an experience and an observation: as a means of taking the viewer along with the drawer. This is just one aim, of course: many drawings are not shared, and are produced in order to think, to work through an issue with a design, to spend some time with a context or event. Sharing is often fraught with fears of judgement and exposure, demonstrating just how honest and open a drawing can be.

The interpretation of Heidegger by Ingold can be adapted to the theme of drawing. Speaking of dwelling – which in Heidegger can be taken as a subset of Being – drawing can be understood as similar to dwelling within an environment: 'Dwelling in the world, in short, is tantamount to the ongoing, temporal interweaving of our lives with one another and with the manifold constituents of our environment' (Ingold 2000: 348).

This is part of a discussion of the skill of weaving, the idea that the world around us is in a perpetual state of coming into being, rather than a final and fixed state of completion. The influence of a skilled practice such as drawing, particularly one that can bring images into being, is that it qualifies and adds detail to precisely *how* we dwell within the world. The practice of drawing continually informs that inhabitation and constitutes a subset of being once an individual is sufficiently skilled in its production.

A graphic anthropology of Namdaemun Market, Seoul

This project makes explicit use of a set of observational strategies gathered together as 'Graphic Anthropology'. This is a term that is not stable, having been formed through a series of conversations asking the question why anthropologists have abandoned drawing as an observational practice in favour of lens-based media such as video and photography. This is a question familiar within architectural discourse as there is a continual crisis around a 'death' of conventional drawing. Reports of this demise are rather premature (Scheer 2015) of course, and a more nuanced position is to consider that drawing's role might be changing – and that the practice of drawing has grown to encompass a range of computer-based practices as different forms of drawing.

Drawing, then, remains an option for the architect and researcher.[3] My work as both an anthropological and architectural researcher in Namdaemun Market[4] in Seoul city centre serves as a case study here. The space in any marketplace is socially produced. It is a combination of temporary and permanent structures with territory maintained by cooperation and contested by competition. Noteworthy are the pragmatics of the drawing process in research: Drawings are largely post-situ rather than in-situ. The reasons for this are practical. For instance a densely occupied space often precludes the possibility for detailed, meaningful drawings to be made. Sketches and notes can be attempted, but prove to be largely useless for the overall project. Photography and video recording are important parts of the process. Notably, in this case study, the photographs are considered as records of the context rather than being taken for their own merits (as a professional photographer might). This means that clarity is important, that the aperture is narrow, with as much of the scene in focus as possible. Typically, several photographs are needed to compose each drawing. Each case study will place its own demands on the researcher, of course, necessitating alternative modes of production, including but not limited to in-situ sketches, digital drawings and models based on survey, or notations describing movement.

The resulting drawings use orthographic or parallel projection conventions. Crucially, rather than default to the sketch-perspective mode (often associated with direct observation), more can be learned about the dimensions and spatial relationships by drawing axonometrics, elevations and sections. Each convention has its affordances, representing some relationships over others: so a choice must be made appropriate to the case in hand. The geometry of the structures

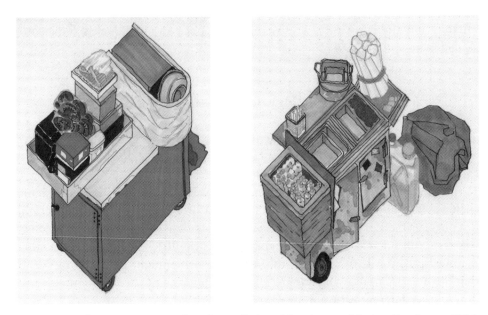

Figures 1 and 2: Axonometrics of market stalls from Namdaemun Market, Ray Lucas, 2015.

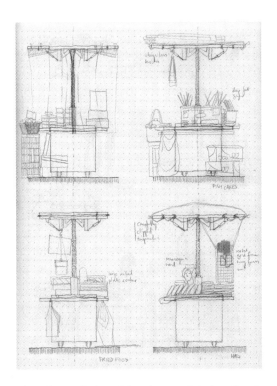

Figure 3: Elevations of market stalls from Namdaemun Market, Ray Lucas, 2015.

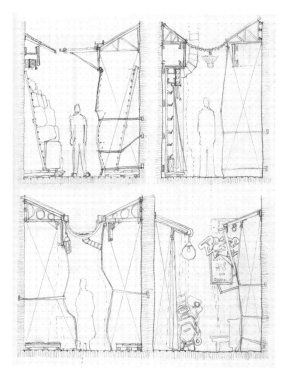

Figure 4: Sections through alleyways of Namdaemun Market, Ray Lucas, 2014.

must be understood in order to make each drawing. People are not shown in the axonometric drawings. That is to say, people are not always explicitly represented: instead remaining implicit within the drawings, a skilled reader can populate the drawing by extrapolation. Each drawing exists as a tangible, unique and personal observation. These drawn observations enter into a dialogue with the written text and are designed to sit alongside it. Each drawing has a narrative that effectively reinserts the vendors and buyers. The alleyway sections include some figures as a proxy for scale. The axonometric drawings are in colour. The marketplace is such a vibrant context that colour is important to its depiction. The sections and elevations are in a clearer series, with a repeated module represented over and over to depict the variety of how these are populated with goods and paraphernalia.[5]

The drawings are supplemented with diagrams. Several of these are simple adaptations of flow and space syntax diagrams (Dovey 2007) in order to show the structure of the urban environment for various actors within the market system. The most notable diagram is an adaptation of Alfred Gell's matrix of artist and agency (1999: 29) from his important text on the anthropology of art. This adaptation builds on the drawing practices of other anthropologists[6] who have borrowed the technique to describe other situations. This diagramming method is

AGENT	Artist	Index	Prototype	Recipient
	vendor / seller	*produce/goods/ material*	*orders*	*buyer*
PATIENT				
Artist *vendor / seller*	Seller A → Seller P *sellers cooperate - shared meals, social space, lookouts, games. LOOKOUT/ SOCIAL SPACE*	Produce A → Seller P *produce dictates how it is sold.* *LIVE FISH*	Order A → Seller P *sales must be bulk orders to ensure profit* *BULK DEALER*	Buyer A → Seller P *seller prepares food ordered* *STREET FOOD STALL*
Index *produce/goods/ material*	Seller A → Produce P *seller makes goods to a pattern.* *CRAFT STORE A*	Produce A → Produce P *produce skillfully prepared for sale* *PREPARED SASHIMI*	Order A → Produce P *seller as middle-man* *WHOLESALE DEALER / NO-STOCK HELD*	Buyer A → Produce P *place order not from stock - seller has sources* *SHOWROOM*
Prototype *orders*	Seller A → Order P *seller makes goods directly - and has materials for sale - stud store, jewellery* CRAFT STORE B	Produce A → Order P *constrained by available produce* *PIG TROTTER STALLS*	Order A → Order P *buying to sell on in bulk* *SPECULATION*	Buyer A → Order P *reporting of bad deal to market authority* *MARKET REGULATION*
Recipient *buyer*	Seller A → Buyer P *captivations - performance based.* *PLACARD / LOUDHALER*	Produce A → Buyer P *buyer's response is due to prestige of goods* *JEWELLERY STORE / HANBOK*	Order A → Buyer P *buyer's experience primary - tourist at market, celebration purchases* *RETAIL SEAFOOD*	Buyer A → Buyer P *buyer hired to negotiate deals* *PROFESSIONAL BUYER*

Figure 5: Agency matrix of marketplace, Ray Lucas, 2015 (after Alfred Gell, 1999).

ideally placed to discuss visually the various forms and qualities of agency present within each marketplace.

The drawings in the case study represent a kind of arrested or accumulated perception. This might be described as a meditation on a moment, settling in to it in order to unpick each of the simultaneous events taking place at a given moment. Drawing includes editing and elision: even in the most photorealistic representation, something is left out. This decision-making can be one of the creative acts in an inscriptive practice, much in the manner that Sergei Eisenstein argues for montage as the creative act in film. The point (spatially or temporally) at which we hold our attention to a scene is crucial to our perception of it. The use of conventions allows the drawings to enter into the wider social system of inscriptive practices. By drawing according to a set of stable and established rules, the moment described can be compared with all other drawings conducted according to that convention. The alleyways can be compared with all other spaces that have been drawn in section; the individual carts can be compared with other axonometric drawings.

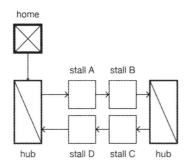

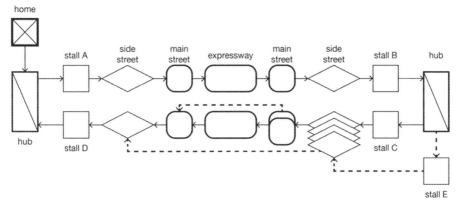

Figure 6: Syntax diagrams of marketplace for manual porters (a) and motorcycle couriers (b), Ray Lucas, 2015 (after Kim Dovey, 2007).

Architectural drawing conventions also serve to elevate oft-ignored practices of building to the status of architecture. This is contentious, given the tradition in architecture to differentiate buildings and architecture along a variety of lines. This drawing operation includes the market carts and accretions of vending or display surfaces in the realm of architecture. It explicitly marks them out as worthy of our attention, study and understanding.

Projected future work includes a composition of the entire market area under a variety of conditions. Given that the occupation of the market precinct varies according to the day of the week, it is appropriate to re-draw it accordingly. More interestingly, the idea of composing a more inclusive work addresses the relationship between the parts and the whole. This speaks again to the experience of the marketplace as initially observed to be chaotic when it might more accurately be considered as a series of overlapping simultaneous orders. Each is relatively straightforward, but attempting to understand the entire context as a totality is too complex. Anthropologists, as noted above, tend towards sketch perspectives,

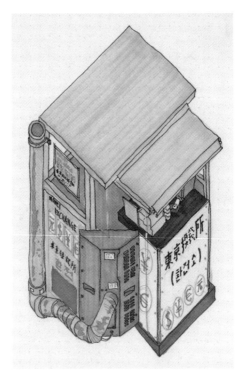

Figure 7: Axonometric of market stall from Namdaemun Market, Ray Lucas, 2015.

schematic plans, diagrams of kinship and more recently comic book conventions. The aim of this project is partly architectural, so the conventions of architectural drawing carry the desired information.

   The aims of this series are relatively straightforward: to see a socially produced space, arguably vernacular in nature, as worthy of architectural attention. The implications of this are rather less simple, of course: the nature of design and its relation to what constitutes architecture are one emergent issue: the market cart has been arranged according to a design that responds to an existing module in many cases, and the precise layout is a practice that is enacted every day: the placement of goods is initially established through experimentation, trial and error, by copying others in the market; until the ideal arrangement for the goods and selling style is arrived at. It is then unpacked every day and arranged carefully, maintained over the course of the day as goods are sold, and packed away again in the evening. The market is a space of mobility: in a manner more associated with the various architectural avant-gardes of the 1960s and 1970s, but conducted in a pragmatic manner. Architecture has a great deal to learn from the resilience of this marketplace, which continues to exist despite colonial occupations, rapid modernization and more recently the forces of gentrification by way of infrastructural intervention and development. Contemporary architecture can explore the possibilities of these agile structures as responses to contemporary conditions of permanence/impermanence, stability, mobility and transience.

Drawing as being

To move from considering drawing as one of many inscriptive practices towards a status as being is a substantial shift. Having justified a practice status and then understood it as a *habitus*, drawing is conceptualized here as a way of knowing about the world: a means by which research can be conducted on alternative terms. There is a logic in understanding drawing practices in this way, particularly those so closely associated with the academic discipline of architecture: it is an activity that allows us to design. The conflation of being and *habitus* will not be appropriate to every practice of course, but drawing is so closely embedded in practices of perception, in how we organize a range of senses: not only the visual, but the kinetic and the temporal, the haptic. It is in this way that once one has learned to draw, it becomes part of how the world is understood, and therefore constitutes an element of our being.

An interesting argument is developed with regard to practised space in Michel de Certeau's work (1984). The notion that space is existential and that existence is spatial lies at the heart of de Certeau's applicability to architectural and urban space. If spatiality is elevated to existentialism, then we are speaking of it as nothing less than a mode of being. This is fundamental to understand the importance of context. Where we are and how we act there are intertwined with our very core, our existence.

Drawing (not restricted to architectural drawing) is more spatial than visual. The visual element of drawing, which so often garners most attention, is merely a function of the trace left behind by the gesture of drawing (Ingold 2007: 72); more or less enduring depending upon the media used.

> A space exists when one takes into consideration vectors of direction, velocities, and time variables. Thus space is composed of intersections of mobile elements. It is in a sense actuated by the ensemble of movements deployed within it. Space occurs as the effect produced by the operations that orient it, situate it, temporalize it, and make it function in a polyvalent unity of conflictual programs or contractual proximities.
>
> (de Certeau 1984: 117)

Figure 8: Samples of source photography of Namdaemun Market, Lucas 2014.

Ingold discusses the process of learning to write (2007: 135), noting from Walter Ong (1982) and Yuehping Yen (2005) that there is an important distinction between learning to draw the individual letters, and their deep sedimentation that allows language and writing to flow. The act of drawing the letters accurately is not enough to be considered as writing. Similarly, Eisenstein (2000) writes engagingly of the similarity with learning to dance: the shift from instructing the student on the placement of their feet – towards the flow of movements that can be considered as dancing. This has a correlation with how one learns to draw: it is not enough to make the marks, they must be embedded as a practice, an embodied knowledge that then has an impact on other areas of life.

My argument then is simple: that as someone who draws (and deliberately avoiding language such as artist or draughtsman), this practice influences how I observe the world around me even when I do not have a pencil and paper to hand, paying attention informed by the *habitus* of drawing. Drawing becomes part of identity, of being, all the more apparent in the case of the autographic mark (Goodman 1976). This is addressed to an extent by artist William Kentridge in an interview with Rosalind C. Morris (2013: 8) when he states:

> Yes, we were talking about the excess of making, the promiscuity of making. When one speaks, one is aware one is doing a massive edit of all the different thoughts that are going through one's head in order to generate a single line of speech or text. So one says 'All right, that is the sense I want to make.' But there is a huge, unspoken part which is different from, say, the unconscious part. Even after the unconscious part, there is a choice between all the different things that might have been said. Then, one says one thing only.

An established element of my professional and academic practice, drawing constitutes a part of being to the extent that I can – for example – differentiate the photographs I take as source material and those I consider to be photographs in their own right; I can reverse engineer drawings by others in order to understand the sequence of gestures, their speed and force, in order to read them and reconstruct them in my own practice. I am composing drawings that I may or may not make when I am in the field: this projective imagination is one of many possibilities afforded by drawing.

Thus drawing is a part of being-in-the-world. Drawing is one of the ways in which it is possible to make sense of the world. This is complementary to other practices, such as ethnographic participant observation, noted for its longitudinal nature and process of gradually reducing distance, eliciting responses about the everyday and ordinary that would not emerge from a formal interview. I make no claims for drawing as ethnography because the two practices are distinctive from one another. Architectural drawing can be used anthropologically, however: and it is in that sense that graphic anthropology can be said to emerge as a series of possibilities rather than a closed procedure.

REFERENCES

Bourdieu, P. (1990), *The Logic of Practice*, Oxford: Polity Press.

Causey, A. (2012), 'Drawing flies: Artwork in the field', *Critical Arts*, 26:2, pp. 162–74.

de Certeau, M. (1984), *The Practice of Everyday Life*, Berkeley, CA: University of California Press.

Dovey, K. (2007), *Framing Places: Mediating Power in Built Form*, London: Routledge.

Eisenstein, S. M. (2000), 'How I learned to draw (A chapter about my dancing lessons)', in Catherine de Zegher (ed.), *The Body of the Line: Eisenstein's Drawing*, New York: The Drawing Center.

Farnell, B. (2009), *Do You See What I Mean?: Plains Indian Sign Talk and the Embodiment of Action*, Lincoln, NE: University of Nebraska Press.

——— (2014), *Dynamic Embodiment for Social Theory*, London: Routledge.

Geismar, H. (2014), 'Drawing it out', *Visual Anthropology Review*, November, pp. 97–113.

Gell, A. (1998), *Art and Agency: An Anthropological Theory*, Oxford: Oxford University Press.

——— (1999), *The Art of Anthropology: Essays and Diagrams*, London: Athlone Press.

Gibson, J. J. ([1966] 1983), *The Senses Considered as Perceptual Systems*, Westport, CT: Greenwood Press.

——— (1968), *The Ecological Approach to Visual Perception*, New York: Psychology Press.

Goodman, N. (1976), *Languages of Art*, Indianapolis: Hackett Publishing.

Heidegger, M. (1978), *Being and Time*, London: Blackwell.

——— (1993), 'Building dwelling thinking', in F. Krell (ed.), *Basic Writings*, London: Routledge, pp. 344–63.

Ingold, T. (2000), *The Perception of the Environment: Essays in Livelihood, Dwelling and Skill*, London: Routledge.

——— (2007), *Lines: A Brief History*, London: Routledge.

——— (2011), *Being Alive: Essays on Movement, Knowledge and Description*, London: Routledge.

——— (2013), *Making: Anthropology, Archaeology, Art and Architecture*, London: Routledge.

——— (2015), *The Life of Lines*, London: Routledge.

Kentridge, W. and Morriss, R. C. (2013), *That Which Is not Drawn*, London: Seagull Books.

Lucas, R. (2006), 'Towards a theory of notation as a thinking tool', Ph.D. thesis, Aberdeen: University of Aberdeen.

——— (2012), 'The Instrumentality of Gibson's medium as an alternative to space', in S. Verraest, B. Keunen, and K. Bollen (eds) (2012), *Special Issue* 'New work on landscape and its narration', *CLCWeb*, 14:3, https://doi.org/10.7771/1481-4374.2039. Accessed 26 August 2019.

—— (2014), 'The sketchbook as collection: A phenomenology of sketching', in A. Bartram, N. El-Bizri and D. Gittens (eds), *Recto-Verso: Redefining the Sketchbook*, Farnham, Surrey: Ashgate.

—— (2016), *Research Methods for Architecture*, London: Laurence King Publishers.

Merleau-Ponty, M. (2002), *The Phenomenology of Perception*, London: Routledge.

Mörtenbröek, P., Mooshammer, H., Forman, F. and Cruz, T. (eds) (2015), *Informal Market Worlds: Reader*, Rotterdam: NAi/010 Publishers.

Nancy, J.-L. (2013), *The Pleasure of Drawing*, New York: Fordham University Press.

Ong, W. (1982), *Orality and Literacy: The Technologizing of the Word*, Baltimore: John Hopkins University Press.

Pallasmaa, J. (1996), *The Eyes of the Skin*, London: Academy Editions.

—— (2005), *Encounters: Architectural Essays*, Helsinki: Rakennustieto Oy.

Sansi, R. (2015), *Art, Anthropology and the Gift*, London: Bloomsbury.

Schatzki, T. R., Knorr Cetina, K. and von Savigny, E. (eds) (2001), *The Practice Turn in Contemporary Theory*, London: Routledge.

Scheer, D. R. (2015), *The Death of Drawing: Architecture in the Age of Simulation*, London: Routledge.

Schwänhausser, A. (ed.) (2016), *Sensing the City: A Companion to Urban Anthropology*, Basel: Birkhauser.

Sudnow, D. (2001), *Ways of the Hand: A Rewritten Account*, Cambridge, MA: The MIT Press.

Taussig, M. (2011), *I Swear I Saw This: Drawings in Fieldwork Notebooks*, Chicago: The University of Chicago Press.

Yen, Y. (2005), *Calligraphy and Power in Contemporary Chinese Society*, London: Routledge.

NOTES

1. Be that drawing considered as a design, artistic or research practice; each of which have their own audiences and viewing conditions. The contact between each audience and the drawing produces meaning.

2. Drawing as image, in Belting's schema, is considered somewhat problematic but beyond the scope of this chapter.

3. See Lucas (2016: 175–78) for further practicalities on the uses of drawing as a research method.

4. Further architectural interest in marketplaces has been detailed recently in Mörtenbröek et al. (2015).

5. The drawings began in sketchbooks, and are re-drawn on heavy Bristol board. The surface is prepared with a printed grid of dots to assist in measurement and to assist with line drawing key to the orthographic and parallel projections used. In the axonometric drawings, mechanical pencil is used initially, followed by fine line pen. The colour is applied with illustration marker pens in a wide range of colours. In this case, the character of the objects

is important, showing the wear and tear as well as vibrantly coloured plastics and tarpaulin against more utilitarian timber and steel. The elevations are intended to be cleaner, pencil lines looked sufficiently clear, with red and graphite used to differentiate between the stable module of the cart and red lines to show how goods are displayed as well as accretions and modifications to the cart.

6. Taussig (2011), Causey (2012) and Schwänhausser (2016) represent the contemporary use of drawings, whilst Geismar (2014) discusses key historical examples. Farnell (2009) is notable for her use of Laban movement notations more commonly found in modern dance and ballet, and Alfred Gell demonstrated a commitment to diagramming as part of his work (1998, 1999).

5

Learning to see: Otto Neurath's
Visual Autobiography

Valeria Guzmán-Verri, Ph.D, University of Costa Rica

From Hieroglyphics to Isotype: A Visual Autobiography was published posthumously (2010) drawing on drafts from the 1940s. Narrated from Otto Neurath's position as a child and youth in the domestic and urban context of *fin de siècle* Vienna, the book sets out the ways in which 'learning to see' crystalized for the author. Attentive to modalities of seeing in a period brimming with advertisements, cinema and museum exhibitions, and convinced that knowledge through images would play an increasing role in the future, Neurath assembled an account of his visual experiences that sought to encapsulate the development of a 'visual consciousness' (Neurath 1944: 1).

Three themes can be identified in the *Autobiography*: experiences of seeing, visual education and the democratization of knowledge. The present examination will be guided by the conceptual distinction between *prendre position and prendre parti* ('taking position/taking sides') elaborated by Georges Didi-Huberman (2009), who in turn follows Walter Benjamin's philosophical concern for actualizing the political and epistemological dimensions of *Erfahrung* ('experience').[1] Despite the considerable distance between Didi-Huberman and Neurath's approaches, this conceptual distinction allows the tensions in the act of seeing throughout the *Autobiography* to be highlighted; tensions explored in the notion of visual education, in techniques and styles of visualization, in the childhood games described therein, and in the playful and mobile condition of the child's visual memories. Once they are recognized as inherent to visual experience and knowledge, these tensions may be grasped in their potential political dimension.

The *Autobiography* is here situated in relation to contemporary studies on visuality and knowledge,[2] and is attentive to modalities whereby contemporary architecture still activates some of Neurath's most problematic aims, notably in the relationship between uses of graphic language and an aspiration to enhance democratic societies. Harun Farocki's video-installation *Deep Play* is then presented as a counter-position, putting at stake the opposition between taking position and taking sides: a decisive distinction when considering the political and the visual in architecture.

The thematic structuring of the book is chronological, tracking what Neurath calls the development of an 'eye consciousness' or 'visual consciousness' (Neurath 2010: 5). It traces his childhood years from 1882 to 1891, his youth from 1892 to 1906, and his adult life, specifically his university years and his 1923 appointment as director of the Visual Education Institute. Neurath seeks throughout to channel memories of his visual life into the parameters of visual communication, understood as the means by which visual materials may be transformed into information bearing agents. This taking sides in relation to the visual (restricted to factual information to be communicated) feeds into with how the visual is grasped in his *Wiener Methode der Bildstatistik* (project by Neurath 1933), which from 1935 became the Isotype project (Neurath [1936] 1980).[3]

Neurath maintained that Isotype was an international mechanism for visual education. Crucially, he believed that translating information into visible and accessible form would enhance democratic systems. Given his interest in ways of seeing that would be intelligible, the *Autobiography* formed an integral part of the urgent task of making visual media 'digestible' for the common man (Neurath 2010: 4). To develop 'eye consciousness' (Neurath 2010: 5) is to shape seeing into accessible comprehension and communication using visualization techniques, in conformity with what Isotype claimed to render visible.

Lesson/game

In the *Autobiography* the visual seems to be restricted chiefly to a 'visible grasp' (Didi-Huberman 2005: 192), that is, to a production of stable units of meaning through which 'a narrative sequence appears before our very eyes to offer itself for reading' (2005: 13). However, this will not preclude the detection of moments that, by Neurath's account, disrupt the stability of the visible world. These moments are inherent to the very notions of the 'development of eye consciousness' and 'visual education', though on the one hand, any development of a visual consciousness – knowing how to see well – is the development of a knowledge that must at least in part elude consciousness, while on the other

> [...] *la pédagogie de la lecture, – qui va de pair* [...] *avec la pédagogie des images – est elle-même un champ de bataille où se recontrent puissances d'asservissement et puissances de libération, contraintes morales et agencements ludiques, chaînes de la leçon et déchaînements du jeu.*
>
> (Didi-Huberman 2009: 198)[4]

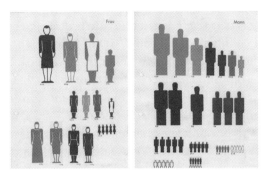

Figure 1: Figures of 'man' and 'woman' from the *Isotype Picture Dictionary*, I.C. 4/3, Otto and Marie Neurath Isotype Collection, University of Reading.

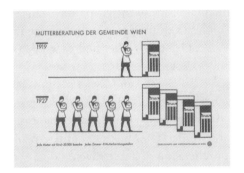

Figure 2: MUTTERBERATUNG DER GEMEINDE WIEN. *Gesellschaft und Wirtschaft*, I.C 5/3, Otto and Marie Neurath Isotype Collection, University of Reading.

Figure 3: Drawings made by primary school children, I.C. 3.2/87, Otto and Marie Neurath Isotype Collection, University of Reading.

The *Autobiography* is effectively located in a tension between *jeu ouvert* ('open game') and *parcours obligé* ('forced route') (Didi-Huberman 2009: 211). On the one hand, there is the experience of a forced form of reading, the standardization of the sign and the establishment of coordinates of the visible in series of graphic arrangements. Neurath calls this the 'technique of visualization' of Isotype (in Neurath and Cohen 1973: 246). To take one example, human figures selected from the *Symbol Dictionary* (the catalogue of standardized Isotype signs) may be arranged by size, colour, position and quantity, to reveal as a whole that, in the 'Consulting service for mothers in the Vienna community', between 1919 and 1927 the number of visits increased (Figures 1 and 2). On the other hand, there is the *playful* experience in Neurath's childhood games that eludes any homogenization of the sign or technique of visualization. When Neurath's group conducted investigations in schools to study the potential scope of the graphic system (Figure 3), though some human figures in the children's drawings loosely followed the stated instructions (to make sequenced chains of lessons), other figures were dispersed across treetops and trunks, thus playfully sidestepping a forced route.

The question arises as to where the child's act of apprehension is to be located. It is not about verifying a lesson learned by putting the figures together in the right order, but rather about drawing, which is a play with figures, even a play with signs. Playing with signs prior to understanding their content evokes the *Primer*, a book which facilitates the apprehension of letters over and above the understanding of the message they carry (Didi-Huberman 2009: 198). 'Playful seeing' here gives rise to learning, and Neurath himself mentions how he would 'visually absorb' images and maps in books (Neurath 2010: 24) even before learning to read. He also relates his encounter with images that were to generate ideas or further images, later associated with further experiences or sites, adding: '… one ought never to overlook the possible educational importance of such details, which do not belong to any of the usual subjects covered by a well-arranged curriculum, but rather come to us by chance' (2010: 12).

Playful agencements

> My most rudimentary activity in the field of combining elements was when, as a small child, I turned over my mother's mending boxes to select the most attractive buttons of various kinds […] I imagined the carpet to be a large piece of country on which the buttons, carefully grouped, could move about. Sometimes they represented armies with commanders […] The rugs I imagined as little islands, sometimes even as the home of Robinson Crusoe.
>
> (Neurath 2010: 13)

As a child, Neurath already knew how to identify the streets of his city on a map; a reading experience learnt walking through the Vienna streets. Creating geometric forms on the carpet with buttons and, later, lead soldiers enabled him to understand battles and military exercises represented in schematic form in books (2010: 15). A rich series unfurls: the carpet of his childhood home, his mother's box of buttons, storybooks with maps, the city of Vienna, schematic drawings of battles. 'Learning to see' brings with it the potential of an association of experiences that passes by way of play, objects, places and times. There is something here of Walter Benjamin's 'untidy child', who does not collect things just to file them away in drawers, but so that imagination can proliferate.[5]

> Each stone he finds, each flower picked and each butterfly caught is already the start of a collection, and every single thing he owns makes up one great collection [...] His drawers must become arsenal and zoo, crime museum and crypt. 'To tidy up' would be to demolish an edifice full of prickly chestnuts that are spiky clubs, tinfoil that is hoarded silver, bricks that are coffins, cacti that are totempoles and copper pennies that are shields.
>
> (Benjamin 1979: 73–74)

This potential propagation of imagination is evinced also in other games that Neurath recounts in relation to the Isotype mission.[6] Particular attention is paid to games where new combinations can be created out of given forms: matching together cut-out figures on a background, concocting market scenes and Alpine or desert landscapes, combining given elements by cutting and assembling.

Assembling separate units is a key activity in Isotype, but there they form a specific order governed by linking up standardized printed symbols to create 'visual arguments' (in Nemeth and Stadler 1996: 292). For example, 'Economic Scheme' (Figure 4) presents four principal levels of occupation differentiated by colour, showing 'everything that the whole population uses, under the present technical conditions in an industrialized country' (Neurath 1939: 146). The different boxes contain pictograms displaying the number of people in each group and their occupation. One can read and compare the proportion of workers for each occupation and make connections between uses of resources, notably their quantity and distribution across the different levels. For Neurath this affords a 'bird's eye view of the interconnections between all parts of a society in action [...]' (Neurath 1939: 65), facilitating analysis of the state of the world or of a country.

Reading 'Economic Scheme' comprises a network of 'visual arguments' (in Nemeth and Stadler 1996: 292) that require familiarity with the protocol

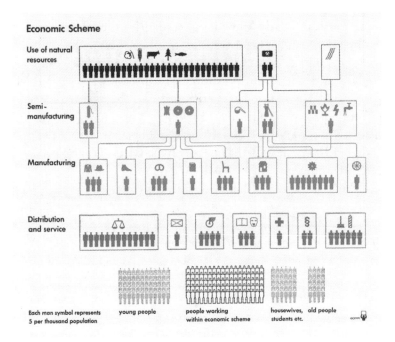

Figure 4: Economic Scheme. *Modern Man in the Making*, 1939, p. 65, Otto and Marie Neurath Isotype Collection, University of Reading.

of equivalences between quantity and symbol so that readers can perform quantitative comparisons, draw conclusions, and formulate questions or further discussion. With Isotype, Neurath is promoting a graphical approach that encourages the development of argumentative capacities based on a predefined reading protocol.

Elisabeth Nemeth asserts that the work of decipherment entailed by reading these pictograms supposes a liberation of the imagination (Nemeth 2011: 73), but this form of imagining implies both discovering meanings and establishing their content. Quite different from Benjamin's 'untidy child', whose playful and mobile position upsets the order of things, this position is at once spatial, epistemological and political. For the imaginative, there is always an aspect of *'jeter en l'air les lettres du discours, dispenser joyeusement les balises de la doctrine préexistante, puis tout reprendre de A à Z'* (Didi-Huberman 2009: 239).[7]

Although the 'geographical games' in the *Autobiography* are indicative of how a proliferation of associations allows for a visual experience that exceeds the Isotype way of seeing, the position of the child that Neurath chooses in the text is, in the main, that of a child in control of what he sees. What he sees is a source of neither confusion nor perturbation. For instance, when

Neurath visits Vienna's *Kunsthistorisches Museum* and is impressed by copies of Egyptian tomb murals,

> I could see what the men and women were doing without being troubled by vague backgrounds and obscure corners. Everything was simple, easily perceptible and told its story clearly. What the little hieroglyphic signs added, I neither knew nor even cared very much, I must confess. What pleased me was that the drawings did not baffle me.
>
> (Neurath 2010: 70)

We see here a desire to restrict visual experience to the non-conflictive 'informative character' (Neurath 2010: 72) of the visible world. As a child he enjoyed reading figures in inkblots on folded paper and in hand shadows, a modality of seeing concerned less with formless stains than with well-defined contours: 'I think my liking for both hieroglyphs and shadows on the wall led me gradually to enjoy silhouettes [...] A silhouette forces us to look at essential details and sharp lines; there are no vague backgrounds or superfluities' (Neurath 2010: 93).

The child's blot-reading game led to the adult Neurath's reinforcement of these figures and outlines as his 'forms' of reasoning. Neurath's visual education plan entails a commitment to single outline forms, and further on he will claim: 'children are mainly interested in the clear visualization of something' (Neurath 2010: 49).

Yet the project of seeing only what it is necessary to see, eliminating 'superfluous' details, does not prevent him from commenting on those moments when the enigmatic detail does catch his attention. Here is his boyhood impression of Brueghel's *The Conversion of Saint Paul* in the museum's galleries: 'I was always struck by the soldier in the foreground who is walking along looking very tired, carrying his helmet and some of his armour, just like a woman carrying her shoppingbasket' (Neurath 2010: 76).

The fortuitous detail attracting his gaze offers an indication of how the effect of the detail, loaded with potential significance, is already an act of the child's non-submission to a clear-cut visualization of things. In this short passage, a position can be glimpsed that is not that of the child who identifies and renders legible what he sees, but rather a mobile position: the child's gaze drifts around, settling on the inessential and the enigmatic, without shutting it in place once and for all.

The authority of the line

By Neurath's reckoning, knowledge should be used in the context of visual education '[...] only for indicating a more or less connected group of statements

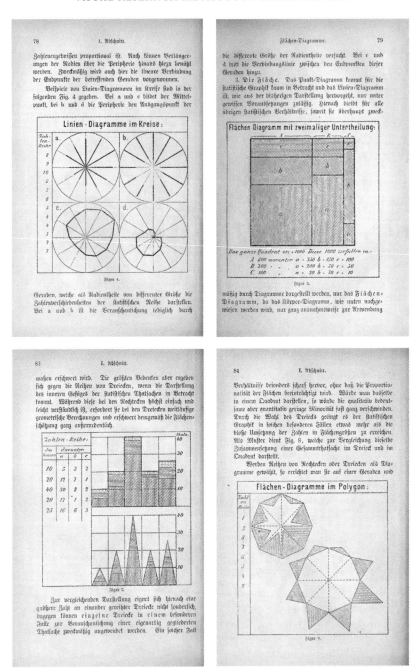

Figure 5: Pages 78, 79, 82 and 84 from Georg von Mayr, *Die Gesetzmässigkeit im Gesellschaftsleben, statistische Studien*, München: Oldenbourg, 1877 (electronic resource), http://archive.org/details/diegesetzmssi00mayr. Free eBook from the Internet Archive http://www.openlibrary.org/books/OL24237960M.

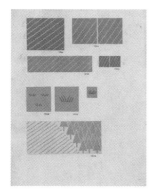  

Figure 6: Textures for 'field' or 'land' from the *Isotype Picture Dictionary*, I.C. 4/3, Otto and Marie Neurath Isotype Collection, University of Reading.

and arguments of a factual kind' (in Nemeth and Stadler 1996: 255).[8] Seeing is restricted to knowing how to translate factual statements, namely statistical information, into arguments. Because factual knowledge is common to all human beings, Neurath maintains, its transmission and communication must be possible. Here, then, resides the political project of this language: to offer the common man unambiguous statements in Isotype language so that discussion, opinion making and transformation of reality become possible.

The search for a common language of communication took root in nineteenth-century Europe (Figure 5), where statistical forms had already reorganized an experience of seeing and understanding materials, aligned with the aspiration to an objective viewpoint that would picture implicit order in social, urban and natural phenomena (Palsky 1996; Guzmán-Verri 2010, 2013). Furthermore, statistical facts enhanced democratic systems in their demand for fairness and impartiality, quantification lending political decisions the impression of being impersonal (Poovey 1998; Porter 1995).

By the time Neurath theorized the *Visual Representation of Architectural Problems* (Neurath 1937) he had already been promoting a regime of line and texture over surfaces and defined contours as a means of translating statistics for social and urban phenomena into readily legible order (Figure 6). This consisted of a visual organization of the various elements of city planning (photographs, graphics, models, cartoons, etc.) into 'an informative whole' or 'coordinated scheme' (Neurath 1937: 58) so that possible correlations of factors could be rendered visible to each individual, whether layman or specialist.[9] The visual representation of architectural problems went on to become a new chapter in the Isotype encyclopaedia.

The typographical aspect of this modality of seeing is especially noteworthy. In the context of incunabula and a new form of advanced visual reasoning, Renzo Baldasso highlights how the authority of the printed line on the page created an accurate typography that 'guarantee[d] the epistemological soundness of visual arguments' (Baldasso 2007: 280). The plates of Ptolemy's 1478 *Cosmographia* attest to this: with their precise lines based on a set of coordinates calculated from terrestrial and celestial data, typographic choices and clear labelling create a graphic, mathematical abstraction, absent from previous manuscripts.

Neurath commits to a precise typography, to the lineal, flat and diagrammatic qualities of representation, as though graphical precision were equated with precise communication,[10] in apparent disregard for the kind of disruption of the authority of line effected years earlier by the likes of Max Ernst in the collages of *La femme 100 têtes* (Ernst 1929), where details exceed or burst into a clear visualization, creating conflict and using line against itself.

An education in citizenship

In the *Autobiography*, Neurath presents visual experience first and foremost as an experience that 'takes sides', that is, as constituting a programme. By providing information and promoting consensus, the Isotype pictograms can strengthen democratic systems. Visual communication is deemed to bridge gaps and reduce antagonism, contributing to 'the creation of a brotherhood of man' (Neurath 2010: 8) in which '[…] a certain store of factual knowledge is common to all, and it may be transferred in as neutral a manner as possible' (in Nemeth and Stadler 1996: 250).

This taking sides in favour of visualization of information, communication and democratic progress is being updated in today's 'information age' and 'information society'. These slippery terms give emphasis to different phenomena (Webster 2006: 8–31), treated by ongoing debates on the manipulation of information, from the emergence of public opinion management (Bernays 1955) to the dynamics of the media apparatus and its supposed role as guardian of public interest (Curran 2002). Following Mario Perniola, this 'taking sides', linked to the communicative capacity of language as purposed to the enhancement of democratic systems has lost its efficacy: 'Di tutte le mistificazioni della comunicazione indubbiamente la più grande è stata quella di presentarsi sotto le insegne del progressismo democratico, mentre constituisce la configurazione compiuta dell'oscurantismo populistico' (Perniola 2004: 6).[11]

What was intended to be a space of discussion – as understood in Jürgen Habermas's notion of public sphere where the forming of public opinion was via rational debate – has become a chaotic accumulation of voices. Contents have dissolved in the face of excessive and uncontrolled exposure of every variable of a message. Yet Neurath's project is still in part active, at least in the field of architecture.[12]

According to Win Jansen, revisions of the Isotype system have occurred mainly in the fields of art and design, while it has virtually disappeared in statistical domains (Jansen 2009). Traces of the project's educational dimension for the architectural field can be found in the 2006 Venice Architecture Biennale *Cities, Architecture and Society*, devoted chiefly to presenting statistical maps and graphs showing differential aspects of cities: proportions of young and old, literacy rates, GDP, energy consumption, CO_2 emission etc. It was assumed that visitors would connect the different aspects of the information, drawing their own conclusions. Conditions of seeing, reading and learning are here restricted to a didactic chain of infographics, limiting the relationship between knowledge (the complexity of cities and societies) and form (graphics) to a programmed discourse.[13]

Other contemporary projects highlight bonds between people, city, digital information technologies and big data, associated within network (Ratti et al. 2013), organic (Ratti 2011) and democratic models (Nabian and Ratti 2012). Senseable City Laboratory (SCL) asserts the possibility of creating 'info-scapes' (in Nabian and Robinson 2011: 20) made from digital traces left by Internet users: for example, documentation of cell-phone activity during massive urban events (e.g. concerts) reveals areas of traffic congestion, numbers of people leaving the area, actual transport demand and so forth (Vaccari et al. 2010).

> [...] these info-scapes provide citizens with a better knowledge of their environment, and allow them to make more informed decisions. Indeed, this seems to be the most promising characteristic of the future, which becomes 'smart' through the collaborative activity of the sentient, self-reporting agents who are its citizens. It will be a desirable place to live and work, since it offers a platform for reinforcing identity and culture through collaboration.
>
> (Nabian and Robinson 2011: 20)

For SCL, cities can come to operate as 'realtime control systems' (Nabian and Robinson 2011: 8) where the visualization of information becomes a continuous mapping of use patterns.[14] Urban complexity is reduced to the efficacy of information and its forms of visualization, which are supposed to be understood 'intuitively' by the community at large (Claudel et al. 2016). Info-scape becomes a new 'visual consciousness' of this 'intuitive' way of seeing. Though this is merely a preliminary consideration of info-scape, one cannot but ask: is this not a categorical *taking sides*?

A tentative answer can be found by counterposing to this the work of Harun Farocki. In the video installation *Deep Play* (2007), twelve projections show simultaneously the final match of the 2006 World Cup. The images of the match come with graphs analysing the movement of each player, the speed and trajectory of the ball and the positions of the footballers. Their movements during the match and across the space of the field become information that is meticulously rendered in graphic form. This visual material, obtained from FIFA (Farocki 2009: 237), is supposed to be synonymous with analysis, calculation and decision-making, and as such becomes a way of conceiving, organizing and directing the event, yet in the installation the info-scapes are stripped of their managerial tasks: the graphs are on the screen, but not the managerial imperative implied in them. With the images now devoid of their implicit function, the viewer has to relearn how to see them; she is solicited anew in her capacity to articulate images with images, with sounds and with texts.[15]

At a time when architects insist on explicitly inserting themselves into pseudo-democratic discourses, what can be unlearned in architecture from a text like Neurath's *Visual Autobiography*? The attempt to create a lesson for learning to see, to create an 'eye consciousness', is in tension with the playful position of the child who cuts through and across the order of things, repositioning herself into a situation of not knowing, where the visual material (her visual memories or assemblages) will not be turned into illustrated politics.

Acknowledgements

I would like to thank the kind assistance of the Department of Typography & Graphic Communication at University of Reading in facilitating access to the archival material in their Isotype Collection, and both the Ph.D. Programme at the Architectural Association and the Faculty of Fine Arts at the University of Costa Rica for fruitful discussions generated when they hosted lecture versions of this text.

REFERENCES

Agamben, G. (2011), 'Identity without the person', in W. Hamacher (ed.), *Nudities* (trans. D. Kishik and S. Pedatella), Stanford, CA: Stanford University Press, pp. 46–54.

Annink, E. and Bruisma, M. (eds) (2008), *Lovely Language, Words Divide, Images Unite*, Rotterdam: Veenman Publishers.

Baldasso, R. (2007), 'Illustrating the book of nature in the Renaissance: Drawing, painting, and printing geometric diagrams and scientific figures', Ph.D. thesis, New York: Columbia University.

Benjamin, W. (1979), 'One-way street', in *One-Way Street and Other Writings* (trans. E. Jephcott and K. Shorter), London: New Left Books, pp. 45–104.

———(2014), *Radio Benjamin* (ed. L. Rosenthal, trans. J. Lutes, L. H. Schumann and D. Reese), London and New York: Verso.

Bernays, E. L. (ed.) (1955), *The Engineering of Consent*, Norman, OK: University of Oklahoma Press.

Blau, E. (2006), 'Isotype and architecture in Red Vienna: The modern projects of Otto Neurath and Josef Frank', *Austrian Studies,* 14, pp. 227–59.

Buck-Morss, S. (1997), *The Dialectics of Seeing: Walter Benjamin and the Arcades Project*, Cambridge, MA and London: The MIT Press.

Burdett, R. and Sudjic, D. (eds) (2008), *The Endless City: The Urban Age Project by the London School of Economics and Deutsche Bank's Alfred Herrhausen Society*, London: Phaidon.

Burke, C., Kindel, E. and Walker, S. (eds) (2013), *Isotype: Design and Contexts 1925–1971*, London: Hyphen Press.

Cartwright, N., Cat, J., Fleck, L. and Uebel, T. E. (1996), *Otto Neurath: Philosophy between Sciences and Politics*, Cambridge: Cambridge University Press.

Chung, C. J., Inaba J., Koolhaas, R. and Tsung Leong, T. (eds) (2002), *Harvard Design School Guide to Shopping*, Köln, London, Madrid, New York, Paris and Tokyo: Taschen.

Claudel, M., Nagel, T., Ratti, C. (2016), 'From origins to destinations: The past, present and future of visualizing flow maps', *Built Environment,* 42:3, pp. 338–55.

Curran, J. (2002), 'Media and democracy: The third way', in J. Curran (ed.), *Media and Power,* London and New York: Routledge, pp. 214–246.

Didi-Huberman, G. (1990), *Devant l'image: Questions posées aux fins d'une histoire de l'art*, Paris: Minuit.

——— (2005), *Confronting Images: Questioning the Ends of a Certain History of Art* (trans. J. Goodman), Philadelphia, PA: University of Pennsylvania Press.

——— (2009), *Quand les images prennent position. L'œil de l' histoire*, Paris: Minuit.

Ernst, M. (1929), *La femme 100 têtes*, Paris: Éditions du Carrefour.

Farocki, H. (2007), *Deep Play*, Germany: Harun Farocki Filmproduktion.

——— (2009), 'Written trailers', in A. Ehmann and K. Eshun (eds), *Harun Farocki Against Whom? Against What?*, London: Koenig Books, pp. 220–41.

Guzmán-Verri, V. (2010), 'Pensar con figuras numéricas', *Revista Reflexiones*, 90:2, pp. 145–64.

——— (2013), 'Form and fact', *Jefferson Journal of Science and Culture*, 3, pp. 94–109.

Hartmann, F. and Bauer, E. K. (2006), *Bildersprache. Otto Neurath, Visualisierungen*, Vienna: WUV.

Hochhäusl, S. (2011), *Otto Neurath-City Planning, Proposing a Sociopolitical Map for Modern Urbanism*, Innsbruck: Innsbruck University Press.

Hüser, R. (2004), 'Nine minutes in the yard: A conversation with Harun Farocki', in T. Elsaesser (ed.), *Harun Farocki: Working on the Sight-lines*, Amsterdam: Amsterdam University Press, pp. 297–314.

Jansen, W. (2009), 'Neurath, Arntz and ISOTYPE: The legacy in art, design and statistics', *Journal of Design History*, 22:3, pp. 227–42.

Kinross, R. (1979), 'Otto Neurath's contribution to visual communication (1925–45): The history, graphic language and theory of Isotype', M.Phil. dissertation, University of Reading.

—— (1990), 'Emigré graphic designers in Britain: Around the second world war and afterwards', *Journal of Design History*, 3:1, pp. 35–57.

—— (2008), *Isotype: Recent Publications*, Hyphen Press, London https://hyphenpress.co.uk/journal/article/isotype_recent_publications. Accessed 10 December 2013.

Kraeutler, H. (2008), *Otto Neurath. Museum and Exhibition Work, Spaces (Designed) for Communication*, Frankfurt am Main, Berlin, Bern, Bruxelles, New York, Oxford and Wien: Peter Lang.

Krampen, M., Götte, M. and Kneidl, M. (2007), *Die Welt der Zeichen: Kommunikation mit Piktogrammen* (*The World of Signs: Communication by Pictograms*), Ludwigsburg: av edition GmbH.

Lee, Jae Y. (2008), 'Otto Neurath's Isotype and the rhetoric of neutrality', *Visible Language*, 42:2, pp. 159–80.

Leonard, R. J. (1999), '"Seeing is believing": Otto Neurath, graphic art, and the social order', *History of Political Economy*, 31, pp. 452–78.

Lupton, E. (1986), 'Reading Isotype', *Design Issues*, III:2, pp. 47–58.

Maas, W. (1999), *Metacity/Datatown*, Rotterdam: 010 Publishers.

Nabian, N. and Ratti, C. (2012), 'A collaborative approach to architecture', http://senseable.mit.edu/papers/pdf/20120302_Nabian_Ratti_CollaborativeApproach_Marklives.pdf. Accessed 6 November 2016.

Nabian, N. and Robinson, P. (eds) (2011), *The Senseable City Guide*, Cambridge, MA: SA+P Press, http://senseable.mit.edu/papers/pdf/2011_Senseable_City_Guide.pdf. Accessed 20 February 2013.

Nemeth, E. (2011), 'Scientific attitude and picture language: Otto Neurath on visualization in social sciences', in R. Heinrich, E. Nemeth, W. Pichler and D. Wagner (eds), *Image and Imagining in Philosophy, Science and the Arts*, vol. 2, Frankfurt, Lancaster, Paris and New Brunswick: Ontos Verlag, pp. 59–83.

Nemeth, E. and Stadler, F. (eds) (1996), *Encyclopedia and Utopia: The Life and Work of Otto Neurath (1882–1945)*, Dordrecht, Boston, MA and London: Kluwer Academic Publishers.

Neurath, M. and Cohen, R. S. (eds) (1973), *Empiricism and Sociology: Sociology/Otto Neurath. With a Selection of Biographical and Autobiographical Sketches*, Dordrecht: Reidel.

Neurath, M. and Kinross, R. (2009), *The Transformer: Principles of Making Isotype Charts*, London: Hyphen Press.

Neurath, O. (1933), *Bildstatistik nach Wiener Methode in der Schule*, Wien/Leipzig: Deutscher Verlag für Jugend un Volk.

—— (1937), 'Visual representation of architectural problems', *Architectural Record*, July, pp. 56–61.

—— (1939), *Modern Man in the Making*, New York and London: Alfred A. Knopf.

—— (1944), *From Hieroglyphics to Isotype: A Visual Autobiography* (Carbon copy of the second draft, 8 Nov), Isotype Collection, IC 3.2/79, Reading: University of Reading.

—— ([1936] 1980), *International Picture Language*, Reading: University of Reading.

——— (2010), *From Hieroglyphics to Isotype: A Visual Autobiography* (eds M. Eve and C. Burke), London: Hyphen Press.

Palsky, G. (1996), *Des chiffres et des cartes: naissance et développement de la cartographie quantitative* française *au XIXe siècle*, Paris: Ministère d'Enseignement Supérieur et de la Recherche, Comité des travaux historiques et scientifiques.

Perniola, M. (2004), *Contro la comunicazione*, Torino: Eunaidi.

Poovey, M. (1998), *A History of the Modern Fact: Problems of Knowledge in the Sciences of Wealth and Society*, Chicago: The University of Chicago Press.

Porter, T. M. (1995), *Trust in Numbers: The Pursuit of Objectivity in Science and Public Life*, Princeton, NJ: Princeton University Press.

Ratti, C. (2011), 'Architetti Imparate da Wikipedia', *Il Sole 24 Ore*, 27 January, pp. 32–38.

Ratti, C., Haw, A., Picon, A. and Claudel, M. (2013), 'The power of networks: Beyond critical regionalism', *Architectural Review*, 23 July, pp. 22–23.

Salzani, C. (2009), 'Experience and play: Walter Benjamin and the Prelapsarian Child', in A. Benjamin and C. Rice (eds), *Walter Benjamin and the Architecture of Modernity*, Melbourne: re.press, pp. 175–98.

Sandner, G. (2015), *Otto Neurath: eine politische Biographie: Eine politische Biographie*, Wien: Zsolnay.

Smith, S. and Watson, J. (2002), 'Autobiographical acts', in *Reading Autobiography: A Guide for Interpreting Life Narratives*, Minneapolis and London: University of Minnesota Press, pp. 49–81.

Tsiambaos, K. (2012), 'Isotype diagrams from Neurath to Doxiadis', *Architectural Research Quarterly*, 16, pp. 49–57.

Twyman, M. (1975), *Graphic Communication through Isotype*, Reading: Department of Typography and Graphic Communication, University of Reading.

Vaccari, A., Martino, M., Rojas, F. and Ratti, C. (2010), 'Pulse of the city: Visualizing urban dynamics of special events', in *GraphiCon'2010*, St. Petersburg, Russia, 20–24 September, http://senseable.mit.edu/papers/pdf/2010_V accari_et_al_Pulse_city_GraphiCon.pdf. Accessed 6 June 2014.

Vossoughian, N. (2006), 'Mapping the modern city: Otto Neurath, The International Congress of Modern Architecture (CIAM), and the Politics of Information Design', *Design Issues*, 22, pp. 48–65.

——— (2008), *Otto Neurath: The Language of the Global Polis*, Rotterdam: NAi Publishers.

Webster, F. (2006), 'What is an Information Society?', in F. Webster (ed.), *Theories of the Information Society*, Oxon and New York: Routledge, pp. 8–31.

NOTES

1. For an overview on Benjamin's insights on childhood in the context of its revolutionary power, see Salzani 2009. For a more general view, see Buck-Morss 1997: 262–86). A 1929 radio talk on children's literature suggests that Benjamin was aware of Neurath's pictograms:

> The extraordinary timeliness that all attempts to develop instruction based on visualization possess stems from the fact that a new, standardized, and wordless system of symbols seems to be arising in very different areas of life – in traffic, art, statistics. Here, a pedagogical problem touches upon a wide-sweeping cultural one, which could be expressed with the slogan: For the symbol, against the word!
>
> (Benjamin 2014: 253)

2. This study does not seek to offer insight into Neurath's life – the person 'Neurath' and the 'autobiographical I' do not necessarily coincide (Smith and Watson 2002: 49–81) – nor does it explicate his visual project in detail. On the life of Neurath, see Neurath and Cohen (1973: 1–83); Nemeth and Stadler (1996: 15–28); Cartwright et al. (1996: 1–82); Neurath and Kinross (2009); Sandner (2015). On Isotype, see Twyman (1975); Kinross (1979); Lupton (1986); Leonard (1999); Hartmann and Bauer (2006); Krampen et al. (2007); Annink and Bruisma (2008); Lee (2008); Neurath and Kinross (2009); Nemeth (2011); Hochhäusl (2011); Tsiambaos (2012).

3. Isotype translates social and economic statistical data into pictograms or 'number-fact pictures' to be made public through museum exhibitions and printed media (Kraeutler 2008; Vossoughian 2008; Neurath and Kinross 2009; Burke et al. 2013).

4. '[...] the pedagogy of reading – is on a par [...] with the pedagogy of images – is itself a battlefield on which there is an encounter between forces of enslavement and forces of liberation, between moral constraints and playful *agencement*, between lessons in a sequenced chain and unchained playfulness'. All translations of this text to English are my own. The term *agencement* has been left in French in reference to Deleuze and Guattari.

5. For the crucial distinction between imagination and sheer fantasy, see Buck-Morss (1997: 256–62) and Didi-Huberman (2009: 254–56).

6. Such as stamp collections, stencils, small publicity images, chemical experiments, the 'shinies' young Neurath sticks into his scrapbook, as well as his toy woodblocks and cardboard figures with changeable clothes (Neurath 2010: 13).

7. An aspect of 'throwing the letters of discourse up in the air and joyfully breaking apart the codes of preexisting doctrine so as to resume from A to Z'. All translations of this text to English are my own.

8. Neurath was a member of the Vienna Circle, whose project had its theoretical bases in empiricism, positivism and the logical analysis of language.

9. For the episode Neurath-CIAM, see Nemeth and Stadler (1996: 167–82; Blau 2006; Vossoughian 2006; Hochhäusl 2011: 95–113).

10. This is emphasized over and again in the *Autobiography*, when he refers not only to scientific texts, such as René Descartes' *Optics* or Thomas Henry Huxley's *Physiography*, but also to the illustrations of Aubrey Beardsley and the vignettes of Wilhem Busch.

11. 'Of all the mystifications of communication, the major one was without doubt to present itself under the banner of democratic progressivism, when in reality it constitutes the outmoded configuration of populist obscurantism'. All translations of this text to English are my own.

12. A number of institutions in England, the Netherlands and Austria are working with Isotype. For a list of publications and exhibition projects, see http://isotyperevisited.org/; http://www.stroom.nl/webdossiers/webdossier.php?wd_id=2615745; http://www.zeitlosezeichen.at/timelesssigns.html. Accessed 28 September 2015.

13. A number of publications in architecture stand as representatives of a renewed interest in statistical data and its forms of representation (Burdett and Sudjic 2008; Maas 1999; Chung et al. 2002, amongst others).

14. Answers are still pending to fundamental questions such as: is the information produced by an Internet user conceptually the same as the participation of a citizen? Does information boost identity? Following Agamben's discussion on biometric data, what seems to be favored is 'identity without person' (Agamben 2011: 67–78).

15. As Farocki suggests: '[…] when you turn photographs or other still images into something, you don't compete with the omnipresent narrative machine. When you show a boy who starts talking to a girl at a coffee shop, you are immediately subjected to standards: does it look like Neighbourhood TV, like an independent film or like the work of a student? When it's about putting stills into a sequence, to read them, a new kind of competence arises' (Hüser 2004: 313).

6

Duration and anexactitude: What is at stake with data-based urban drawing in research?

Miguel Paredes Maldonado, University of Edinburgh

Half a decade after the apparent consolidation of the 'Digital Turn' in architecture and its associated spatial practices (Carpo 2013), it seems clear that computational thinking has become particularly prevalent when addressing issues of design and governance at the urban scale. Whereas the Smart Cities paradigm is nowadays the most widely recognized set of data-driven practices of urban spatial intelligence, it is by no means the only framework for articulating data-based enquiries into the urban field. This chapter endeavours to prove this point by outlining urban research methodologies that stem directly from a critique of the modes of operation, control and representation of Smart Cities. Formalized as data-based drawing tools and practices, these methodologies reveal fine-grain urban conditions and subjectivities that would otherwise remain obscured under mainstream modalities of digital operation.

Smart Cities constitute powerful representational frameworks for both urban design and urban governance. Technically speaking, they are simply an overlay of integrated digital infrastructures that tap into big data streams from mobile apps, sensor networks, social media feeds and transport information, with the goal of making urban features more responsive to changing conditions (Coyne 2017). One of their most critical aspects is that – for the sake of efficiency – this complex overlay can only be manifested above certain scalar thresholds. In other words: the subject of the Smart City is a single, large-scale, continuous metropolitan body (as opposed to an assemblage of constituent, interconnected elements). In order to articulate such a representational subject any smaller, individually heterogeneous components are 'averaged' into a homogeneously readable 'whole' for the purposes of global observation (De Landa 2016; Krivý 2016).[1] This resonates with recent New Materialist perspectives on design research, which suggest that cities and their infrastructures could be regarded as metropolitan-scale 'bodies' and humans as robotic 'carriers' of matter, energy and information operating within them (Oosterhuis 2017). This is not at all dissimilar to the representational structure of the Smart City paradigm: Thanks to the pervasiveness of digital sensing, data harvesting and computational technologies, the spatial datasets that articulate the 'smart' city are both drawn and controlled as interdependent flows of matter, energy and information. Constituencies like the MIT SenseAble City Lab explore the potentials of this representational approach, identifying recurrent urban flow patterns and rendering them visible, with a view to developing strategies to optimize flow-based urban resources (Offenhuber and Ratti 2014). However, whereas such a flow-centred paradigm has been enthusiastically embraced by cities all over the world, it is important to note that it is far from free of caveats and contradictions.

First, the political neutrality of 'sensed' or 'harvested' data streams and their representations is a highly contested matter. Smart Cities stand on the fiction that their representational tools lead to objective and impartial decisions on urban design, policy and governance (Picon 2015: 49). Observing these tools through Manuel De Landa's reading of the work of Deleuze and Guattari (De Landa 1998), we can easily ascertain that, in fact, the opposite is true: such mediated, singularized representations of data are highly stratified processes of selection and organization, consolidating urban narratives of control that fall under the category of what Guattari (2008) would refer to as urban 'subjectifications'. In other words, different ways of selecting and organizing data generate radically different narratives, and therefore different responses, actions and policies. Thus data-based drawing representations are non-neutral operations in the articulation of the urban field: what we sense, measure or read cannot be reduced to a purely technical issue. In spite of this, the representational mechanisms of Smart Cities conflate 'smartness' with the fulfilment of numerical standards of efficiency and optimization of intertwined flows. Thus, anything that cannot be numerically 'sensed' and represented as a form of 'flow' simply falls outside their infrastructural framework of action and governance (Krivý 2016). In other words, whatever 'flows' must 'flow' better and, consequently, if something does not 'flow' it cannot be considered as a 'subject' for the purposes of the Smart City.

Second, the Smart City paradigm is grounded on a conventionally established distinction between top-down and bottom-up spatialized intelligences (Picon 2015: 78–100), thus suggesting that information (and power) may flow in either direction of the scalar hierarchy.[2] However, it seems clear that, by tackling the assembled 'whole body' of the city as their locus of operations, Smart City practices

VISUAL RESEARCH METHODS IN ARCHITECTURE

foster a technocratic form of urban subjectivity that is decidedly top-down. The consequence of addressing the city-whole as the sole subject of scrutiny and organization is that of averaging the agencies of discontinuous, finer-grain subjects – namely those of individual citizens – into much larger metropolitan-scale, flowing 'subjects'.

Figure 1: Downtown Caligiari as a subjective visual data-scape: Mapping of geo-localized public images of the city, extracted from Flickr. Image by Miguel Paredes Maldonado.

Figure 2: Mapping subjective urban flows: Flyover of downtown Cagliari towards the docks. Image by Miguel Paredes Maldonado.

In light of these shortcomings in the mainstream project of digitalized urban spatial intelligence, we may wonder: Is it possible to articulate a data-based counter-project of design research that subverts these urban narratives of optimization, efficiency and top-down 'smartness'? Can we steer the representation of data flows towards the emergence of multiple, heterogeneous individual subjectivities? How do we resituate these subjectivities back into the locus of design research agency? In response to these questions, this chapter presents a visual research methodology that foregrounds the individual, multiplicitous subjectivities of the urban through productive transferences between architectural drawing and philosophical thinking in the context of a digital, robotic design environment. In doing so it also intends to highlight how urban drawings can be mobilized as enablers for speculative thought, thus tapping into Bernard Cache's understanding of philosophy not as a contemplative activity, but rather as a mode of production: a 'calculation of reason and forms' that defies established productive paradigms (Cache 2011a: 21). For Cache, data-driven architectural drawings are the 'other means' through which philosophy can be engaged as a mode of production. As a modality of visual practice, this chapter's methodological approach explores how this engagement is orchestrated (how thinking can be conducted by architectural means) but also what kind of knowledge is actually revealed in the process. The productive capabilities of digital computation and robotic fabrication are radically leveraged by the processing power of current technologies. However, we might still wonder: Is there a non-computable element of thought? And how could it be revealed?

The unpacking of this data-driven urban drawing research practice starts with a description of the digital, robotic drawing environment that constitutes the locus of productive knowledge in this chapter. The word 'environment' intentionally emphasizes its plurality, for in line with Gilbert Simondon's taxonomy of technical devices it is not a singular 'technical object', but a 'technical ensemble' constituted by multiple machinic systems transferring information to one another. As Simondon (1989: 145) noted, a critical aspect of this ensemble is that throughout its embedded processes of transference between machines, information is shifted, modulated and translated, thus allowing for the emergence of associated forms of productive indetermination. The technical ensemble presented in this chapter is designed to enact the geometric operations underpinning the development of data-based digital drawings. Therefore, in this ensemble 'drawing' is understood as a dynamic action – something that develops over time, gradually unfolding in front of us. But, equally importantly, the original source of information to be processed through this technical ensemble is also dynamic in nature. It consists of an animated urban plan, tracing 79 geo-localized paths of individual displacement (corresponding to the author and his students from the University of Cagliari in Sardinia) that were collectively captured via GPS-tracking smartphone apps throughout a single day in April 2017. The resulting traces – part of a larger exercise on subjective urban data collection – re-draw the fabric of Cagliari as a summative accumulation of the individual urban geographies of group members, rendering them as dynamic urban plans that are formalized as quantized vector video clips.

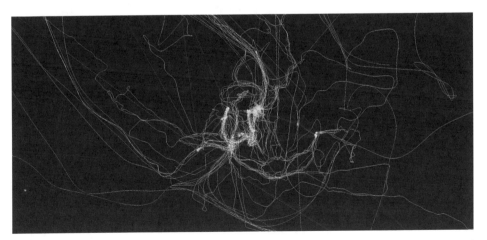

Figure 3: Mapping collective circulation. Still frame from animation showing pathways of university staff and students through downtown Cagliari districts. Image by Miguel Paredes Maldonado.

From this starting point, the first machine in the ensemble (a technical object consisting of a piece of digital parametric code) breaks down the source geometry of each individual path and subsequently reconstructs it as a single, incremental sequence of similarly sized fragments, to be gradually fed into a second machine. This second, code-based technical object translates the animated sequence into sets of coordinates, which are, in turn, transferred – at an appropriate rate and as a series of points in space – into a third, hardware-based machine. This is an extended Arduino circuit that transforms the incoming digital stream into an analogue signal to modulate the rotation of two electric stepper motors. These mechanical motors, in turn, constitute the core of the fourth machine: A flatbed physical device where rotational movements become biaxial displacements of a drawing head. Thus, we are looking at a technical ensemble that is composed of four individual technical objects, operating in a range of digital and analogue conditions. As suggested by Sébastien Bourbonnais (2012) in his observations on Simondon's work, the indetermination between machines appears in the form of information relays when shifting, modulating and translating information from one to another. In the particular case of our drawing ensemble, relays appear due to the different rates at which information flows across machines (which is, in turn, a factor of the data processing capabilities, buffers etc. of each individual technical object) but also due to the losses and additions of information occurring as a consequence of the accumulative conversions across different formats (from lines to fragments, to points, to rotations and finally to axial coordinates). Moreover, and as Simondon (1989: 137) emphasized, yet another set of relays emerges through our own ability as 'living beings' to orchestrate the transferences of information across the different components of the ensemble. In other words, we place ourselves between machines to interpret their functioning in terms of information, and adjust their interactions with pertinent projective goals in mind.

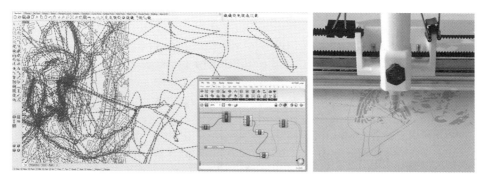

Figure 4: Re-drawing data: Two components of the drawing machine as a relayed technical ensemble (digital technical object and flatbed physical apparatus). Image by Miguel Paredes Maldonado.

As soon as this setup is put to work, we can quickly ascertain what kind of thought – computational as well as non-computational – is manifested through this productive process. As noted above, the original source material for this ensemble is a trans-scalar, data-based dynamic drawing, which can be considered as an assemblage of geometries emerging from GPS logs and installed into Euclidean space (Cache 2011b).[3] Once this installation is dynamically re-enacted through the relayed technical ensemble, these geometries start to approach what can be referred to as 'anexact' in the context of Jacques Derrida's reading of Edmund Husserl's seminal essay 'The origin of geometry'. For Derrida (1978) the anexact was manifested through vague morphological types, giving rise to a form of descriptive science based on the observation of objects being perceived as a whole. Using the work of Husserl and Derrida as a conceptual scaffolding, Greg Lynn (1993) formulated a distinction between exact, inexact and anexact geometries that is particularly useful here: According to Lynn, exact geometries can be reduced to fixed mathematical systems, therefore allowing for their precise reproduction. On the contrary, inexact geometries lack the necessary rigor and precision to allow for their measurement and, consequently, our ability to reproduce them is limited. Finally, anexact geometries are irreducible to specific points and dimensions; however, they are rigorous insofar as they can be described with precision. Whereas the exact deals with geometries that are reproducible due to their idealized, abstract nature (for example circles or squares), anexact geometry deviates from idealized form while still allowing for precise replication. Another critical aspect of the anexact is the fact that its geometrical construction takes place within the 'real space' of what is perceived. For the purposes of this chapter, this 'real space' is the flatbed surface of the robotic drawing apparatus. In light of this, we can argue that our technical ensemble allows for a slippage of the exact into the anexact to be enacted in real time, and in front of us. Throughout its relayed processes, references to standard geometrical primitives (circles and squares but also linear segments, arcs etc.) and their location with regard to a global, metric spatial set are gradually erased from the stream of information. Instead, a regime of local relationships is established, whereby a single linear sequence emerges via the addition of a multiplicity of fragments over time. In resonance with the conceptual scaffolding of the anexact, each individual fragment is solely referenced to its preceding element in the sequence, and in turn constitutes the sole spatial and dimensional reference for its succeeding element. Each fragment does cover an individually measurable distance. However, the geometry of the linear sequence as a whole is not drawn from an overarching metric scheme, but rather develops in a self-referential manner as an anexact-but-rigorous construction based on the dynamic, accumulative occupation of the surface of the paper.

The relayed ensemble of the drawing environment does not simply reproduce the original data-based urban traces, but also re-enacts their gradual unfolding over time. This reveals much more than final forms: All the operations that need to be undertaken for the target geometries to emerge are also physically traced. By re-enacting an originally digital territory as a gradual, accumulative occupation, the drawing machine becomes an updated version of the gothic *compagnon* or 'journeyman' as conceptualized by Deleuze and Guattari (1987: 364–65, 367–69), for, in both cases, they proceed by rendering visible the full set of discrete instructions that they are meant to carry out.[4] In the particular case of the robotic drawing ensemble, these instructions take the form of CNC code. Thus, the drawings emerging from the machinic process presented in this chapter can be regarded as partial registrations of urban displacement, rendered into anexact-but-rigorous geometry through accumulative translations and relays of procedural information.

For the purposes of this chapter anexactitude is heavily inflected by the passing of time as a vehicle for gradual, accumulative development. On the one hand, the anexact describes a process whereby continuity is enforced – both geometrically and procedurally – via sequential exchanges established within the technical ensemble. On the other hand, and tapping again into Simondon's lexicon, the informational relays built into those exchanges modulate this continuous development via moments of compression and expansion of the informational flow (Bourbonnais and Rose 2012). Therefore time – or, more precisely, 'the passing of time' – is revealed here as a viscous pulse, a continuous flow of heterogeneous transformations. This allows the other non-computable element of thought enacted by means of the machinic urban drawing environment to surface: Henri Bergson's elusive notion of 'duration', or the process of perpetually becoming-other through modalities of development that are simultaneously continuous and heterogeneous (Deleuze 1991: 37).

The potential of the robotic technical ensemble as a medium to highlight this durational 'pulse' in connection with its anexact character is even more apparent once closer attention is paid to the implications of using a dynamic source of geometrical input such as the collectively constructed urban plans of Cagliari. As in mainstream Smart City representations, the gradual unfolding of these data-based urban traces articulate a form of 'urban flow' through the interactions of heterogeneous sets of components incorporating matter, energy and information. However, the effect of running this dynamic digital material through the relayed drawing protocol produces the distinct effect of critically reinstating time-as-duration as a fundamental component of the collectively constructed multiplicities that it attempts to represent. Thus, 'urban flow' is no longer articulated as a homogeneous, totalizing 'assembled whole', but as a continuous-yet-heterogeneous occupation of the urban landscape.

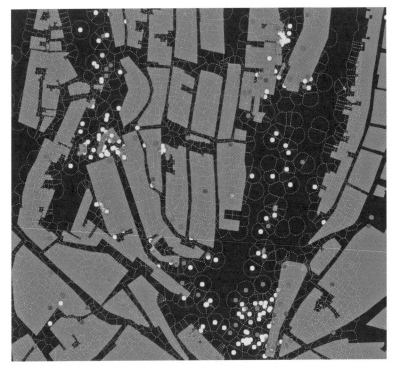

Figure 5: Collectively assembled urbanities, or the spatial agency of images: geo-localized data points of publicly shared pictures – extracted from Flickr – and their areas of influence in the urban fabric of Cagliari. Image by Miguel Paredes Maldonado.

It is also interesting to note that the relayed ensemble is not completely 'up to the job': The drawing head endlessly chases the moving targets of the 79 traced pathways as they gradually 'play out at once'. As soon as the pen closes in on a point, it is forced to move on to the next position in the spatial sequence. The process does not flow seamlessly, being instead punctuated by abundant machinic 'stuttering' occurring whenever the transfer rates of any two given relays in the ensemble are temporarily misaligned. As a consequence of this, the machinic urban plans emerging from the process become actualized solely on the physical surface of the drawing paper. By watching their traces emerge we can catch a glimpse of the continuous-but-heterogeneous dynamics of duration affecting the gradual unfolding of collective displacements across Cagliari. Whereas this time-based, machinic environment is originally installed into Cartesian space and Euclidean geometry, its protocol of digital actions gradually resituates it into the hybrid category of the anexact. This hybrid digital-analogue scenario of dynamic drawing conveys the simultaneously heterogeneous and continuous character of the collectively assembled urban processes that originated it: Never static, always *becoming other*.

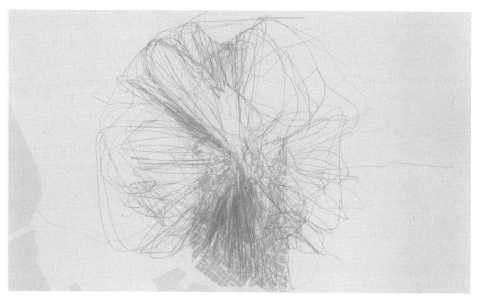

Figure 6: Anexact urban drawing depicting the durational output of the technical ensemble. Image by Miguel Paredes Maldonado.

Smart Cities and other related data-driven modalities of spatial intelligence have successfully co-opted Félix Guattari's notion of the mechanosphere (2012: 73–74) by presenting their integrated approach to urban infrastructure as a globalizing, efficient intermeshing of architectural, mechanical and biological processes exponentially facilitated by connective layers of digital technologies. However, as Guattari also argued 'machines do not just revolutionize the world: they can completely recreate it – in many, radically different directions' (Guattari and Lotringer 2009: 74). On the one hand, Smart Cities produce very specific forms of (capitalist) subjectivity, which emerge primarily from the articulation of their representational (media) mechanisms. On the other hand, powerful counter-narratives of collectively assembled urban subjectivity can potentially emerge via hybrid media methodologies akin to the one presented in this chapter. Following media archaeologist Jussi Parikka's conceptualization (2012: 38) these technical ensembles articulate sets of topological relationships between digital and physical objects and interfaces. As active visual representations they can open up spaces of resistance to the homogeneous, technocratic 'smartness' of contemporary urban governance. The relayed digital-analogue drawing process is mobilized to address the domain of the commons as a subject that emerges gradually and collectively. In doing so, the institutional narrative of the neutral, efficient flow is confronted with a narrative of collectively assembled citizenship. Two critical aspects of this narrative emerge as 'non-computational elements of thought', revealed through the relayed machinic process. These aspects are anexactitude (as both the form of urban multiplicities and a tool to overcome technocratic narratives of numerical optimization) and duration (as both an index of the continuous heterogeneity deployed collectively by urban subjects and a counterpart to the homogeneity of the 'assembled whole'). Borrowing again from Manuel De Landa's lexicon (2016: 22), this visual research methodology does not 'fold' the urban into singular, homogeneous 'assembled whole', but rather unpacks it as an assemblage of heterogeneous components. Within this framework for design research – and as Felix Guattari would put it (2012: 231–39) – forms of spatialized enunciation emerge from collective angles, with an emphasis on what is common to our individual experiences.

Acknowledgements

The body of work presented in this chapter was supported by funding provided by the Università degli Studi di Cagliari and the Erasmus+ Programme (via the University of Edinburgh).

REFERENCES

Bourbonnais, S. and Rose, J. (2012), 'Information relay: The indetermination between machines', *Log*, 25, pp. 63–70.

Cache, B. (2011a), 'Objectile: The pursuit of philosophy by other means?', in *Projectiles*, London: AA Publications, pp. 20–30.

——— (2011b), 'Plea for Euclid', in *Projectiles*, London: Architectural Association, pp. 31–59.

Carpo, M. (2013), 'Twenty years of Digital Design', in *The Digital Turn in Architecture 1992-2012*, London: John Wiley & Sons, pp. 8–14.

Coyne, R. (2017), 'Share city | Reflections on Technology, Media & Culture', richardcoyne.com, https://richardcoyne.com/2017/09/12/share-city/. Accessed 10 January 10 2018.

Deleuze, G. (1991), *Bergsonism*, New York: Zone Books.

Deleuze, G. and Guattari, F. (1987), *A Thousand Plateaus: Capitalism and Schizophrenia*, Minneapolis: University of Minnesota Press.

Derrida, J. (1978), *Introduction to the Origin of Geometry*, Stony Brook, NY: Nicolas Hays.

Guattari, F. (2012), *Schizoanalitic Cartographies*, London: Bloomsbury.

Guattari, F. (2008), *The Three Ecologies*, London: Bloomsbury.

Guattari, F. and Lotringer, S. (2009), *Soft Subversions: Texts and Interviews 1977–1985*, Los Angeles: Semiotext(e).

Krivý, M. (2016), 'Parametricist architecture, smart cities, and the politics of consensus', *Ehituskunst: Investigations in Architecture and Theory*, 57, pp. 22–45.

De Landa, M. (2016), *Assemblage Theory*, Edinburgh: Edinburgh University Press.

—— (1998), 'Deleuze and the genesis of form', *Art Orbit*, 1, http://www.artnode.se/artorbit/issue1/f_deleuze/f_deleuze_delanda.html. Accessed 30 August 2019.

Lynn, G. (1993), 'Multiplicitous and in-organic bodies', *Architectural Design*, 63:11/12, pp.30–37.

Offenhuber, D. and Ratti, C. (2014), *Decoding the City: Urbanism in the Age of Big Data*, Basel: Birkhäuser Verlag.

Oosterhuis, K. (2017), 'Emotive embodiments', in A. Radman and H. Sohn (eds.), *Critical and Clinical Cartographies*, Edinburgh: Edinburgh University Press, pp. 168–83.

Parikka, J. (2012), *What Is Media Archaeology?*, Cambridge: Polity Press.

Picon, A. (2015), *Smart Cities: A Spatialised Intelligence*, London: Wiley.

Simondon, G. (1989), *Du mode d'existence des objets techniques*, Paris: Aubier.

NOTES

1. Manuel De Landa refers to this totalizing configuration as the state corresponding to 'territorialized strata' in the context of his characterization of assemblages as parametric continuums. Maros Krivý also refers to this particular mode of understanding the city as a continuum that overcomes the limitations of 'objects' in the context of the 'projective turn' in architectural theory.

2. Top-down (practices emerging from institutions or corporations) and bottom-up (practices emerging from groups of individuals, organized or not). We should however note that top-down and bottom-up informational systems very often coexist within the same plateau of digital technology platforms.

3. Euclidean geometry refers to the geometrical system for the abstract description of space emerging as a systematic synthesis of formerly isolated theorems, developed by earlier Greek and Egyptian mathematicians and compiled by Euclid in his book *Elements*. It is primarily based on five axiomatic postulates, which originally extended into a series of formal proofs and eventually evolved into a comprehensive, saturated, self-consistent system of 21 axioms compiled by David Hilbert in Grundlagen der Geometrie (1899). Two of its most critical axiomatic postulates are metric measure – the understanding that distances between all components of a given spatial set are defined – and parallelism – the existence of parallel lines within the aforementioned spatial set.

4. Rather than producing a set of representational scale drawings, the journeyman would proceed by directly delimitating boundary regions as full-scale traces drawn on the ground, thus determining the internal and external outlines of the building on site. In tune with previous distinctions between the exact and the anexact, the work of the journeyman is non-Euclidean, albeit not necessarily less rigorous than that emerging from Euclidean geometries assembled through modern scale drawing conventions. Nonetheless, a key difference between these two modes of operation is that, by directly negotiating the nuances

of the site as a full-scale, non-neutral surface, the journeyman has no use for the stasis of idealized geometrical models. On the contrary, he proceeds dynamically by occupying the site with the marking-off of limiting traces, which define themselves gradually and continuously over time.

PART II

PHOTOGRAPHY: PRESENCE AND POSITIONING AS A RESEARCHER

Figure 2 (from Introduction): Siegfried Giedion's formatting of his own photographs of the Pont Transbordeur in Marseille (taken in January, 1927). pp. 62f of *Bauen in Frankreich* as published in Harbusch (2015: 605) (copyright: gta Archives/ ETH Zurich). + Journal of Architecture/Harbusch.

> I have found it preferable, in order to arrive at a true and complete understanding of the growth of the new tradition, to select from the vast body of available historical material only relatively few facts. *History is not a compilation of facts, but an insight into a moving process of life*. Moreover, such insight is obtained not by the exclusive use of the panoramic survey, the bird's eye view, but by isolating and examining certain specific events intensively, penetrating and exploring them in the manner of the close-up.
>
> (Giedion [1946] 1967: vi, Foreword to the first edition; italics in original text)

7

Looking at photographs:
Thinking about architecture

Hugh Campbell, UCD Architecture, Dublin

I

Photography frames pieces of the world we live in, constructing limits that seem to confer order and significance on whatever comes within them. It would seem therefore to have a fundamental affinity with architecture, which is also concerned with framing human behaviour, and which must also proceed from the given conditions. The affinity between the two disciplines has been evident since the advent of photography in 1839 and has played out in practice and in theory ever since. In recent years particularly, there has been a considerable increase in research, scholarship and publication dealing with the relationship between photography and architecture (Woods 2009; Higgott and Wray 2012). However in much of this work one or other of the disciplines tends to be the dominant partner. This means, in turn, that the research paradigms and methods used tend to be dictated by the dominant discipline. Thus, on the one hand, photography could be analysed in relation to the culture and discourse of architecture; on the other hand, the role that architecture plays in the making and reading of photographs could be explored. A good example of the former is Claire Zimmerman's 2014 publication *Photographic Architecture in the Twentieth Century*, where, as photography's adjectival status in the title suggests, architecture is the dominant partner. An example of the latter would be the 2014 exhibition curated by Elias Redstone and Alona Pardo *Constructing Worlds – Photography and Architecture in the Modern Age* (2014), in which, as the non-alphabetical order connotes, photography takes the lead.

Both are considerable in their achievements. In her analyses of photographs of Mies van der Rohe's Tughendhat House, for instance, Zimmerman folds an understanding of photography as a technical practice into a historically and theoretically inflected account. She seems to be, if not siding with, then certainly alert to photography as technical practice. However, the images' formal and aesthetic qualities count for little except to the extent that they relate to the formal and aesthetic qualities of the architecture. Ultimately photographs seem to be considered as conduits through which information and messages can pass, and photographic practice becomes merely an appendage to the serious business of making and marketing buildings.

In the *Constructing Worlds* exhibition and catalogue, the emphasis is on documentary photography on the one hand and fine-art photography on the other, rather than on architectural photography as it is usually understood. The story of the relationship with architecture is set within a trajectory that leads from Walker Evans and Berenice Abbott to Nadav Kander and Simon Norfolk. Architecture serves in various ways as subject matter and content but what is primarily at stake is what photography gains from this engagement. How the processes and practices of architecture might be concomitantly enriched remains unexplored.

While the two examples are successful on their own terms, and can be used to establish a somewhat schematic dichotomy, they might equally be seen to point towards some possible shared ground. This would be founded on the idea that the conceptual impulse, the technical practice and the formal artefacts relating to each discipline in fact share many qualities. Pierre Bourdieu's concept of *habitus* – defined as 'a system of dispositions which generate perceptions, attitudes and practices' – might provide a model for unifying the different aspects of the two disciplines (Bourdieu [1980] 1990: 53). And, picking up on the exhibition title, the term 'constructing' could serve to establish a common currency. *Constructing Worlds* reveals the ongoing propensity of some photographers to construct in images that which humans have constructed in the world. The act of constructing is central to both. Zimmerman finds a kind of concordance between buildings, images and publications, as if they were borne of the same conceptual principles, organized according to similar logics, and possessed of similar qualities.

II

Building upon this hastily established premise of a shared disciplinary disposition, in this chapter I aim to articulate some alternative ways of thinking about the architecture/photography relationship. These derive largely from my experience in teaching a course in this area along with a colleague, Alice Clancy. Entitled 'Space framed – Photography and the human habitat', the module has evolved over a number of years but there have been a number of constants running through it.[1] First, it roots itself in the discourse of photographic practice, criticism and curating. It starts from the simple point of view that photographs have value and are worthy of study in their own terms. This distinguishes it from other approaches that originate from the discipline of architecture and seek to establish links back to photography. It also distinguishes it from certain strands of photographic theory and discourse, which require of photographs that they stand for something other than themselves, that they emblematize aspects of the human condition. Those staples of the canon Susan Sontag's *On Photography* (1977) and Roland Barthes' *Camera Lucida* (1981) might be said to fall into this category. On the other hand, the works of historians and theorists, including David Campany (2015), James Elkins (2011) and Michael Fried (2008), who invest in close readings of photographic images and consider their making and their meaning in equal measure have proved extremely useful in establishing theoretical frameworks.

In addition, we have made extensive use of two seminal teaching primers: John Szarkowski's *The Photographer's Eye* (1966) and Stephen Shore's *The Nature of Photographs* (1998). Each is brief, eloquent, lucid and forceful; each provides descriptive and analytical tools, with which to develop an understanding of photographs and how they work. Szarkowski, a celebrated photographer in his own right and renowned as curator of photography at MoMA from 1962 to 1991, brings to bear a fine curatorial discrimination in his selection of images. These are organized thematically in order to offer a sort of typology of the photographic image (the thing itself, the detail, the frame, time etc.), with each theme introduced by a brief text. In his text, Shore establishes a series of levels at which photographs can be considered: the physical, the depictive and the mental. They are to be understood first as artefacts, second as describing aspects of the world and third as thoughtful constructs. These key texts provide analytical tools that are straightforward and potent. They equip students to look critically at photographs.

The seminar charts a course through twentieth-century photography. Extending beyond the realms of architecture per se, it deals with work that captures the relationship between people and their environment. The purview is necessarily wide: after all, the space of photography is, in essence, the space of human occupancy. In order for a photograph to be made at all, the location depicted must have been visited by the photographer – although in the digital age this truth has been questioned to interesting effect, as can be seen for instance in the recent use of Google Streetview to capture images by Michael Wolf and Doug Rickard (2012), among others. But beyond this most basic level, photographs offer a rich and complex meditation on the ways in which we occupy space.

Much of the material covered falls within the standard canon of photographic history – from Walker Evans and Berenice Abbott in the early decades of the twentieth century to Thomas Struth and Candida Hofer at its end. Along the way, many of the defining themes and developments in practice are dealt with:

the 'documentary style' of Evans, the credo of the decisive moment, the age of street photography, the rise of the 'New Topographics' (Salvesen 2009) and the Dusseldorf School (Gronert 2009). The students also engage with contemporary photography, discovering work that resonates with the historical and theoretical perspectives established. In parallel, the students are introduced to a range of photographic equipment, including medium and large-format cameras, in order to better understand how the specific parameters imposed by technique and technology determine how images are made and how they work.

The focus is on specific projects, exhibitions and photobooks – coherent bodies of work rather than single images. This allows students to understand how a photographer can bring to bear upon a subject and a setting a particular set of formal and intellectual preoccupations, and how this practice can evolve over time. It also allows them to explore parallels and equivalencies with their own research and design methods. Thus while the explorations as set out above are strongly rooted in the history, theory and practice of photography, the relationship to architecture is always at play, and becomes the subject of specific interrogation in the various assignments undertaken by students. The seminar is premised on the idea that a deep engagement with one discipline will produce new insights that apply back to the other discipline. And while at times the subjects selected are overtly architectural – looking, for instance, at the relationship between Harry Callahan and Mies van Der Rohe in Chicago or at the practice of Iwan Baan – more often the focus opens out to encompass the designed and inhabited landscape more broadly conceived.

The students' explorations have engendered a greater alertness to both the temporal and spatial aspects of inhabitation, and a greater openness to the techniques by which those aspects might be depicted and analysed. These insights derive not only from close readings of photographs but also from an appreciation of the space and time involved in, for instance, making portraits with a large-format camera in a busy urban setting, or tracking patterns of movement across a public space. Photography is thus appreciated as a spatio-temporal practice. The technical aspects of taking and producing of photographs, and the limitations and possibilities thereby opened up, also come to the fore. Fundamentally, students learn to look differently at inhabited space and at the relationship of people to their settings.

III

In his seminal essay on *The Decisive Moment*, Henri Cartier-Bresson defined 'l'instant decisif' as the point at which action and situation coalesce into significant form (Cartier-Bresson 1952, unpaginated introduction, section titled 'Composition'). His own photographs offer endless evidence of this perfect concordance of activity and the place it happens, from the man jumping over a puddle behind the Gare St Lazare (his silhouetted form mirrored in the water and echoed by the figure on the poster on the hoarding behind) to the cyclist seen from the top of some steps speeding round a corner in the tight streets of Hyere (Cartier-Bresson 1952). But his philosophy also sets in motion two tendencies that govern the approach to photographing the human habitat over the subsequent decades – the first alighting on action, the second on situation.

Thus, dynamic shots of moments of urban life characterized the street photography of Garry Winogrand and others which dominated American photography in the 1960s whereas an interest in the formal, composed situation, informed the work of Stephen Shore, Robert Adam and others whose work was gathered together in the 'New Topographics' exhibition of 1972, and which proved enduringly influential. And while for the former tendency the high-speed Leica and 35mm camera were the chosen instruments, the latter involved a revival of interest in medium- and large-format cameras. These necessitated a much more deliberate framing of shots, which, in turn, produced more formally constructed images. This seam of work has extended up to the present through

Figure 1: Untitled, from the series *Illuminance* 2007 © Rinko Kawauchi.

the photographers associated with the Dusseldorf School (Thomas Struth, Candida Hofer and Andreas Gursky) and through subsequent generations of US photographers working with large format (Richard Misrach, Mitch Epstein, Gregory Crewdson). Meanwhile, the 'snapshot' aesthetic has also continued to exert an influence. And while Cartier-Bresson had evinced an approach in which the moment achieved a perfectly balanced equipoise, for subsequent generations a more open, informal, seemingly casual aesthetic emerged. In the work of William Eggleston, for instance, conventional framing and subject matter seems to fall away, replaced by a freewheeling, almost aleatoric mode. 'I am at war with the obvious', Eggleston famously said, describing himself as 'photographing democratically [...] outdoors, nowhere, in nothing' (Eggleston 1989: 171, 173). But from such offhand, undefined methods and such unprepossessing material, Eggleston could consistently conjure vivid moments of magic.

The two modes of photography emerging here might be summarized as the constructed scene and the wondrous moment. Both, it can be argued, have the capacity to respond to, and to speak back to architecture. The former makes evident the lineaments of occupation, of how we use and inhabit space. The latter illuminates those fragmentary points of connection that embed places and settings in our experience and our memories. Taken together they offer an enriched understanding of what it is to inhabit and, by extension, how such inhabitation might be conceived and designed. Photographers pay attention to the world: their photographing is the enactment of that attention, their photographs the evidence of that enactment. Architecture can augment its visual methodologies by becoming more alert to the discoveries provided by the photographer's attention.

This essay concludes with brief case studies of two contemporary practitioners working within the two modes outlined above. The first, Alec Soth, operates within the tradition of social documentary and the constructed scene, the second, Rinko Kawauchi, is intent on pursuing moments of wonder. Both fall outside the usual repertoire used to connect architecture with photography. But by looking at the work of both, we might arrive at an understanding of how the study of such photographic practices might enrich architecture's visual methodologies.

IV

'Just when it seems that everything has been photographed in every possible way, along comes a photographer whose work is so original that the medium is renewed' (Badger and Parr 2006: 316–17). This strong claim for the quality and originality of the work of Japanese photographer Rinko Kawauchi was made by Gerry Badger and Martin Parr who included her first published collection *Utatane* in the second volume of their series *The Photobook: A History* (2006). The pictures in the book were mostly taken with a Rolleiflex camera, and made potent use of its distinctive square format and the slightly disembodied view its top-mounted viewfinder encourages. In the resulting photographs, colours are typically washed out; the light is bright but diffuse. Views vary between close-ups and wider vistas but are mostly fragmentary and open-ended rather than whole and completely composed (Kawauchi 2001).

Although working within a heavily urbanized culture, Kawauchi is drawn to nature and to evidence of natural processes. A typical sequence from her 2011 publication *Illuminance* gives us a half-open umbrella, a pale snail seen from above, an open tub of yoghurt, then jets of water rising to a blue sky (Figures 1–3). The subject matter is endlessly varied and yet somehow seems consistent, because the images are bound together, each to the next, by compelling, often witty formal rhymes and by a sensibility that is always alert to wonder and seems to find it everywhere. In all of Kawauchi's work, there is the feeling (alluded to by Parr and Badger) of seeing things for the first time. We are made to understand that, seen from a certain vantage point, things are more similar than different. This might be

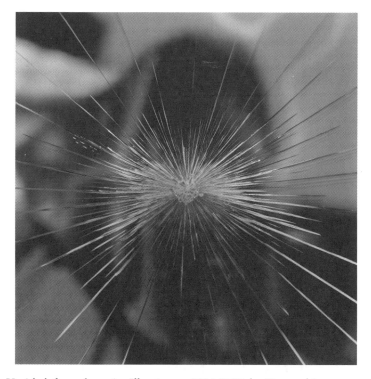

Figure 2: Untitled, from the series *Illuminance* 2011 © Rinko Kawauchi.

an alien's view, or that of a young child, for whom things are not yet categorized or ordered in terms of their purpose, their nature or even their size and shape. These are the beginnings of descriptions.

Kawauchi has been prolific in her rate of publication and exhibition. The idiom that she established in *Utatane* has been extended and augmented through subsequent collections such as *Aila* (2004), *Cui Cui* (2005), *Illuminance* (2011) and *Ametsuchi* (2013). While the work has developed in terms of its range and complexity, and while Kawauchi's star has risen in the art-world, her work retains a private, contemplative quality, as if we are inhabiting her daydreams (the title *Utatane* means siesta). Over a number of years, Kawauchi has also posted photographs daily to an online diary, further accentuating the personal character of her images (http://rinkokawauchi.tumblr.com). But if there is something confessional and intimate about her photographs, they are nonetheless capable of opening up larger insights about the world as encountered. Following Maurice Merleau-Ponty's description of Paul Cézanne's work, she might be said to be photographing 'the way the world touches us' (Merleau-Ponty [1945] 1993: 59). The soft, lambent, sometimes blurred quality of the images removes us from the hard reality of the facts being recorded, and brings us closer to the moment of the sensation being perceived. We are within the act of seeing, inhabiting the space between sensation and perception, a terrain that Nicholas Humphrey has referred to in his studies of consciousness as 'the thick present' (Humphrey 2006: 47).

While the images are alert to the phenomenology of experience, they also address the world at large, suggesting that things, irrespective of scale or purpose, regardless even of whether they are naturally occurring or manmade, share a latent order. Kawauchi alights upon underlying patterns, which produce a kind of willed concordance between quite disparate phenomena. We look in succession at a woman's iridescent raincoat, the veined back of an elderly man's hand, a stack of bicycles, a tangle of tree roots: we register a common pulse running through them. In other words, such segues and juxtapositions might descend into formal game-playing, but the evident instinctiveness of the image-making militates against this. The world all hangs together, Kawauchi seems to be saying, if you only drop your guard and open your eyes.

Where Rinko Kawauchi alights on vivid moments, Alec Soth surveys the social scene. Considered to be among the most significant photographers currently working in the United States, Soth sits within the lineage of social documentarians stretching from Walker Evans through Robert Frank, to Stephen Shore and Joel Sternfeld. It comes as no surprise that he was taught by Sternfeld at St. Lawrence College. Soth recounts how he became confirmed in his mission as a travelling photographer when Sternfeld pointed to the presence of his own truck in his picture of Gatlinburg, Tennessee (Engberg 2010: 40). The photograph is one

Figure 3: Untitled, from the series *Illuminance* 2009 © Rinko Kawauchi.

of those collected in Sternfeld's 1987 publication *American Prospects*, a book that was deeply influential on a generation of photographers, not only for the pioneering way in which it used large-format colour photography but also for the way in which it accommodated complex social landscapes within coherent compositions (Sternfeld [1987] 2003). Drawing inspiration from Pieter Breughel the Elder's so-called 'world paintings' – in which, for example, Icarus could fall to the sea from his ill-fated flight while a farmer ploughed on regardless – Sternfeld used framing and composition to allow his images to combine several registers, to reveal social disjunctions and, repeatedly, to set the raw edge of settlement as it extended into the landscape against the confident purpose of its inhabitants. He showed a particular gift for the situated portrait and a capacity to find character and specificity in any setting.

Soth follows suit. In his first book, *Sleeping by the Mississippi*, he moved from his home state of Minnesota up and down the great river, seeking out those living along its edges and photographing them in their milieus (Soth [2004] 2011). One of the first images in the book, and the photograph that clarified the project in Soth's mind, shows the bed of Charles Lindbergh at his boyhood home in Little Falls, Minnesota. The picture gains its particular poignancy from the disjuncture between the humble dishevelment of the setting, and Lindbergh's later

Figure 4: Alec Soth, Peter's Houseboat, Winona, Minnesota, 2002.

fame and heroic stature. But apart from this and a shot of Johnny Cash's boyhood home, for the most part Soth's images feature people who are not destined for greatness. Preachers, strippers, musicians, convicts, his subjects are more akin to the picaresque characters Huckleberry Finn and Jim encountered on their journey down the great river.

In a pattern that would characterize all his subsequent work, Soth switches his gaze between people and their physical settings. But in his portraits, the space that his subjects occupy is as important as the subjects themselves, while where the human subject is absent, the setting acts as a synecdoche of its inhabitant. Beds, for instance, become a recurring motif – sometimes as emblems of abandonment, sometimes as strange sites of fantasy. Chairs and couches – the equipment of domesticity – appear too, often deployed in improvised and unlikely ways. Soth is interested in the way people establish meaning and significance for themselves; how a life is constructed physically and psychologically. Often in making portraits, he would ask sitters to write down what their dream was, thinking that the act alone would transport them from immediate circumstance to a richer mental realm; a realm often represented through mementos, notes and pictures. His preoccupation with the dream-state provides an interesting overlap with Kawauchi's work (Figure 4).

Figure 5: Alec Soth, Untitled, from *Broken Manual*, 2011.

Soth also understood that he was operating in a critical relationship with an inherited pictorial tradition. In treating the Mississippi itself as a peripheral presence rather than a defining geographical feature Soth was reacting against the romantic landscape tradition that dominated nineteenth-century American painting, and that informed subsequent generations of photography – 'This', he says, 'is not a book about the Mississippi, it is a book about the idea of the Mississippi' (Soth 2005).[2]

Continuing his critical engagement with this tradition, Soth turned to one of North America's greatest natural spectacles, the Niagara Falls, for his next project (2006). However, for him the spectacle of the falls was, again, marginal to the predominant settings of the book – the proliferation of cheap motels and wedding parlours, which had sprung up in the adjoining town. Calm, detailed images of these banal settings combine with respectful portraits of their inhabitants to set out the lineaments of a whole culture.

From this point onwards, Soth's practice becomes more varied and compendious. He sets up a blog and a publishing company, Little Brown Mushroom, and establishes an alter ego, Lester B. Morrison, who writes prose and poems, to accompany his photographs. He experiments with different forms of publishing, producing zines and, in 2008, a cheap newsprint publication called *The Last Days of W*, which documents 'ordinary' American life in the dying days of the Bush presidency. Soth is pushing against the edges of photographic practice – extending and supplementing it, exploring its margins. But all the while, he is consciously extending his project of documenting the American social landscape, a project with roots extending back, at least to the Farm Services Administration photography of the Great Depression.

In his more recent work *Broken Manual* (2006–10), Soth brought to bear a larger battery of techniques upon a more extreme version of his familiar subject matter. Prompted by his research into the Olympic Park Bomber, who, after attacking the Atlanta games in 1996, lived in hiding for years in the Appalachian wilderness, Soth began, as Siri Engberg explains, 'to investigate the notion of vanishing from civilization more broadly, seeking out reclusive individuals – drifters, monks, survivalists – who chose to escape society for spiritual, legal or environmental reasons' (Engberg 2010: 47). These were characters living truly marginal, strange lives. Equally strange were their habitats, often extremely crude and basic but sometimes providing odd disjunctions of the banal and the bizarre: a cave equipped with coat-hangers, a mirror ball in a forest. Soth's expanded range of techniques – from infrared photography to large-format – began to open up new conceptual and narrative possibilities. 'What excites me about the medium isn't pure documentary or pure fiction', he says, 'I like exploring the murky middle place in hopes of finding what Werner Herzog calls the "ecstatic truth"' (Soth 2013, n.pag.) (Figure 5).

In their different ways, Kawauchi and Soth use their photographs to reveal and celebrate how it is to live in the world, whether by focusing on ephemeral encounters with the lived environment or by portraying the social scene. The world as encountered is given back to us freshly minted. These models of engagement with the lived world offer valuable lessons to architecture. They propose that, if we are alert to a given setting, its incidental pleasures and its intrinsic patterns, and if we attend to the way life unfolds within those settings, we might, in turn, engender more specific, modulated design strategies. This combination of alertness and attentiveness – so often evident in photography – could become a potent tool in understanding contexts, in understanding the nature of human and social behaviour, in becoming attuned to patterns of inhabitation, in creating environments that allow life to flourish.

Acknowledgement

I am grateful to Alice Clancy, who collaborated on the Space Framed seminar discussed in the chapter.

REFERENCES

Badger, G. and Parr, M. (2006), *The Photobook: A History*, vol. II, London: Phaidon.

Barthes, R. (1981), *Camera Lucida: Reflections on Photography*, London: Vintage.

Bourdieu, P. ([1980] 1990), *The Logic of Practice*, Cambridge, MA: Polity Press.

Campany, D. (2015), *A Handful of Dust*, London: Mack Books.

Campany, D., Pardo, A. and Redstone, E. (2014), *Constructing Worlds – Photography and Architecture in the Modern Age*, London: Prestel.

Campbell, H. (2015), 'Review of Zimmerman, photographic architecture in the twentieth century and redstone, pardo, constructing worlds – Photography and architecture in the modern age', *Journal of Architecture*, 20:1, pp. 152–59.

Cartier-Bresson, H. (1952), *The Decisive Moment*, New York: Simon & Schuster.

Eggleston, W. (1989), *The Democratic Forest*, New York: Doubleday.

——— ([1976] 2002), *William Eggleston's Guide*, New York: Museum of Modern Art.

——— (2003), *Los Alamos*, Zurich: Scalo.

Elkins, J. (2011), *What Photography Is*, London: Routledge.

Engberg, S. (2010), *Welcome to Utopia*, in S. Engberg (ed.), *From Here to There: Alec Soth's America*, Minneapolis: Walker Arts Center.

Fried, M. (2008), *Why Photography Matters as Art as Never before*, New Haven, CT: Yale University Press.

Gronert, S. (2009), *The Dusseldorf School of Photography*, London: Thames & Hudson.

Higgott, A. and Wray, T. (eds) (2012), *Camera Constructs: Photography, Architecture and the Modern City*, London: Ashgate.

Humphrey, N. (2006), *Seeing Red: A Study in Consciousness*, Cambridge, MA: Belknapp.

Kawauchi, R. (2001), *Utatane*, Tokyo: Little More.

——— (2005a), *Aila*, Tokyo: Foil.

——— (2005b), *Cui Cui*, Tokyo: Foil.

——— (2011), *Illuminance*, New York: Aperture.

——— (2013), *Ametsuchi*, New York: Aperture.

——— (2017), 'Rinko diary', http://rinkokawauchi.tumblr.com. Accessed 28 February 2017.

Merleau-Ponty, M. ([1945] 1993), Cézanne's doubt, in G. Johnson (ed.), *The Merleau-Ponty Aesthetics Reader: Philosophy and Painting*, Evanston, IL: Northwestern University Press.

Raban, J. (1987), *Old Glory*, London: Picador.

Redstone, E. and Pardo, A. (curators) (2014–15), *Constructing Worlds – Photography and Architecture in the Modern Age*, Barbican Art Gallery, London, 25 September 2014–11 January 2015.

Rickard, D. (2012), *A New American Picture*, New York: Aperture.

Salvesen, B. (ed.) (2009), *The New Topographics*, Tucson, AZ: Centre for Creative Photography (expanded edition of original 1975 exhibition catalogue).

Shore, S. (1998), *The Nature of Photographs*, Baltimore, MD: Johns Hopkins Press.

Sontag, S. (1979), *On Photography*, London: Penguin.

Soth, A. (2006), *Niagara*, Gottingen: Steidl.
—— ([2004] 2011), *Sleeping by the Mississippi*, Munich and Gottingen: Steidl.
—— (2013), *Broken Manual*, Gottingen: Steidl.
—— (2015), *Songbook*, London: Mack.
Walker Art Center (2017), Alec Soth with Andrei Cozescu, https://www.youtube.com/watch?v=Vwol1tb8BF4. Accessed 28 February 2017.
Sternfeld, J. ([1987] 2003), *American Prospects*, New York: DAP.
Szarkowski, J. (1966), *The Photographer's Eye*, New York: Museum of Modern Art.
Woods, M. N. (2009), *Beyond the Architect's Eye: Photographs and the American Built Environment*, Philadelphia: Penn Press.
Zimmerman, C. (2014), *Photographic Architecture in the Twentieth Century*, Minneapolis, MN: University of Minnesota Press.

NOTES

1. We have used a blog to share reference material and student assignments, which over time has become a useful archive and repository for source material: www.spaceframed.blogspot.com. The module has also given rise to a number of conference presentations, publications and to a major symposium entitled *Constructing the View*, held in late 2013 (http://constructingtheview.org). Contributors included Thomas Struth, Michael Wolf, Shelley MacNamara, John Gerrard and Alexandra Stara.

2. Jonathan Raban, in *Old Glory*, his great account of a journey down the river described how, in the nineteenth century, 'the river was the best embodiment of the sheer space and variety of American life; nothing else in the country could match it for its prodigious geographical reach […]'. He recalls the 1840s craze for painting vast panoramas of the river which were unfurled as moving dioramas in darkened rooms - proto-movies (Raban 1987: 214–15). In Soth's book, this whole pictorial tradition is reduced to a postcard stuck on a wall in Cape Girardeau, showing a dramatic view of an oxbow lake, recalling both Ansel Adams' famous image of Snake River and the fervid renderings by the painters Thomas Moran and Frederick Church of such celebrated sites as the Grand Canyon and the Niagara Falls.

8

Architecture's discursive space: Photography

Marc Goodwin, Architectural Photographer

Photography has affected the collective memory in ways that are neither neutral nor mechanical (Bate 2010; Fried 2008). Architecture is no exception. Far from being objective documents, architectural photographs are increasingly viewed as *Constructed Worlds* (Pardo and Redstone 2014), *Camera Constructs* (Higgott and Wray 2012), *Constructing a Legend* (Cefererin 2003) or *Constructed Views* (Rosa et al. 1994). However, this argument is often forgotten when photography is taken as a means to an end, such as in the presentation of architecture in promotional media.

Architects have written most of the books about architectural photography. A short list would include: *Building with Light* (Elwall 2004), *Architecture Transformed* (Robinson and Herschman 1987) and *The Edifice is Colossal* (Sobieszek 1986). It might also extend to the many encyclopaedic histories of architecture starting with *Histoire de l'architecture* (Choisy 1899). Through meticulous research, they have paid tribute to the great practitioners in the field.[1] That history contains a large blind-spot, therefore, because it is comprised mainly of images taken by the most renowned photographers working with the most celebrated architects, producing the iconic, which is by nature exceptional. Whilst informative and compelling, such a study says little or nothing about the everyday in architectural photography. It overlooks a discursive regularity constructed through the omission of errors that do not fit within the bounds of standard practice. That oversight is growing with the scale of publication. This presents a new opportunity for photography as a visual methodology through which to interpret architectural discourse.

K. Michael Hays and Krista Sykes have identified a decline in the influence of theory as a productive, critical force in architecture (Hays 2000; Sykes 2010).[2] What if that decline were reframed as a shift to images, a move widely invisible to an academic tradition focused on written texts? Theory itself has started to look more and more at images (Pallasmaa 2005; Leach 1999). Perhaps those two opposed vectors might have similar points of origin. If photography is a discursive frame shaped by art historians, as John Tagg (2009) argues through Foucault, is its rise possibly coterminous with the decline indicated by Hays and Sykes? Perhaps photography can reveal something about that discourse and the mechanisms behind it. If photography is architecture's principal discursive space, much is at stake, and several opportunities stand to arise from such a discovery.

So, pulling all of these strands together, I will ask whether the decline of theory in architecture and the rise of image might not be reconceptualized as a movement from word to image as the discursive space of architecture. I will look specifically at the use of commercial architectural photographs to assess, quantify and visualize certain conventional practices in architectural photography. In doing so I will ask what might be the discourse producing that standard. I will argue that conventions which amount to code of best practice are mired in cliché that stereotypes architectural creation and leaves it devoid of a sense of place.

Grids offer a new perspective (again)

I have worked as an architectural photographer for over ten years, ample time and cause for reflection into my practice. However, it was not until undertaking a doctoral research project in partnership with architects in Finland and Denmark in 2011 that I started to see photography's potential as a tool for investigation as well as the value of practice-based research. I discovered that colour is content.

Figure 1 contains the preferences of nine clients, each of whom selected nine images out of a sample of several hundred images. Images are ordered into three columns of daytime exteriors (left), three columns of interiors (middle) and three columns of evening exteriors (right). Each row is assigned to a given architect.[3] This grid shows what each client thought was worth saying with images – worth money, in fact. It lends visual support to two assertions made by theorist Mark Wigley: that white walls are the most obvious element common to contemporary architecture (Wigley 1995) and that 'good architecture is associated with good weather' (Wigley 1998: 20). This arrangement of images suggests a visual convention. Has architectural photography moved from black and white to blue and white? Keeping colours to a minimum is a way of cleaning up and ordering the world visually (Wigley 1998: 25). One might also argue that the lack of full-spectrum colour shows that these photographs are not the photo-realistic, objective documents the architects I interviewed for my research claimed to prefer. Instead they are the decedents of a long line of architectural drawings, a dream about

ARCHITECTURE'S DISCURSIVE SPACE

Figure 1: Preferences and purchases. Photographs by Marc Goodwin.

space turned into line and shade (Wigley 1998: 27) as well as a reflection of many societies' shared ideal of life at the beach.

Figure 2 contains leftovers from the same set of jobs: images not chosen by clients. It shows 81 images that nine separate clients thought were unusable. They are monochromatic (but not blue) and feature both empty and populated scenes. These images are organized along a greyscale from white to black, shot at different times of the day and year. The main difference between these two grids is the weather: rain, clouds, snow, black night skies were all rejected. Because the images in these grids were produced entirely in Northern Europe, the absence of such weather in the photographs is significant, because it shows a preference for a certain kind of atmosphere that is not reflected in the climate.[4] Here the individual images are reminiscent of pixels or perhaps tesserae of a mosaic. The building in each is too small to be seen. Only the predominant colour remains. This approach is in line with Saint-Martin's notion of the coloreme as the basic unit of the visual language (Saint-Martin 1990: 3) as well has his assertion that 'any work of visual language achieves existence essentially through colour organisations, as does reality itself' (Saint-Martin 1990:18). Clearly colour counts – perhaps it is as much the subject matter of an architectural photograph as the architecture itself.

Figure 2: Errors. Photographs by Marc Goodwin.

Of course, this might have been a fluke. These findings could well represent nothing more than my own preferences or those of my clients. A larger sample was needed for the sake of comparison. For this, the *Phaidon Atlas of Contemporary World Architecture* was a valuable reference tool for obtaining a global perspective. The Atlas is described in a promotional blurb as: '[t]he only resource of its kind [presenting ...] over 1,000 of the most outstanding works of architecture from all over the world built since 1998 [... it] includes every building type and each project has been nominated by a panel consisting of 150 leading names in the international field of architecture'.[5]

The book is not without its shortcomings, however, when viewed from the perspective of photographic diversity. Because the projects are presented through photographs, I conducted content analysis to count the number of projects featuring photographs with blue skies (daytime and evening, interior and exterior) and projects using grey-scale images. The following is a count from countries and regions studied:

    Australia   97 blue/21 greyscale
    China   48 blue/29 greyscale
    S. Korea   22 blue/21 greyscale

Finland	33 blue/9 greyscale
Denmark	40 blue/11 greyscale
United Kingdom	141 blue/32 greyscale
Africa	47 blue/8 greyscale
United States	85 blue/15 greyscale
S. America	62 blue/6 greyscale

This count provides an overview indicating a preference for, or at the very least a greater dependence on, blue images that corresponded to the grids of my own work. Nordic, equatorial, tropical and subtropical climates all appear to be the same in this publication. The correlation between global findings in the atlas with my own praxis acts as the vertical and horizontal axis of this research, producing a new image of certain conventions in architectural photography. Of course, this is not a photography book, but rather one that relies upon an 'objective', standardized picture style to purvey architecture to a niche public and convey it to them in the clearest manner possible. However, conventional practices may actually do the reverse, creating a uniform, homogeneous image that complicates the reading of each architectural work and its site as unique. That disastrous result would be as bad for the understanding and appreciation of architecture as it is for the potential richness of photographic art.

The importance of colour can be seen in photographs of interiors, too. In Figure 3, images of different spaces line up neatly into three colour bars, showing once again how predominant colour has much to do with the space you see in an architectural photo. In this particular example, colours represent a brief history of theatre design that went from gilded to white, finally ending in a black box.

Of course, this grid does not represent photographic choices per se, as the predominant colour comes from the colour of the room. Apart from desaturating and brightening white walls, few choices are at the photographer's disposal. For that reason, frame and lens choice should also be looked at. To do this I shot the same scene repeatedly with 17mm, 24mm and 45mm tilt-shift lenses that were used to capture images stitched together into panoramas. I believe they show both the homogenizing effect of repeated wide-angle photographs as well as the overall significance of focal length. The horizontal lines are of the same place, but vertical similarity is also apparent. Different spaces appear more similar than they might to the naked eye due to the fact that they were shot with the same lens from the same vantage point. This grid demonstrates how a space in a frame is not the same as a space you walk through. In an image, space becomes an arrangement of lines and shades. In short, how you configure space within a frame through a set of photographic procedures has important consequences for the sense of place – when a formula is repeated, the sense of difference is eroded. Places are homogenized

Figure 3: Interiors. Photographs by Marc Goodwin.

into a uniform standardized product called architectural photography. As with the reliance on a repeated set of weather conditions addressed in the first two grids, reliance on too few compositional techniques and the same wide angle lenses, the same vantage points means that a single atmosphere is reproduced, in favour of the limitless others that might have been pursued. Space here is produced by the graphic lines that are the basic constituent parts of photographic composition you learn during a first year photography course. When you look at an architectural photograph you are not really looking through it to the building, you are seeing the reconfiguration of lines, colours and textures determined by the lens, format, composition as well as seeing the post-production work involved. In short, you are seeing the set of conventions already identified as an architectural atmosphere – one produced by photographs. Yes, they are photographs of something, but the sense of place transmitted has as much to do with the photograph as the things photographed. That sense of place is reduced by the repetition of the one-size fits all approach, which is conventional architectural photography. These theatres are an example of that reduction, revealed through repetition.

ARCHITECTURE'S DISCURSIVE SPACE

Figure 4: Camera works. Photographs by Marc Goodwin.

A key finding of this research is that there is much repetition in architectural photography. That the repetition of preferred colours and views can be used to reveal systemic repetition across a network of practitioners is particularly satisfying for its neat simplicity. Added together, these grids show how repetition can stereotype. Of course, the grid is a kind stereotype machine (Krauss 1985). Perhaps it leads us down a dangerous path of translation or transformation instead of revealing something about architectural photography. However, this visual methodology is not aimed at discerning the particular qualities of each individual image, but rather at seeing how they fit into a tradition. For that the grid is ideal.

Why the grid?

Grids have a well-established track record in the study of the built environment. *Learning from Las Vegas* by Venturi et al. (1977) is an example of architecture theory that uses photography and the grid as an epistemic device. The authors look at selection of hotels, motels and petrol stations[6] laid out in a grid of photographs

(Venturi et al. 1977: 32–47) to deploy their 'scale / speed / symbol' argument which states that the Las Vegas strip, when viewed from an automobile, requires a different scale and different symbols than say an eastern bazaar or medieval street viewed at the pace of a pedestrian. Significantly, the archives of Venturi and Scott Brown were exhibited in the 2015 Rencontres Photography Festival in Arles, France. Dan Graham's *Homes for America* (1966–67) is perhaps nearer to the discursive analysis of architecture through photography that I am concerned with. The project features a series of photographs of suburban American homes that emphasizes similarities between the repetitive standardized housing developments and the serial approach of minimalist art of the period. In addition, the work parodies the mores of 'house beautiful' magazines whilst at the same time challenging the hegemony of the white cube gallery as the means of exhibiting fine art. I have attempted to use photography of spaces with this same critical spirit. However, Graham's work is not strictly deployed as a grid, though a matrix of images does appear across the printed page.

Several artists working in the photographic medium have used systems of grids for exhibition and publication. Berndt and Hilla Becher, Karl Blossfeldt and Richard Avedon are three well-known examples. What is significant about their grids is not so much the layout on a wall or page, but their premeditated fabrication of repetition through the strict application of a set of rules. The Bechers worked out the atmospheric conditions for white skies and soft shadows as well as the correct vantage points for feasible repetition across several locations (Stimson 2004). Blossfeldt's photographs were intentionally taken as documents in order to catalogue plants and flowers. For that reason again you find in his work a reduction of variables in order to show the subject of each image in precisely the same light. Avedon, whether working outdoors with a mobile studio or in a classic photographer's studio with lighting equipment, was able to do much the same with white backgrounds and a set of instructions for his printer (a previsualization of his project that informed those instructions).

This method that both unifies and subdivides has been selected to visualize some of the most significant discoveries of modern times: the Punnet Square, the periodic table of elements, 'Alberti's window' and so on. But why? Perhaps it is because, as Rudolf Arnheim has claimed, '[v]ision is not a mechanical recording of elements, but the grasping of significant structural patterns' (Arnheim 1974: viii).[7] The grid allows us to see such patterns through regularity and repetition, where complexity or chaos might impede comprehension. It has certainly been the case with images looked at here. This need for regularity and repetition for comprehension is discussed in both the process philosophy of Whitehead et al. (1978) and in Feyerabend's paratactic aggregates (1993). *A Pattern Language* (Alexander et al. 1977) is but one of many architectural texts concerned with patterns.

Discursive regularity in architectural photography

In addition to its utility in arts and science, the grid allows for the emergence of a pattern that points to what Michel Foucault (1971) would call organized conditions of possibility for certain norms or symbolic codes. Seen from this perspective, grids potentially take on the aspect of a cage. Are we, as consumers of architectural photography, limited in our freedom by discursive regimes, whereby the visibilities – what we can see – and enunciations – what we can say – about architecture, namely its atmospherics, are always already regulated by complex sets of sociotechnical and institutional conditions? Not necessarily. For Foucault (1973), any principle of legitimation also has at the same time the possibility of throwing any discourse into error or contradiction, in which paradoxically lies the possibility of alterations to the history of the formation of knowledge and objects, and thus installing an avenue of freedom from the present. This is why I focus here on two archives of my own work: one of commissions and publications and the other of rejected and erroneous photographs. Objects of discourse deemed as errors and rejected become the very surface that points to on one hand the conditions of possibility of the formation of architectural photography as discursive objects, and on the other, provides a reason and means to reconsider my part in a chain of commercial practices. Attention paid only to the successful images, however, will only reinforce the notion that a set of familiar conventions are a form of optical truth instead of a clear instance of discursive formation predicated on a frame whose very ontology presupposes exclusion. One way to view this is that disciplinization closes our vision as 'every discipline is made up of restrictions on thought and imagination' (White 1978: 126) confining discourse to certain types of evidence and discourse. These are analytical restrictions, which are defined by the historian or genealogist as regulatory mechanisms that produce the discursive object. The ways in which we choose to look at disciplinary discourses and texts are affected by the discipline itself as well as the methodology subscribed to look at them.

This discussion of photography through Foucault leads naturally to the work of John Tagg and his recent book, *The Disciplinary Frame* (2009). There he develops the idea of photo-graphing 'subjecting light to the punctual rule of the room's inbuilt geometrical law' where the camera is useful as 'a device for producing and preserving text' (Tagg 2009: 1). Tagg's reading of photography is crucial, for Foucault claims that he applies his method only to 'verbal performances' (Foucault 1973: locations 3782–88). Of particular relevance to the subject of architectural photography, Tagg refers to both the camera and the panopticon as 'the truth machine' though with some degree of implied doubt about the veracity of such a claim. Another elision is made between the camera and the filing cabinet that together form a completed unit for the capture, taxonomy and storage of information. Building on his work in *The Burden of Representation*, Tagg looks at how photography is used by institutions and the state, as well as analysing how art history has constructed the disciplinary frame through which photography is viewed. He questions and problematizes the notion that documentary photography is transparent and universal, a window on the world, instead of a series of moves responding to standardized tropes or the specific requests of a photographic brief (his example is the Farm Security Administration, not architecture). Documentary emerges from and produces discourse in the service of political, social and economic powers. This final topic leads to the key, albeit startling, claim that 'discourse for Foucault is not a purely linguistic phenomenon, for the elements of a discursive system may not be in words at all'. Furthermore, he argues: 'Confessional rituals [...] involve not just certain kinds of speaking and hearing but also specially designed spaces [...] And we can readily see how this could be extended to the rituals of connoisseurship or art historical judgment' (Tagg 2007: 243). As I will now argue in the next section, discourse can take on many forms but need not be as total and severe a prison as the Panopticon.

Discourse in decline?

In her book, *Constructing a New Agenda,* Krista Sykes writes, 'during the period spanning the mid-1960s through the mid-1990s, there did exist a prevailing discourse that, despite varying methods of approach, sought to reformulate the discipline and carve out a niche for architecture' (Sykes 2010: location 183–88). It ended with the final issue of the journal *Assemblage* in 2000, of which K. Michael Hays was editor-in-chief. Sykes and Hays have identified a long trend moving from language-based arguments connected to academic research to 'the new pragmatism' in architecture (Sykes 2010; Saunders 2009). Simply put, new pragmatism puts emphasis on business. A key component is the use of images in order to sell building designs. Sykes acknowledges that pragmatism is itself a discourse, albeit one less influenced by cultural theory, structuralism, deconstruction, phenomenology than by codes of conduct for publication.[8] Publication takes us back to the triumvirate of famous photographers working to put famous architects in famous journals. In this sense, highly skilled photographers have distinguished themselves by showing their unique vision of the world.[9] It is most of their work that fills the pages of the *Phaidon Atlas*. So why do so many of their images resemble each other in that publication? They are the discursive space of a world where fame is critical for commercial success. How that discourse is reified by the activity of photographers, editors and architects is in need of greater investigation. Yet it seems clear here that whilst each photographer has their signature, certain stylistic conventions are common to most practitioners. This may be true of other commercial fields. However, it is hard to imagine what fashion photography would look like if all models wore white clothes standing before blue backgrounds. Such adamant repetition is at best a glaring oversight for a practice that is about the visual appreciation for and understanding of place, place-making, the genius loci and atmosphere. At worse it is a form of discursive regularity that insists we direct our eyes and imagination away from much of phenomenological experience of the world.

Showing more

This has been a Luddite solution, the slow and fallible plodding of a sole researcher. But it could be extended to all major publications for the sake of falsification. Technology could do much of this work. Current developments in object recognition[10] suggest that deep learning will allow for computers to not only identify image types according to a predetermined rubric but learn to identify new images via past experience.[11] Such experiments are expensive and not currently available to modest research projects. Yet the furore around big data suggests access might be democratized before long.[12] Hence, in addition to visualizing data through artistic methods, treating image as data via scientific methods appears to be a near reality. Responses to that sea change will undoubtedly be diverse if not utterly polemic.

However, the technological production of grids on the Internet is a present reality and one less likely to be divisive. The issue is addressed in *October* in the article 'On aggregators' (Joselit 2013). The point the author makes is that a new sort of online aggregate has emerged, where 'curated search engines' such as Contemporary Art Daily, Arch Daily, Architizer etc. act as a kind of personal selection tool that takes a step beyond the impersonal algorithms of Google. Filters, such as tags and keywords, are working to create countless grids of images that change the way images are used, understood, shared and consumed. Be it the aggregators of Joselit's article or the aggregates of images found in Google searches, Pinterest, Instagram, endlessly shuffled and reshuffled through keyword searches, this new sort of fluid grid figures largely in the future of photography. For this reason, it seems, Daniel Rubenstein argues in his 2009 article in *Photographies*:

> The classroom study of photographic masterpieces by selected 'masters of photography' feels more and more outdated. Contemporary digital photography is characterized not by the outstanding work of the few but by the middling

work of the many. Rather than a system of the production of work of art, photography today is a system of dissemination and reproduction.

(Rubenstein 2009: 139)

Urging increased dialogue between photographers, editors and architects is a desirable outcome of such research. Publications such as *Archizines* (Redstone 2011) and exhibitions such as the *Constructing Worlds* in the London Barbican Centre (2015) suggest that such a need has been identified and change is already underway. But this topic presents ample opportunities for the kinds of photographic studies called for in *Photographies* by Rubenstein. Along those lines photography might serve researchers and educators as a means of critical engagement with the general cultural and scientific milieu and not continue to look inwards upon itself as either a specific technology or a particular sphere of visuality, but rather 'place the study of the digital photograph at the centre of a culture which is based on reproduction, multiplication and copying' (Redstone 2011: 135). Tellingly, Rubenstein concludes that rather than continuing to look primarily at the work of the masters of photography, we should teach photography focus on discourse created by all producers and users of images (Redstone 2011: 141). This too presents an opportunity for architecture. What if photographic and architectural studies were truly interdisciplinary, informing and enriching each other in an age of online expansion? What if each discipline contributed instead of retreating from that space?

Conclusion

The repetition of practices is what makes them important, here. That is true of both photography and architecture. The repetition of stylistic conventions homogenizes the diversity of places we call the world. Taken individually, photograph by photograph, the repetition of conventions I've attempted to address is easy to overlook. By putting them alongside one another, I hope to have made the conventions in practice more visible. It is not a building you see when you look at an architectural photograph. You see the way the photographer represented it according to the rules of architecture's discursive space.

In writing about photography as a visual methodology, I have been given the opportunity to articulate commercial photographic practices that receive little attention in current research. All too often photography is written about as an index, a product of mechanical reproduction or a click of the shutter. The first two topics are so fascinating that they have interested nearly everyone ever since their first publication. The last is so omnipresent that for researcher and laymen alike the snapshot is almost synonymous with photography. But that is not the case for people who dedicate their lives to the practice. None of those photographic topics takes into account the days, weeks and sometimes months spent either side of the click of the shutter in order to produce a finalized image.

Grids reveal an aggregate of beliefs and practices that show how the discursive space of architecture as one that is increasingly photographic. Discursive regularity creates a biopolitical control of the way of seeing architecture through photographic norms. That those norms are in part the heritage of architectural representation, in part the result of beliefs about best documentary practices goes without saying. Yet the conventional atmosphere of architecture goes beyond that. It visualizes preferences for certain, ideal conditions that when repeatedly published globally become the industry standard. That standard promotes certain atmospheres to the exclusion of others. Grids have provided a method for looking at repetition in order to examine discursive regularity and errors. This is just one example of how photographic practices can be used for critical engagement with architecture. As technology democratizes both the practices of photography and publishing, this presents new opportunities for critiques of commercial uses of photography as well as the means of constructing new and more diverse spaces through the discourse that photography can create. Instead of being the enabling dispositif of the systems of control exposed by Feyerabend, Foucault and Tagg, photography might be used to turn them on their heads like the image in the ground glass of a large format camera, still used by some architectural photographers. That counter-intuitive image elegantly reveals how our eyes work to see what we will in an architectural image. As Errol Morris cleverly put it: believing is seeing.

REFERENCES

Phaidon Press (2004), *The Phaidon Atlas of Contemporary World Architecture*, London: Phaidon.

Alexander, C., Ishikawa, S. and Silverstein, M. (1977), *A Pattern Language: Towns, Buildings, Construction*, New York: Oxford University Press.

Arnheim, R. (1974), *Art and Visual Perception: A Psychology of the Creative Eye*, Berkeley, CA: University of California Press.

—— (1988), *The Power of the Center: A Study of Composition in the Visual Arts*, Berkeley, CA: University of California Press.

Čeferin, P. (2003), *Constructing a Legend: The International Exhibitions of Finnish Architecture, 1957–1967*, Helsinki: SKS.

Choisy, A. (1899), *Histoire De L'architecture*, Paris: Gauthier-Villars.

Bate, D. (2010), 'The memory of photography', *Photographies*, 3:2, pp. 243–57.

Elwall, R. (2004), *Building with Light: The International History of Architectural Photography*, London: Merrell.

Feyerabend, P. (1993), *Against Method*, London: Verso.

Fried, M. (2008), *Why Photography Matters as Art as Never Before*, New Haven, CT: Yale University Press.

Frampton, K. (1991), 'Towards a critical regionalism: Six points for an architecture of resistance', in H. Foster (ed.), *The Anti-aesthetic: Essays on Postmodern Culture*, Seattle, WA: Bay Press.

Foucault, M. (1971), *The Order of Things: An Archaeology of the Human Sciences*, New York: Pantheon Books.

Hayes, Michael K. (ed.) (2000), *Architecture Theory since 1968*, New York: Columbia Books of Architecture.

Higgott, A. and Wray, T. (2012), *Camera Constructs: Photography, Architecture and the ModernCity*, Farnham, Surrey: Ashgate.

Joselit, D. (2013), 'On aggregators', *October*, 146, pp. 3–18.

Krauss, R. E. (1985), *The Originality of the Avant-garde and Other Modernist Myths*, Cambridge, MA: The MIT Press.

Leach, N. (1999), *The Anaesthetics of Architecture*, Cambridge, MA: The MIT Press, http://search.ebscohost.com/login.aspx?direct=true&scope=site&db=nlebk&db=nlabk&AN=24396. Accessed 23 November 2015.

Norberg-Schulz, C. (1980), *Genius Loci: Towards a Phenomenology of Architecture*, London: Academy Editions.

Pallasmaa, J. (2005), *The Eyes of the Skin: Architecture and the Senses*, Chichester: Wiley-Academy.

—— (2009), *The Thinking Hand: Existential and Embodied Wisdom in Architecture*, Chichester: John Wiley & Sons Ltd.

—— (2011), *The Embodied Image: Imagination and Imagery in Architecture*, Chichester: John Wiley & Sons Ltd.

Pardo, A. and Redstone, E. (2014), *Photography and Architecture in the Modern Age*, London: Barbican Art Gallery.

Redstone, E. (2011), *Archizines*, London: N.P.

Redstone, E. (2014), *Shooting Space: Architecture in Contemporary Photography*, London: Phaidon.

Robinson, C. and Herschman, J. (1987), *Architecture Transformed: A History of the Photography of Buildings from 1839 to the Present*, New York: Architectural League of New York.

Rosa, J., Shulman, J. and Mccoy, E. (1994), *A Constructed View: The Architectural Photography of Julius Shulman*, New York: Rizzoli.

Rubinstein, D. (2009), 'Towards photographic education', *Photographies*, 2, pp. 135–42.

Saint-Martin, F. (1990), *Semiotics of Visual Language*, Bloomington, IN: Indiana University Press.

Saunders, W. S. (2007), *The New Architectural Pragmatism: A Harvard Design Magazine Reader*, Minneapolis, MN: University of Minnesota Press.

Sobieszek, R. A. (1986), *This Edifice is Colossal: 19th Century Architectural Photography*, Rochester, NY: International Museum of Photography at George Eastman House.

Stimson, B. (2004), 'The Photographic Comportment of Bernd and Hilla Becher', *Tate Papers*, 1 April, Issue 1, http://www.tate.org.uk/research/publications/tate-papers/photographic-comportment-bernd-and-hilla-becher. Accessed 30 August 2019.

Sykes, K. (2010), *Constructing a New Agenda for Architecture: Architectural Theory 1993–2009*, New York: Princeton Architectural Press.

Tagg, J. (2007), *The burden of representation: essays on photographies and histories.* Basingstoke: Palgrave MacMillan.

Tagg, J. (2010), *The Disciplinary Frame: Photographic Truths and the Capture of Meaning.* Minneapolis, MN: University of Minnesota Press.

Van Leeuwen, T. (2010), *Handbook of Visual Analysis*, London: SAGE Publications.

Venturi, R., Scott Brown, D. and Izenour, S. (1977), *Learning from Las Vegas: The Forgotten Symbolism of Architectural Form*, Cambridge, MA: The MIT Press.

White, H. V. (1978), *Tropics of Discourse: Essays in Cultural Criticism*, Baltimore, MD: Johns Hopkins University Press.

Wigley, Mark (1998), 'The architecture of atmosphere', *Daidalos*, 68, pp. 18–27.

—— (1995), *White Walls, Designer Dresses: The Fashioning of Modern Architecture*, Cambridge, MA: The MIT Press.

—— (1993), *The Architecture of Deconstruction: Derrida's Haunt*, Cambridge, MA: The MIT Press.

Whitehead, A. N., Griffin, D. R. and Sherburne, D. W. (1978), *Process and Reality: An Essay in Cosmology*, New York: Free Press.

NOTES

1. Thanks to them we still know of Bedford Lamere, Dell and Wainwright, Robert Elwall and Eric de Maré in the United Kingdom; Max Dupain and David Moore in Australia; Cervin Robinson, Ezra Stoller and Baltazar Korab in the United States; the Bisson brothers, Edouard Baldus and Dominique Roman in France. To say nothing of the great fame of photographers like Le Grey, Negre, Le Secq, Atget, Abbott and Evans whose subject matter was largely the built environment, or Julius Shulman and Lucien Hervé who worked commercially as architectural photographers.

2. Of course, critical debate on the subject of architecture can still be found in *Architectural Review*, *Architectural Design*, peer-reviewed journals and many of the publications found in *Archizines*, such as Mas Content. Architects such as Michael Sorkin argue for the continued importance of theory: http://www.architectural-review.com/essays/critical-mass-why-architectural-criticism-matters/8663075.article. But perhaps none of these could be said to replace journals such as *Oppositions* or *Assemblage*.

VISUAL RESEARCH METHODS IN ARCHITECTURE

3. From top down: Helin and Co, JKMM, KHR, 3XN, AOA, Alvar Aalto for Aalto University, PLH, JS Siren for the Finnish Parliament and Studiopuisto. Six of the nine clients started out as partners in my research who ended up purchasing the images indicated. These purchases acted as a catalyst for this research.

4. It may be useful to compare the photographic atmospheres of the *Phaidon Atlas* with actual Meteorological data. The point I hope to make is that there is greater atmospheric variety in the world than in the world of the architectural photograph. Annual rainfall and sunshine are two means of documenting that variety, though mass observation data is also a useful source of information, such as can be found here: http://www.massobs.org.uk/index.htm

Average precipitation in depth (mm per year) 2005–2014:

Australia	524
China	645
Finland	536
Denmark	703
United Kingdom	1,220
United States	15
South Korea	1,274
South Africa	495
Ethiopia	848
Guinea	1,651
Libya	56
Central African Republic	1,348

Annual Hours of Sunshine:

Australia	1,750–3,500
Finland (Helsinki)	1,780
Denmark	1,495
United Kingdom	1,154
United States (D.C)	1,783
South Korea (Seoul)	2,066
South Africa	2,500

5. http://de.phaidon.com/store/architecture/the-phaidon-atlas-of-contemporary-world-architecture-9780714843124/.

6. Hotels: Sahara, Riviera, Stardust, Caesar's Palace, Dunes, Aladdin, Tropicana; stations: Gulf, Texaco, Shell, Texas, Union 76; motels: Gaslite, Mirage, Wedding chapel.

7. In short, we are hot-wired to see things through patterns; hence, repetition of photographic practices will homogenize architectural spaces, as I am arguing. To overlook this built-in tendency is to ignore the physics and psychology of optics – in short, to ignore Arnheim's argument.

8. Clearly, success has always mattered to practising architects and debates continue to rage in academic journals. It is only the increased importance of a certain type of image and the decreasing influence of a certain type of writing that are at stake here.

9. A cursory glance at global photographic practice shows that: the world is vibrant and bustling in the images of Iwan Baan, poignant and beautiful in the work of Hélène Binet, silent and sculptural in the images of Agata Madejska, visionary and far-fetched in the creations of Victor Enrich and Filip Dujardin, dense and urban according to Michael Wolf, exists on the anonymous fringe when shot by Bas Princen, is a strange, sad fantasy in the work of Geert Goiris, is a seemingly limitless source of inspiration for Frank van der Salm, can be viewed from several points all at once in the work of Barbara Probst, or reduced to exceptional graphic beauty in the work of Janie Airey and Josef Schulz. This is to say nothing of respected, successful, contemporary practitioners such as Hufton and Crow, Roland Halbe, Richard Bryant, Simona Panzironi, Fernando Guerra, Duccio Malagamba, John Gollings, Adam Mørk, Miko Huisman, Adrià Goula, Brigida Gonzalez, Grant Mudford, Nick Guttridge, Dennis Gilbert, Erieta Attali, Morley Von Sternberg, as well as the many other photographers represented by the agencies: View, Arcaid and Esto.

10. http://www.cs.jhu.edu/~hager/Public/teaching/cs461/ObjectRecognition.pdf.

11. http://deeplearning.net/reading-list/.

12. http://www.sas.com/content/dam/SAS/en_us/doc/whitepaper1/big-data-meets-big-data-analytics-105777.pdf.

9

Desert Cities

Aglaia Konrad, Independent Artist

I came across these cities on a trip from Cairo to Alexandria by taking the Cairo-Alexandria Desert Road in 1992, endless housing complexes passing by like a mirage. Nothing reminding me of the mythological Egyptian history one would expect encountering; I have seen only desert roads and *Plattenbau*. It took twelve years until I returned to Egypt to extend the basic interest (I was already interested but it took time to take on the project) in the phenomenon of these sixteen new-built cities, each for 250 up to 500 thousand inhabitants, in the middle of the deserts of Egypt.

My work isn't just recording the world, it is an active search for reading back decision making on a political and economic level, departing from architecture and urbanistic phenomena, and a translation of these into a foremost artistic vocabulary. The whole story of the development of the desert cities is very complex and complicated.

The idea of the 1970s master plan (still under Anwar Sadat) was to build 'independent cities', away from the Greater Cairo Region to provide new development poles. In the mid-1980s, the approach shifted to building satellite cities, as residential settlements for the excessively growing population. The real-estate boom of the 1990s and early twenty-first century changed everything. While speculative builders are doubling the size of Cairo, the government is proposing to duplicate the Nile Valley. In less than fifteen years, the urbanized area of Cairo has almost tripled in size and a new urban world has been created at Cairo's gates.

The 'Desert Cities' project is a complex matter with an endless number of possible perspectives and objectives. Issues arise concerning matters of gender, migration, immigration, segregation, exclusion, neo-liberal order, globalization, transnationalism, government agencies, securities, privatization – to name a few. Nevertheless, I don't want to be an artist who also acts as an anthropologist, or a geographer, or a *journaliste*. The perspective of my Desert Cities project is mainly based on the fundaments of my own artistic practice. This suggests a reflection on architectural and urban phenomena that articulates my view on the organization of society from my photographic endeavour.

Acknowledgements

The project 'Desert Cities' was awarded and supported by the Grand Prix de la Photography, Vevey 2004. The book *Desert Cities* has been published by JRP Rignier, Christoph Keller editions, Zürich, 2008 and has been made possible by the Albert Renger Patzsch Award, 2006. The book was awarded with the Infinity Award by the International Centre for Photography, New York, 2009. All the original photographs are in colour.

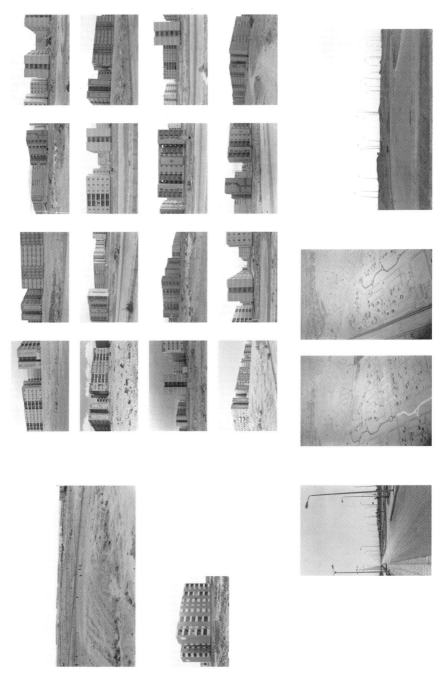

PLANCHE 01

PLANCHE 02

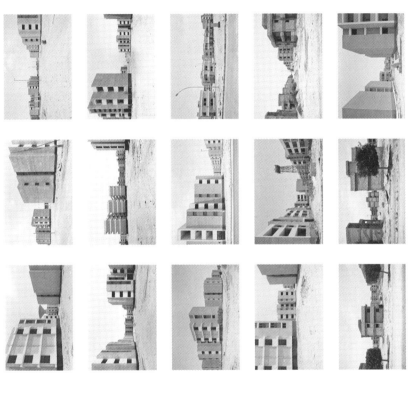

Figure 9.1: Desert Cities Series. Photographs and arrangement by Aglaia Konrad.

PLANCHE 03

PLANCHE 04

Figure 9.2: (Contd.)

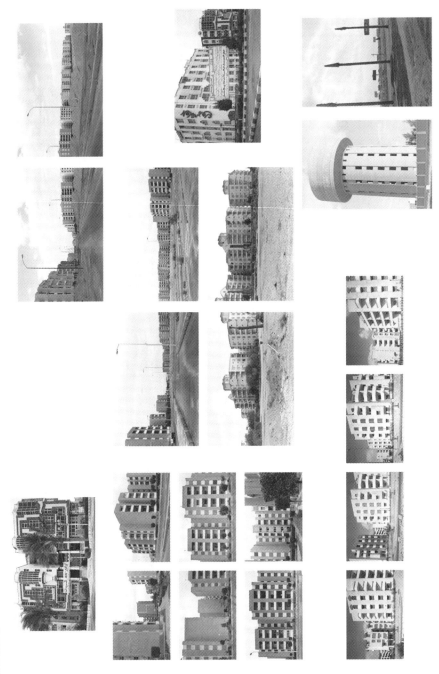

PLANCHE 05

PLANCHE 06

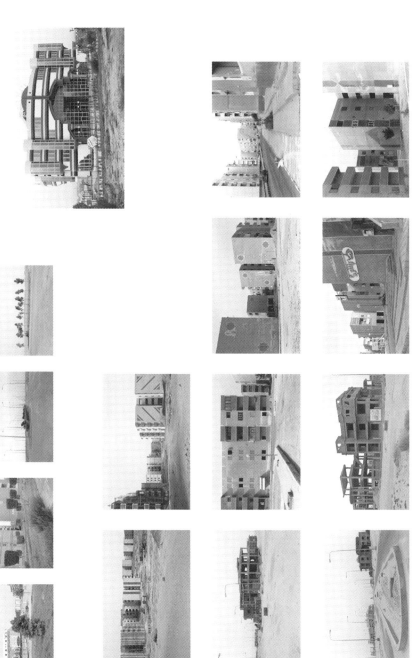

Figure 9.3: *(Contd.)*

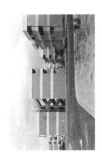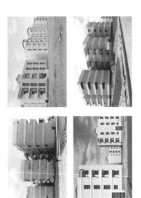

PLANCHE 07

PLANCHE 08

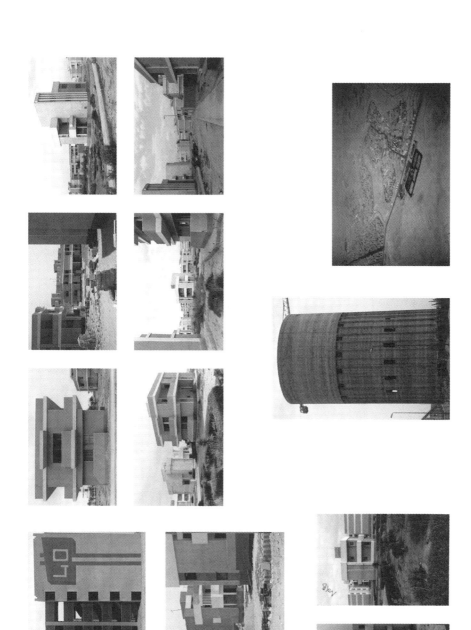

Figure 9.4: *(Contd.)*

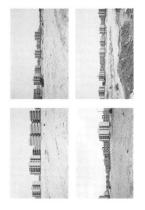

PLANCHE 09

PLANCHE 10

Figure 9.5: *(Contd.)*

PLANCHE 11

PLANCHE 12

Figure 9.6: (Contd.)

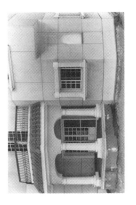

PLANCHE 13

PLANCHE 14

Figure 9.7: (Contd.)

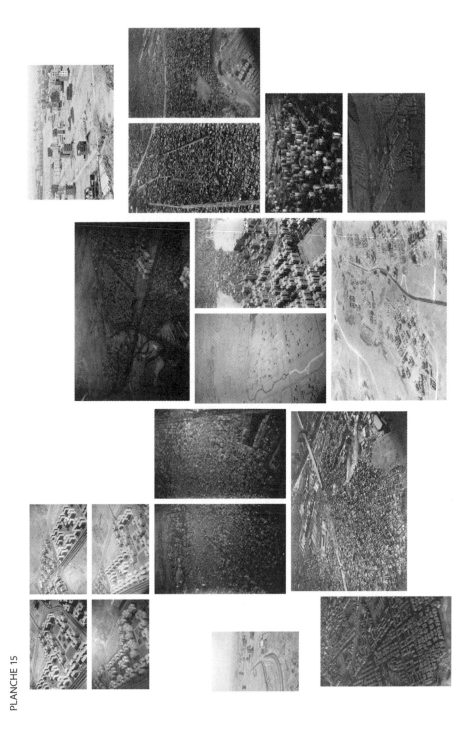

PLANCHE 15

PLANCHE 16

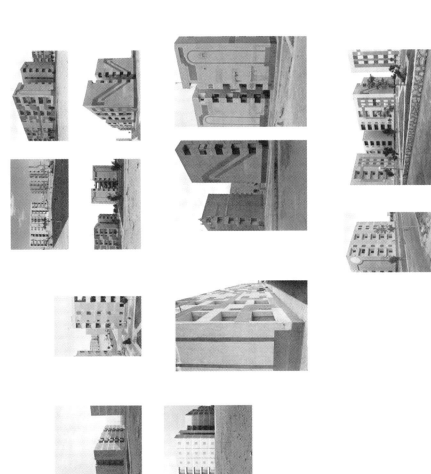

Figure 9.8: *(Contd.)*

175

10

Visual methodology on display: Taking photographs of *Separation*

*Shelly Cohen, David Azrieli School of Architecture,
Tel Aviv University*

Haim Yacobi, Development Planning Unit, University College London

In the midst of the surge of violence that began in Israel in October 2015, the Israeli police set up a temporary wall in one of the Palestinian attack sites in East Jerusalem, the Jabel Mukaber neighbourhood close to the Jewish Armon Hanatziv neighbourhood. The police announced that the wall was intended to prevent the Palestinians from throwing Molotov cocktails, shooting fireworks and aiming stones at passing vehicles and houses in the neighbourhood (Hasson and Ravid 2015: 1, 3). The setting up of the temporary separation wall attracted a great deal of public attention and demonstrated the fragility of the shared texture of life in the mixed cities, in which Jews live alongside Arabs in Israel.

The Palestinian neighbourhoods in East Jerusalem are segregated spaces, characterized by an absence of development, a tremendous shortage of space for housing and public gathering, defective infrastructures and destruction decrees against residents' houses (Cohen-Bar 2015: 39–43). But at the same time, the Palestinian residents of Jerusalem are greatly present in the life of Western Jerusalem, both in the workforce and in the commercial areas, such as the western city centre and the large malls. In addition, at the junction where the wall was set up, there are Palestinian shops that used to benefit from commerce and relations between Jews and Arabs (Hasson and Ravid 2015: 3). The concrete wall attracted a great deal of media attention in Israel, but little has been said about its design: the six concrete slabs that were placed in the street were mobile precast slabs with an external finish of chiselled stone. An urban by-law that dates from the time of the British

Mandate (1917–48), and which is still valid today, requires that every external wall that is built in Jerusalem should be covered in chiselled stone. The technique of building with an external finish of chiselled stone is called 'Jerusalem Stone' and has become one of the distinctive characteristics of the city. Thus, even though every concrete slab of the mobile wall that has been placed in Jabel Mukaber has the words 'Temporary Mobile Police Barricade' written on it, the mobile wall has a local character that ascribes it to Jerusalem's permanent architectural culture. This sets it apart from the Separation Wall that has been under construction in Israel since 2002, built to prevent the unauthorized transition of Palestinians to population centres in Israel. This permanent security wall that passes through East Jerusalem is made of prefabricated slabs of bare concrete.

The security rationale is only one aspect of the totality of political considerations that are employed in determining the path of the separation barrier. The temporary wall that was set up in Jabel Mukaber led to stormy responses including, according to media reports, some in the political-security cabinet as well, due to its controversial implications undermining the integrated spatial conditions. The right-wing ministers in the government criticized the decision to build a temporary wall because it implied that the government had renounced its sovereignty over the Palestinian neighbourhoods of Jerusalem, and was de facto dividing the city (Hasson and Ravid 2015: 3). Indeed, the logic of separation has been dominant in the recent political discourse in Israel, peaking at the beginning of the 2000s with the building of the separation barrier and the temporary wall in East Jerusalem about fifteen years later. We argue that it has played a significant part in shaping spatial planning and architecture in Israel.

Israeli territory is characterized by ethnic, national and class divisions. Spatial demarcation distinguishes between Jews and Arabs, Mizrahi Jews who migrated from Middle Eastern countries and Ashkenazi Jews who migrated from Europe, between rich and poor, thus giving rise to different types of social power relations (Tzfadia and Yacobi 2011: 107). The population in the outlying immigrant development towns consists mainly of Mizrahi Jews and new immigrants from the former Soviet Union. Set apart geographically, they are distant from the metropolitan centre. Other forms of spatial separation are also evident in mixed cities where there is educational and occupational segregation, with the affluent citizens setting themselves apart and closed off in discrete developments. While the Separation Wall, which the Israel government calls the Security Barrier, was being built between Israel and the Palestinian Occupied Territories (though partly annexing Palestinian land into the 'Israeli' side), fences and walls were used not only in Israel's external borders, but impassable physical partitions have become a readily available spatial solution inside the country as well.

The exhibition *Separation,* presented in 2005 in The Architect's House Gallery, home of the Israel Association of United Architects, explored these issues arguing that spatial and physical demarcation intersect different types of social power relations within the Israeli society and often reproduce them. The *Local* series provided the framework for the presentation of the exhibition. Presented between the years 2001 and 2013 at the Architect's House Gallery in Jaffa, the series has included seventeen exhibitions. *Local* has aimed to examine Israeli architecture and environment, not through architectural achievements, extraordinary buildings and leading architects, but rather by focusing on planning procedures and on the social and political conditions of architecture that are unique to the place. *Local* received public funding from the Israeli Ministry of Science Culture and Sport, and from the Culture and Art Department of the Tel Aviv-Jaffa municipality. With these resources, the Architect's House Gallery has created a relatively protected alternative space that enables young architects, scholars and artists to develop a moral discussion of architecture, set apart from the world of practice.

Theoretical processes in the 1990s expanded the discussion of culture, underscoring the power relations associated with it, largely contributing to the critical and postcolonial transition in the research of Israeli architecture. *Local* joined the social discussion on architecture; in many respects, it even spearheaded that shift. In times of a growing split between a group of researchers, who were committed to social issues but ignored material aspects of architecture, and the majority of architects, who were committed to technology and form but refrained from social questions (Cohen 2008: 116–17), it is noteworthy that the series was featured in the home of the Israel Association of United Architects and that it appealed directly to an audience that is not necessarily convinced of the architect's moral role.

The exhibition was initiated by Shelly Cohen, chief curator of the gallery at the time, who invited Haim Yacobi, a researcher of urban space and social justice and an architect, to explore the effect of the recently built separation fence on the Israeli landscape, as a curatorial project. Initiating *Separation* originated from our observation that the act of spatial planning is generally perceived as an enlightened process, which is a part of democratic political reality driven by the belief that proper planning can improve the quality of life, the economy, environment and the sense of community. This is obviously only partially true as it can disregard the need to comprehend spatial phenomena as an expression of power relations. The exhibition therefore attempted to question and undermine assumptions of the processes occurring in the space as obvious developments or as the result of circumstances reflecting normality in the relationships between different groups. Alongside the exhibition's visual evidence of the prevalence of spatial separations in the contemporary Israeli condition, the question arises: do planning practices themselves – architecture, urban planning, civil engineering and landscaping – indeed generate separation and normalize it in the built environment?

Photographing separation

In order to answer this question, we, the curators, invited three photographers to document sites across Israel in which there is a discernible spatial separation. We also approached architects, planners, sociologists and social activists, asking them to address these sites in writing. The exhibition comprised twelve photographs, each representing one of the selected sites. A book was published following the exhibition (Yacobi and Cohen 2007). Methodologically, we followed Sarah Pink's (2004: 2) approach, which suggests that visual ethnography is *done*, rather than conducted. In this project too, the best – if not the only – way to understand our relations with the landscape of separation is through a journey, performed by a photographer and a curator together, in and through the visual documentation of designed and planned objects. In other words, the 'journeys' that were presented in the exhibition document objects that are often considered to be 'neutral' expressions of technical arrangements in space, rather than objects that address the inter-relations between these structures and the persons inhabiting the urban, sub-urban or rural space.

The exhibition layout in the small Gallery space mixed the images made by all the photographers, thus mixing different image-formats, and depicting different types of separation in the sites. Three photographs, though not hung next to each other, showed walls that faced the photographer and the viewer frontally and actualized the concept of separation in the gallery itself: the Separation Fence between the Jewish neighbourhood of Ganey Dan and the Arab neighbourhood of Juarish, both neighbourhoods in the mixed city Ramla (Figure 1), and the Separation Wall between Pardes-Snir, an Arab neighbourhood on the outskirts of the city of Lod, and the Jewish village Nir-Tzvi (Figure 2). The two walls are built cement walls, and alongside them there is a photograph of the dirt dyke between the Jewish town Caesarea and the Arab village Jisr az-Zarka (Figure 3). These three photographs (taken by different photographers) created a kind of typological series, in the spirit of the famous typologies that were created by the artists Brand and Hilla Becher and their followers from the 1960s onwards: collecting, grouping, and naming members of the same type, usually industrial structures (Freidus et al. 1991). This typological photography has influenced Israeli photography of landscapes and cityscapes from the late 1990s onwards (Maimon and Herzogenrath 1998: 1). Siman-Tov and Geron, two of the Separation

Figure 1: Orit Siman-Tov, *Ramla*, 2005, colour photograph, 75×110 cm.

Figure 2: Amit Geron, *Lod-Pardes-Snir*, 2005, colour photograph, 120×150 cm.

Figure 3: Yair Barak, Jisr az-Zarka-Caesarea, 2005, colour photograph, 70×140 cm.

photographers, also participated in 'Living Space' (Maimon and Herzogenrath 1998) – one of the early key exhibitions presenting this type of local photography.

The three main photographs focused on the wall as a discrete and identifiable object. When the exhibition headline was attached to these images, they directly formulated the exhibition's central argument that the logic of separation – as a political, cultural and spatial concept – is intrinsic to rural and urban landscape design in Israel. The other photographs presented less obvious complex urban conditions of separation (Figures 4–6), delimited gated neighbourhoods (Figures 7 and 8), communities of Jewish Ethiopian immigrants in Beer-Sheva or excluded Bedouin communities in the Negev (Figures 9 and 10), as sites of latent exchange or differentiation. The ostensibly banal elements of the separation syntax – wall, rampart, road, public building and construction project – and their contexts in popular, suburban or high-end residential areas generated a cumulative effect that marks diverse sites in Israel as fenced off, closed and impassable.

Architectural exhibitions make it possible to present political arguments through visual tools. In *Separation*, the power of the images was their documentation of a spatial phenomenon with a social meaning. This sociospatial realism has a visual agency derived from the indexical relationship of the photographic image to its object (Krauss 1985: 198, 203). In the semiotic theory of Charles Sanders Peirce ([1897] 1932), the index is one of the three fundamental sign categories, depending on a physical relation between the sign-vehicle and the object (Pierce [1897] 1932 in Silverstein 1976: 27). In photography this relation is maintained between the photographed object and the resulting image, derived from the transformation of a light-sensitive negative caused by light reflecting off the object (Krauss 1977: 203; Gunning 2004: 39–40). This process as described by Roland Barthes (1981: 76–77) depends on the presence of 'the real thing which has been placed before the lens, without which there would be no photograph' (Barthes 1981: 76). Barthes formulated the expression 'That-has-been' (Barthes 1981: 77) to describe the essence of photography as a depiction of reality: the photographed subject and the image produced are directly related and this exchange takes place in

VISUAL METHODOLOGY ON DISPLAY

Figure 4: Amit Geron, *Jerusalem*, 2005, colour photograph, 80×100 cm.

Figure 5: Amit Geron, *Haifa*, 2005, colour photograph, 80×100 cm.

Figure 6: Orit Siman-Tov, *Modi'in-Maccabim-Re'ut*, 2005, colour photograph, 40×60 cm.

Figure 7: Orit Siman-Tov, *Arsuf*, 2005, colour photograph, 40×60 cm.

Figure 8: Amit Geron, *Jaffa*, 2005, colour photograph, 80×100 cm.

Figure 9: Orit Siman-Tov, *Beer-Sheva*, 2005, colour photograph, 40×60 cm.

Figure 10: Yair Barak, *Amra-Omer*, 2005, colour photograph, 70×140 cm.

analogue photography on film (two of the photographers, Orit Siman-tov and Yair Barak, used film photography). At the same time, this is of course photography that interprets reality rather than merely documenting it. In the photographic process the photographers attempted to edit, extract and emphasize the separation situation as a logic and as an identified condition differentiated from the everyday and banal situation in front of their eyes, through the placement of the camera, the design of the frame composition, and emphasis on the aesthetics of the photographed subject. In addition, the selection of a single photograph from each site for the exhibition was made through a combination of considerations of content and form. Out of all the photographs that were taken on site, the one photograph that the curators and photographers chose for the exhibition together, was the strongest manifestation of the political argument of the exhibition in aesthetic terms. For example: The image of the Katamonim neighbourhood housing projects, which were built in Jerusalem between the 1950s and the 1970s and were populated by Jews of Eastern origins (Figure 4), was taken from a distance that made it possible to capture them as comprising a fortified wall against the Jordanian threat. Other photographs developed the exhibition's argument through implicit social and environmental transgressions: for example, the Tunnels Road, which bypasses Palestinian Bethlehem and connects Jerusalem to Hebron for Jewish vehicles, was photographed with the sunrays lighting the elevated road that penetrates the shadowed landscape of the Palestinian town of Beit Jala.

The photographers, Yair Barak, Amit Geron and Orit Siman-Tov, present physical separation and the central role it plays in Israeli spatial experience and construction, yet they differ from one another in the types and objects of their gaze. Amit Geron criticizes the neutrality of traditional architectural photography that is centred on an architectural façade dissociated from its context and inhabitation. His frontal photographs document distinctive, monumental and threatening separations. Thus, for example, the façade of the Carmel Beach Tower in Haifa (Le Meridian) fills the entire frame, leaving no air (Figure 5). The neglect is conspicuous in front of the monumental western façade of the Andromeda Hill project in Jaffa and its margins (Figure 8). Pedestrian figures in both photographs emphasize the absence of human scale in both buildings and their foreignness to their surroundings.

Yair Barak photographs sites where the power relations are latent. His gaze seeks the manner in which the aesthetics of separation generate the illusion of 'life as usual'. Barak lingers on the rhythm of the rows of trees and irrigation pipes on the embankment in Jisr az-Zarka (Figure 3). His photographs manifest the aesthetic role of photography in drawing the viewer's eye and heart to an encounter with reality. Barak's interest in the material surface of separation reminds us of the chiselled stone surface of the temporary wall in East Jerusalem.

A closer look at his photographs reveals the cracks in the harmonious picture of the world: the sand dunes cover some of the ramparts as nature resists the separation efforts.

Similarly, in the sites documented by Orit Siman-Tov the spatial context of separation is not apparent at first sight. Thus, the fences at the Nurit immigrant absorption centre in Beer-Sheva, housing Ethiopian newcomers, resemble the fences of state institutions where strict discipline applies. The figures populating the space undermine the image's neutrality, abruptly introducing questions and quandaries: Who are these people crowding by the fence? Why do they idly stand there? Why does one of them stretch his hand towards the viewer? Who controls the walls? Siman-Tov thus reinstates the physical setting with human experience and inhabitation, and with the help of the exhibition's declaration of intent, opens the door to a social critique of space (Figure 9).

Visual and spatial interpretation

The images shown in the exhibition were prioritized over the texts; they were presented in the gallery space, not attached to the texts. However, the exhibition viewers were also invited to read the story of each of the photographed sites from a booklet of texts that was handed out in the exhibition. The short texts were written by twelve different writers. Urban planner and social activist Yuval Tamari described how the walls erected between the Jewish neighbourhood Ganei Dan in Western Ramla and the adjacent Arab neighbourhoods Juarish with the 'minority quarters' were initially used as a protective wall against internal Arab strife over control of narcotic traffic, but later transformed from a protective means into a feargenerating fact (Figure 1). The photograph captured a moment in which Arab children pushed their way under and through the concrete fence in Ramla, perhaps on their way home to Juarish from the Jewish neighbourhood, and a dissonance is created between the fear that led to the construction of the wall and the innocent children trying to cross the barrier.

Thus, in addition to the rational facet of the arguments explaining the erection of fences, walls and other barriers, the texts in the exhibition also addressed another level, elusive yet significant, associated with the fears invoked by the encounter with the 'other'. These feelings are rarely expressed directly and explicitly, but the fear of the other, as indicated by the projects on view, is a central element in the political-spatial discourse. Furthermore, the existence of fear in the space is not a reflection of the social reality; rather, it constructs that reality (Sandercock 2002: 215). In other words, construction of the sense of fear in certain groups serves political interests that reflect the power relations in society. The mundane context of this reality is visualized in the exhibition in relation to Ramla, Lod and Jaffa – mixed Arab-Jewish cities where the nationalethnic homogeneity is interrupted.

The sense of fear is reinforced in temporal and spatial junctions where the space is transformed in manners that influence the political discourse, such as the arrival of immigrant groups with conspicuous visibility (Sandercock 2002: 208), for instance migrant workers in Tel Aviv or Ethiopian immigrants in Beer-Sheva city in the south of Israel. The social and political construction of fear highlights the question of what and who to fear, while changes are created in the space that benefit certain communities and exclude others. Sites typified by physical and social neglect and by social and moral chaos are considered as sites that must be either ignored or cleansed (Sibley 1995: 90). In this context, the fear has a spatial significance: where to go and where not to go; who lives 'there'; who are they in moral terms; and who hides behind the Wall?

Displaying politics

Israeli discourse on architecture and urban planning has shifted from a perception of architecture as a purely professional practice focusing on an aesthetic and stylistic interpretation of architecture, to a kind of research that examines the ethical and social dimensions of architecture. In the past two decades a new generation of architectural researchers has begun to address the connection between architecture, society and politics. Architectural phenomena are being studied as evidence of clear traces of power relations; phenomena such as spatial discrimination and neglect of national and ethnic groups have been studied (Yacobi et al. 2016: 3).

Galleries and museums have been a central site in which the critical image of the Israeli space has been established (Cohen 2004: 342). In the intersection between theory and practice, the gallery space enables suspension of construction for the purpose of posing critical questions. The photographic exhibition makes for a quick and focused response to reality, suggesting both its reflection and its interpretation (Cohen 2008: 116).

The exhibition, *Separation*, held in a public architectural gallery, is therefore to be understood as a participant in political criticism of Israeli space. It exposes the impact of planning processes on the built reality, contributing new insights to the social discussion. According to *Separation*, architecture not only reflects an inequitable social condition but also plays an active role in polarizing and splitting Israeli society. Many of the exhibitions in the *Local* series have featured photography. The participating photographers have documented the constantly evolving Israeli space, and their work in *Local* belongs to the practices of critical photography that thrived in Israel, particularly at the end of the twentieth century and the beginning of the twenty-first century. The exhibitions' architectural framing presented the ostensibly neutral photographed space as the outcome of planning.

Other exhibitions in the *Local* series went back to the sites presented in *Separation*, and documented manifestations of gentrification and the blocking of national and ethnic groups: Two exhibitions addressed Jaffa, in which the Architect's House Gallery, which hosted the *Local* exhibition series, resides. The exhibitions, *A House in Jaffa* Cohen-Bar, E. (2015) and *Ten Gazes from Jaffa* (Dabit et al. 2009), address the feelings of the Arab and poor residents of Jaffa, for whom the development momentum in Jaffa does not meet their most urgent need for attainable housing in their community. The exhibition *Moving Israel's Coastal Highway* (Cohen 2010) addressed the inadequacy of the road infrastructure of Jisr az-Zarka, a Palestinian Arab village that is currently at the bottom of the social-economic scale in Israel. This work on display creates a rich research body that demonstrates various dimensions of separation and enclosure in the Israeli space.

Separation received feedback and mentions in the daily press (Zandberg 2005), demonstrating its traction beyond the architectural field, and into critical writing about Israeli society. Writers noted the mixture of neo-liberalist and ethno-nationalist forces causing the construction of various kinds of barriers (Tzfadia 2006; Shenhav 2007). In our estimation, the immediate connection between the concept and the various sites of separation supported the exhibition's core argument regarding the prevalent conditions of spatial separation in Israel, and became consensual almost immediately.

While the exhibition's visual means and mode of argument clearly displayed the actuality of separation, the work of building fences and walls along the borders of Israel continues. As in the case of the setting up of the temporary separation wall in east Jerusalem, which was described in the beginning of this chapter, it appears that the new walls along the borders of Israel continue to reflect the government's attitude against groups inside Israel – work immigrants and refuge seekers from African countries, and the Palestinians. The two groups constitute a threat to the Israeli demographic balance and arouse national and ethnic tensions among disadvantaged populations in Israel. As the trend of building external borders develops, the work of addressing the social and spatial polarizations inside Israel by visual and written methods has to be pursued.

REFERENCES

Barthes, R. Roland R. (1981), *Camera Lucida: Reflections on Photography*, London: Vintage.
Cohen, S. (2003), 'A house in Jaffa', http://shelly-cohen.com/exhibition/local-7-a-house-in-jaffa/. Accessed 15 December 2017.

—— (2004), 'A moment of change? Transformation in Israeli architectural consciousness following the Israeli Pavilion Exhibition', in H. Yacobi (ed.), *Constructing a Sense of Place: Architectural and the Zionist Discourse*, London: Ashgate, pp. 329–51.

—— (2008), *Local: 10 Exhibitions, The Architect's House Gallery*, Tel-Aviv: Israel Association of United Architects.

—— (2010), 'Moving Israel's Coastal Highway', http://shelly-cohen.com/exhibition/local-14-moving-israels-coastal-highway/. Accessed 15 December 2017.

Cohen-Bar, E. (2015), *Trapped by Planning, Israeli Policy, Planning, and Development in the Palestinian Neighborhoods of East Jerusalem*, Jerusalem: Bimkom.

Dabit, B., Zandberg, E., Cohen, S. and Meishar, N. (2009), 'Ten gazes on Tel Aviv's centenary celebrations from Jaffa', http://shelly-cohen.com/exhibition/local-12-ten-gazes/. Accessed 15 December 2017.

Freidus, M., Lingwood, J. and Slemmons, R. (1991), *Typologies: Nine Contemporary Photographers*, Newport Harbor, CA: Newport Harbor Art Museum Publication.

Gunning, T. (2004), 'What's the point of an index? Or, faking photographs', *NORDICOM Review*, 16:1-2, pp. 39–49.

Hasson, N. and Ravid, B. (2015), חומה מוקמת בג'בל מוכבר: עיריית ירושלים דנה בהפרדת חלקי העיר ,הארץ, ('Erecting of barriers in East Jerusalem: Jerusalem municipality discusses the division of the city'), *Haaretz*, 19 October, pp. 1, 3.

Krauss, R. E. (1985), *The Originality of the Avant-Garde and Other Modernist Myths*, Cambridge, MA: The MIT Press.

Maimon, V. and Herzogenrath, W. (1998), מרחב מחיה - רחוק קרוב (*Living Space, Distant and Close*), Herzliya: Herzliya Museum of Contemporary Art.

Peirce, C. S. ([1897] 1932), *Collected Papers of Charles Sanders Peirce*, edited by C. Hartshorne and P. Weiss, Cambridge, MA: Belknap.

Pink, S. (2004), 'Introduction: Situating visual research', in S. Pink, L. Kürti and I. Afonso (eds), *Working Images: Visual Research and Representation in Ethnography*, London: Routledge, pp. 1–10.

Sandercock, L. (2002), 'Difference, fear and habitus: A political economy of urban fears', in J. Hillier and E. Rooksby (eds), *Habitus: A Sense of Place*, Farnham, Surrey: Ashgate, pp. 203–18.

Shenhav, Y. (2007), 'Why not "The Occupation", preface', *Theory and Criticism*, 31, Winter, pp. 5–10.

Sibley, D. (1995), *Geographies of Exclusion: Society and Difference in the West*, London and New York: Routledge.

Silverstein, M. (1976), 'Shifters, linguistic categories and cultural description', in K. H. Basso and H. B. Selby (eds), *A Meaning in Anthropology*, Albuquerque: University of New Mexico Press, pp. 11–55.

Tzfadia, E. (2006), 'When the logic of late capitalism meets the logic of ethnonationalism: An exhibition review of "Separation"', *Hagar: Studies in Culture, Polity and Identities*, 7:1, pp. 49–54.

Tzfadia, E. and Yacobi, H. (2011), *Rethinking Israeli Space: Periphery and Identity*, London: Routledge.

Yacobi, H. and Cohen, S. (eds) (2007), הפרדה: הפוליטיקה של המרחב בישראל (*Separation: The Politics of Space in Israel*), Tel Aviv: Xargol and Am Oved.

Yacobi, H., Ventura, J. and Danzig, S. (2016), 'Walls, enclaves and the (counter) politics of design', *Journal of Urban Design*, 21:4, pp. 481–94.

Yiftachel, O. (2006), *Ethnocracy: Land and Identity Politics in Israel/Palestine*, Philadelphia, PA: University of Pennsylvania Press.

Zandberg, E. (2005), 'Separation seems to have spread everywhere', *Haaretz*, 4 August.

11

Visaginas: Looking at the town through photography

Povilas Marozas, Landscape Architect, Lithuania

I have photographed the housing block in Partizanai street during a long stroll through the town's pedestrian boulevards in the winter of 2013. It comes in a series of photographs that were meant to document the contemporary state of Visaginas' architecture and present it to the audience that was not aware of the town's existence. The photographs that I produced before exploring local photographic archival resources and engaging in theory informed photography interpretation reflect uncritical and detached engagement with the town's architecture. At the time I was fascinated by the exotic character of the place and it led me to picture the buildings in a peculiar manner while adopting certain popular standards of photographing aged post-Soviet environments. Omitting any signs of life, exploiting particular weather conditions and meticulously framing the view of the buildings enabled me to present Visaginas in a similar manner to the works of many photographers documenting similar post-Soviet environments.

Visaginas – the youngest town in Lithuania – is a strange example of late Soviet modernist urban settlement. It was conceived as a satellite town for the once most powerful atomic power plant in the world, and for the past four decades it has been home to a culturally mixed crowd of engineers and builders who had been operating the nuclear facilities until its closure in 2009. This top-down planned Soviet town was erected in only two decades and its full life-cycle of building and inhabitation has been witnessed by only one generation.

Figure 1: Povilas Marozas, *Housing blocks in Partizanai street in Visaginas*, 2013.

The town of Visaginas (initially called Sniečkus) is a material remnant of architectural and urban regimes of a specific historical period – the years when Lithuania was part of the Soviet Union (1944–1990). When, in the early 1970s, plans for a new atomic power plant on the shores of Lake Drūkščiai emerged, all decisions relating to design, construction, operation and service of the facilities were centralized in Moscow due to its scale and strategic significance. The project's scale quickly attracted the attention of professional engineers and skilled builders who were loyal to the ministry responsible for managing and delivering the construction of the nuclear power complex. People who worked across similar sites spread in the vast territories of the USSR started pouring in while the involvement of the local population was very limited. The first settlers moved in on Lenin's birthday in 1977 and the first reactor of Ignalina Nuclear Power Station came online in 1983.

Built in the middle of formerly uninhabited woodlands, Sniečkus was an amalgam of a mechanically reproduced version of Soviet mono-industrial towns and locally specific architectural interventions that were led by ambitions to adapt to the peculiarities of the landscape. With the local architectural community fighting against the gigantic designs of Leningrad's team of architects and claiming their rights to contribute to the development of the town, initial aspirations to build a consistent Soviet modernist urban settlement deviated into a far looser assembly of different buildings. Housing blocks of various shapes and materials were arranged in a few distinct layouts with oversized pedestrian avenues and vehicular roads bisecting the town. The subsequent development slowed down due to delays in the construction of the nuclear power plant itself and came to a final halt at the outset of the newly independent Republic of Lithuania in 1990. The original plans to build the settlement double in size were never implemented.

Visaginas was conceived as a stark imperial gesture. This got broken amidst the fall of the Soviet Union and the town's transformation was subsequently driven by a market economy and new political regroupings. As a result, the town has been vulnerable to historical circumstances and marked by frictions and conflicts between various parties. During Soviet Rule the initial plans were challenged by local specialist institutions such as Lithuanian Academy of Sciences and professional architecture bodies. After the Chernobyl Power Station disaster in 1986 it attracted the attention of wider publics when a local environmentalist group was joined by an emerging nationalist political movement and successfully protested against the construction of the third reactor. The flip of powers at the outset of Lithuania's independence in 1990 was marked by a far more serious confrontation, when the administrative bodies of Ignalina Nuclear Power Plant declared civil disobedience in response to newly constituted laws instituted by the Supreme Council of the Republic of Lithuania. They subsequently passed a resolution that demanded the resignation of Lithuania's government. When these conflicts were resolved by Russian officials as many as 6,000 people left the town and the new country, most heading east (Kavaliauskas 2003: 303–05).

After Lithuania's declaration of independence, substantial political decisions were taken concerning the nuclear complex. Due to the doubts of the international scientific community about the safety of the Ignalina nuclear facilities, in 1994 Lithuania accepted funds from the European Bank for Reconstruction and Development agreeing to conditions that precluded the country from exploiting the power station after its exploitation date expired in 2010 (Storm 2014: 90–91). Later, the country's negotiation for EU membership was also conditional on the European community's insistence that all the units of the power station would be closed. Parliament approved the plans to close the first reactor in 2005 and to fully cease operating the plant by the end of the same decade. Today, with the second reactor shut down, this remote and ethnically diverse urban settlement of less than 21,000 people is involved in the long process of decommissioning the nuclear facilities, while its built environment is eternally stuck in the Soviet past and slowly deteriorates amidst the dense woodlands of this north eastern part of Lithuania.

Ever since I arrived in Visaginas in 2007 scouting for a more exotic site for my university architectural design assignment, I have been fascinated by the way in which the lives of the people who live there are intertwined with its architecture. I set out to explore this relationship in greater depth during my architectural history studies a few years later by examining various photographs of the town. Due to the

Figure 2: Vasilij Chiupachenko, *Construction site of the first school of Visaginas*, 1977. Image sourced from V. Chiupachenko archive currently held at Visagino Kultūros Centras, Lithuania.

inconsistency of local archival sources and the inaccessibility of archives within the institutions responsible for planning, constructing and administrating the town, the photographs of Visaginas made by people who lived there, or visited the town, emerged as significant primary source material to work with. Further, with only one scholarly history of the town, written within a specific institutional and ideological context and mostly relying on the memories of people who live there, photographic images offered additional evidence to be interrogated (Kavaliauskas 1999, 2003).

Vasilij Chiupachenko depicts a dynamic scene at the construction site of the first school of Visaginas. The locally based teacher-photographer captures a mixed crowd of builder-troops, men and women builders, levellers and engineers, assembling and arranging the entrance area of the school in the shadow of the construction crane. Some of the workers are laying concrete blocks in front of the main door while others supervise them. Some are levelling, planning their work or consulting the drawings, whilst others are resting or simply wandering aimlessly. As the soldier in the right side of the image looks into the camera, the viewing subject itself appears as a part of the crowd, an active participant who also has certain duties in this complex process. Photographed at eye-level this image presents a close-up view of the building processes as evolving in various construction sites around the town. Although today the image could be seen as proof of inefficient working methods of construction in the Soviet Union where shortage of sophisticated building technology was compensated by excessive human labour, with this image the photographer celebrates the communal efforts of the crowd in generating architecture. He depicts the reciprocal relationship between people and the built environment, where architecture is being produced by the crowd and the crowd itself is produced by the architecture.

The works of the few photographers from Visaginas included in various local publications suggested consistent first-hand documentary accounts that captured this Soviet modernist settlement throughout the different stages of its development (Kavaliauskas 1999, 2003; Bogdanovich and Bogdanovich 2009). The photographs taken by Vasilij Chiupachenko, a local teacher, picturing the everyday life of the town during the first few decades of its construction, and a similar account of Visaginas in the late 2000s by Vitaly Bogdanovich seemed to display a clear visual narrative of the place. But only after finding the book, *Raktai į Lietuvos miestus* (*Keys to the Cities of Lithuania*) by Lithuanian photographer, Gintaras Česonis, which showed images of a completely different version of the town, and, subsequently, the photographs of Visaginas' Hotel made by Polish-Swiss photographer Nicolas Grospierre, did the idea of the unbiased and neutral nature of any visual narrative about the town of Visaginas became evidently questionable. Seen within the complex context of the Visaginas' history, the apparent partiality of these views requires more comprehensive study of the peculiar circumstances within which they were made. Theoretical ideas developed by artist and writer, Victor Burgin, published in *Thinking Photography* (Burgin 1982), offer relevant critical tools to engage with this visual material and examine its bias.

Burgin proposes that the object of photographic theory should include practices of signification and suggests that photographic images should not be analysed by addressing an objective reality reproduced by the photograph, but rather by interrogating 'the relationships between visually apparent functions of image elements as they come together to constitute a dominant social discourse' (Streitberger 2009: xvi–xvii). He highlights the significance of hidden ideological contexts of production, dissemination and reception of photographic images and employs theories of semiology and psychoanalysis to explore it.

In an essay, 'Photographic practice and art theory' (Burgin 1982: 39–83), Burgin situates photography within the realm of language. The author suggests that photography operates within the wider intelligible system of relationships that are organized by the use of language and claims that:

> Forms of artefacts, as much as forms of language, serve to communicate ideologies [...]. All that constitutes reality for us is, then, impregnated with

meanings. These meanings are the contingent products of history and in sum reflect our ideology.

(Burgin 1982: 46–47)

In order to decipher how these meanings, 'contingent products of history', are constructed through photographic representation, Burgin suggests to employ semiotical methods to analyse forms of communication in photography. By drawing on the works of Roland Barthes and Umberto Eco, Burgin probes the codes of analogy by which 'photographs denote objects in the world, the codes of connotation through which denotation serves a secondary system of meanings, and the "rhetorical" codes of juxtaposition of elements within a photograph or between different but adjacent photographs' (Burgin 1982: 143).

While a proposed linguistic analysis of photographs provides a productive mode of interpreting the ideological intentions behind certain images, the author further addresses the social and historical contexts within which the practice of decoding is carried out by employing psychoanalytic theory. In his essays, 'Looking at photographs' (Burgin 1982: 142–53) and 'Photography, phantasy, function' (Burgin 1982: 177–216), Victor Burgin considers how the viewing subject is constituted through photographic practice and centres on the analysis of the relationship between the subject's psychic investments and ideology, which unfolds in the act of looking at a photographic image. Without denying the intentionality in image production and its embededness within specific ideologic contexts, Burgin points to the significance of the active role of the reader whose psychic and social formations are always at play in the construction of meaning of a photographic work. The author explains that each individual photograph

> becomes the point of origin of a series of psychic 'pans' and 'dissolves', a succession of metonymies and metaphors which transpose the scene of the photograph to the spaces of the 'other scene' of the unconscious, and also, most importantly, the scene of popular preconscious: the scene of discourse inseparable from language.
>
> (Burgin 1982: 211–12)

If in his previous writings Burgin attended to the claim that image is ideological message, here he is preoccupied with the way this message is transmitted and how, at the level of decoding, the subject recognizes the discourse as its own. As a result, the author claims that 'it is neither theoretically necessary nor desirable to make psychologist assumptions concerning the intensions of the photographer', but rather suggests to attend to 'the pre-constituted field of discourse which is the substantial "author" here' (Burgin 1982: 207).

Burgin's comprehensive inquiry into the ideology at work in the production of meaning through the creation, dissemination and reading of photographs appears to be particularly important when interpreting the photographic images of Visaginas – a site where different ideologies, powers and worldviews have been continuously clashing and where one's own position in relation to them defines particular ways of seeing the town through photography. In my analysis of the photography of the town, I focused on the photographic works that were carried out either as part of an individual photographer's initiative or as comparatively unrestrained artistic projects without, or limited, intermediate institutional conditions. Following Burgin, I attempted to locate the photographic practices of Vasilij Chiupachenko, Vitaly Bogdanovich, Gintaras Česonis and Nicolas Grospierre within specific ideological and institutional contexts and to explore how the varying adopted positions in relation to the photographed subject – the town of Visaginas – conditioned the way it was represented through their images.

Figure 3: Nicolas Grospierre, Olga Mokrzycka, *Hotel Visaginas*, 2003.

The linguistic/semiotic mode of analysis proposed by Burgin was particularly important for interpreting the photographs taken by the two local cameramen, Vasilij Chiupachenko and Vitaly Bogdanovich. Their reportage images that were made during two different periods in Visaginas' history displayed direct ties to the contemporary official culture. Vasilij Chiupachenko's photography of the town voluntarily documented everything between the late 1970s and early 1990s, from the erection of the nuclear power plant, to Visaginas' buildings, to the everyday life of the town's community, public events and visits by important party members. He celebrated the construction of the town. By presenting the built environment as an outcome of the heroic communal efforts of the people with the socialist state, he promoted the successful implementation of the communist project. A few decades later, in the late 2000s, Vitaly Bogdanovich attempted to document material symbols of the town's expiring identity in the face of the closure of the Ignalina Nuclear Power Plant. In these images he contrasted the town's ageing architecture with the colourful activities of its youth, in order to negotiate a space for their future under new historical circumstances. Albeit documentary in their nature, these works that captured the intimate relationship between the people of Visaginas and the town's built environment share the same tendency to foreground the collective achievements of the town. Both photographers were careful to select their subjects and the occasions and to locate viewing subjects in a particular way in order to display recognizably collective versions of town.

Swiss-Polish photographer, Nicolas Grospierre, photographed the interior spaces of Aukštaitija hotel for his project *Hotel Visaginas* with Olga Mokrzycka in 2003. In one of the rigidly composed photographs of this prominent building, the photographer depicts the deteriorating leisure venue's two old bowling lanes tightly framed by the walls on each side. An excessively decorated ceiling of a strict diagonal grid wood pattern is rhythmically interrupted by the fluorescent lamps. The unusual sport device sharply contrasts with the dullness of standardised materials, so widely used in most modernist Soviet buildings. The symmetry of this composition is interrupted by dismantled floor tiles stacked to the side of one of the lanes, indicating that this place has seen its best days. Although the photographer applies strict rules of framing, the previous uses of this room are conjured. The unusual venue under Soviet rule would not be accessible to everyone and must have been used by important party members during visits. The viewer is offered entrance to the exclusive pastime activities of nomenklatura officers, high-rank party members, engineers and other significant guests of the town. The author uses equipment and techniques widely applied to the photography of new buildings. If commercial architectural photography aims to represent sterile and neat newness of the built environment to celebrate the work of masters, excluding any signs of use, in Grospierre's work the specifically staged sterility draws attention to the former inhabitants that shaped the architecture. The building and its interiors are presented as the material evidence of the past where all the traces of the present have to be suppressed. The photographer creates an uncanny repetition of details that reappear in different images in the Hotel series. This sense of uncanny strangeness is reinforced by the absence of human subjects and by the abstraction of these scenes. Grospierre offers a detached and voyeuristic view of the past petrified in architecture.

By contrast with Chiupachenko and Bogdanovich, Gintaras Česonis and Nicolas Grospierre have drawn a far darker picture of Visaginas by seeking to engage with latent registers of the fantasy, memory and knowledge of the viewing subjects. By abstracting the town's architecture and capturing lonely human figures, or omitting any signs of life altogether, both photographers tried to evoke associations to particular pasts and to represent Visaginas as a mysteriously alien and exotic site for the pleasurable consumption of a disengaged viewer. Whether consciously or not, both Gintaras Česonis and Nicolas Grospierre employed what Burgin calls the 'popular preconscious' of the viewing subject, in order to create and control the specific atmospheres of their photographs. Stripped of any clues of the actual and contemporary character of the town, and not pretending to provide documentary accounts, more than anything the works of these photographers aim to capture viewers' projections of what could be called a failed Soviet utopia onto a distorted view of Visaginas architecture.

While the theorized interpretation of the photographs of Visaginas suggests a constructive way to question the seemingly indexical character of this visual material, it also inevitably points to the obscure nature of the process of interpretation that one performs while looking at the photographs – as a viewer and as a researcher. I turn to Donna Haraway's ideas on embodied knowledge production and Irit Rogoff's notion of criticality to attend to this peculiar problem and to outline a potential strategy to address it in relation to this active visual interpretation.

In her seminal text, *Situated Knowledges: The Science Question in Feminism and the Privilege of Partial Perspective* (Haraway 1988), Donna Haraway attempts to define feminist objectivity in scientific discourse. She uses the metaphor of vision to insist on the embodied nature of knowledge production. The author opposes the myth of neutral vision – 'the power to see and not to be seen, to represent while escaping representation' – and instead calls for 'the particularity and embodiment of all vision' that 'allows us to construct a usable, but not an innocent, doctrine of objectivity' (Haraway 1988: 582–83). The embodiment of vision points to the significance of positioning in knowledge production: embodied, partial, locatable critical knowledges conscious of their own limitations as opposed to selfless, unlocatable and therefore irresponsible knowledge claims that are unable to be called into account. Positioning implies responsibility and accountability of the knowing self and locates the production of knowledge within a wider political and ethical domain. It also underlines the importance of webs of connections through which shared practices of objectivity are performed.

Haraway's ideas of embodiment of vision and knowledge production relate to the concept of criticality developed by writer and cultural theorist, Irit Rogoff. In her writings and talks on academic knowledge production in the cultural field, Rogoff suggests the use of the term, 'criticality', to mark a reflective shift from the analytical to the performative mode of observation, where meanings are not excavated but instead take place in the present. She claims that within a relatively short period of time,

> we have moved from criticism which is a form of finding fault and of exercising judgement according to a consensus of values, to critique which is examining the underlying assumptions that might allow something to appear as a convincing logic, to criticality which is operating from an uncertain ground of actual embeddedness.
>
> (Rogoff 2006: 8)

According to Rogoff, within the logic of criticality 'we are always already embedded in the problematic we are dealing with, living out its conditions, sharing its effects while being able to think it through' (Rogoff 2006: 8).

In the light of Donna Haraway's call for visualizing practices aware of their own partiality with their claims answerable to a wider community of knowing selves and Irit Rogoff's proposed performative mode of criticality that acknowledges its entanglement in problematics that it seeks to critique, I use my own photographic work of Visaginas as part of my research methodology that addresses the inevitable flaws of interpretative processes. While the four photographic accounts of Visaginas present valuable archival material for interpreting the town's past, it is hard to dismiss the hidden agendas behind each of the authors' work. And although theorized interpretation of these works provides the critic with deeper insights into certain hidden contexts of their production and, in turn, presents a constructive way of confronting their 'neutral' status, it is through the act of collecting these reflections into a specific narrative that the meaning is created. If Victor Burgin is right by claiming that '*it is neither theoretically necessary nor desirable to make psychologist assumptions concerning the intentions of the photographer*; it is the pre-constituted field of discourse which is the substantial 'author' here, photograph and photographer are its products; and, in the act of seeing, so is the viewer' (Burgin 1982: 207, original emphasis), then the specific contexts within which the interpretation of these images takes place should not be left obscure.

Having argued that photography is a mode of knowledge production that is an embodied and situated practice, my photographic work enables self-reflexive questioning of the town's social/political struggles as a form of interpretative critique, alongside more conventional text as theorized interpretation. While the photographs made by the four selected photographers of Visaginas provide rich source material for critical analysis, my 'active interpretation', which is itself situated and performed within other ideological and institutional contexts, not only encompasses but also extends this source material into a research narrative. I step between the position of interpreter of visual material and that of photographer, and my own photographs of Visaginas aim to actualize my adopted position towards the town, from which I make my theorized interpretation, while avoiding taking sides. I invite readers to critically reflect upon the contexts within which my own interpretations are situated. They are not intended to directly respond to the other photographs, but including my images of Visaginas alongside those made

Figure 4: Povilas Marozas, *Lift hall in hotel 'Aukštaitija' in Visaginas*, 2013.

by the other photographers, I seek to activate my position from which I interpret their work. Taken together, the photographs visually 'look at' the town in order to animate and realize distinctive, albeit partial versions of it.

The image made at the lift hall of Visaginas' hotel 'Aukštaitija' captures a fragment of the interior and shows children toys stored next to fake antique cabinet with small Lithuanian flag placed on top of it. The twelve storey hotel – one of the largest buildings at the centre of the town – has been sparsely inhabited over past decade due to the closure of Ignalina Nuclear Power Plant. During my stay there I was fascinated by the eerie atmosphere of the empty building, but here my attention was drawn to subtle signs of Visaginas' troubles of defining its own identity. After Lithuania's declaration of independence in 1990 there were more and more Lithuanian's taking part in town's administration and Visaginas underwent certain symbolic integration into the structures of the nation state. The official nationalist narratives were projected onto the former new socialist industrial town and the subtle signs of uneasy adoption of new national character while neglecting the origins of the settlement are visible in various spaces of the town. Made during one of the first study trips to Visaginas this work subsequently led me to document these barely visible signs of change in public spaces of the town.

Acknowledgements

This text was written during the author's Architectural History studies at the Bartlett School of Architecture, University College London, UK. The author wishes to thank Professor Jane Rendell for her guidance and help carrying out the research.

REFERENCES

Bogdanovich, T. and Bogdanovich, V. (2009), *Visaginas: Europos Miestai. Goroda Yevropy. European Cities*, Visaginas: Media Primus.

Borden, I. (2007), 'Imaging architecture: The uses of photography in the practice of architectural history', *The Journal of Architecture*, 12:1, pp. 57–77.

Burgin, V. (ed.) (1982), *Thinking Photography*, Houndmills and London: Macmillan Press Ltd.

Česonis, G. et al. (2010), *Raktai i Lietuvos Miestus (Keys to the Cities of Lithuania)*, Kaunas: Miesto IQ.

Cinis, A., Drēmaitē, M. and Kalm, M. (2008), 'Perfect representations of Soviet planned space: Mono-industrial towns in the Soviet Baltic republics in the 1950s–1980s', *Scandinavian Journal of History*, 33:3, pp. 226–46.

Drėmaitė, M., Petrulis, V. and Tutlytė, J. (2012), *Architektūra Sovietineʹje Lietuvoje*, Vilnius: Dailės Akademijos Leidykla.

Elwall, R. (2004), *Building with Light. The International History of Architectural Photography*, London and New York: Merrell Publishers and RIBA.

Haraway, D. (1988), 'Situated knowledges: The science question in feminism and the privilege of partial perspective', *Feminist Studies*, 14:3, pp. 575–99.

Higgott, A. and Wray, T. (eds) (2012), *Camera Constructs: Photography, Architecture and the Modern Cities*, Farnham, Surrey and Burlington, VT: Ashgate.

Kavaliauskas, A. (1999), *Visaginas (1975–1999)*, Vilnius: Jandrija.

Kavaliauskas, A. (2003), *Visaginas. Istorijos Fragmentai (1972–2002)*, Vilnius: Jandrija.

Kavaliauskas, A. (2009), *Po Išskleistais Gervės Sparnais*, Utena: Utenos Indra.

Nilsen, M. (2009), *Architecture in Nineteenth-Century Photographs*, Farnham, Surrey and Burlington, VT: Ashgate.

Rogoff, I. (2006), 'Academy as potentiality', in A. Nollert et al. (eds), *A.C.A.D.E.M.Y.*, Berlin: Revolver, pp. 1–9.

Storm, A. (2014), *Post-Industrial Landscape Scars*, Basingstoke and New York: Palgrave Macmillan.

Streitberger, A. (ed.) (2009), *Situational Aesthetics: Selected Writings by Victor Burgin*, Leuven, Belgium: Leuven University Press.

12

Writing with pictures: Reconsidering Aby Warburg's *Bilderatlas* in the context of architectural scholarship, education and Google Images

Willem de Bruijn, Arts University Bournemouth

Introduction

Within the context of evaluating the role of the visual in architectural scholarship and education, it is necessary, so this chapter argues, to revisit the work of art historian Aby Warburg (1866–1929). Necessary, because the increasingly image-driven acquisition of knowledge today demands that we as scholars and educators develop a critical method of analysis based on images. Warburg's work, in particular his famous *Bilderatlas Mnemosyne* (known in English as the *Mnemosyne Atlas*), pioneered a means of 'doing' art history by juxtaposing images (mostly photographic reproductions of works of art) mounted onto large panels to build an argument in pictorial terms (Warburg 2003). Warburg's primary concern, in building the *Bilderatlas*, was to trace the survival (*Nachleben*) of ancient pictorial motifs (*Pathosformeln*) formed of gestures, flowing garments and other features expressive of strong emotions in the art and visual culture of the Italian Renaissance (van Eck 2012: 138). When Warburg died in 1929, his work on the *Bilderatlas* was unfinished and despite careful documentation, remained for long unpublished (Warburg 2003). Yet Warburg's influence is unmistakable in the development, during the 1970s, of Visual Studies as a discipline, in the related use of the term 'visual culture' (Grafton and Hamburger 2012: 9) and in the use of collage in texts such as John Berger's *Ways of Seeing* (1972) and John Hejduk's *The Silent Witnesses*, a 'photo-essay' first published in 1976 (Søberg 2012: 117–18).

Following the publication of the (unfinished) *Bilderatlas* in 2003, Warburg's work has received greater recognition and widespread critical attention within the domain of art history and cultural theory (Michaud 2007; Didi-Huberman 2011; de Mare 2012; Weigel 2013) – a process that can be traced back to the early 1990s following the first public display of reproductions of the *Bilderatlas* panels in Vienna in 1993 (Weigel 1995). Within the context of architectural history and theory however, Warburg remains a somewhat shadowy figure. For although he wrote very little on architecture, as architectural historian Caroline van Eck points out, Warburg's novel approach to the study of images influenced architectural scholars such as Rudolf Wittkower (who taught at the Warburg Institute), Nikolaus Pevsner and others, who made use of pictorial juxtapositions in support of their writing (van Eck 2012: 134). Yet, as van Eck observes, 'Wittkower and his students by no means exhausted the potential of Warburg's thought for architectural history' (van Eck 2012: 146). Indeed, publications such as Wittkower's *Architectural Principles in the Age of Humanism* (1952) still follow the conventional format of an illustrated book, where the (photographic) image remains in service of the word (van Eck 2012: 136). A similar observation can be made with reference to more recent studies, which often rely on elaborate verbal argumentation to highlight the role of pictures in the mediation or 'production' of architecture (Colomina 1994; Evans 1997; Rattenbury 2002; Pallasmaa 2011). So, to unlock the potential of Warburg's thought for architectural education and scholarship, we shall have to return to the *Bilderatlas* and the immediate context of its construction.

Warburg's Mnemosyne Atlas *(1927–29): Mnemonic collage and pictorial argumentation*

Although Warburg began juxtaposing images as early as 1905 in the context of a lecture on Albrecht Dürer given at a conference in Hamburg, it was not until after his recovery from a period of mental illness in the mid-1920s that he began exploring the technique of 'pictorial argumentation' (*Bildargumentation*) with sustained and critical attention (Fleckner 2012: 1). The collages Warburg created during these years are referred to as *Bilderreihen* (Warburg 2012), which can be translated as *Image-series*, and culminate in the creation of the *Bilderatlas Mnemosyne* (1927–29), which, as the title indicates, is concerned with memory (*mnemosyne* in Greek). Drawing on a vast collection of photographic reproductions of paintings, sculptures, maps and buildings, Warburg explored a variety of themes by placing images in 'suggestive combinations' (Koerner 2012: 104), first on a table and then mounting them onto large panels covered in black cloth. The panels were put on display inside the main reading room of the library that Warburg built as an extension of his home in Hamburg, known today as the Warburg-Haus. The reading room, oval in shape, was the concrete materialization of a *Denkraum*, that is, a mental space or 'thought space' (Didi-Huberman 2012: 55), where ideas in the form of images could physically circulate and be kept in motion as part of a dynamic understanding of history. That is to say, for Warburg, images are not merely mnemonic devices, i.e. visual records of the past prompting a process of recollection; rather, the past survives in them *as* history (see also Weigel 1995: 144). In this respect, Warburg's *Atlas* differs radically from the earlier, narrative-based histories of art exemplified by the work of Johann Joachim Winckelmann and Jacob Burckhardt, for whom images serve as an illustration to a story told in chronological fashion. Warburg, by contrast, used images 'to reveal their interconnected meanings across time and space' (Grafton and Hamburger 2012: 9). Architecture forms an integral part of this attempt to redefine historical thinking. Among the *Bilderreihen* developed by Warburg in 1927, there are two panels that focus on the work of the Florentine architects Filippo Brunelleschi (1377–1446) and Leon Battista Alberti (1404–72) respectively. Although both panels deserve to be looked at more closely, I shall focus here on the Alberti panel (Figure 1), for Warburg elaborates its argument further with a second panel in the *Mnemosyne Atlas*.

Figure 1: Leon Battista Alberti and the Roman Arch (1927). WIA III, 108.7.3 (Heydenreich 2). Copyright and photo: The Warburg Institute, London.

Alberti and the Tempio Malatestiano (c.1453)

Warburg's interest in Alberti forms part of an investigation into the recurrence of the architectural motif of the triumphal Roman arch, illustrated in the top left corner of the collage by a picture of the Arch of Augustus (27 BC) in Rimini, the oldest surviving arch of its kind. Warburg contrasts this early example with pictures of various religious buildings in Italy, including the cathedrals of Parma, Pisa and Orvieto, to trace the 'survival' of the motif in Italian Renaissance architecture. The most important of these, illustrated directly below the Arch of Augustus, is Alberti's Tempio Malatestiano in Rimini, a church dedicated to St Francis but named after the local ruler Sigismondo Pandolfo Malatesta (1417–68), who commissioned Alberti to re-design the church in 1453 and who was later buried in the church. A picture of the medal commemorating Malatesta's commission shows Alberti's original design for the church, which included a Pantheon-like dome that was never built. Warburg thus emphasizes the historical continuity between Alberti's design and the architecture of ancient Rome whilst mapping the very thought process by which the Tempio can be understood as the subtle transformation of a religious building (the original church) into a pagan structure (Malatesta's 'mausoleum').

Figure 2: Aby Warburg, *Mnemosyne Atlas* (1929), Panel 25. Copyright and photo: The Warburg Institute, London.

Warburg continues his investigation of Alberti's Tempio Malatestiano with the creation of Panel 25 for the *Bilderatlas* (Figure 2). Views of the exterior and interior of the Tempio are placed in quick succession at the top of the panel, followed by close-up photographs of sculpted reliefs representing allegorical personifications, planetary and other, below. Some of the reliefs are also shown in clusters, which are integrated within the series of photographs meandering across the surface of the panel. This 'meandering', or snake-like movement across the panel, is marked by the widening gaps between the horizontal rows of images and serves to transform our viewing into a form reading that begins in the top left corner and gradually makes its way down (and back up again). This reading unfolds without any reference to a text – it is one. That is to say, it is a way of *narrating* the temple (to the viewer) that allows for an experience that is both mnemonic (a recollection) and concretely spatial, like the building itself. As Michaud points out with reference to this panel:

> One suddenly realizes that the panel constitutes in reality a visit to the temple and is developed like an interior monologue: it is the chronicle of thoughts and associations that went through the historian's [i.e. Warburg's] mind as he worked.
>
> (Michaud 2007: 258)

Panel 25 offers us, in other words, a type of 'mnemonic' presentation of architecture that includes Warburg's own references and associations pointing to other buildings, including the Oratorio di San Bernardino in Perugia, based again on the common architectural motif of the Roman arch. Yet, the focus of Panel 25 is no longer the Roman arch, but the allegorical personifications that appear in the reliefs, consisting predominantly of female figures dressed in loose, flowing garments. These figures are connected by Warburg to the mythical maenad, who appears in a drawing copied from an ancient Roman relief (Figure 3). This ancient motif of the ecstatic girl dancing her way to a sacrificial altar haunts Warburg's entire oeuvre and anchors the panel within the project of the *Atlas* as a whole (Michaud 2007: 28). But with respect to the earlier panel devoted to Alberti, she also serves to draw out with greater force the pagan character of the temple, for her presence is accentuated by a vertical gap to the left of the picture. The maenad thus serves to visually animate the succession of images: placed at a crucial junction in the composition, she creates a literal *turning point* in the meandering arrangement of photographs. And as her arched body performs this turn, she sets the otherwise static images in motion; she ensnares them (and us, viewers) in a dance across the surface of the panel. *She*, then, can be understood as *triumphant* within the triumphal setting of the panel, as she is the one who represents the 'living presence'

Figure 3: The dancing maenad, detail of Panel 25 in Aby Warburg, *Mnemosyne Atlas* (1929). Copyright and photo: The Warburg Institute, London.

(van Eck 2012: 138) within the context of death and its architecture (Malatesta's 'mausoleum').

Google Images: The rise of the online image-atlas

Warburg's argument about the recurrence of paganism in Renaissance architecture could of course have been made verbally and illustrated with pictures, but the collage method serves to keep the interconnections between the buildings visually at play and open to interpretation. This is signalled in Panel 25 by the 'unexplained' entry of the maenad, as she performs a similar role to the figures in animated dress that enter the paintings of Domenico Ghirlandaio (1449–94), which Warburg had studied and for whom they served as evidence for the survival of expressive movement in otherwise motionless pictures (Michaud 2007: 68). Indeed, Warburg's argument about the persistence of pagan elements in Renaissance art and popular culture (i.e. the *Pathosformeln*) hinges on her. To reinforce this point it is useful to compare Panel 25 for a moment with the image-related results of a Google-search for the term 'Tempio Malatestiano' (Figure 4). When we look at the results, it can be noted that many of the images are practically identical to the images used by Warburg. The arrangement of

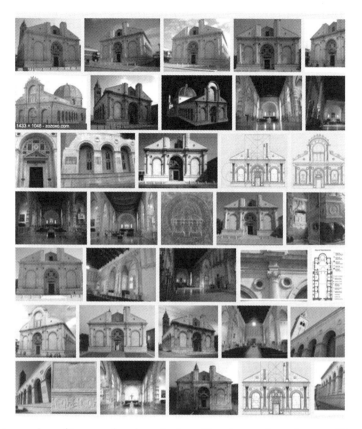

Figure 4: Screenshot of image-related results for a Google-search on the term 'Tempo Malatestiano' (created 24 January 2015).

the images in rows also bears some resemblance to the collage, with the exterior views coming in at the top and the reliefs following below (after some scrolling). Even the commemorative medal made for Malatesta is of the party. Not the dancing maenad, however. She only appears within Warburg's composition, not as an alien figure within the composition, but as the pivotal picture around which his argumentation revolves, both literally and conceptually. Google, being a machine, lacks this ability to make meaningful connections that set images and thought in motion. It can only produce an endless accumulation of the same and self-same images.

Yet, behind each Google-powered search lurk complex mechanisms sifting potentially relevant data, ranging from the use of a general 'Index' (where web-pages are indexed according to key information), algorithms (designed to refine a search) and over two hundred factors determining the order of appearance of results (Google 2016). Moreover, search engines like Google are becoming ever more sophisticated in sifting potentially relevant data among the ever-growing amount of data stored on servers worldwide. Google and other search engines like Bing (which produces very similar results for a Tempio-related search) have created 'advanced' search options and ways of clustering results relating to (what they identify as) key terms associated with the search. For the Tempio Malatestiano these include 'Interior', 'Arial View', 'Duccio', 'Relief' etc. From a scholar's perspective this might seem like a welcome refinement of the tool. Yet, in ramifying the search along key terms, search engines produce atlases within atlases that increase degrees of separation between results. In any event, the likelihood of a maenad ever appearing in any of the Tempio-related results is extremely small. And even if she would appear, by way of some algorithmic miracle or glitch in the system, the dancing maiden would find herself lost among a multitude of similar-looking images, not knowing how to set them in motion.

The comparison between Warburg's *Bilderatlas* and Google Images further serves to highlight the subtleties of Warburg's pictorial method, in particular the way in which the space between the photographs is carefully negotiated, using paperclips to force the closest possible connections between images. This attention to spacing, rhythm, direction and flow, I would argue, defines Warburg's iconography furthermore as a form of writing, in the sense that each panel is also a pictorial *script* that can be read. Online search-results can only ever be viewed, not read. As script, but also as map, Warburg's *Atlas* implies a conception of writing that is different from the conventional articulation of a text using words. This has led some to argue that Warburg's method implies a move away from the word, aimed at freeing scholarship from the laborious 'craft of writing' (Koerner 2012: 105). Yet, when we look at the preparatory sketches that Warburg made for his panels, we sense the presence of a deeper connection between writing and imaging that is preserved in the initial conception of each panel (Figure 5). In these preparatory sketches, the photographic reproductions of works of art appear *as* words (verbal prompts) set within rectangular frames. It would be misleading, I think, to interpret these indexical markers as mere labels. The frequent adjustments in these sketches, visibly indicated by erasures, crosses, arrows and the use of differently coloured pencils, are all evidence of a crafting at work – one that blurs the distinction between writing, sketching and drawing.

Warburg's *Bilderatlas* can therefore be taken as a model for a type of architectural writing that is performed with pictures and drawings as well as with words. Herein also lies the value of Warburg's method as a means to develop arguments through visual means. For, within the humanities and social sciences, the 'visual' is still predominantly a verbal affair: most, if not all, academic publications featuring the term 'visual research' are illustrated textbooks (see, for example, Pink et al. 2006). Of course, verbalizations of research and theory are needed; this chapter forms no exception, but the comparison between Warburg's *Atlas* and Google Images on which my argument hinges, is a visual one. Pictorial forms of argumentation could,

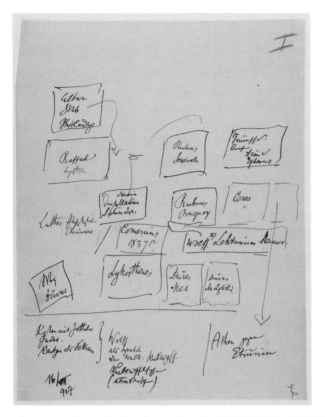

Figure 5: Sketch for a panel from the Heydenreich series (06/07/1927). WIA III, 97.2 fol. 37. Copyright and photo: The Warburg Institute, London.

therefore, redress the balance in favour of visualizations of architectural thought, not just in history and theory, but also in practice. I have designed The Collage Workshop as a response to this problem for the context of architecture education.

The architectural collage: Tool in support of academic writing

Over the past five years I have been exploring ways to develop students' academic writing skills within an architectural education context. I have drawn on Warburg's *Bilderatlas* as a reference to design a workshop aimed at a visual mapping of ideas and themes through the making of a collage (Figure 6). In so doing, I wanted to extend the use of images in the teaching of critical thinking skills (Cordell 2015) and to address students' anxieties around academic writing. The Collage Workshop was introduced as part of History and Theory programmes at undergraduate and postgraduate levels, first at the University of East London, to assist students in the

Figure 6: Tomohiro Himeno, *Gradation with Multi-Layer* (2014). Copyright: Tomohiro Himeno. This collage explores the themes of light and space through the notions of 'gradation' and 'layering' to draw unexpected connections between a range of architectural referents.

development of their undergraduate essays or Master dissertations. Using images as vehicles for thinking about architecture and reflecting on architectural issues has proven beneficial to all students, even to those who already felt comfortable in writing. The Collage Workshop proved to be particularly useful to non-native English speakers, for whom images could assist in the communication of ideas, and so-called 'visual learners' (Bywater 2006; James and Brookfield 2014), students who feel more at home in visually oriented studies, whilst also prompting 'verbal learners' to think about the role of images as other than illustrative of a text.

I encourage the use of Google and other online resources such as ArtStor as a means to find relevant imagery, in addition to more traditional media such as books and magazines. The collected images are then cut out, placed on the sheet of paper and moved around in search of 'suggestive combinations' based on formal similarities, thematic connections and other possible links. I always make sure each student gets the opportunity to discuss combinations in conversation with myself and fellow students. Once the suggestive combinations appear to form a whole, the collage is fixed and pinned up for presentation, at which point a first attempt at verbalizing its 'argument' is made.

As the architectural collage draws on both visual and verbal skills in the building and presentation of an argument, it is aptly placed to negotiate between the activities of designing, drawing and writing that architecture students engage in. In particular the attention given to the positioning, placing and spacing of images serves to develop students' awareness of their argumentative and critical force. In so doing, the collage may reflect a specifically architectural sensibility towards writing that emphasizes the position of the writer in relation to the space or 'site' of their writing (Rendell 2005: 2). Hence, the use of the preposition 'with' in the title of this chapter – writing *with* pictures – is not only a means to bring writing 'into close proximity' (Rendell 2005: 7) with architecture and its representation, but also to account for the pictorial and spatial nature of the architectural text itself (Chmielewska 2013). Moreover, in spatializing the relation between writing and image, the collage also represents a conception of architectural history freed from the 'tyranny' of chronology, acknowledging the co-presence of works of architecture from the past in the present. This type of architectural collage, practised as a visual research methodology, thus offers a means to develop a concrete space to attend to image and writing (and image-writing) that exists outside the digital environment. As the pressure on academia to adapt its working methods, strategies and outputs to the digital environment is growing, this concrete space for an embodied and sustained attention to the image and to writing is ever more relevant.

Conclusion

Although deeply rooted in the historical and biographical moment of its creation, Warburg's *Mnemosyne Atlas* is far from outdated. In a world where images have become a searchable category of information, the *Bilderatlas* stands out as work of 'epistemological significance' representing a radical 'change of method' that concerns images of all kinds (Didi-Huberman 2012: 66). This 'change of method' aims to work directly *with* images, understood as the currency of memory (*mnemosyne*) within human culture. As architecture is increasingly caught up in the circulation of uncontextualized images, we as educators and scholars are called upon to develop visual methodologies that can critically engage with the domain of pictures. This chapter argues for a return to Warburg and his *Bilderatlas*, past and beyond the work of his successors, as a way to develop anew an architectural writing and historiography that situates architecture visually within a broader context of cultural production. Warburg's panels form an invaluable tool in this context for the writing, with pictures, of architectural histories that are visual as well as verbal. So, I think we *can* speak of a 'Warburgian approach to architectural history' (van Eck 2012: 135), but this approach, I argue, will have to gain the status of a *common* as much as a *critical* practice located in a *Denkraum* or space – literally a 'room for thought' (Weigel 1995: 147) – where students can expand their thinking and develop new forms of architectural inquiry.

Acknowledgements

I am particularly grateful to Renée Tobe for supporting and promoting The Collage Workshop as part of the MA Architecture: Interpretation and Theories programme at the University of East London. I would also like to thank all the students who participated in the workshops and who produced such wonderful and intellectually stimulating collages. Thanks are also due to Eckart Marchand and Claudia Wedepohl for their assistance with my research at the Warburg Archive in London.

REFERENCES

Berger, J. (1972), *Ways of Seeing*, London: BBC and Penguin Books.

Bywater, J. (2006), 'Theory after theory: The effective facilitation of verbal-conceptual learning appropriate to creative practitioners', in A. Davies (ed.), *Enhancing Curricula: Contributing to the Future, Meeting the Challenges of the 21st Century in the Disciplines of Art, Design and Communication*, London: The Centre for Learning and Teaching in Art and Design, pp. 444–52.

Chmielewska, E. (2013), 'Writing with the photograph: Espacement, description and an architectural text in action', in A. Dahlgren, N. Lager Vestberg and D. Patersson (eds), *Representational Machine: Photography and the Production of Space*, Aarhus: Aarhus University Press, pp. 83–105.

Colomina, B. (1994), *Privacy and Publicity: Modern Architecture as Mass Media*, Cambridge, MA: The MIT Press.

Cordell, D. M. (2015), *Using Images to Teach Critical Thinking Skills: Visual Literacy and Digital Photography*, Santa Barbara, CA: Libraries Unlimited/ABC-Clio.

Didi-Huberman, G. (2011), *Atlas ou le Gai Savoir Inquiet*, Paris: Les Éditions de Minuit.

—— (2012), 'Warburg's haunted house' (trans. S. Lillis), *Common Knowledge*, 18:1, pp. 50–78.

Eck, C. van (2012), 'The Warburg Institute and architectural history', *Common Knowledge*, 18:1, pp. 134–48.

Evans, R. (1997), *Translations from Drawing to Building and Other Essays*, Cambridge, MA: The MIT Press.

Fleckner, U. (2012), 'Ohne Worte: Aby Warburg's Bildkomparastik zwischen wischenschaftlichem Atlas und kunstpublizistischem Experiment', in A. Warburg, *Bilderreihen und Ausstellungen* (eds Uwe Fleckner und Isabella Woldt), Berlin: Akademie Verlag, pp. 1–18.

Google (2016), 'How Google search works', https://support.google.com/webmasters/answer/70897?hl=en. Accessed 13 November 2016.

Grafton, A. and Hamburger, J. F. (2012), 'Introduction: Warburg's library and its legacy', *Common Knowledge*, 18:1, pp. 1–16.

James, A. and Brookfield, S. D. (2014), *Engaging Imagination: Helping Students Become Creative and Reflective Thinkers*, San Francisco, CA: Jossey-Bass.

Koerner, J. L. (2012), 'Writing rituals: The case of Aby Warburg', *Common Knowledge*, 18:1, pp. 86–105.

Mare, H. de (2012), *Huiselijke Taferelen: De veranderende Rol van het Beeld in de Gouden Eeuw*, Nijmegen: Vantilt.

Michaud, P-A. (2007), *Aby Warburg and the Image in Motion* (trans. S. Hawkes, foreword by G. Didi-Huberman), New York: Zone Books. Originally published as *Aby Warburg et l'image en mouvement* (Éditions Macula, 1998).

Pallasmaa, J. (2011), *The Embodied Image: Imagination and Imagery in Architecture*, Chichester: John Wiley.

Pink, S., Afonso, A. I. and Kürti, L. (eds) (2006), *Working Images: Visual Research and Representation in Ethnography*, London and New York: Routledge.

Rattenbury, K. (ed.) (2002), *This Is Not Architecture: Media Constructions*, London and New York: Routledge.

Rendell, J. (2005), 'Architecture-writing', *The Journal of Architecture*, 10:3, pp. 1–10.

Søberg, M. (2012), 'John Hejduk's pursuit of an architectural ethos', *Footprint*, 6, pp. 113–28.

Warburg, A. (2003), *Der Bilderatlas Mnemosyne*, herausgegeben von Martin Warnke unter Mitarbeit von Claudia Brink, Berlin: Akademie Verlag.

—— (2012), *Bilderreiher und Ausstellungen*, herausgegeben von Uwe Fleckner und Isabella Woldt, Berlin: Akademie Verlag.

Weigel, S. (1995), 'Aby Warburg's *Schlangenritual*: Reading culture and reading written texts' (trans. J. Gaines and R. Wallach), *New German Critique*, 65, pp. 135–53.

—— (2013), 'Epistemology of wandering, tree and taxonomy: The system figuré in Warburg's Mnemosyne project within the history of cartographic and encyclopaedic knowledge', *Images Re-vues*, Hors-série 4, pp. 1–20, http://journals.openedition.org/imagesrevues/2934. Accessed 7 August 2019.

PART III

FILM: AFFINITIES AND APPROPRIATIONS FOR RESEARCHING CONTEMPORARY CULTURE

Figure 3 (from Introduction): Preparation for Las Vegas Deadpan film shoot, Las Vegas, 1968. Photo by LLVRS. Copyright: Princeton University, School of Architecture.

'You don't think, you shoot', she [Scott Brown] says. 'Because by the time you've worked out with yourself why you want that thing, it's gone'.

(Scott Brown cited in Anna Fixsen 2016)

The idea of an affinity between architecture and film is implicit in both *The View from the Road* and *Learning from Las Vegas*. The potentially distracted – cinematic – gaze of the car driver confronts the roadway engineer with the task of framing and directing the automobilized observer's perception of the city: 'The cinema tells its story with dramatic changes in the separation between camera and actor, from close-up to long shot depending on what is being said. So it is one the city highway: the designer can decide what he wants to emphasize – a total skyline, a distinct character, a single landmark – and adjust the viewing distance accordingly. As in the cinema, contrasting distances will keep his sequences legible and eventful' (Lynch *et al.* 1964: 11). Engineer and architect become directors of the gaze. The films produced by Venturi and Scott Brown and their students in the *Learning from Las Vegas* Research Studio attest to this attitude, which makes the visual survey of the existing city a prerequisite for architectural design.

(Stierli 2013: 184)

13

Next to nothing: Psychogeography and the 'film essay'

Gavin Keeney, Independent Scholar, USA, and

David Jones, Deakin University, Australia

Figures 1–8: Dream Line. Stephanie Ho, 'Point Henry' (2014). Video stills, SRL731 Landscape Narrating & Meaning (Instructor: Gavin Keeney), in association with SRL733 Indigenous Narratives & Processes (Instructor: David Jones), School of Architecture & Built Environment, Deakin University, Geelong, Victoria, Australia. All images © Stephanie Ho. Full video available at https://vimeo.com/147295123.

Protocols of the 'Third Landscape'

The term Third Landscape does not allude to the Third World, but to the Third Estate. It is a referral to Abbé Sieyès' question: 'What is the Third Estate? Everything – What role has it played to date? – None – What does it aspire to? – Something'.

(Clément 2009)

Graduate of the prestigious L'École Nationale Supérieure de Paysage (School of Landscape Architecture) at Versailles, Gilles Clément was more than willing to sit around for hours, days, weeks and/or months in his Planetary Garden at La Vallée, Creuse, France, watching the wind and sun cross the meadows stirring the foliage and illuminating the grasses and wildflowers. Sometimes to do next to nothing is to do more than meets the eye. Indeed, landscape architects might take a page from Clément's 'book', in particular the film *Le jardin en mouvement* (Comte 2013), and try sitting around observing '*la belle nature*' (a term derived from the theory of the Fine Arts associated with French philosopher Charles Batteux's *Les beaux arts réduits à un même principe* [1746]), versus installing yet another utterly de-natured, ethically bereft landscape, typically requiring one form or another of permanent life support (e.g. irrigation, maintenance, replacement and other costly measures) divorced from nature. Such is indicative of the rather sad state of affairs today for urban landscape making, in particular, that which extends outward towards exurbia, the suburbs, and – one day soon enough – to the last vestiges of semi-wild or semi-domesticated 'Third Landscape' (Clément 2003) left on the planet.

> Picking up the threads of thinker and clergyman Sieyès' question, 'Qu'est-ce que le tiers-état?' ('What is the Third Estate?'), as embodied in his 1789 political pamphlet, Clément has appropriated Sieyès' argument that the Third Estate constituted a complete nation within itself – which had no need for the 'dead weight' of the two other orders, the first and second estates of the clergy and aristocracy – and reinterpreted it as human-influenced landscape transformative periods. While Sieyès believed that the French people wanted genuine representatives in the Estates-General, equal representation to the other two orders taken together, and votes taken by heads and not by orders, Clément perceives that such is 'the sum of the space left over by man to landscape evolution – to nature alone', it is 'a privileged area of receptivity to biological diversity'
>
> (Clément 2016)

That which manifests meaning and spirit in landscape imbued with post-industrial archaeology and ruin often struggles to address place, ecology and Indigenous culture. Industrialization has mass-commodified cities into huge de-humanized structures in eclectic forms, shapes and materials to service progress and consumerism. What does that have to say for most so-called modernist landscape-architectural practice, present and past?

Clément's concept of 'Third Landscape' would seem to include a valorization of what Dutch architectural theorist and urbanist Rem Koolhaas once called 'junkspace', which 'is the residue mankind leaves on the planet. The built [...] product of modernization is not modern architecture but Junkspace. Junkspace is what remains after modernization has run its course or, more precisely, what coagulates while modernization is in progress, its fallout' (Koolhaas 2016). Thus, to Koolhaas every natural protrusion except for one token hill has been levelled in the place that is Singapore:

> There is, Koolhaas writes, no nature left in Singapore; the green of the outside is a planned, parklike greenery identical to the atrium-garden of a corporate headquarters. He predicts that architecture will take us 'beyond the naive assumption that contact with the exterior – so-called reality – is a necessary condition for human happiness'. In case his audience has not yet succumbed, Koolhaas asks, tauntingly: 'Aren't the disadvantages of the exterior – ozone-depleted, carbo-charged, globally heated – by now well established?'
>
> (Wolf 2006)

Thus, this Singaporean landscape is the diaspora of human intervention and industrial mechanization of a landscape. This landscape is an interruption of scenery by technology due to industrialization, echoing the literary tropics of Leo Marx's seminal book, *The Machine in the Garden: Technology and the Pastoral Ideal* (1964).

Ever the contrarian, Koolhaas found refuge in the world of virtuality. This, in turn, cued – in his often over-heated architectural imaginary – the value of 'junkspace'. 'The superficial variety and fundamental monotony of junkspace is, if anything, even more extreme in virtual space. Moreover, the virtual and the physical incarnations support each other in a mutual feedback loop: 'As physical territory is absorbed into junkspace, the glow of the computer and the PDA becomes a cheap replacement for the vanishing natural world' (Wolf 2006).

The protocols of design generally require strenuous moves to justify intervention and to qualify the work *as* 'Landscape Architecture'. Leaving the landscape as a regenerative platform (Roös 2014) or to reinstate its originary nature, whatever that might be perceived to be, or to simply let it die are invariably not options because the discipline's spirit is about positive interventions, epitomized by the American Society of Landscape Architects (ASLA) principles of 'dedication to the public health, safety, and welfare, and recognition and protection of the land and its resources' (ASLA 2015). This is utility combined with American 'Manifest Destiny' writ large. Whether this also inflates the cost and enriches all concerned is a moot point. One cannot argue for leaving things alone with those who prefer to impose their will on natural processes – especially if such versions of economic determinism are enforced by the design professions proper.

John Dixon Hunt (2014) may call all landscape-architectural interventions 'feigned truth' (*pace* Shakespeare), but that hardly excuses the misappropriations of the given for profitable and/or arrogant purposes. 'McHarg concluded that "processes are expressive" and "natural processes are deterministic, they respond to [nature's] laws", and that humans are fractious disturbers (McHarg 1966). All landscape architecture is essentially and *excitedly* a "lie", a falsehood, or what Shakespeare calls a "feigned truth"' (Hunt in Grant 2014, emphasis added).

If contemporary urban landscapes are any sign, most instances of urban natural processes are now proverbial dead horses – to be flogged from time to time, but also ceremonially bemoaned, even if the present-day penchant for strategizing urban ecologies presents a fashionable discourse in the guise of another stake driven through the heart of urban nature. The crisis of the urban has now become truly global or planetary (IPCC, UN 2014) and the Great Collapse, with attendant mass migrations, is expected to begin around 2030 (Oreskes and Conway 2014).

Therefore, a shift in pedagogy is called for, and landscape architects must re-consider their collective and individual forms of design praxis using the slenderest means possible. This would require most landscape-architectural and landscape-urbanist works to remain in the realm of the Fine Arts – as proposals (e.g. 'film essays', storyboards) versus realized projects. It would require a voluntary refusal to participate in the last conquests of what's left of so-called undisturbed or 'wild' nature and would, paradoxically, give new life to morally and ethically challenged design professions through a revivification of purely theoretical work.

'Asymptomatic ellipses'

'Asymptomatic ellipses' in design are tell-tale *caesuras*, or semaphores towards a psychogeographical summary of possible ways out of the current stalemate through new theoretical paradigms. Such is illustrated by the accompanying set of still images (Figures 1–8) drawn from a student video, by Stephanie Ho, part of inquiries that evolved in a trimester-long Master's seminar entitled 'Landscape Narrating & Meaning', conducted at Deakin University, Australia, in 2014. The premise of such intentional caesuras is to erase or minimize narration, and permit things to speak for themselves. This does not, however, exclude subjectivity. In fact, subjectivity comes to the foreground in Ho's Point Henry video, in the form of a posse of hooded figures prowling the post-industrial site (and strangely suggestive of students conducting 'field research'). In other student videos associated with this project, subjectivity inhabited the middle or far ground of design, in a manner similar to the mysterious, neoclassical paintings of Nicolas Poussin. Notably, Ho's video opens with a quote from Edmund Burke's famous treatise on the Sublime, *A Philosophical Enquiry into the Origin of Our Ideas of the Sublime and Beautiful* (1757).

These video investigations focused upon a semi-naturalistic, industrialized waterfront site in Geelong. Deakin's Waterfront Campus affords distant views northeast across Corio Bay to the low-lying Point Henry Peninsula, a site effectively recently 'abandoned' by Alcoa Australia after 50 years of aluminium smelting. The now-decommissioned industrial enclave became the centre of the design inquiries – Alcoa being the sole inhabitant of the rather unusual north-facing peninsula. The seminar was conducted in tandem with a parallel seminar entitled 'Indigenous Narratives & Processes', and several of the video projects were informed by stories that the Point Henry site under investigation is a segment of an extant Aboriginal dream line overseen by the *Wadawurrung* community of the *Kulin* Nation (Powell et al. 2019). The resultant 'film essays' (versus site or master plans), as asymptomatic ellipses, provide gaps in normative research as such, but are productive, *as gaps*, of something normally seen only in peripheral vision, as mirage.

As the current generation of up-and-coming designers of the built environment grapple with the various protocols of sustainable projects in the face of climate change, social and economic chaos, and attendant cultural issues, it is not surprising to find many projects today premised on the discursive and non-discursive dialectic of the 'film essay', tacitly invoking elements from the history of the 'film essay', from Jean-Luc Godard and Chris Marker to Tacita Dean and Harun Farocki.

The *idea* of the 'film essay', inaugurated by a 1948 essay by Alexandre Astruc on the camera as a type of stylus that writes with light (Astruc [1948] 1968), has since the 1960s been re-positioned in-between documentary and art-house filmmaking. Chris Marker, who more or less perfected the form in the 1950s and early 1960s, passed this 'essay' form on to a new generation represented foremost by Dean and Farocki. The signature discordant harmony of word and image in the Markerian 'film essay', while dark and often forbidding, is also consistent with the intellectual rites of passage for such works. Thus, discursive aspects (even if minimized) are positioned against an existentialist register (i.e. lived experience or potential lived experience) that invokes the age-old dyadic construction, Thanatos/Eros (Death/Desire).

While hardly based in either Structuralist (i.e. linguistic) or Freudian (i.e. psychoanalytical) theory, the appropriation of the 'film essay' in design studies has a type of embedded history that teases forth unconscious or half-conscious arguments for and against the general or specific programmatic and utilitarian biases of modern environmental design.

Thanatos and Eros, in turn, as foundational and, perhaps, psychological and psychogeographical coordinates for the development of the vision plan, lead (as they do in the film-essayists noted above) to Thanatos and Logos. Arguably of a higher order or modality (intelligibility *plus* sensibility), this semi-abstract and semi-archaic idealist function, embedded in cultural production, has been more or less discredited through postmodernist disputation with master narratives and/or authorized histories. Yet this dynamic function ('X') is symptomatic of many of the unresolved problems associated with cultural production as cultural heritage, insofar as the presence and supposed superiority of the word has haunted both progressive and regressive forms of ideology and ideation since at least Augustine – or Plato.

The word, when positioned as paradigmatic (versus merely syntagmatic), and the ideological or ideational, when considered from a non-repressive perspective (e.g. as neo-platonic ideality), counters the idolatry of the image used to circumvent and, paradoxically, de-nature the word and quite often the world in the process.

Yet the word here must also be understood at the level of the pure idea, versus the level of a mere linguistic sign or part of an imposed ideological formation. In this sense, as in the film essays of Godard and Marker, the word is held in tension with the image, while in the artistic and theoretical matrix of the 'film essay' neither typically is privileged.

The existential register operates as a field in which the classical figural elements of design are weighed though not fully deployed. They are, in fact, *critically withheld* – and the resulting work resembles the classic 'open work' (which, in turn, justifies the term *vision plan*). Initially there is generative hesitancy, while there is also an underlying nobility and strength through resistance to the coded visual language of environmental design as the production of commercial or cultural property per se.

The non-discursive image

The apparent non-discursivity of the avant-garde image deployed in service to landscape-architectural production that nominally eschews programmatic concerns has a quiet and even secret relationship to another order of discursivity that is existentialist, or which connotes subjective versus objective (projective) states – viz. identity per se versus sociocultural production.

This tension in the image, in part, depends on the situational spirit of the singular image within design presentations – e.g. as part of a 'film essay' or as stand-alone still image used in more conventional design media. Pages from *Vogue* in both 1997 and 2015 oddly illustrate the premises of such a theory of the image for Landscape Architecture, while also invoking problems that suggest the missing link for design disciplines, generally, is rigorous self-analysis.

Peter Lindbergh's set of images, entitled 'Couture's Glorious Excess' (1997), of flamboyantly attired female models strolling through European formal gardens served as both an index for the products being sold – a model for exclusivity and wild abandon (or, 'what money can buy') – and a larger, unacknowledged apparatus associated with subjective states and the stylization of the natural world. Similarly, Hermès' Fall/Winter 2015–16 'Flâneur Forever' advertisement campaign, inclusive of a set of images by Harry Gruyaert, of a solitary, elegantly attired female model lingering in the shadowy passageways and narrow *calli* of Venice, Italy, served as touchstone for late-modern *flâneurie*, a practice associated with late nineteenth-century Paris and *fin-de-siècle* Parisian decadence – *flâneurie* generally reducible to 'wandering aimlessly'.

In Lindbergh's case, the timeless imagery is mysteriously, by association, applicable to modernist and anti-modernist theories of milieu and anti-milieu – e.g. the highly discursive readings of environments, habitats, speciation and biomimicry associated with French Surrealism and its sociopolitical discontents. In the case of Gruyaert's imagery, the entire history of the urban *flâneur* is invoked, in addition to all of the problems associated with so-called public and private urban space, past and present. As exemplary images from contemporary media – i.e. fashion media – these images show that the mid-twentieth-century Situationist conception of psychogeography is intimately related to the psychological ambitions of modern advertising, at least in retrospect. Yet biomimicry and *flâneurie* are directly appropriated through the constructive and generative aspects of the image without the attendant discursive baggage. How they operate on the consciousness of the consumer is the entire point, *for* the world of fashion; while how they function as indices for larger, often inscrutable sociocultural states is a matter of how they are existentially assimilated, *for* or *against* haute couture.

Therefore, how might rigorous and reverie-based self-analysis affect the design and production of contemporary landscape architecture?

Foremost in answering this question is the historical curiosity of Frederick Law Olmsted and Calvert Vaux's deployment of a hierarchy of roads in their design of Central Park, New York City, to instil an educative class envy, something that no doubt came over via Vaux from London's royal parks. This flawed, but then liberal-minded manoeuvre is valid today nonetheless as object lesson for measuring how contemporary landscape is also based on inclusion and exclusion, or often-subtle forms of programmatic hubris that overly condition what might otherwise be universally accessible. Non-programmatic landscapes that alleviate or neutralize the very mechanisms of desire and consumerist fantasies embedded in overt regimes of the manipulation of subjectivity via socio-economic scenography are the very antithesis of 'spectacle'. This, of course, also implicates narrativity in landscape-architectural pedagogy; as the global proliferation of codified or interpretive landscapes has proceeded to engulf and submerge any nominally abstract or use-less designed landscape types associated with Modernism (e.g. passive parks), and most especially in the case of post-industrial sites, where program is often equal to fetishized ruins plus interpretive gloss. Inescapably complex as such ruined sites are, as most require massive remediation to be otherwise rehabilitated for other uses or 'no use', post-industrial parks are often examples of de facto neo-liberal capitalist hegemony in the guise of an ecologically inflected design ethos – i.e. representing a total lack of respect for leaving land to heal itself and/or returning it to semi-natural states that cannot be monetized or turned to immediate so-called passive use (e.g. view corridor or borrowed landscape for high-end real estate). In many ways the landscape-architectural project *is* the production of real estate, and therein lies half the problem.

Regarding *flâneurie* and urban landscape, there is perhaps no better critical summary than Hannah Arendt's remarks in her somewhat controversial Introduction to a book she also edited, Walter Benjamin's *Illuminations* (1968). Her summary – which in some ways is more useful than reading Benjamin's essay on the subject of *flâneurie* – problematizes the negative reception of Benjamin's work by the Frankfurt School. In doing so, Arendt points to the non-dialectical operations of Benjamin's essayistic work in general. It is the 'poetical thinking' that she assigns to Benjamin that makes his work unassimilable to then-prevalent Marxist critiques of cultural production. His historically determined extensive, yet erratic writing in many senses was a form of literary *flâneurie* (or, according to Arendt, 'pearl diving').

Benjamin's refusal to make connections between abstract and particular sociocultural phenomenon is useful towards self-analysis for the discourse of Landscape Architecture. The image is the manner of the refusal; as the image in his writing is what made it poetical versus sociopolitical. This form-of-image has since been discussed and theorized as thought-image (*Denkbild*), something akin to an intellectual icon versus the conventional, essentially discursive symbol or sign. In its positive form, the thought-image induces reverence through reverie, not utility. The thought-image is, in fact, an iconological versus iconographic or analogical form of expression; and it is rooted in everyday, quotidian experience. This lowly, everyday aspect of the thought-image, combined with its meta-poetic capabilities, is what makes it magical-realist as well; for it collapses artificially maintained high and low orders or rules, for and towards poeticized reverie and revelation.

Crisis and self-analysis

How then can we raise landscape-architectural cultural production to the level of self-analysis in relation to a discipline mired in a post-theoretical, self-inflicted identity crisis?

The now not-quiet urgency of overlapping socio-economic, sociopolitical and environmental distresses suggests that classic Marxist or Frankfurt School analyses of structure and superstructure are far from defunct. Instead, they require the incorporation of the thought-image to break out of the false binds of socio-economic determinism associated today with the production of so-called everyday space, a vital social conception that has devolved since Henri Lefebvre's seminal *La production de l'espace* (1974) to everyday banality. The fact that the thought-image crosses back-and-forth from literary criticism to film criticism is hardly a coincidence. Both literature and cinema are highly noetic and meta-poetic disciplines and substantially capable of synthesizing discordant intellectual currents, such discord being that which perpetuates the circular regimes of thought and self-serving argumentation given to neoliberal academia and design disciplines caught in the endless and ethically bereft game of servicing Capital.

The methodologies and programmatic biases of landscape-architectural design have hardly shifted since the incorporation of vague and pilfered post-Marxist cognitive-mapping strategies in the 1990s. This late-postmodern design insurgency was aimed at toppling 1980s formalist or artistic biases and favoured, in terms of representation, a *mélange* or mash-up of appropriated imagery that was derived, in part, from theories for visualizing information. Its attendant focus on incommensurate flows and theories of emergence derived from ecology and systems theory underscores the general avoidance of theories of visual agency proper. This manoeuvre sidesteps subjectivity entirely, while hiding the fact that the hidden hand of architectural and landscape-architectural design is as capricious as any other hidden hand.

These pseudo-objective practices (i.e. primarily visual-rhetorical practices) were intimately tied to the emergence of both Landscape Urbanism and, its successor cult today, Ecological Urbanism. On the other hand, it is easy for landscape urbanists to ignore landscape-historical discourses that perpetuate Early Modern and Modern mythologies of artistic genius or genius of place. This conflict between artistic ego, often valorized as Romantic madness, and the impersonal genius of place (nominally derived from antiquity and forms of Aristotelian vitalism) is at the heart of postmodern, nihilist dualism and its inability to synthesize much of anything on behalf of Reason – or its higher surrational function, Revelation. Yet personal agency now crashes into monstrous forms of neoliberal impersonal agency, and landscape-architectural practice is implicated as long as it adheres to the production of vast simulated environments – the signature late-modern crisis in urban identity and processes of subjectivization being the production of precarity on a massive, if not global scale.

The anti-intellectualism of post-critical design disciplines today is generally upheld as a badge of courage, even when it is the primary cause of the corruption by Capital of the professions from both within and without. Old arguments about 'theory and praxis' no longer work (much like 'word and image', as above), especially given that the 'smooth' or 'liquid' spaces of neoliberal capitalism are essentially constructed to make operational difference all but impossible (or, better yet, appropriable if marketable). This pervasive anti-intellectualism of the design professions is further propped up by new pseudo-scientific justifications for analysis and execution of environments. As a result, much design today qualifies as the analysis and 'crucifixion' of environments on behalf of Capital.

The nature of the image is, therefore, the key. The architectural image endlessly returns to its object status, un-dynamic and un-accountable to nature, no matter how it is presented or re-presented. The landscape-architectural image endlessly returns to the *mélange*. Such unfortunately comes about through forcing too many programmatic aspirations and too much economic value upon environments. The discord is notable: the architectural image reverts to the status of 'tomb', while the landscape-architectural image reverts to the status of 'field'. The resultant, late-modern synthesis of these dual biases is the lexical anomaly, 'tomb in the field', supplanting the older, equally anomalous 'Machine in the Garden' ethos of high modernism articulated by Marx (1964), by way of – incidentally – Henry David Thoreau and the reverie-soaked *Walden* (Thoreau 1854). Returning to the subject of post-industrial landscape, is not 'tomb in the field' the primary image for post-industrial landscape itself, a semi-tragic outcome no matter how picturesque it may be? Thus emerges a field of possible operations whereby a landscape is used as a model and basis for urban and ex-urban interventions that are *operative* (via the dynamic and Trinitarian economy of nature, culture and subjectivity) in defiance of purely representational or static landscape deliverables. How then to sound such depths – to produce the self-analysis required as exit strategy?

Tarrying with the negative

Thomas Ruff's 2015 exhibition *Nature morte* at Gagosian's diminutive storefront gallery on Davies Street, in Mayfair, London, England, indexed something rather bizarre in relation to the economy of the image as icon.

Ruff's images of plants, as still-life photography, are part of a series called 'Negatives' (part of a larger series called 'Photograms and Negatives') produced digitally by collapsing the process of photographic printmaking (Freedberg 2015). Ruff uses positives (found prints) to produce new positives (manufactured prints) that are images of non-existent negatives. The head hurts just to think about it, and it is all done via the juju-craft of the computer. In essence, a found historical image (a positive) is scanned and converted to a digital negative through the mediation of a computer. It is then printed, yielding a positive image of the spectral, 'missing' negative, which in the age of digital photography no one remembers anyway. Because the found prints are sepia-toned albumen prints of a 'semi-archaic' quality, the whole operation suggests a faux-historical or faux-archaeological project on Ruff's part. The *mise-en-abyme* nature of this project is more than obvious – and somewhat profound. In fact, what the images indicate is an immense reserve function in photography for commenting both upon itself and upon its implicit and irreducible spectrality.

In this rather cunning set of images resides the question of how the singular image operates in tension with its putative source. Of course, Ruff erases the source by using the found image as source. In doing so, he is also invoking that crisis noted above that involves the reversion of inexorable processes to object status – the object in this case the apparent still-life photograph, which is only a simulation or facsimile. These images register at several levels the multiple layers of agency given to the photographic image since the invention of photography, and the subject of the images (ostensibly 'dead nature') has a lachrymose elemental discord only representable by the fact that they are captive subjects in the ongoing history of art photography. This is meta-photography, and what it suggests is that representational orders are guilty of certain things that they, in turn, might redeem or at least play out through the artist-practitioner. Might not Landscape Architecture, as discipline or profession, undertake the self-same analysis through meta-critique? 'Next to nothing', therefore, connotes a neo-Hegelian 'tarrying with the negative', and/or erasing things through exposing other things.

For Landscape Architecture, '*Nature morte*' crosses over into an affective and somewhat claustrophobic regime of representation and mimesis that it can only exit by accepting that the Benjaminian veil hiding truth includes mimetic games of chance that may or may not be sincere – or games of chance that may be Surrealist or Surrealist-inspired. Morality sometimes hides behind amorality. Such was the secret chord of both Dada and Surrealism.

Ruff's sincerity is only suspect if one also suspects photography of post-humanist misanthropy, a type of death drive that seems embedded in the production of images formed from images – a will to expire. The repertoire resembles a Borgesian house of mirrors. How to escape this circularity is the primary question his production of these works asks. The answer is definitively 'outside' of the images proper (here a series of mirages). The iconicity of the thought-image is the veil, built or unbuilt.

What, then, is this veil to be comprised of, if it is to counter trends in global precarity, re-introduce non-instrumentalist orders to the design of the environment, and function as self-analysis for landscape architects and landscape urbanists? Ruff provides clues, yet it remains to be seen what will work for design professions otherwise plugged straight into the dark manoeuvres of the neo-liberal-capitalist exploitation of Life itself.

REFERENCES

American Society of Landscape Architects (2015), *ASLA Code of Professional Ethics*, http://www.asla.org/ContentDetail.aspx?id=4276&RMenuId=8&PageTitle=Leadership. Accessed 23 November 2015.

Astruc, A. ([1948] 1968), 'Naissance d'une nouvelle avant-garde: La caméra-stylo' ('The birth of a new avant-garde: La Caméra-stylo)', in P. J. Graham (ed.), *The New Wave: Critical Landmarks*, Garden City, NY: Doubleday, pp. 17–23.

Batteux, C. (1746), *Les beaux arts réduits à un même principe*, Paris: Durand.

Benjamin, W. (1968), *Illuminations* (ed. H. Arendt, trans. H. Zohn), New York: Harcourt, Brace & World.

Burke, E. (1757), *A Philosophical Enquiry into the Origin of Our Ideas of the Sublime and Beautiful*, London: R. and J. Dodsley.

Clément, G. (2003), *Manifeste du Tiers paysage*, Paris: Éditions Sujet/Objet.

—— (2009), *L'homme symbiotique, commentaire de six dessins*, http://www.gillesclement.com/cat-lhommesymbiotique-tit-L-Homme-symbiotique. Accessed 23 November 2015.

—— (2016), *The Third Landscape*, http://www.gillesclement.com/art-454-tit-The-Third-Landscape. Accessed 28 June 2016.

Comte, O. (2013), *Extrait du film 'Le jardin en mouvement, Gilles Clément'*, Video, Directed by Olivier Comte, A.p.r.e.s. Production, http://vimeo.com/85514662. Accessed 23 November 2015.

Freedberg, H. (ed.) (2015), *Thomas Ruff: Nature Morte*, London: Gagosian Gallery.

Grant, K. (2014), 'The lie of the land – John Dixon Hunt', http://melbourneartnetwork.com.au/tag/garden-design/. Accessed 1 August 2019.

Intergovernmental Panel on Climate Change (IPCC), United Nations (2014), *Fifth Assessment Report 2014*, http://ipcc-wg2.gov/AR5/report/. Accessed 23 November 2015.

Koolhaas, R. (2016), *Junkspace*, http://oma.eu/publications/junkspace. Accessed 28 June 2016.

Lefebvre, H. (1974), *La production de l'espace*, Paris: Anthropos.

Marx, L. (1964), *The Machine in the Garden: Technology and the Pastoral Ideal in America*, Oxford: Oxford University Press.

McHarg, I. (1966), 'Ecological determinism', in F. F. Darling and J. P. Milton (eds), *Future Environments of North America*, Garden City, NY: Natural History Press, pp. 526–38.

Oreskes, N. and Conway, E. M. (2014), *The Collapse of Western Civilization: A View from the Future*, New York: Columbia University Press.

Powell, B., Tournier, D., Jones, D. S. and Roös, P. B. (2019), Welcome to Wadawurrung Country, in D. S. Jones and P. B. Roös (eds), *Geelong's Changing Landscape: Ecology, Development and Conservation*, Melbourne, Australia: CSIRO Publishing, pp. 44–84.

Roös, P. (2014), 'Design with nature: A proposed model for coastal settlements in Australia adapting to climate change and extreme weather events', *UHPH 2014: Landscapes and Ecologies of Urban and Planning History: Proceedings of the 12th Australasian Urban History Planning History Conference*, edited by M. Gjerde and E. Petrović, Australasian Urban History / Planning History Group and Victoria University of Wellington, Wellington, New Zealand, pp. 649–64.

Sieyès, Comte E. J. ([1789] 1963), *What is the Third Estate?* (ed. S. E. Finer, trans. M. Blondel), London: Pall Mall Press.

Thoreau, H. D. ([1853] 1973), *Walden; or, Life in the Woods*, Garden City, NY: Anchor Press/Doubleday.

Wolf, G. (2006), 'Exploring the unmaterial world', *Wired Magazine*, 1 June, http://archive.wired.com/wired/archive/8.06/koolhaas.html. Accessed 23 November 2015.

14

Ciné-Cento: Eisenstein's visual methodology and the space of film

Niek Turner, Queen's University Belfast

Introduction

Just as the entire mode of existence of human collectives changes over long historical periods, so too does their mode of perception. The way in which human perception is organized – the medium in which it occurs – is conditioned not only by nature but by history

(Benjamin 2008: 23)

In his 1936 essay 'Art in the age of mechanical reproduction', Walter Benjamin suggests that new mass media technologies such as newspapers, radio, photography and film are intimately tied to the modern way of experiencing and seeing the world. This new way of seeing is brought about by changes to the individual's spatial experience and new modes of travel, such as the train and the motor car, and the city, where work, living and entertainment are grouped together in an intimate montage of visual events.

Film, more than any other medium, was intimately tied to this experience of modernity in its ability to accurately represent the ever-shifting light, form and time of modern space. In the early part of the twentieth century, the Soviet Union led the way in exploring the potential of this medium, with its avant-garde using it to address the question of past, present and future space, which had taken on extra significance following the revolution and the establishment of a new communist state (Widdis 2003: 1–18; Efimova and Manovich 1993: xix–xxxi).

Leading this new wave of revolutionary filmmakers was Sergei Eisenstein, whose examination of montage in film and theory directly addressed the potential of cinema's new way of seeing. Significantly, Eisenstein had a background in architecture, which began with his father Mikhail Eisenstein, a prominent architect in Riga at the turn of the century, and continued when he opted to study architecture at the Petrograd School of Engineering in 1915. Whilst the revolution cut short his studies, this background in architecture and the construction of space continued to play an important role in his thinking as evidenced by numerous references to the subject in his writings, and meetings with prominent architects of the time, such as Le Corbusier. In fact, when Le Corbusier visited the USSR and Moscow for the first time in 1928, he attended a private showing of Eisenstein's *Bronenosets Potemkin* (*Battleship Potemkin*) (1925) and preliminary shots of a work in progress, *The General Line*, which would ultimately become Eisenstein's fourth film *Staroye i Novoye* (*The Old and the New*) (1929). Following the viewing Le Corbusier declared in an interview,

> Architecture and the cinema are the only two arts of our time. In my own work I seem to think as Eisenstein does in his films. His work is shot through with the sense of truth, and bears witness to the truth alone. In their ideas, his films resemble closely what I am striving to do in my own work.
>
> (Le Corbusier cited in Cohen 1992: 49)

This combination of a background in architecture paired with working with the new visual medium of film contributed to Eisenstein producing several innovative theoretical essays throughout his career. This includes 'Montage and architecture' (Eisenstein 2010a: 59–81) and 'Piranesi or the flux of form' (Eisenstein 1987: 123–54), which employed visual research, as opposed to traditional text-based exploration, as a method to explore space in both the real world and the mediated image.

In the years that have passed since Eisenstein's death in 1948, technology has continued to develop exponentially and with it so too has the potential for Benjamin's new 'modes of perception' and Eisenstein's innovative visual research methods. Computers have allowed us to engage with space in both the immediate and wider context in innumerable different ways via the multitude of screens (cinema, television, computer, phone and watch) that now dominate our waking lives. Consequently, new visual research methods are emerging that utilize the potential of computer technology to store, display and analyse large amounts of visual data. Lev Manovich is a pioneering academic working in this area who, alongside writing several books on the subject, has led various experiments into the potential of these techniques with the *Software Studies Initiative* (2015). In *Language of New Media*, Manovich (Manovich 2002: 330) directly addresses the question of how new media has altered our perception from the time of Benjamin and argues that 'we should explore the aesthetic possibilities of all aspects of user's experience with a computer, this key experience of modern life: dynamic windows of GUI, multi-tasking, search engines, databases, navigable space, and others'.

Taking inspiration from Benjamin, Eisenstein and Manovich, this chapter introduces a series of new visual methods being developed as part of a research project examining the role that space played in Eisenstein's most famous and enduring film *Bronenosets Potemkin* (*Battleship Potemkin*) (Eisenstein 1925). It aims to contest the traditional qualitative history and theory approach that dominates the study of architecture and film and demonstrate how new ways of seeing, made possible by ongoing development in computers and software, can offer unique opportunities to study film not just as text, but to move through the screen and explore its spatial and architectural properties. In a world where visual technologies are becoming more and more ubiquitous, researching the role that visual space plays is important not only for filmmakers, but also for architectural practice and theory.

Eisenstein's method as a visual approach

Glasnost and the ultimate dissolution of the USSR in 1991 (Kenez 2006: 253–57) led to the broader international availability of Eisenstein's films and writings – a fact that is evidenced by the British Film Institute's release of a large selection of previously unseen theoretical writings over four volumes between 1988 and 1995 (1995, 2010a, 2010b, 2010c). Wider access to Eisenstein's oeuvre has led to a resurgence of interest in him in the past quarter of a century. The resulting research examines Eisenstein and his work from several viewpoints, ranging from new biographies, such as Oksana Bulgakowa's (2001) *Sergei Eisenstein: A Biography*; reappraisals of his films and theory, as in David Bordwell's (1993) *The Cinema of Eisenstein*, to the discussion of a selection of Eisenstein's writings by architectural researchers, such as in Anthony Vidler's (2000) *Warped Space*. Whilst these, and other pieces of research, discuss a wide range of topics relating to Eisenstein's filmmaking, none reveal the central role that visual methods played in Eisenstein's thinking.

Visual/Montage as a new language for research

Sergei Eisenstein was multilingual, and could read, write and converse in Russian, English, German and French. However, it was in images not text where Eisenstein's true linguistic skill lay. This imagistic thinking is revealed early on in his writings through his exploration of Chinese and Japanese script in articles such as 'An unexpected juncture' (Eisenstein 2010b: 115–22) and 'Beyond the shot' (Eisenstein

233

2010b: 138–50) written in 1928 and 1929 respectively. Eisenstein's belief in the discursive power of the image over text is made evident when he states:

> The point is that the copulation – perhaps we had better say the combination – of two hieroglyphs of the simplest series is regarded not as their sum total but as their product, i.e. as a value of another dimension, another degree: each taken separately corresponds to an object but their combination corresponds to a *concept*.
>
> (2010b: 139, original emphasis)

Eisenstein's command of this imagistic language is demonstrated by the enduring worldwide appeal of *Bronenosets Potemkin* (*Battleship Potemkin*) (Eisenstein 1925). It is noteworthy that this reliance on the image as a discursive tool is not limited to Eisenstein's filmic work but also played a significant role in Eisenstein's thinking at a more fundamental level. Jay Leyda and Zina Voynow's (1985) *Eisenstein at Work* reveals this by gathering together a range of documents from throughout his life and career, as filmmaker, teacher and theorist. In this summary overview of Eisenstein's output, it is not text, but images, in the form of sketches, pictures and diagrams that dominate the book. Ted Perry (in Leyda and Voynow 1985: vii) acknowledges the importance of the image to Eisenstein in the introduction, when he states on the first page of the book; 'To think through an idea, to give it discernible form, was to sketch it. Abstractions were encountered, grappled with, and rendered as visual ideas'.

What is significant for a researcher of Eisenstein's time is that this visual mode of thinking is not limited to sketchbooks but becomes a research tool in its own right. Consequently, Eisenstein's theoretical writing is interspersed with numerous tables, diagrams, sketches, and images. This visual method is particularly marked in arguably his most complete book, *Towards a Theory of Montage* (Eisenstein 2010a), which was compiled many years after his death. In the chapter 'Vertical Montage' (Eisenstein 2010a: 327–399), written between the years of 1937 And 1940, Eisenstein utilises extensive visual analysis to deconstruct the visual and musical composition of a battle sequence in one of his later films *Aleksandr Nevskiy* (*Alexander Nevsky*) (Eisenstein 1938). Whilst in this diagram Eisenstein largely explores the compositional contours of the image plane, there are several occasions when his visual analysis moves through the surface of the image to examine the filmic space beyond. Key examples of this are the aforementioned essays, 'Piranesi or the flux of form' (Eisenstein 1987: 123–54) and 'Montage and architecture' (Eisenstein 2010a: 59–81) alongside others such as 'Yermolova' (Eisenstein 2010a: 82–105). In doing so, Eisenstein not only engages directly with the common elements of film and architecture (light, form and time), but also addresses the question of how does one explore the space of the two-dimensional image. This leads him to deploy various original techniques, from re-configuring the spatial composition of a (Giovanni Battista) Piranesi etching, to re-reading Auguste Choisy's sequential analysis of the Acropolis in Athens as a cinematic sequence, or exploring how the Russian painter Valentin Serov captured the body in space using subtly shifting viewpoints.

Re-envisioning Eisenstein's visual method

> Movies influence the way we construct images of the world, and in many instances they influence how we operate within it.
>
> (AlSayyad 2006: 1)

In our everyday lives, we experience space in many formats both actual, through our surroundings, and virtual, via various screens and frames. This invasion of mediated space, which originated with photography and film in the early 1900s, has grown exponentially over the past century with screens invading first our homes, through the television, then the office, through the computer and now our own personal space, with the smartphone. Despite living in this ubiquitous mediated environment, architectural history and theory research has largely failed to engage with the opportunities that these new visual technologies offer us. Instead, for the most part, researchers have continued to rely on the written word as their principal medium. Consequently, we are confronted with the question of how Nezar AlSayyad's study *Cinematic Urbanism: A History of the Modern From Reel to Real* (2006) might have differed had he applied his above thinking to his methodological approach?

What my preceding exploration of Eisenstein's theory reveals is the variety of forms that visual research can adopt to expose previously unseen information embedded within the mediated image. One academic who is exploring how such visual research might be evolved using contemporary technology is computer scientist, Lev Manovich. Manovich, who like Eisenstein began his career studying architecture, has spent the past decade developing visual research techniques that utilize the computers' potential to offer new ways of seeing media. This has generated a broad range of experiments that deploy the computers' unique processing power to gather, analyse and then display a large amount of visual information. Examples of his research outputs can be found on both his own (Manovich 2015) and the Software Studies Initiative website (2015), which include among other things, a visual study of two of Dziga Vertov's films and a visual analysis of the covers of *TIME* magazine over the past century. Much like Eisenstein's visual research, Manovich's techniques are most successful when they pair an innovative visual research method with a visually arresting output.

Exploring the space of the individual shot

Taking inspiration from both Eisenstein and Manovich, this research harnesses the computer's ability to process the large amount of visual information contained within the moving image to explore the complex construction of space within *Bronenosets Potemkin* (*Battleship Potemkin*) (Eisenstein 1925).

Whilst Eisenstein is principally known for developing montage theory, one of the most arresting elements of his films is in fact the individual shot. This is suggested by his mentor, and originator of montage theory, Lev Kuleshov (1974: 138–39), who observed shortly after the release of Eisenstein's first film *Stachka* (*The Strike*) (1925):

> He is more a director of the *shot* – tasteful and expressive – than of montage and human movement. Eisensteinian shots always overpower the rest; in the main, it is they that constitute the success of his works. It is enough simply to remember the hosing episode in *Strike*, the infinite savoring of these photogenic pieces of film, to become absolutely convinced of the director's fine '*eye*,' of his particular love of the plastically expressive shot.

The importance of the individual shot was not lost on Eisenstein and he devoted much attention to the subject in both his theory and teaching. This is evident, in that he devotes the first third of his book *Towards a Theory of Montage* (Eisenstein 2010a) to this very subject. Following Eisenstein's example this research into the *Bronenosets Potemkin* (*Battleship Potemkin*) (Eisenstein 1925) proposes a three-stage visual method to explore the use of space in the individual shot.

Stage 1: Ciné-Cento or identifying spatial characteristics of the shot

Approaching the question of Eisenstein's use of space in the individual shot I was acutely aware of the extent of visual information embedded within films – an issue

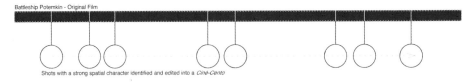

Figure 1: 'Stage 1 – Ciné-Cento – Identifying spatial characteristics of the shot', © Niek Turner, 2015.

that is compounded in early Soviet cinema, and especially Eisenstein's films, by the rapid montage editing of footage. This results in the 72-minute *Bronenosets Potemkin* (*Battleship Potemkin*) (Eisenstein 1925) consisting of over 1500 shots.

This sheer amount of information has led researchers to disregard a holistic visual analysis of films in favour of a detailed analysis of short sequences (Bordwell 1993: 46–47). An approach adopted by Eisenstein himself in the previously discussed compositional analysis of a sequence in *Aleksandr Nevskiy* (*Alexander Nevsky*) (Eisenstein 1938). However, as Manovich's research shows, computers are fundamentally altering our ability to manipulate and analyse large amounts of data. Adopting this principle, my research set out to examine how space was used in the individual shot throughout the whole film as opposed to one short sequence. In the first stage of the process this involved devising a technique that would create an overview of how Eisenstein approached space in the individual shot throughout the film.

The inspiration for my initial approach came from an article by Eisenstein entitled 'Laocoön' in which he relates the montage editing of film to contemporary and historical techniques from art. One such example cited by Eisenstein is a classical form of poetry called the 'Cento' which he describes as 'a work compiled from verses or prose extracts drawn from one or several authors' (Eisenstein 2010a: 179). Eisenstein relates this technique to cinema by referring to the films of pioneering Soviet filmmaker and editor, Esfir Shub as *ciné-centos* (Eisenstein 2010a: 178). Shub constructed narrative films, such as *Padenie dinastii Romanovykh* (*The Fall of the Romanov Dynasty*) (Shub 1927), by combining newsreel footage from various sources, thus creating a filmic equivalent of this ancient poetic technique.

Adopting this approach for my own study of *Bronenosets Potemkin* (*Battleship Potemkin*) (Eisenstein 1925) offered the potential to create a distilled view of how Eisenstein used space in the individual shot. Thus, I used film-editing software to wander, like Walter Benjamin's flâneur, through the landscape of Eisenstein's film and explore the space of the moving image. This process was concluded with the construction of a *ciné-cento* of *Battleship Potemkin* that drew together individual shots of the film that exhibited a strong spatial character (Figure 1).

Aside from revealing the sheer volume of shots in the film that exhibited a strong spatial character, this output allowed me to reflect on Eisenstein's use of space in the individual shot unencumbered by the original narrative of the film. Ultimately this process of engagement revealed that the film was largely constructed from just six principal spatial shot types. Each of which displayed a very clear approach to arranging and capturing space. Stills taken from my *ciné-cento* demonstrate these types (Figures 2–7), which I have classified as Perspectival, Fore/Middle/Background, Geometric, Flat, Unfamiliar and Intimate Space. What these definitive spatial approaches to the shot suggest is that Eisenstein deployed space in a deliberate way in his films as well as his thinking. Importantly these spatial shot types also reveal an approach to capturing space that is not contingent on the architectural style of the *mise-en-scène*. Whether on a warship, a factory or street, space and how it is captured is defined by the narrative and the emotional response that Eisenstein is attempting to trigger in the viewer.

Figure 2: 'Perspectival Space' – Still from *Bronenosets Potemkin* (*Battleship Potemkin*) (Eisenstein 1925) Soviet Union / Berlin: Stiftung Deutsche Kinemathek / Transit Film GmbH.

Figure 3: 'Fore/Middle/Background Space' – Still from *Bronenosets Potemkin* (*Battleship Potemkin*) (Eisenstein 1925) Soviet Union / Berlin: Stiftung Deutsche Kinemathek / Transit Film GmbH.

Figure 4: 'Geometric Space' – Still from *Bronenosets Potemkin* (*Battleship Potemkin*) (Eisenstein 1925) Soviet Union / Berlin: Stiftung Deutsche Kinemathek / Transit Film GmbH.

Figure 5: 'Flat Space' – Still from *Bronenosets Potemkin* (*Battleship Potemkin*) (Eisenstein 1925) Soviet Union / Berlin: Stiftung Deutsche Kinemathek / Transit Film GmbH.

Figure 6: 'Unfamiliar Space' – Still from *Bronenosets Potemkin* (*Battleship Potemkin*) (Eisenstein 1925) Soviet Union / Berlin: Stiftung Deutsche Kinemathek / Transit Film GmbH.

Figure 7: 'Intimate Space' – Still from *Bronenosets Potemkin* (*Battleship Potemkin*) (Eisenstein 1925) Soviet Union / Berlin: Stiftung Deutsche Kinemathek / Transit Film GmbH.

Stages 2 and 3: A new patchwork or mapping the film and analysing the output

> Protagonists are to be eliminated, because they are precisely what stays in the spectators' memory, instead of the settings and the meaning of the action. My task was the opposite: to make the viewer remember the meaning of action and setting.
> (Eisenstein cited in Ryabchikova 2008)

Eisenstein refers to his early silent films of the 1920s as 'mass films', in that the narrative unfolding on screen affects numerous people as opposed to the individual. As the above quote taken from the Hyperkino Edition of *Stachka* (*The Strike*) (Eisenstein [1925] 2008) reveals, Eisenstein employed this approach to allow space to become a central character in the events unfolding on screen.

Whilst my *ciné-cento* approach revealed how Eisenstein captured space in the individual shot, it did not reveal to what extent and why each shot type is used. The second and third stages of this research address these questions by suggesting how these shot types might be mapped and then analysed against the film's narrative structure.

In the appendix of David Bordwell and Kristen Thompson's (2008: 431–38) *Film Art: An Introduction*, the authors offer a short summary of how to write a critical analysis of film. Under the heading 'Draw up a segmentation of the entire film', they adopt an architectural analogy to convey their approach to the reader, stating:

> Analyzing a film is a bit like investigating a building's design. When we walk through a building, we notice various features-the shape of the doorway,

the sudden appearance of an immense atrium. We may not, however, have a very strong sense of the building's overall architecture. If we are students of architecture, though, we want to study the design of the whole building, and so we'd examine the blueprints to understand how all the individual parts fit together. Similarly, we experience a film scene by scene, but if we want to understand how the various scenes work together, it's helpful to have a sense of the film's overall shape.

(Bordwell and Thompson 2008: 431–32)

Bordwell and Thompson suggest that '[m]ovies don't come equipped with blueprints […] so we have to make our own' (2008: 432). As such, they advise that the film student should write a summary, or 'segmentation' as they call it, of the films overall structure to aid with their analysis. As someone approaching filmic research from an architectural background, this analogy suggests a method that is more than just a written summary of the film's structure. Instead, it brings to the fore the qualities that a 'blueprint' possesses to visually convey the overall spatial qualities of an object or building.

Using this as inspiration, the second stage of my visual analysis will involve creating an overview of the film by mapping the use of the previously identified spatial shot types throughout the film. The potential of mapping measurable data from films is something that has been explored previously by Barry Salt. In his book, *Film Style and Technology: History and Analysis* (1992), Salt collates quantifiable information from films, such as shot length, camera position and movement, and then uses this outputted numerical data to compare a variety of films. This research method, which has subsequently become known as Cinemetrics (2015), has undergone further development in recent years by film academics such as Yuri Tsivian on his website of the same name. Whilst my research method draws inspiration from Salt and Tsivian's technique of data collection, it reframes the approach, as much of Manovich's work does, to represent this data in a more visual way.

Thus, by creating a matrix of still images for every individual shot of the film arranged chronologically from left to right, the visual mapping technique proposed in the second stage of my research allows for the simultaneous interpretation of data and image (Figure 8). This method, which builds on Manovich's research in a project entitled *Visualising Vertov* (Manovich 2015), allows not only the classification of each of the individual shots against the suggested spatial shot types, but also the production of a new method of engaging with the film. Re-imaging the film as a patchwork garment, as Eisenstein's cento reference suggests, provides an alternative way of visually engaging with the space of this film.

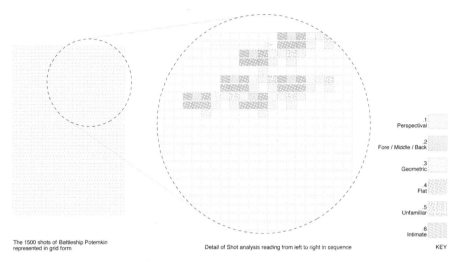

Figure 8: 'Stage 2 – A new patchwork – Mapping the film', © Niek Turner, 2015.

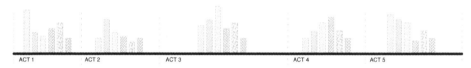

Figure 9: 'Stage 3 – Analysing the output', © Niek Turner, 2015.

Once this spatial shot type data mapping is complete, the third and final stage of my analysis will involve collating this information to explore how Eisenstein's use of space varies throughout the narrative structure of the film. Eisenstein had a background in theatre, which ultimately led to him adopting a classical five-act structure for the film. In the final analytical diagrams (Figure 9) I will visually map these five acts and reveal whether these different spatial shot types are used consistently throughout the film or if their density varies according to the narrative effect that Eisenstein aims to achieve.

Conclusion

> The Acropolis of Athens could just as well be called the perfect example of one of the most ancient films. [...] It is hard to imagine a montage sequence for an architectural ensemble more subtly composed, shot by shot, than the one which our legs create by walking among the buildings of the Acropolis.
>
> (Eisenstein 2010a: 60)

The above quote is taken from Eisenstein's article, 'Montage and architecture' (2010a: 59–81). In it Eisenstein, using Auguste Choisy's visual analysis of the Acropolis in Athens, relates the spatial experience of architecture as *path* to a filmic sequence. This subtle reframing of Choisy's visual study by Eisenstein has been cited by several influential theorists as demonstration of the underlying links between architecture and film (Vidler 2000; Bruno 2002). What my process of visual engagement with Eisenstein's films suggests is that Eisenstein's interest in architecture and space extended beyond his theoretical writing to the conscious construction of space in his films. For Eisenstein, the opportunity to recast space through the two-dimensional surface and the frame of the screen gives him the ability to inject meaning and narrative into the film.

Furthermore, this research into the space of the individual shot of *Bronenosets Potemkin (Battleship Potemkin)* (Eisenstein 1925) highlights an inherently visual approach to Eisenstein's theory. By pairing Eisenstein's visual method with more contemporary examples, such as those developed by Manovich, the research demonstrates the potential that a visual method has to reveal unexplored information about spaces' important role in film.

Looking beyond the confines of this particular study, it is beneficial to question how this visual method might be refined or adapted for other uses within architectural design and research. Through its dissection of one of the most revered films of all time, this research reveals the important role that the arrangement and capturing of space has to play in the narrative and ultimately the impact of a film. In a broader sense, it shows how one can utilize the computer's ability to process, store and display a large amount of information, to construct a semi-automated technique to reverse engineer the filmmaking process to create a digitized sequential overview of the visual grammar of the film. This could be used by architectural researchers and filmmakers alike as a tool to reflect on specific qualities of a single film. Whilst this research has focused on space and its arrangement in the shot, there are endless visual characteristics of the shot that could be analysed from colour, to lighting or indeed movement, as I am myself doing in other areas of my research on Eisenstein. Furthermore, once such visual information has been extracted from films, there is no reason why it could not, in similar way to Barry Salt's previously discussed cinemetrics, be utilized as a comparative tool for a collection of films.

Finally, whilst this research project has focused principally on film as its site of exploration, there is an inherent reciprocity between the subjects of architecture and film. Since the moving images' inception, numerous architects have commented on and worked in the medium. This is demonstrated by Le Corbusier's citation of the same section of Choisy's *Histoire de l'Architecture* (1899), as Eisenstein in his seminal work, *Towards a New Architecture* (1927: 43). The ever-increasing role that media plays in our daily interaction with our surroundings has inevitably led to renewed interest in this relationship between the realms of the architecture (physical space) and film (mediated space), pioneered by Eisenstein and Le Corbusier. In the past couple of decades books such as Beatriz Colomina's, *Privacy and Publicity: Modern Architecture as Mass Media* (1994), or Richard Koeck's, *Cine-Scapes: Cinematic Spaces in Architecture and Cities* (2013), have suggested how media, from print to film, has influenced the history of architecture and our perception of it respectively. Central to Koeck's argument is that we should look at cities through a filmic lens as a method to understand our postmodern urban landscape, or to use his own words (2013: 6), 'Architectural and urban sites can have a filmic, or even scenographic, dimensions, which might not be obvious in our everyday passive perception of cities'.

This raises the important question; how could my research technique be reframed as a tool for architects as opposed to film practitioners? It is conceivable that by pairing my analytical process with custom-made films it would be possible to study existing buildings and sites with express purpose of understanding how the sequential arrangement of space might alter one's perception of an environment. In fact, this approach, which was pioneered by Choisy over a century ago, is not uncharted territory and was examined in relation to urban planning by Gordon Cullen in his and his colleagues' work on *The Concise Townscape* (1971). Cullen's research contested the then predominantly plan-based method of urban planning by reappraising it from eye level. This led him to coin the phrase 'serial vision' as an expression for the unique way in which space unfolds within urban landscapes.

> The human mind reacts to a contrast, to the difference between things, and when two pictures (the street and the courtyard) are in the mind at the same time, a vivid contrast is felt and the town becomes visible in a deeper sense. It comes alive through the drama of juxtaposition.
>
> (Cullen 1971: 9)

Aside from striking similarities to elements from Eisenstein's early theoretical writings, which suggested the use of visual and other shocks to concentrate the audience's attention (2010b: 34), Cullen's quote highlights the potential of this visual research method as a design tool. As architects we, like the urban planners, are still often influenced by the modernist obsession with plan at the expense of the experiential qualities of space. Contemporary engagement with the world around us is dominated more than ever by the visual via actual and virtual engagement with space through devices. As such it is not difficult to imagine how the techniques developed here might be adapted and reframed, as

Eisenstein did in 'Montage and Architecture', to help architects understand more comprehensively how the individual shot might visually engage with the spaces of their buildings.

Acknowledgements

This research project has been made possible through the support of the Arts and Humanities Research Council. I would also like to thank Stiftung Deutsche Kinemathek / Transit Film GmbH for the use of the stills from their painstakingly restored version of *Bronenosets Potemkin* (*Battleship Potemkin*) (Eisenstein 1925). Finally, I would like to acknowledge the ongoing support of The University of Liverpool, The Centre for Architecture and the Visual Arts (CAVA) and my supervisors Professor Richard Koeck and Professor Iain Jackson.

REFERENCES

AlSayyad, N. (2006), *Cinematic Urbanism: A History of the Modern from Reel to Real*, New York: Routledge.

Benjamin, W. (2008), *The Work of Art in the Age of Its Technological Reproducibility, and Other Writings on Media* (eds M. W. Jennings, B. Doherty and Thomas Y. Levin), Cambridge, MA: Belknap.

Bordwell, D. (1993), *The Cinema of Eisenstein*, Cambridge, MA: Harvard University Press.

Bordwell, D. and Thompson, K. (2008), *Film Art: An Introduction*, 8th ed., New York: McGraw-Hill Higher Education.

Bruno, G. (2002), *Atlas of Emotion: Journeys in Art, Architecture, and Film*, New York: Verso.

Bulgakowa, O. (2001), *Sergei Eisenstein: A Biography*, Berlin: Potemkin Press.

Choisy, A. (1899), *Histoire de l'Architecture*, Paris: Gauthier-Villars.

Cinemetrics. (2015), http://www.cinemetrics.lv. Accessed 27 November 2015.

Cohen, J. L. (1992), *Le Corbusier and the Mystique of the USSR: Theories and Projects for Moscow, 1928–1936*, Princeton, NJ: Princeton University Press.

Colomina, B. (1994), *Privacy and Publicity: Modern Architecture as Mass Media*, Cambridge, MA: The MIT Press.

Cullen, G. (1971), *Concise Townscape*, Abingdon: Architectural Press.

Efimova, A. and Manovich, L. (1993), *Tekstura: Russian Essays on Visual Culture*, Chicago, IL: The University of Chicago Press.

Eisenstein, S. (1925), *Bronenosets Potemkin* (*Battleship Potemkin*), Soviet Union and Germany: Stiftung Deutsche Kinemathek and Transit Film GmbH.

—— ([1925] 2008), *Stachka* (*The Strike Hyperkino Edition*), Soviet Union and Russia: Sovkino and Ruscico.

—— (1938), *Aleksandr Nevskiy (Alexander Nevsky)*, Soviet Union: Mosfilm.

—— (1987), *Nonindifferent Nature* (trans. H. Marshall), Cambridge: Cambridge University Press.

—— (1995), *Beyond the Stars: The Memoirs of Sergei Eisenstein* (ed. R. Taylor, trans. W. Powell), Calcutta: Seagull Books and London: BFI Publishing.

—— (2010a), *Towards a Theory of Montage: Sergei Eisenstein Selected Works: v. 2* (eds. M. Glenny and R. Taylor, trans. M. Glenny), London: I.B. Tauris.

—— (2010b), *Writings, 1922–1934: Sergei Eisenstein Selected Works: v. 1* (ed. and trans. R. Taylor), London: I.B. Tauris.

—— (2010c), *Writings, 1934–47: Sergei Eisenstein Selected Works: v. 3* (ed. R. Taylor, trans. W. Powell), London: I.B. Tauris.

Kenez, P. (2006), *A history of the Soviet Union from the beginning to the end*, 2nd ed., Cambridge: Cambridge University Press.

Koeck, R. (2013), *Cine-scapes: Cinematic Spaces in Architecture and Cities*, London: Routledge.

Kuleshov, L. (1974), *Kuleshov on Film: Writings by Lev Kuleshov* (ed. and trans. R. Levaco), Berkeley, CA: University of California Press.

Le Corbusier. (1927), *(Vers une architecture) Towards a New Architecture ... Translated from the Thirteenth French Edition with an Introduction by Frederick Etchells*, London: John Rodker.

Leyda, J. and Voynow, Z. (1985), *Eisenstein at Work*, London: Methuen.

Manovich, L. (2002), *The Language of New Media*, Cambridge, MA: The MIT Press.

—— (2015), http://manovich.net. Accessed 25 November 2015.

Ryabchikova, N. (2008), '3. Cast: The collective of the 1st Workers' Theatre', *Stachka/The Strike: Hyperkino Edition*, DVD Extras, Soviet Union and Russia: Sovkino and Ruscico.

Salt, B. (1992), *Film Style and Technology: History and Analysis*, 2nd ed., London: Starword.

Shub, E. (1927), *Padenie dinastii Romanovykh (The Fall of the Romanov Dynasty)*, Soviet Union: Sovkino.

Software Studies Initiative. (2015), http://lab.softwarestudies.com. Accessed 25 November 2015.

Vidler, A. (2000), *Warped Space: Art, Architecture, and Anxiety in Modern Culture*, Cambridge, MA: The MIT Press.

Widdis, E. (2003), *Visions of a New Land: Soviet Film from the Revolution to the Second World War*, New Haven, CT: Yale University Press.

15

Constructing an architectural phenomenography through film

Ruxandra Kyriazopoulos-Berinde, Department of Architecture,

Cambridge University, UK

Introduction

The path towards constructing a potential architectural phenomenography started through an enquiry into how meaning and memory of home are communicated through select films by Andrei Tarkovsky.

They include *Ivanovo detstvo* (*Ivan's Childhood*) (Tarkovsky 1962), *Andrey Rublyov* (*Andrei Rublev*) (Tarkovsky 1966), *Solyaris* (*Solaris*) (Tarkovsky 1972), *Zerkalo* (*Mirror*) (Tarkovsky 1975), *Stalker* (Tarkovsky 1979), *Nostalghia* (Tarkovsky 1982), *Offret* (*The Sacrifice*) (Tarkovsky 1986). Written autobiographies, work notebooks with drawings for film sets, lectures, screenplays, published short stories and poems, diaries, interviews, professional or personal letters, biographies written by family members and anecdotes from the filming process were also examined. In addition to this textual material, the visual content of the seven films, photographs taken with or by Tarkovsky, as well as documentaries, informed a reading of his various homes. In order to cover both the textual and visual, an appropriate methodology fit to respond to such diverse research data was sought.

Tarkovsky's highly poetical visual universe constitutes direct research material for exploring phenomenological issues, due to its spatial qualities, of notable architectural interest. Tarkovsky's seven major cinematic works display a substantial connection with memory of place and architectural phenomenology, with an almost obsessive interest in retracing the memory of childhood as multisensorial remembrance of places once inhabited. There is also a record of vivid and creative empathy with newfound filming locations. This interest is visible and nearly palpable in his films, through images that the viewer can almost inhabit. These films constituted a highly abundant source of research, when studied in connection with biographical information and the poetically spatial descriptions from autobiographical writings. As such, they provide a threshold into the world of experience, allowing a systematic and more comprehensive understanding of how a place becomes identifiable as a home, how architecture is meaningfully dwelled in, how it lingers in the memory of those who had once lived in it.

In phenomenographic research, the products are a flux of descriptions that grasp into more depth the plurality of modes inscribed in the experience itself. The attempt to map Tarkovsky's filmic experiential lived space revolves around certain characteristics that are evident on a first view of his seven-film oeuvre: creative variation and a certain recurrence of experiential themes. The focus on the variation in the representation of lived space befits a phenomenographic endeavour. The research material is formed from a fluctuating stream of house icons. These moving images are treated not as mere depictions of familiar spaces, but as hypostases of the recollected archetype, in which sensorial perception is interwoven with experiential memories and emotional associations. Traces of this recollected archetype can thus emerge in non-autobiographical works in the form of spatial characteristics, space configurations or associative textures and fragments.

Phenomenology versus phenomenography

In 1954, during the flourishing times of the phenomenological movement, philosopher and psychologist Ulrich Sonnemann introduced a new term, aimed at demarcating what he considered the two main distinct categories of phenomenology (Sonnemann 1954). Sonnemann introduced the term *phenomenography* in order to make a distinction between existential phenomenology and the sort of phenomenological approach developed by psychiatrist Karl Jaspers, at the start of the twentieth century. By definition, first-person experience was an imperative for any phenomenological attempt, but Jaspers had been interested in understanding his patients in more depth (Spiegelberg 1975: 36–45). His 1913 work on *General Psychopathology* opens with a chapter entitled 'The subjective phenomena of the abnormal life of the psyche (phenomenology)' (Spiegelberg 1975: 36–45) in which he asserts a re-defined understanding of the task of phenomenology: 'to make present intuitively the mental states which actually only the patients experience' (Jaspers 1963: 55). Jaspers' approach essentially differs from the previous ways in which phenomenology was defined. He does this by methodologically leading the way into the world of the other. By renaming Jasper's phenomenology as *phenomenography*, Sonnemann thus thinks of the description of experiences as less hermetic, more communicative and intersubjective. 'The problem of intersubjectivity is precisely the problem of other minds. That is, the problem is to explain how we can access the minds of others. According to this supposition, this is a problem of access because other minds are hidden away, closed in, behind the overt behavior that we can see' (Gallagher 2005: 209). Thus, with an innate intersubjectivity in the very method of inquiry, *phenomenography* opens an epistemological approach to the world of the other.

Sonnemann's term remained underexplored until the 1980s. At that time, a research group from the education studies department of Gothenburg University, led by Ference Marton, had been performing phenomenological studies on student experience of taught subjects, but they were constantly realizing that 'to provide a grounding for empirical research in other people's experience rather than one's own, it was necessary to transcend the original form of phenomenology' (Richardson 1999: 63). They reclaimed the term *phenomenography*, utilizing it 'to describe the qualitatively different ways in which a phenomenon is experienced, conceptualized or understood, based on an analysis of accounts of experiences as they are formed in descriptions' (Dall'alba and Hasselgren 1996: 202). In time, the term and the method have become identifiable with the empirical research on education and on how theoretical concepts are learned in various fields of human activity. The emphasis has shifted from the experience itself to the importance of variation in this experience (Marton and Booth 1997: 117).

Nowadays researchers define phenomenography as an empirical research method that allows the study of variation in experiencing phenomena of the world around. Both phenomenology and phenomenography are therefore related to the experience of phenomena, but the main difference between them lies in the object of interest: while phenomenology aims to tackle the essence of the experience, phenomenography is interested in the qualitatively diverse ways in which one phenomenon can be experienced by a number of people (Figure 1). The research quality in phenomenology is experience of the researcher her/himself; the research quality in phenomenography is the description of ways of experiencing, as accounted by participants in the study. The research outcome of a study by a phenomenologist is a description of directly experienced phenomenon so as to provide depth and thickness. The phenomenographer gathers descriptions of the ways in which the phenomenon is experienced by participants in the study and seeks patterns, parallels and differences that can be identified under certain themes. They then narrow them down and group the categories of description. Accuracy of the findings is considered to ensue from variation, the overlapping themes and categories identified. A renewed, diverse and more comprehensive image of the phenomenon studied results from acknowledging the multiple ways in which it can be experienced.

VISUAL RESEARCH METHODS IN ARCHITECTURE

	PHENOMENOLOGY	PHENOMENOGRAPHY
starting point	phenomenon as experienced	
unit of research	the experience of the phenomenon	the ways of experiencing the phenomenon
mode of enquiry	first order: appearance of the phenomenon as experienced by the researcher	second order: analysis of the ways of experiencing, as described by participants
focus of enquiry	individual level	collective level
main method applied	phenomenological reduction (bracketing)	identifying and refining relevant categories of descriptions, through repeated (cross-) readings
research outcome	detailed description of the experience	categories of ways of experiencing
main aim of research	understanding the ESSENCE of the experience	understanding the VARIATIONS in experiencing
strength	depth and thickness of the description	comprehensive view of the phenomenon, in the light of varying ways of experiencing it
weakness	increased subjectivity; blindness to other ways of experiencing the same phenomenon	lack of depth in individual accounts; tendency for facile generalizations; omission of context

Figure 1: Summarized comparison between phenomenological and phenomenographic research methods; table © R. Berinde, January 2015.

In phenomenographic research, the semi-structured interview represents the most common form of data collection. With a certain theoretical hypothesis in mind, the researcher formulates a set of open questions to incite unpredicted answers. Data collection through video recordings of the participants is deemed to be a method that is thought to overcome the limitations of verbal expression, warranting 'a more complete well-structured experiment' (Wellington and Ward 2010: 3). In the case of data collection through interviews, where most methodological developments have been made so far, the analysis of the transcripts is made through seven consecutive steps: a first reading of transcripts; an additional reading, having a certain line of questioning in mind; followed by a labelling of the answers that are subsequently grouped into categories. In turn, these categories are refined, named, described. The final product of the analysis, the list of categories thus identified and described, is enriched with quotes from the transcripts, and aims to verbally illustrate the spectrum of variation in living and encountering the researched phenomena.

Although comparable in some aspects to grounded theory and ethnography, phenomenography differs from the former through its highlighted focus on how phenomena are experienced, and, unlike ethnography, it does not require a day-to-day immersion within the social processes it studies. However, the factor that best distinguishes phenomenography from either of the afore-mentioned methods or from phenomenology is the focus on the variation of experience, and the steps performed to map out its range, limits and patterns.

So how could this variation of experiencing a phenomenon be drawn out of visual material?

Phenomenography as Phenomenon+Graphein: A writing of phenomena

In the form in which it has developed as a qualitative method, phenomenography so far disregards the visual element as potential research material. The embedded discursive nature of phenomenography does not comply with data based on photographs, moving images, representations of experiences. Moreover, although phenomenographers have mentioned there is potential in applying the method on historical, narrative or biographical material, there is so far no record of such an experiment. Nevertheless, visual content bypasses hindrances such as the risk of 'interpreting linguistic differences and choice of words among interviewees as differences in meaning of conceptual content' (Sin 2010: 308).

The etymology of the term *phenomenography* and the unused potential of its content stand as the very basis for reclaiming it in order to analyse and describe audio-visual material. It is formed of *phenomenon* and *-graphy*, coming from the Greek words φαινόμενον (to appear luminously, to shine) and γράφειν (to inscribe, to write). Upon a literal reading, therefore, it would mean 'a writing of phenomena'. In similarly formed compounds of words, the *-graphy* suffix means respectively 'writing', such as in *calligraphy* (literally: 'beautiful-writing') and *photography* ('light-writing'). It can also mean 'description, account', such as in *biography* ('life-writing'); a 'listing' of elements, such as in *bibliography* ('book-writing'); or a 'mapping description', as in *geography* ('earth writing').

The story of the Greek γράφειν (*graphein*) opens up other fertile paths of interpretation. The term was formed as an onomatopoeic word imitating the sound of the stylus scratching the stone tablet whilst inscribing signs. It thus grasped multiple meanings: the action of inscribing, the visual trace left by the inscription and the audible component of inscribing. The combination of these three incorporates not just the results, but also the experience of inscribing. Moreover, the word γράφειν means 'to record' or store information. In modern language, the same verb is used for video-recording: η κάμερα γράφει meaning 'the camera is recording'. Understood in the context of this research, a re-reading of the term *phenomenography* entails the inherently audio-visual characteristic of γράφειν, which explores the ways in which phenomena are audio-visually communicated as experiences, engulfing the description and the mapping of the phenomenon, as well as the inscription, the remembrance and the writing of the phenomenon through the means of autobiographical film art. This matches the description of film art where director and screenwriter are one and the same person, as given by film critic Alexandre Astruc: 'Direction is no longer a means of illustrating or presenting a scene, but a true act of writing. The film-maker author writes with his camera as a writer writes with his pen' (Astruc 1968).

In this research, the *phenomenon* is broadly defined as experience of space-place, narrowed down to the experience of home. The *graphein* comprised in the given case involves the ways of inscribing, recording and writing experience, peculiar to narrative arts. The main difference between the material comprised in the films, screenplays, poems, short stories and – to some degree – the autobiography of Tarkovsky is their innate narrativity, i.e. the artistic imagination constituting an additional layer that is overlapped over the raw, direct experience that pervades in interview accounts. Imagination, representation and metaphors are thus essential components of the *graphein* of this study.

To exemplify, the cinematic *graphein* of a door implies that the image of a door in one instance of a film may not be understood in its imaginative fullness when separated from other reiterations of the same element. The image of an opening door in an oneiric episode gains its living character only when analysing its spatio-temporal construction in the filmic language that precedes it.

Reclaiming phenomenography

In working with the visual material provided by the aforementioned Tarkovskian films, I tried to paraphrase and adapt the steps of traditional phenomenographic analysis. As such, I started by 'freezing' film stills that contained spatially relevant frames, from all the seven films. I considered these 'frozen' frames as a traditional phenomenographer would consider fragments of interview transcripts and thus, I 'interrogated' the audio-visual material contained therein. What does the image talk about? To exemplify again: does it 'talk' about a door? Does it communicate something experiential about it? Is it a mere background for a scene, or does the character open the door ajar, lean upon the doorframe, peak through, look back from the doorway? (Figures 2–4) Is the door audible? What words are being uttered once the character opens the door? Thus I interrogated images, as if they were living respondents to my research questions, and generally the answers were rich and manifold. It might seem artificial to scrutinize so closely the rationale of the *mise-en-scène*. However, Tarkovsky's own opinion was that no element of the *mise-en-scène* should be arbitrary, but every choice of location should be experientially melded within the overall psychological mood of that scene:

Figures 2–4: Illustrations of film stills depicting doors/standing in the doorway. Figure 2 (left): film still from *Zerkalo* (*Mirror*) (Tarkovsky 1975), © Mosfilm; Figure 3 (centre): film still from *Nostalghia* (Tarkovsky 1982), © Rai2, Sovinfilm; Figure 4 (right): film still from *Offret* (*The Sacrifice*) (Tarkovsky 1986), © Svenska filminstitutet, Argos Film.

> It is sometimes suggested that the actors' position makes no difference: have them standing here by the wall, and talking; [...] One can simply write: 'The characters stop by the wall', and go on to give the dialogue. But what is special about the words that are being uttered, and do they correspond with standing by the wall?
> (Tarkovsky 1987: 74–75)

The analysis was performed in a number of steps. First, an initial viewing of the seven films, while in parallel I was reading the available written sources; extensive notes tracked initial observations on spatial awareness and various preferences of places (for instance, written descriptions of windows and poetic narrations of light coming through –in diaries and screenplays – paired with visual representations of same awareness, in films). During the second viewing, the previously mentioned film stills were extracted and time-coded (leading to a total of 180–280 film stills per film). The actual work initially involved printing and cutting out these images, with the purpose of having them as a palpable and graspable research material (Figures 5 and 6). Later on, the process was entirely digitized with the use of a software[1] which allowed simultaneous selection and tagging, together with adding explanatory notes (Figure 7). Having gathered digital or material piles of film stills, the process involved a verbal description of their visual content, thus labelling each one according to their relevance in depicting spatial and architectural experience: from the configuration of landscapes, the location of the house in the landscape and the appearance of the house as an external image, to the entrance of the house, the threshold, the separating elements of walls, floors, ceilings, the mediating elements of porch and stairs, the openings, windows and doors, to elements of furnishing and the way in which these items are configured as relations within and between rooms. Across these spatial categories, some generic qualities were observed: particular uses of light, darkness, sound, music, silence, words, memory and dream as temporal, rhythmic and spatial texture, natural elements – wind, fog, smoke, fire, water, rain.

Figures 5–7: Working with the film stills. Figures 5 and 6 (left and centre): handwritten labelling, on the back of the printed film stills; Figure 7 (right): digital labelling with Zoner software; all photos © R. Berinde, June–September 2015.

In conjunction with the narrative fabric of the film and with the notes that had been taken from biographical and autobiographical written sources, these categories were then repeatedly refined and re-configured (traditional phenomenography recommends a number of 4–5 categorization processes). Pairing direct reading of static film stills with notes on biographical and narrative context, the analysis sought to avoid being an autopsy of chopped films. The written notes situated the images within the order and rhythm of the film, while the repeated number of film viewings made possible to grasp each image as part of a whole. Knowing Tarkovsky's (1987: 120) thoughts about working with film stills – he claims that 'no time truth exists in the separate frames. In themselves they are static and insipid' – the labelling of images started only after having established a strong familiarity with the overarching environment of his films and biography. In this manner, the images became prompts, which, although still, were now invisibly playing the fragment of film inside the mind of the researcher.

The final, and most important, analysis step brought back into discussion the factor of architectural experience. If all the previous steps had involved an identification of the architectural visual elements present within the static image of the film still, this final step returned to the flowing audio-visual content of the moving image. I considered these images, then, to embed the inhabitable notions of filmic space, which constructs an imaginary building for the viewer. Through the synesthetic experience triggered by the act of watching, the viewer is transposed in the position of walking from room to room, of looking outside its windows, hearing sounding floors and feeling the light falling on the table, touching the rugged surface of walls and being caressed by curtains slowly moving in the wind. The filmmaker in this case is not a builder of functional architecture, but a builder of architectural experience, thus providing shelter not for the physical needs of the viewer, but for the emotional and ontological need for dwelling. And, ultimately, providing raw experiential data for a researcher wondering how the phenomenon of home is experienced and represented.

The list of phenomenographic categories

The results of my phenomenographic analysis on Tarkovsky's films identified 41 spatially relevant categories (Figure 4). These 41 categories were grouped under six main headings: Place, Construction (im)materials, Spatial elements, Furnishing, Fragments/triggers and Spatial Organization. At the beginning of the analysis a set of categories were drafted, envisaged as what could be main headings of an architectural textbook, hoping to fill them, one by one, with the appropriate film stills. However, this initial set was greatly altered as the viewing of the films progressed, due to the relationships emerging when images taken out of different films were put together. Some of the a priori devised categories initially contained a significant number of cards, but there were no strong resemblances between stills taken from different films. For instance, the element 'roof', which could hypothetically be experienced as looked at, climbed on, fallen from, pointed to, appeared in a number of film stills as simply a static background image. This led to the deletion of the category 'roof', considered invalid for the scope of the analysis.

As such, categories that remained in the final stage of the analysis, for instance 'door', signify not only that the element 'door' appears with much poignancy throughout Tarkovsky's oeuvre, but that among all the scenes that feature doors in his movies there are internal relationships and affinities. The more one way of experiencing or of portraying 'doors' was repeated throughout the films in a very similar moving image, the clearer a subcategory was formed. To exemplify, for the element 'door', five subcategories concern static, formal characteristics of doors that repeat throughout the films, whereas ten subcategories concern verbs, which not only describe ingenious dynamics of the film shot, but – due to the very fact that they repeat with persistence in different films – seem to embody a way of experiencing. For this reason, inside each category, an increased importance is given to these subcategories labelled 'verbs', the movements and actions within the shot that are directly related to the spatial fragment contained therein and that fluidly describe its experiential qualities (see 'door' subcategory in Figure 8).

Inverting the process of architectural phenomenology, the phenomenographic analysis explored how the filmmaker operates through the perceptual and associative regimes of the film in order to 'build' spatial experience and render habitable the rooms of moving images. Choosing phenomenography as a working method allowed for an understanding of the seven films as a continuum, rather than as separate narratives, opening up new readings, parallels, hierarchies. Unveiling the separate categories has in fact been an endearing walk through the rooms of a lived memorial house, unusually habitable, warm and familiar.

VISUAL RESEARCH METHODS IN ARCHITECTURE

Figure 8: The categories of cinematic architectural experience, resulted from the phenomenographic analysis of the films, © R. Berinde, May 2015.

Conclusion

These fragments of architecture built as part of film sets, and the way they are combined together to form a whole, are in fact direct expressions of the filmmaker's spatial understandings, spatial memories and emotions, phenomenological experiences of architecture, and therefore offer direct insight into the way spaces are perceived, experienced, remembered and conceived in their represented form. Film as an art form can thus be an open expression of architectural experience, and for the researcher who studies its audio-visual representation, it can provide an open book, a catalogue of encounters with architecture, at the most intimate and familiar level. The spatiality of the set itself, the *mise-en-scène*, the lighting, the textures, materials and movements of the camera and of the actors within the set, but not least, the way scenes from a set are stitched together with images of other places and, through careful editing, create a continuous flowing new and illusory architectural configuration ... all of these artificial mechanisms communicate intricate experiences. The gaze of the camera, mediating between the representational mind of the filmmaker and the visual/spatial perception of the viewer, adds the person-experience dimension to any portrayed space. As such, places in autobiographical films are not abstract or detached, but are already visualized experiences of place, and could thus be understood as cinematic phenomenographies of place.

As Bachelard (1987: 71) writes:

> through the brilliance of an image, the distant past resounds with echoes, and it is hard to know at what depth these echoes will reverberate and die away. Because of its novelty and its action, the poetic image has an entity and a dynamism of its own.

The strength of phenomenography as a method in analysing such poetic images is its ability and potential to map experience in a broad palette, structured and narrowed down to distinct, overlapping foci of condensation. The method is replicable for other auteur filmmakers, by observing closely the way in which the space – and particularly the space of home – is written on film. Each such endeavour would yield a different set of categories and a broad variation of sub-categories, potentially bringing a significant contribution to architecture's field of knowledge, shedding a little more light on how the space of home is perceived, remembered and represented, and how abstract spatial elements are lived in the bittersweet everydayness of home.

Applying an architectural phenomenographic reading to these studied films allowed for at least one definite conclusion to emerge: that if the filmmaker had himself finely grasped the essence of dwelling phenomena, his films will be carrying his experiences as a paper carries the inscribed meanings of a text. These meanings can, in turn, be understood, decoded and experienced by the viewer. From the specific case of Tarkovsky's films read through the phenomenographic method, there springs the conclusion that the architectural worlds that we carry within us, constructed on the course of time from memories that we are aware or unaware of, are structured around some definite and luminously real material and spatial elements. These material elements, after having sunk in the inner worlds of our minds and souls, embody more than just the function attributed to them in pragmatic thinking; they are the carriers of experience, meaningful, genuine, awakening experience.

Their images, reiterating over time, rediscovered in unknown emplacements, in some secluded corners of the memory, and in the photographic or cinematic choices we make, are moving fragments of the invisible homes we all carry within us.

REFERENCES

Astruc, A. (1968), 'The birth of a new avant-garde: La Camera-Stylo', in P. Graham (ed.), *The New Wave*. London: Secker/ BFI, pp. 17–23

Bachelard, G. (1987), *On Poetic Imagination and Reverie* (trans. C. Gaudin), Dallas: Spring Publications.

Berinde, R. (2016), 'Moving Images of HOME: Tracing an architectural phenomenography through the films of Andrei Tarkovsky and Ingmar Bergman', Ph.D. thesis, Sheffield. School of Architecture, University of Sheffield.

Bowden, J. (1996), 'Phenomenographic research – Some methodological issues', in G. Dall'Alba and B. Hasselgren (eds), *Reflections on Phenomenography: Towards a Methodology?* Göteborg: Acta Universitatis Gothoburgensis, pp. 49–66.

Dall'alba, G. and Hasselgren B. (1996), 'Reflections on phenomenography: Towards a methodology?', *Gothenburg Studies in Educational Sciences*, volume 109.

Gallagher, S. (2005), *How the Body shapes the Mind*, Oxford: Oxford University Press.

Jaspers, K. (1963), *General Psychopathology* (trans. from German by J. Hoenig and M. W. Hamilton), Manchester: Manchester University Press.

Marton, F. (1981), *Phenomenography: Describing Conceptions of the World around Us, Instructional Science* 10, Amsterdam: Elsevier, pp. 177–200.

———(1986), 'Phenomenography: A research approach to investigating different understandings of reality', *Journal of Thought*, 21:3, pp. 28–49.

Marton, F. and Booth, S. (1997), *Learning and Awareness*, Mahwah, NJ: L. Erlbaum Press.

Pallasmaa, J. (1996), 'The geometry of felling: A look at the phenomenology of architecture', in K. Nesbitt (ed.), *Theorizing a New Agenda for Architecture: An Anthology of Architectural Theory 1965-1995*, New York: Princeton Architectural Press, pp. 451–52.

Richardson, J. T. E. (1999), 'The concepts and methods of phenomenographic research', *Review of Educational Research*, 69:1, pp. 53–82.

Sin, S. (2010), 'Considerations of quality in phenomenographic research', *International Journal of Qualitative Methods*, 9:4, pp. 305–19.

Sonnemann, U. (1954), *Existence and Therapy: An Introduction to Phenomenological Psychology and Existential Analysis*, New York: Grune & Stratum.

Spiegelberg, H. (1975), *Doing Phenomenology*, The Hague: Martinus Nijhoff.

Tarkovsky, A. (1987), *Sculpting in Time: Reflections on Cinema* (trans. K. Hunter-Blair), New York: Knopf.

Wellington, C. and Ward, R. (2010), 'Using video to explore programming thinking among undergraduate students', *The Journal of Computing Sciences in Colleges*, vol. 25, pp. 149–155

Filmography

Tarkovsky, A. (dir) (1962), *Ivanovo detstvo (Ivan's Childhood)*, Russia: Mosfilm.
—— (1966), *Andrei Rublev (Andrey Rublyov)*, Russia: Mosfilm.
—— (1972), *Solyaris (Solaris)*, Russia: Mosfilm.
—— (1975), *Zerkalo (Mirror)*, Russia: Mosfilm.
—— (1979), *Stalker*, Russia: Mosfilm.
—— (1982), *Nostalghia*, Italy: Rai 2, Russia: Sovinfilm.
—— (1986), *Offret (The Sacrifice)*, Sweden: Svenska Filminstitutet, France: Argos Film.

NOTE
1. Zoner Photo Studio 16 (released autumn 2013, © Zoner Software).

16

An animated portrait of Casa Malaparte: Filmic practice as design research in architecture

Popi Iacovou, University of Cyprus

Encountering Casa Malaparte

In 2005, on a trip to Naples, I visited Capri to see Casa Malaparte (1938–42), the house that starred in *Le Mépris/Contempt* (Godard 1963). Looking at the house for the first time, from the cliff above (Figure 1), had a strong impact on me. Its decisive gesture, refreshing simplicity, colour, theatrical staircase and the way it relates to the landscape, seemed to me, at the time, a fascinating hybrid between theatre and architecture. This break of disciplinary boundaries triggered my curiosity and I decided to look at Casa Malaparte in more depth.

I first visited the house as a participant at a five-day workshop organized by the Catholic University of America at Casa Malaparte, in June 2008. Two years later, in 2010, I stayed at the house as a guest researcher to conduct further fieldwork. Living in the house for a week gave me insights from the perspective of a user of the space, unavailable through only historical, archival and theoretical research. This was an opportunity to discover more about the house's interior, which remains in many ways unknown due to restricted access – as the house is a private property – and to the overemphasis on its iconic exterior. The relative inaccessibility of the house, on one hand, and the overexposure of its exterior form, on the other, has impacted on the academic research conducted on the house to date.

Casa Malaparte's authorship has been in debate amongst architecture historians up until now. For many years the house was attributed to Italian architect Adalberto Libera. However, Marida Talamona's book *Casa Malaparte* (1992) provides evidence that questions Libera's authorship over Casa Malaparte and

AN ANIMATED PORTRAIT OF CASA MALAPARTE

instead renders its owner the author of his own house. Through on-site, archival and historical research, my work expands Talamona's research on the authorship of the house and it is also the first attempt to theorize Malaparte's architectural practice. For the unfolding of Malaparte's creative method and understanding of the house, the collection and analysis of visual material is an important element of the work, something that existing research on the house lacks.

I employ a visual filmic methodology based on the use and development of mixed media animation techniques – where I combine photographs, videos and digital line drawing – to interpret the house's compositional logic and thematics on which it was conceived. In addition I use the filmic methodology to convey aspects of my experience of the house, which I use as a source of knowledge. I want to make visible the transient conditions of atmosphere, affect and imaginary, all outcomes of my encounter and temporal occupation of the house.

Built on the rocky promontory of Punta Massulo overlooking the broad horizon, the house an elongated rectangle in Pompeian red is organized in four levels: the rooftop, first floor, ground floor and lower ground level. Below is a list of the spaces that compose each level:

Cliff Passage
External Staircase

Roof terrace

1st Floor
Hall
Storage Room
Maid's Room
Salon
T-Corridor
Favorita's Room
Favorita's Bathroom
Malapate's Bathroom
Malaparte's Room
Writing room

Ground Floor
Entrance Hall
Interior Staircase
Tavern
Kitchen

Kitchen Storage
Maid's Room
Corridor
Guest Room 1
Guest Room 2
Guest Room 3
Guest Room 4
Bathroom 1
Bathroom 2

Lower Ground
Cellar 1
Cellar 2
Cellar 3

Unlike the conventional production of most buildings, Casa Malaparte was built in an improvisational manner that incorporated in situ decisions, thematic framings, theatrical staging of objects and views, material collage and assemblage. The construction started in 1938 and by 1942 the house took the form it has today.

Living in the house while working on it, Malaparte's life became the script of the house. But the house was never finished and so I would like to argue that it was meant to be an ongoing built script. Rather than static, fixed and stable, the house was physically as well as imaginatively in motion: informed, transformed and reformed by Malaparte's life and imagination. The house is understood as a living picture of its owner. Video stills from the following animation *Performing Casa Malaparte* explore and describe the idea of architecture as 'living pictures' re-enacted from my experience of the house as a visitor.

Performing Casa Malaparte

Performing Casa Malaparte (11 minutes and 28 seconds, 2012) is an animated portrait of Casa Malaparte reconstructed after my visits and seven-day occupation of it. It is made as a mixed media animation combining video, photography and digital drawing. *Performing Casa Malaparte* focuses on the interior of the house including the passage on the Cliff of Punta Massulo, which I consider as an extended entrance. The building portrait interprets the house's compositional methods and animates spaces, views and fragments of it in a series of cinematic tableaux each capturing a specific theme of the house: *Raining Windows, Salon, T-Corridor, Raining Windows, Writing Room, Boat*.

Figure 1: View of Casa Malaparte from the Cliff of Punta Massulo.

Figure 2: Film stills, *From Naples to Capri*, 2008.

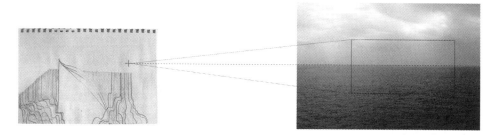

Figure 3: Cut: Horizon, diagram by the author.

Figure 4: 'On the Boat', Film still from *Performing Casa Malaparte*, 2012.

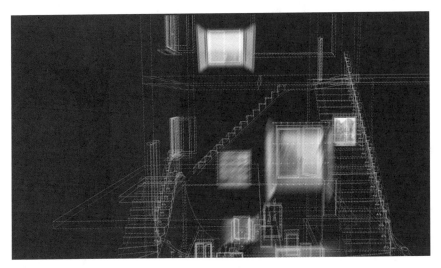

Figure 5: 'Raining Windows', Film still from *Performing Casa Malaparte*, 2012.

This building portrait is part of a larger project that includes a video installation *From Naples to Capri* (17 minutes and 47 seconds, 2008). It depicts in two juxtaposed projections my boat journey from Naples to Capri and backwards (Figure 2). The boat journey is an integral part of the experience of Casa Malaparte that prolongs the encounter with the iconic house. There are overlapping moments between the two projects that draw poetic analogies between the boat journey and the house (Figures 3 and 4).

Figure 6: 'Salon', Film still from *Performing Casa Malaparte*, 2012.

Figure 7: 'Salon', Film still from *Performing Casa Malaparte*, 2012.

Performing Casa Malaparte aims to go beyond the house's common iconic exterior image. Rather, this portrait endeavours for an intimate point of view of the interior, which has been neglected in Casa Malaparte's historical analysis and theoretical discourse.

Figure 8: 'T-Corridor', Film still from *Performing Casa Malaparte*, 2012.

Filmic process

Knowledge derived from the affective and intimate encounters of space in lived experience rarely gets communicated visually in architecture. Traditional architectural tools, like drawing and modelling, provide limited means for exploring the relation between architecture and its lived experience. Dalibor Vesely (2004: 4) in *Architecture in the Age of Divided Representation* writes that:

> What we normally refer to as reality, believing that it is something fixed and absolute, is always a result of our ability to experience, visualize, and articulate – in other words, to represent so as to participate in the world.

The participatory role of architectural representation is largely undermined, contributing to further detachment between the built and the lived experience of space. The way architects observe and interpret space influences the way they design. As a response, I introduce the concept of the *architect-performer*, an active subject attuned to movement that has multiple roles: a user, an observer and a filmmaker who both interprets and designs. The architect-performer interweaves knowledge acquired from direct place experiences with insight from historical, theoretical and design research. My interest in making connections between drawing and the lived experience of space urged me to explore how video, sound and photographs can be mixed with line. In this research, I ask how the lived experience of a place becomes a performative practice for critically reading and reconstructing a site that draws on its temporal qualities. And then, how can the temporal dimensions understood through the architect's performative actions on-site be meaningfully documented through the use of film?

The filmic process developed blurs the boundaries between the real and the fictive, the factual and imagined. It is described below in a series of actions: Collecting, Line Drawing, Animating Points of Views, Composing Sounds and Projecting on Black.

Collecting

The starting point of the design research project was the collection of video shots, sounds and photographs from the site, made during my two visits at the house in 2008 and 2010. These visual and audio recordings were catalogued thematically in order to construct an archive. The archive is an audio-visual database that can potentially grow to accommodate more themes and information on the house in the future. The audio-visual archive replaces the storyboard and the script as 'proactive' controlling tools that allow time for planning. The process of collecting creates an open-ended source that can be used for the creation of multiple scripts giving openness to a research process that is not restricted by a preconceived idea or outcome. One of the challenges is the archive's fragmented nature. Multiple staged photographs of various fragments of spaces, views and close-ups of details become available but the spatial transitions amongst the photographic spaces are the missing *gaps* in the database.

Line drawing

The reconstructive possibilities of the archive were explored by introducing the idea of the line drawing, as a means of filling in the gaps between the fragmented pictorial spaces. The line drawing 'completed' the fragmented photographic spaces. The wooden interior staircase of the house was measured on-site and 3D modelled afterwards. It was multiplied several times to create as many vertical connections needed. Several other spaces and architectural elements were modelled in measured dimensions and others were approximated referring to my affective experience of the house.

In the line drawing the walls are dematerialized to foreground over two hundred layers of photographic material. The line drawing, like a scaffolding system, gives order and structure to the images, in this way it replaces the script, it is notational and its role is to stage, give rhythm and animate the photographic spaces. It re-organizes the pictorial spaces of the house in a vertical order rather than horizontal, which is how they are positioned in reality. This references the surrealists' idea of the house as a labyrinth of the mind and its creative imagination.

Casa Malaparte is designed from inside out, as an interior that extends beyond its physical boundaries, incorporating elements of the expanded landscape that is turned into a fictitious place. For example, the picture windows in the Salon that frame Malaparte's 'imaginary landscapes' are thresholds that can be literally inhabited. The body is cut in two: between reality and imagination, the conscious and the unconscious world. This resonates Surrealist's work, like for example Italian artist Alberto Savinio's[1] painting *The Annunciation* (1932) where 'the "objects" we look at through the window are emanations of the unconscious, rather than the features of any exterior view' (Malt 2004: 182). The surrealist window in Casa Malaparte obscures reality to delve into mental journeys, which are neither all fiction, nor all real. In the animation, the *windows are reversible passages* between interior and exterior space that activate imaginary journeys of the house. The line drawing turns the house into a ghostly presence that fictionalizes and restages a labyrinth of fragmentary images that blur the boundary between reality and imagination.

Animating points of view

The movement in the spaces of the animated house is not a person's point of view, 'a walk-through', but an intentionally *impossible* point of view. The a-personal viewpoint constructed in this animation deconstructs the geographical conditions and provides new affective, interior views of the house. This point of view denotes my first encounter of Casa Malaparte. The house is inaccessible to the public and is normally experienced from the walkway traversing the cliff above or from the water and adjacent bays below. The animated building de-territorializes any fixed views and invites the spectators to be immersed in the imagery.

The structure of the successive episodes is circular, as the entrance and exit of the house happen through the same window – the one that frames the horizon. As there is no story to be followed, the viewers are provoked to be immersed in the imagery without necessarily giving their full attention. At any moment, they can leave the room and return, like the way buildings are experienced in everyday life.

Composing sounds

The sound composition, created in collaboration with sound composer Nasia Therapontos, follows the same process as that of the visual research collection methodology. Sounds collected on site – such as the water pipes that are heard while walking on the cliff of Punta Massulo, seagulls, sea water, the rustle of the leaves, sound of the waves hitting the rocks, my footsteps, the tourist's guide voice and the wind – are mixed and processed with additional synthesized sounds created by Therapontos. Again through digital collage, the different collected sounds are overlaid in multiple layers to recreate the soundscape of the place mixed with additional sounds created to express a sense of place. The sound composition also follows certain spatial patterns as those of the animated images, such as fading, retreating, rotating, doubling suggesting movement. It also has characteristics of qualities of sound such as low and high key sound to express the presence of two elements that antagonize etc.

Projecting on black

The animated line drawing is projected against a black background that has multiple functions. On one hand, it stands as a reference to the narcissist traits Casa Malaparte was conceived. In Michelangelo Merisi da Caravaggio's painting, *Narcissus* (circa 1597–99) is depicted kneeling on top of a pool of water looking at his own reflection in it. The only environment around him is his own reflection in the water. The remainder of the painting is darkness, suggesting that his reality is constructed around his projection of the self. Similarly, Malaparte constructs his narcissist gaze, his I/Eye, by integrating the site views into the interior. As such, the house is built as a microcosm of its owner, on an isolated site that becomes an integral part of the building's interior living image. The site views become integral part of the house interior, outside of which is left mere darkness – black empty space. On the other hand, the black background becomes a surface of erasure, on which traces of my experience are inscribed as a means of openness to future views and encounters. Finally, the black surface is a plane of reflections, potentially mirroring the viewer onto the picture plane.

Performing Casa Malaparte explores the potential of mixed media animation techniques as a reflective tool in architectural design research. It examines the relationship between the architect-performer and existing buildings. This comes as an alternative to the most common uses of animation in architectural practice and education that fluctuate mainly between two polarized directions; from photorealistic representations of not yet realized visions to the constructions of fictional worlds, which are not located in real sites. In between these opposing directions there are various other approaches that explore the creative possibilities of animation techniques in regard to speculative building design. However, exploring existing buildings as a form of reflective practice through mixed-media animation provides a design research method that mediates between 'site' analysis and design and takes into consideration the temporal dimension of space.

In the case of photorealistic representations, animation is used to communicate a space through *after* the design is finalized. This has certain advantages in professional practice as the animation communicates directly how a space 'looks', which makes it legible to a broader audience who is not familiar with the coded system of architectural drawings. Through walk-throughs, animations navigate the viewer in spaces as if walking through the building. These photorealistic simulations can be paralleled to the Beaux-Arts' rendered drawings, which describe the experience of the space as a visual spectacle that unfolds along the axis of movement. At the other end of the spectrum, animations are used for the design of fictional worlds that are not based on real sites. These works deviate from the investigation of existing places and buildings. I suggest that through the use of mixed media animation techniques, space can be captured *in time*, enabling the documentation of the lived experience of existing buildings to address qualities of occupation, subjectivity and temporality.

Building portrait as visual methodology

In life, words (written or verbal) are not the only means by which people communicate, learn and explore the world. Gestures are a powerful visual language that animates the body to communicate feelings and thoughts on a conscious or subconscious level. French dramatist and theatre director, Antonin Artaud (1993: 61), who believed that 'a gesture contains its own energy', advocated that theatre should return to 'the idea of a physical knowledge of images'. Rather than leaning on only literary forms, theatre should be composed of images that engage the audience in an affective manner. Moreover, Bertolt Brecht's *gest*, a theatrical technique, interprets gestures as the embodiment of a broader attitude articulated in images to convey a meaning that has a social dimension (Brecht 1966: 104).

Gestures usually accompany speech to complement, enrich and at times even contradict it. In the *Hiroshima Projection* (1999), video artist Krzysztof Wodiczko explores the relationship between gestures and verbal language in his attempt to document the interviews he conducted with Japanese people who experienced the tragic bombing of Hiroshima. Instead of only recording the conversations, Wodiczko also recorded the gestures of his interviewees. He then projects his oral research of the interviewees on the only surviving building at ground zero in Hiroshima, the site where the atomic bomb exploded. Wodiczko also projects onto the building the gestures of the survivors' hands, which were recorded while they were being interviewed, so that the hand gestures accompany the spoken confessions. One of the video sequences shows the speaker's nervous and uneasy hands playing with a pair of eyeglasses. These visual gestures articulate feelings that are not expressed in people's verbal confessions. Thus, in the *Hiroshima Projection*, gestures complement the verbal confessions to reveal what remains unspoken. Metaphorically, the building is animated not only to speak to us about what it has seen but also to show us how it was felt.

If gestures animate the body to express feelings and thoughts as equally important sources of knowledge, I suggest that animated spaces (with the use of mixed media animation techniques as the means of representation) are gestures that speak through visual language and communicate spatio-temporal dimensions that cannot be articulated through words. In addition, the openness and often ambiguous or enigmatic nature of visual language allows for a pluralist reading of the space. The juxtaposition of *Performing Casa Malaparte* as a visual gesture multiplies the lenses and languages through which I study and communicate my research findings of the house.

Performing Casa Malaparte is a building portrait that enacts an intimate and affective view of the house as reconstructed after my house visits and occupation. To make a portrait, you need to get to know the person first. Art critic, historian and curator, Jean-François Chevrier (2013), says that:

> Portraiture is not a genre but a way of thinking, because it is a way of coming very close to somebody else but at the same time staying outside, feeling the experience of the beholder.

He explains that the relationship established between the painter/photographer and the sitter is a 'common ground' developed for the process of making the portrait. Making a portrait is at the same time being inside and outside a subject of study. In this sense the portrait says as much about the sitter as the artist. It is also affected by the gender of the person making the portrait. Curator Chrissie Iles (2012: 21), in her discussion about Marco Anelli's project *Portraits in the Presence of Marina Abramović* where he creates a series of photographic portraits that document Abramović's performance *The Artists is Present* (2010) at The Museum of Modern Art, New York, describes his photographic practice as a 'double event'. Iles frames the act of making a portrait as an event in itself that documents another event, which is the 'performance' of the sitter (even if in stillness). I suggest that making a building portrait is an event where a reciprocal process between exploring a building and the self evolves. The architect-performer engages with a building in a series of filmic actions that overlay the documentation of the building itself.

Going through the process of filming and editing *Performing Casa Malaparte*, my position shifted between that of a *viewer,* when filming the building behind the camera, and that of a *user* of the house. I retrieve insights of the space moving from a distant to an intimate viewpoint. The distant viewpoint is also reinforced by the fact that editing the project does not have the immediacy of the live recording like in the case of *From Naples to Capri,* which comprises of two unedited single long shots of the journey from Naples to Capri and back. Rather the audio-visual material collected on-site creates an archive for constructing multiple compositions afterwards. The audio-visual archive becomes the basis for the construction of a portrait of Casa Malaparte, which foregrounds fragments of the house that are neither visible in the overall views provided by the plan and section drawings of the house, nor from the distant views of the cliff and the adjacent water bays.

The animation of the images is made by overlaying over two hundred photographs, which are digitally collaged in a spatial manner on screen to creatively reconstruct some of the compositional principles of the house and their effect in the experience of it. The pictures are animated with slow movement, fade ins and outs, cuts, on screen collage and sound to convey an intimate and affective point of view. The hybrid technique developed through digital collage enables the combination of video, photography and line drawing. I consider the photographs, videos and audio footage collected on-site as *found views* and *sounds* integrated within drawing. This process opens up a way of working that operates between site analysis and design. This allows me as the researcher to interpret what I see and reconcile it with an abstract diagrammatic drawing that dematerializes the house and reorganizes it, three dimensionally. Also the line drawing spatializes the photographic spaces, by taking into consideration the compositional principles of the house. Vesely notes that:

> The framework in which the communicative role of architecture can be restored must make it possible to reconcile the abstract language of conceptual constructions with the metaphorical language of the visible world. This was a typical task of poetics, replaced in modern times by the science of poetics (known better as aesthetics), which left the creative principles of making unaddressed.
>
> (2004: 8)

For Vesely the poetics do not rely on abstraction and the application of theoretical knowledge, but on 'praxis', a way of putting forward practical knowledge that concerns the way human beings situate themselves in the world. For Vesely (2004: 387), 'the phenomenon of situatedness stands in clear contrast to instrumental thinking and to the subjective experience of aesthetics. It represents deep respect for the given reality of the natural world, manifested in the rich articulation of typical situations'.

In *Performing Casa Malaparte*, the material is not presented as objective, i.e. as a *document* of my experience but is used in a collage-like manner within the diagrammatic animated drawing to create poetic analogies between images. For Chevrier the tableaux (painted or photographic) is a poetic document of an experience. He explains how the *document* became a relevant and important element in art practices that expanded their role beyond art with 'cultural anthropology at the end of the nineteenth century and [...] surrealism, which associated the *poetical document* with the found object' (Chevrier 2006: 54). He writes that tableaux

> [m]ake reference to the most fundamental principle of bearing witness: the author of the testimony is one who can say 'I was there,' in other words 'I am restoring that which I have seen, the event or the phenomenon in which I participated.' But this principle is far from being a sufficient assurance of accuracy. The precision of the testimony provides trustworthiness to the information; it guarantees the adherence of the viewer or the reader within the mode of belief. But the accuracy of the work is situated upon another level; it presupposes an additional elaboration, a construction of information and concomitantly the possibility of a critical distance for the viewer or the reader.
>
> (Chevrier 2006: 56)

In architecture, the *building portrait* can be seen as a poetic document of an experience. When the building portrait is based on a reflective and situated filmic practice, it can open up new ways of re-looking at built space by taking into consideration time, oscillating between the objective and the subjective, memory and imagination. I propose that making a building portrait is a method for getting to know a place more intimately, as well as creating an aesthetic experience that conveys the affective experience from the perspective of the user.

Performing Casa Malaparte emphasizes the self's participatory role in architectural representation by foregrounding the lived experience as a source of knowledge in site analysis and architectural design. 'To experience is to learn; it means acting on the given and creating out of the given. The given cannot be known in itself. What can be known is a reality that is a construct of experience, a creation of feeling and thought' (Tuan 1977: 9). The building portrait is a visual gesture that expresses feelings and thoughts in the form of a documented event that is the outcome from an encounter with a place.

The architect-performer's practice of physical and filmic movement aims to expand the study, representation and, potentially, design processes of architecture. As an architect-performer, you fluctuate between multiple roles: a user, an observer and a filmmaker who both interprets and designs. Behind the camera you can bring to the foreground elusive, subtle and temporal qualities of space that would otherwise be left unnoticed. In this way, the on-site performances and mixed media techniques embedded in Casa Malaparte's portrait contribute a new spatial construction to the existing textual and visual understandings of the building. Through the filmic techniques presented I aim at developing a new means of analysing and designing architecture; one that takes into consideration how movement and time (as history, present and future) are implicated in architecture. The hybrid techniques developed for the spatial montages allowed the combination of photography, video and line drawing. This opens up a creative method of working between documentary and fiction as a means to advance the architectural design by incorporating filmic strategies. With the use of camera and montage techniques, a creative analysis of architectural sites becomes an integral part of the design process that offers a richer understanding of the event-space and its relation to time. As a form of documented event in a prolonged period of time, the on-site performative actions of the architect-performer articulate visually spatio-temporal dimensions and atmospheres that become architectural propositions.

Acknowledgements

From Naples to Capri and *Performing Casa Malaparte* were made with the support of Architecture Research Fund, The Bartlett School of Architecture, UCL.

For the mixed media animation *Performing Casa Malaparte*, I would like to thank Nasia Therapontos for her sound composition, Alessia Rositani for inviting me to Casa Malaparte and Giorgos Artopoulos for his technical support.

REFERENCES

Abramović, M., Anelli, M., Biesenbach, K. and Iles, C. (2012), *Marco Anelli: Portraits in the Presence of Marina Abramović*, Bologna: Damiani Editore.

Artaud, A. (1993), *The Theatre and Its Double*, London: Calder Publications.

Borzello, F. (1998), *Seeing Ourselves: Women's Self-Portraits*, London: Thames and Hudson.

Brecht, B. (1966), *Brecht on Theatre* (ed. trans. J. Willett), New York: Hill and Wang.

Chevrier, J. F. (2006), 'The tableau and the document of experience', in T. Weski (ed.) *Click Doubleclick*, Cologne: Walther König, pp. 51–61.

——— (2013), 'Inside/Outside', https://vimeo.com/67684056. Accessed 17 September 2013.

Godard, Jean-Luc (1963), *Le Mépris/Contempt*, Paris: Rome Paris Films.

Malt, J. (2004), *Obscure Objects of Desire: Surrealism, Fetishism, and Politics*, Oxford: Oxford University Press.

Talamona, M. (1992), *Casa Malaparte*, New York: Princeton Architectural Press.

Tuan, Y. F. (1977), *Space and Place: The Perspective of Experience*, Minneapolis, MN: University of Minnesota Press.

Vesely, D. (2004), *Architecture in the Age of Divided Representation: The Question of Creativity in the Shadow of Production*, Cambridge, MA: The MIT Press.

NOTE

1. Savinio, the brother of Giorgio De Chirico, was a close friend of Malaparte and got involved with the design of tiles for the house.

17

Exploring, explaining and speaking in tongues: Visual scholarship and architectural education

Lesley Lokko, The Bernard & Anne Spitzer School of Architecture,

City College of New York

Site specifics

On the 9th of March 2015, a student protest movement entitled #RhodesMustFall began at the University of Cape Town, directed initially against a commemorative statue of Cecil Rhodes (Flint 2009), the British arch-imperialist who once said 'to be born English is to win first prize in the lottery of life'. #RhodesMustFall garnered national and international support and on the 9th of April, following a UCT Council vote the previous night, the statue was removed. In retrospect, the protest movement was only the beginning. Although the focus of student demands was on the removal of the statue, the roots of the malaise go far deeper. In the wake of countrywide protests that have seen buildings set alight and urgent calls for a radical re-thinking of what we teach, a unique opportunity has arisen to question the terms and nature of architectural scholarship, particularly since the discipline of architecture itself has been called to account. From the segregated spatial ideologies of *apartheid* planning to the legacy of colonial commemorative monuments, the complicity of the built environment professions in maintaining social and economic inequity is now common knowledge.

This chapter aims to situate the re-definition of architectural scholarship through visual methodologies – including, but not limited to, film – in the broad political context of 'change' and 'transformation' as they are currently happening both in South Africa and the wider African continent at large. Here, the terms 'change' and 'transformation' refer specifically to the challenge of 'de-colonizing' knowledge and 'transforming' the racial and cultural landscape of South African universities, not just in terms of student and staff numbers, but more interestingly in terms of canon. The chapter can therefore be read as an attempt to use the opportunity opened up by these enormous political challenges to re-think what we mean by architectural scholarship, particularly in relation to representation and analysis. As I argue throughout, visual methodologies – of all kinds – offer new and different possibilities for cultures and societies engaged in the serious and complex business of 'finding' their own authentic voice(s). It may seem obvious, but education – even in the context of a professional course like architecture – isn't just about the delivery of an approved curriculum, it is also (and perhaps more deeply) concerned with the transmission of values. Here in South Africa, the very idea of a shared culture or values-in-common that might transcend the specificities of place, language, history and even 'race' remains an elusive pipedream. The question of *what* and *how* we might teach our current and future generation of young African architects is equally elusive. The translation of indigenous built environment beliefs, histories, relationships and ways of seeing the world into a functioning, relevant and accessible architectural curriculum remains an on-going process. The complex and rich conditions of African 'space' lend themselves particularly well to new ways of seeing/making/exploring/researching architecture, which might lead to wildly differing outcomes, not just in terms of how we understand space, but, crucially, how we construct and inhabit it.

The visual propositions contained in this chapter, *Speaking in Tongues*, use film and photography to respond to this artificially constructed tension between conventional ways of understanding architecture, particularly in relation to African cities, and more speculative, open-ended means of investigation. Although the site of the project itself is in West, not South Africa, the means through which the project has unfolded over the past ten years are as relevant in Johannesburg as they are in Accra. This chapter examines architectural scholarship (my own) through the lens of the decade-long research project and attempts to situate my findings in the architectural educational context in which I currently work.

A novel idea

At the University of Johannesburg, where I directed the Graduate School of Architecture from 2014–2019, the wider university has been quick to foreground *knowledge* as well as fees as the key issues in the recent protests.[1] To quote from one of the working papers of the Ad Hoc Senate Committee on Decolonisation of Knowledge and Curriculum Reform (2016: 5),

> decolonisation of knowledge at UJ entails building an institutional ethos which
> reflects an African centeredness in curriculum, research, aesthetics and governance

in relevant and globally competitive academic programmes, commensurate with the institutional vision of an international university of choice, anchored in Africa, dynamically shaping the future.

It's a bit of a mouthful but the opportunity for disciplines like architecture to critically and fundamentally examine their pedagogical provenance comes around once in a lifetime (well, at least in mine). The call for academics to 'fundamentally re-think the entire curricula of departments and faculties in order to break the "epistemic violence" that has been a hallmark of the higher education system in South Africa' has repercussions for the entire continent (Rensburg 2016: 21).

To unpack this statement a little more fully, I'd like to step sideways for a moment and speak not about architecture, but about writing, and specifically fiction.

> Novel: mid 16th century: from Italian *novella (storia)*, 'new' (story), feminine of *novella* ('new'), from Latin *novellus*; from *novus* ('new'). The word is also found from late Middle English until the 18th century in the sense of 'a novelty, a piece of news', from Old French novella.[2]

When the word 'novel' entered the languages of Europe via *Don Quixote*, considered to be the first European novel, it had a very vague meaning. It meant – as its name suggests – something new, a form of writing that was formless, that had no rules; that made up its own rules as it went along. It captured – and represented – the collision of a number of different forces: urbanization, the spread of printing, the availability of cheap paper, and it began the tradition of an intimate reading experience that has endured to this day. For cultures *without* the written word – like the majority of African cultures – that relationship between *intimacy* (the solitary act of reading or drawing) and *performance* (those aspects of oral storytelling and communal building) – is one that we grapple with – or at least *should* grapple with – today. But we don't, at least not in any part of the African continent that *I* know of. In the context of African schools, like it or not, staff and students must necessarily act simultaneously as interpreters and investigators, explaining a world that is often invisible to western-trained 'eyes', both to themselves and others, yet at the same time exploring it in all its depth. It's a difficult, complex task. As many scholars from Achille Mbembe, AbdouMaliq Simone to Edgar Pieterse have already noted, there is something deeply interesting and complex happening here (in African cities) if we could only work out how to see it (see Pieterse 2008; Simone 2004).

The question of 'how to see' (and subsequently how to name, make, propose) has been a major preoccupation of mine over the last twenty years. Following Derrida, architecture may be thought of as a language where 'various [...]

programmes can be arranged in various ways, depending on context' (quoted in Wigley 1997), I would also argue that part of the difficulty in 'reading' contemporary African cities, spaces and landscapes has to do with the tools we employ to 'see': the conventional architectural vocabulary (of plan, section, elevation and perspective) allows us to recognize only fraction of what we see. Static architectural drawings imply a world that is both familiar and unchanging: in contexts where the slippage between form and programme, space and use, near and far dominates the gaze, such forms of representation fail to catch or capture the fundamentally unpredictable nature of cities/spaces like Johannesburg, Accra, Dakar ... and any in-depth understanding consequently escapes us. Using the moving drawing as a means of *exploring*, not *explaining*, seems to offer African students of architecture (and here let me only speak about students, not practitioners or professionals) a way out. Speculation as a means of investigation (as opposed to the more pragmatic problem-solving approach) represents a real triumph of will, not only in the context of global speculation about architecture and architectural education, but particularly in the context of Africa, which has never 'deserved' to be speculative. There's a lot of work to be done to re-configure a curriculum that better serves our needs – and here I'm not talking about sanitation upgrades or social housing – but rather that gap between exploration and explanation that visual methodologies capture so well.

The following extracts are from a research project that was undertaken in Accra over a two-year period, primarily as a preamble to a much longer project involving Master's level students at the Graduate School of Architecture, University of Johannesburg, which included two other sites, Stone Town, Zanzibar and Praia, Cabo Verde. The wider research project, entitled *The Eclectic Atlases*, draws on Italian urbanist and architect Stefano Boeri's statement that

> we are in the middle of a transitional period in the disciplines of architecture and urbanism. Most of these symptoms are linguistic, as the weakness of our architectural vocabulary faces the complexity of contemporary urban spaces: we still use generic, vague words to name spatial issues. But we don't only need a new vocabulary. Symptoms of a more profound disease stand in our visual culture, in the ways we usually think about and represent the urban dimension.
>
> (Koolhaas et al. 2001: 224)

Film was specifically chosen for its ability to capture time, place, ambience and mood, and the site – Spintex Road, Accra – was chosen specifically as it resists easy attempts to define its programme: thoroughfare, retail, religious or peripheral? It is all of these, and none.

VISUAL RESEARCH METHODS IN ARCHITECTURE

Extract # 001 September 2006 'A Fine Line'

A Fine Line was originally intended as a straightforward mapping project looking at different activities along a single six-and-a-half mile strip of road. Spintex Road is a narrow but major thoroughfare connecting the capital city, Accra, with the new town of Tema, the port city planned and built by the country's first president, Osagyefo Kwame Nkrumah. Once two distinct cities, Accra and Tema have merged to become one urban conglomeration, linked by arterial routes such as the Spintex Road, which were never designed to carry their current traffic load. Built in 1975 as a single-lane track accessing a handful of industrial estates, today it is estimated that more than a million people live in and around it, a result of the building boom of the 1990s and early 2000s when a surge of middle-class Ghanaians returned 'home' after the political turbulence of the previous two decades. At first glance, Spintex is unremarkable, except perhaps in its ordinary specifically tropical dreariness. With no exit points, no adjoining roads and no turn-offs, there is only one way in and out of Spintex: at its mouth, where the road meets the mall, and at the other end, in Tema. It is also the site of two of the most significant architectural projects of the past decade: at one end, Accra's first western-style shopping mall – Accra Mall – and, halfway along its length, the country's largest and most prestigious charismatic Christian church, Action Chapel. In 2002, before construction of the Accra Mall had properly commenced, it took approximately twenty minutes to traverse its length. Today (2016) the same journey can take up to three hours. Both the mall and the churches have contributed not only to the traffic congestion, but also to its West African counterpart, the roadside market.

The market has produced a number of different spatialities (for want of a better word) that both define and describe a uniquely West African urban condition: opportunistic, fleet-footed, mobile, customer-savvy. *Everything* is for sale along Spintex, from live puppies to nine-packs of toilet roll, from out-dated gym equipment to concrete garden gnomes. Manufacturing zones have sprung up on either (pavement-less) side of Spintex, which also now house the retailers, together with their families. Crèches, food stalls, mobile kitchens, kiosks, ablution blocks, as well as makeshift shelters are the new end-conditions on either side of the road, which is itself beginning to self-widen as more and more mini buses (Accra's privately-owned 'public' transport system) see a new route opportunity and seize it. The site resists easy categorization: it is neither a road, a production strip, a marketplace, a place or worship or a residential zone: rather, it is all of these, at once, simultaneously and subject to rapid and quicksilver change. There are no zoning regulations, no bylaws, no codes [...] this is city- and place-making at its most immediate. Static representations are superfluous and do little to capture the

Figure 1: Traffic along Spintex, 6:30am, © Lokko, L. 2010. *Photograph*.

Figure 2: A 'live-work' zone adjacent to Spintex, momentarily quiet on a Sunday morning, © Lokko, L. 2010. *Photograph*.

essence of the site. It is both destination and through-route: a slice of Accra that is best represented on the move.

The following photographs and videos (available on the Vimeo link https://vimeo.com/home) show the initial mapping exercise, shot over a three-day period in 2010 and again in 2015.

Extract # 002 April 2010. Action!

> Modern man no longer communicates with the madman. There is no common language: or rather, it no longer exists; the constitution of madness as mental illness, at the end of the eighteenth century, bears witness to a rupture in a dialogue and expels from the memory all those imperfect words, of no fixed syntax, spoken falteringly, in which the exchange between madness and reason was carried out. The language of psychiatry, which is a monologue by reason about madness, could only have come into existence in such a silence.
>
> (Foucault [1984] 2009: 131)

No city poses quite as direct a challenge to conventional forms of architectural education, representation and practice as the African City, wherever on the continent that may be. One of the seminal chapters in Koolhaas' edited work, *Mutations,* argues that 'shopping is the last remaining forms of public activity' (Koolhaas et al. 2001: 4). His project, the student-led *Harvard Project on the City* looks at the ways in which shopping has been able to colonize and replace almost every aspect of urban life, including religion. 'Churches are mimicking shopping malls to attract followers' (Koolhaas et al. 2001: 125). The juxtaposition in *Mutations* of classic architectural programmes of 'airport', 'mall' and 'church' provides an interesting exploratory context for Spintex, situated adjacent to the international airport on one side and with Africa's most modern shopping mall and its biggest church located along it. Koolhaas' explorations on Lagos focused primarily on Lagos at a macro scale, from the air (in a helicopter) and through static, all-seeing aerial photography, rather than at the micro, on-the-ground scale of moving images that seem to me, at least, richer and more complex tools of potential analysis. In the same way that Koolhaas looks at shopping as being emblematic of western urban culture, it is hard to talk about public life and space in African cities without referring (explicitly or otherwise) to the charismatic Christian churches that have proliferated across the continent in the years following the economic collapse of many African states. The IMF and World Bank structural adjustment programmes in both Ghana and Nigeria in the 1980s have proved to be amongst the most contentious issues in global economic policy, affecting not only the measurable material health of both countries, but arguably their spiritual wellbeing, evidenced by the explosive growth of 'empowerment' healing and the dominant message of the importance of financial success. In 2009, the then-President of Ghana, John Atta-Mills, (incidentally also an accountant specializing in tax) upheld the government's decision *not* to levy any form of taxation on churches since, as he put it, 'who can tax God?' (Ateba 2009).

Action! began shortly afterwards, towards the end of 2009 and continued until 2013, and looks at the 36 churches that are to be found along Spintex. With the exception of Action Chapel, none of the 36 places of worship along the Spintex Road began life as such: these places of worship have contained a number of disconnected programmes over their (short) lifespan, from abandoned residences to petrol stations. Some started out modestly, as little more than a thatched kiosk located at the side of the road; others seem to have emerged spontaneously, located on the sites of gathering, occasionally occupying and replacing other premises as congregations grew and expanded. Some of these churches appear to 'have found their natural ground and stability' (Foucault 1986) as terrestrial palaces that reference a celestial order. There is no easy or orthodox way to enter these churches as an outsider (in both religious and cultural terms). In some, entrance is strictly forbidden; in others, a donation or expression of interest suffices. I chose the Blessed Givers Church, which, in three short years, had grown from little more than a roadside shack to a substantial two-storey building with a corrugated tin roof, several halls of prayer and (somewhat incongruously), a car wash.

Entering the church, I'm again reminded of Foucault's concept of 'heterotopias', sacred or forbidden places in which individuals who find themselves in a state of crisis in relation to the society in which they live. They have become less spaces of conventional worship than 'safe' spaces of non-confinement in which anything may be said. To witness one of these services is to find oneself in an eerie, uneasy territory located somewhere between crisis and deviance, half church/half asylum in which despair and hope are carefully and skilfully stoked. The four videos that were shot clandestinely inside the Blessed Givers Church do not lend themselves easily to prose description: like all moving images, they rely on sound, light, atmosphere and dialogue, all of which are routinely outside the conventional means of architectural representation. (The videos are available on the following Vimeo link: https://vimeo.com/home). Sounds compete with sounds: the voice of the pastor, amplified over a series of loudspeakers; a radio sermon played at full blast; mounted television screens relaying Baptist American services and clusters of worshippers, murmuring, praying, lamenting, fainting ... speaking in tongues. The ambiance is simultaneously chaotic and cathartic and hard to define.

Figure 3: The two pastors of Blessed Givers wave me off. © Lokko, L. 2013. *Photograph*.

In *Discipline and Punish: The Birth of the Prison*, Foucault (Foucault 1975) traces the evolution of the concept of madness through three phases: the Renaissance, the Classical Age and the Modern experience. In the Renaissance, madmen or 'the mad' were often understood as having some sort of higher wisdom, an understanding of the limits of our world, and were often portrayed in literature as revealing the slippage between what men are, and what they pretend to be. In the mid-seventeenth century, the Age of Reason, the rational response to the mad, who until then had been consigned to society's margins, was to separate them completely from society by confining them, along with all the other undesirables (prostitutes, vagrant, blasphemers) in newly created institutions all over Europe – asylums and madhouses, a process he calls the 'Great Confinement'.

Aside from being interested in the spatiality of confinement – whether it's the prison or the madhouse – I'm also interested in the tension between sanity and insanity. *Speaking in Tongues* looks at these charismatic churches as spaces of *non*-confinement – spaces of slippage between spiritual, social, legal, financial and institutional control. Foucault's modern experience begins at the end of the eighteenth century with the creation of specially designated spaces devoted completely to either curing madness or confining it. For me, in West Africa (which is very different from elsewhere on the continent), the modern experience begins much later, with

EXPLORING, EXPLAINING AND SPEAKING IN TONGUES

independence, and rather than attempt to confine or cure those behaviours that, *for whatever reason*, no longer fit within the modern narrative, such behaviours are left to fluidly find their own level, place and space within it. Although the subject matter is ostensibly religion, I'm actually more interested in the idea of *language* than in *belief* or *faith*, per se. I'm fascinated by the relationship between confusion and translation, between 'babble' and 'meaning', between 'speaking strangely' or 'speaking in tongues', between foreigner and native. What does it mean to be both/and, as opposed to either/or? To be both stranger and intimate? To be hybrid? To be halfway? It's a commonly held belief that language is about communication but, 'language', according to Barthes, 'is actually legislation. Speech is its code' (Barthes 1983). Architecture too is a language, and like any form of it, also contains its codes: drawing codes, building codes, engineering codes, representational codes and so on. When we teach those codes, we bring the legislation and policing of the language of architecture into play. *Glossolalia*, the Latin word for '*speaking in tongues*' is defined as the 'fluid vocalising of syllables that sound like intelligible speech but lack any readily apparent meaning' (Colman 2009: 258). *Speaking in Tongues* is intended as a play on *architectural language*, using notions of fluidity, instability and intuition (as opposed to the more traditional tropes of architectural expression – stability, solidity, grounded-ness, foundations) to uncover new possibilities for architecture in *all* its forms: built, speculative, intimate, urban. I'm interested in looking more closely at the act of *translation* (from idea to drawing, drawing to model, model to building, building to city) as a multi-faceted, multi-layered mechanism that isn't only about a 1:1 direct transfer of meaning, but to see the act rather as a space of fluidity, of play – perhaps even of risk.

This chapter began its 'journey' in South Africa, travelled through example to West Africa and now must return. Nowhere on the African continent are the tensions between North and South, West and the rest, modernity and tradition more deeply and problematically entrenched than at its foot. Architecture is a deeply speculative act, propositional as well as critical, as engaged with the 'real' world as it is with the world of the imagination. In a place where architecture has historically done more harm than good, it seems appropriate to protect the academy as the space in which the re-definition of architectural scholarship may legitimately take place. Learning to use architectural language (spoken, written, built) is a key task of architectural education. The more familiar students are with recognized languages, the more adept they are in adopting or creating their own. It seems to me that this is the key task and challenge of contemporary African architectural education: to find, invent, appropriate or construct a new language of architecture that offers new possibilities for seeing, making, dwelling. Film may not yet be that language: but it appears to come closer to the mark.

REFERENCES

Ateba, S. (2009), 'Pastor T.B. Joshua predicted my victory', *PM News*, 12 January, www. thepmnews/about/atta-mills. Accessed 8 September 2016.

Barthes, R. (1983), *Barthes: Selected Writings*, London: Fontana Press.

Colman, A. (ed.) (2009), *A Dictionary of Psychology*, Oxford: Oxford University Press.

Flint, J. (2009), *Cecil Rhodes*, London: Little, Brown.

Dahaene, M. and de Cauter, L. (eds) (2008), *Heterotopia and the City: Public Space in a Postcivil Society*, London: Routledge

Foucault, M. (1975), *Discipline and Punish: The Birth of the Prison*, New York: Random House.

Foucault, M. and Miskowiec, J. (1986), 'Of other spaces', *Diacritics*, 16:1, pp. 22–27.

———— ([1984] 2009), *History of Madness*, preface to the 1961 edition, pp. xxvii–xxxix (trans. J. Khalfa), New York: Routledge.

Koolhaas, R. et al. (eds) (2001), *Mutations*, New York: ACTAR.

Pieterse, E. (2008), *City Futures: Confronting the Crisis of Development*, Chicago, IL: The University of Chicago Press.

Rensburg, I. (2016), 'Vice-Chancellor's overview and reports of the Ad Hoc Senate Committee on Decolonisation of Knowledge and Curriculum Reform', https://www.uj.ac.za/about/Documents/reports/UJ_AnnualReport2015ONLINE.pdf. Accessed 9 September 2016.

Simone, A. (2004), *For the City Yet to Come: Urban Life in Four African Cities*, Durham, NC: Duke University Press.

Wigley, M. (1997), *The Architecture of Deconstruction: Derrida's Haunt*, Cambridge, MA: The MIT Press.

NOTES

1. Subsequent to #RhodesMustFall, #FeesMustFall was a second, student-led protest movement that began in mid-October 2015 in response to an increase in fees at South African universities. The protests also called for higher wages for low-earning university staff who worked for private contractors such as cleaning services and campus security and for them to be employed directly by universities. Protests started at the University of Witwatersrand and spread to the University of Cape Town and Rhodes University before rapidly spreading to other universities across the country. Although the focus of the protests was centred around fees, as with the #RhodesMustFall movement a year earlier, the demands were linked to a number of other issues, not least the lack of what has been termed 'transformation' in broader socio-economic and racial terms.

2. Definition from the Free Dictionary, http://www.thefreedictionary.com/novel. Accessed 9 September 2016.

18

The plasmatic image: Experimental practices between film and architecture

Morten Meldgaard, Institute for Building, Landscape and Planning, The Royal Danish Academy of Fine Arts School of Architecture

Introduction

The fact is that the new spiritual automatism and new psychological automata depend on an aesthetic before depending on technology.

It is the time-image which calls for an original regime of images and signs before electronics spoils them or in contrast relaunches it.

(Deleuze [1985] 1989: 252)

The task of Kafka the writer was perhaps no different than that of "K." the land surveyor in The Castle and the accused in The Trial. It was, on the one hand, to chart the topography of this peculiar emergent world, to discover the laws of how things combine, and on the other, to trace by trial and error the mysterious principle of its functioning. But at the same time no sketch or figure is anywhere offered up, unless it be one of these deliberately scrambled and inscrutable images like the officers' blueprints for the inscription apparatus in the Penal Colony. For in Kafka, the task is no longer to trace the visible form of the world by recourse to an external schema or representational mode, but to somehow espouse its very substance, to become of the world by becoming one with it.

(Kwinter 2001: Preface)

Figure 1: The motion pictures here depicted probe the relation between image content and 'Out of Field' in three ways: the inside/outside of the frame, the behind/in front of the mask and the before and after of movement in time. Frame grabs from three-panel video installation entitled 'Loop' © Marie Limkilde and Barbara Bohr, 2015. The video was produced as part of a workshop entitled 'How to produce a Time Crystal' taught by Cort Ross Dinesen, Morten Meldgaard, Anders Michelsen and Frederik Thygstrup.

In his famous books on Cinema, philosopher Gilles Deleuze theorized on cinema's initial failure as both technique and medium by pondering the question; 'what was Cinema's position at the outset?' Deleuze (2005: 6–7) came to the conclusion that cinema's failure in the first twenty or so years of its existence presented a double-figure, since neither its analytic or synthetic qualities were in demand by science or the Arts respectively. Today this insight seems astounding *and* perplexing, recognizing that such a distinction between science being analytical and the arts being synthetic seems absurdly redundant. Today science fundamentally relies on moving images, in its ever increasing 'combinat' of surveillance, computation and warfare (Lury 2014), while the Arts have moved beyond any idea of unity or re-assemblage of post-industrial knowledge.

To echo Deleuze, we might add that the idea of the *exposed* and printed negative, which even Deleuze himself took for granted, as an *Original*, informed and restricted a great many traits of classical and modern cinema. That the 'jump cut' and the reuse of material or enlargements of framings ('pistol-cutting') were considered vulgar, was not only derived from the technical problems involved in using the same piece of negative twice, but in a whole ethics of unity, which modern cinema sought to warp but never forsook. With the advent of (MTV) digital editing in the early 1980s, the economic cost of the single individual cut in the negative print went down proportionally with the pace of editing going up. From then on the ubiquity of the Pixel replaced the singularity of the negative.

Today this is all in the annals of history. There is no more negative exposed, printed or otherwise. The pixel plate of Digital Cinema is wholly analytical and wholly synthetic at the same time. While Deleuze grouped different practices of cinema as solid, fluent or gaseous (Bogue 2003: 105), we might in turn discuss the prevailing state of affairs as 'plasmatic' (Meldgaard 2013: 172–82), owing to the ever-increasing flux of media, images and motion pictures *outside* the realm of cinema. Images are no longer bound by what Patricia Pisters (2003: 218–19) coined 'a camera consciousness', nor are they linked to 'the light chamber' that Roland Barthes (1981) made an essential of the artificial image, moulded or modulated (Deleuze 2005: 25) as photography or moving image.

Transvisuality

But what might define such a 'plasmatic' image? First of all we have to ask, what constitutes an environment where they might appear and how do we go about researching them? Perhaps it is due time that we stopped asking images about their meaning and focus instead on how they are being generated and how they operate. Today the agenda of visual studies moves away from traditional boundaries of thematics (gender, minority, cognition) towards a broader understanding of the visual compounds as self-governing systems and stratifications. This development has been coined as 'transvisuality' (Kristensen et al. 2015a). The discourse of the 'transvisual' offers the ambition to ask the how of contemporary image production, realizing that images are no longer a representation of power, but are fully governing and operational strata in themselves (Kristensen et al. 2015: 12–52). Even Henri Bergson seemed to have noted this growing tendency of the *Index*, a moulded or modulated image, when he famously used it as a metaphor: 'Photography, if there is such a thing, is already snapped, already shot, in the very interiority of things and for all the points in space' (Bergson 2005: 38). Today visuality moves away from and beyond traditional borders of representation, power and meaning. Visuality is fully able to create these stratifications as internal operations, within its own combines, while coaxing, connecting and creating independent transversals through media, culture, economics, politics, geographies and zones of privacy. The 'transvisual' is an all-encompassing plethora of image-matter akin to the *Chiasm* of Maurice Merleau-Ponty: Not the word, but the

Image becomes (the) *Flesh* of the world. Ultimately this reversal of the 'facialism' of the 'White wall-Black hole' system means that bodies no longer let themselves be imprinted on images, but that images now imprint themselves as self-governing and sufficient bodies (Deleuze and Guattari 2005: 211–12). This is where the 'when' of genesis and the 'how' of operation become crucial to understanding post-industrial mediascape and the ever-increasing flux of unrestrained image production.

Hence the visual material accompanying this text is not only derived from cinema, but from a combined effort of filmmakers and architects alike, to negotiate different 'scapes' of memory, affect, necessity and desire as we draw transversals and construct chronotopes, which in turn generate an artificial landscape built from textual assemblages, cinematic sequences and diagrammatic constructs of drawing. Easily we might conclude that cinema has moved away from the 'movie house', and that architecture today is cinematic, topological and sequential, but more importantly there seems a shared difference of the frame and the essential discussion of how the visual domain is constituted today. What constitutes architecture's basic drawing framework in a visual domain where representations no longer represent, but form a reality of their own? What is the *architecture* of this 'ocean of [audio-visual knowledge] formlessness'?

In our work we have tried to establish a new hierocracy between architectural drawing, moving image and written word. Deleuze, in his book on Foucault, would have it that the 'seeable' is determined by the 'sayable' (Deleuze 2004: 67) but cannot be reduced to this determination. It is this gap or perhaps more precisely, in this overflooding of the relation between the two that our drawings try to expose. We picture this process analogue to the experience of developing an exposed photographic paper in the vat of the dark chamber filed with developer fluid. The paper has been determined by exposure, but the process of the fluid is so intensive that it has a limit space in where this determination can be negotiated, manhandled or cancelled out.

> Above all, then, Foucault describes how the articulable determines the visible [...] Foucault's project consists in revealing truth as the determination of the visible by the sayable [...] Ironically, the 'light of truth' emerges when light has been contained in any given apparatus (dispositif), when the power grid is so overwhelming as to render the resulting representation seemingly adequate.
>
> (Flaxman 2000: 24–25)

The drawings are not representations (Figure 2), though they may have a very clear *likeness* to other architectural drawings through their occasional resemblance in structure, scale, marking, signature, geometry etc., but just like the seeable itself it cannot be reduced to these determinations of practice (grammar, convention, zweckmässigkeit). That does not mean that our drawings do not produce anything or have no pragmatic measure, they do indeed. The drawing holds together the hodological space of the draughtsman with the computational entity of the world, while it in turn can serve as an underlay for unrolling schematic planar solutions, which can then be developed extremely fast with very basic design competences.

The plasmatic image

In many ways our current understanding and grasp of the state of the image in contemporary culture seem as limited and conventional as early twentieth-century concepts of what cinema actually was and was capable of (Kracauer 2004; Deleuze 2005: 253). Have we actually remembered to ask of the pixel what more it can do? As Jean-Luc Godard (in Lundemo 2004: 380) said of montage, as he disobeyed the rule of reuse, it is much more and of a greater significance:

> Montage is what made Cinema unique [...] The silent movie felt it very strongly and talked about it a lot. No-one found it. Griffith was looking for something like montage, he discovered the close-up. Eisenstein naturally thought that he had found montage [...]. But by montage I mean something much more vast.

The Plasmatic Image arises from Godard's claim that the virtuality of what has not yet been cut, will be cut, cannot be cut. But it is 'Trans-Vertovian', in the sense that it is no longer the camera (and its inherent capability of montage) that extends the human eye and consciousness. No, the pixel exists on its own level, a difference in kind, since it does not include a priori traditional camera values or acts, like exposure, shot, take, lightning, speed, in any way. The Plasmatic Image is no longer 'a cloud of camera eyes'; it is in turn what constitutes *the Cloud*, as a computational necessity of that said digital entity.

Any inclusion or exclusion of current phenomena would be remote from this definition. Everything that could be exposed on a pixel plate, including what has, is and will be exposed, through acts of camera exposure, animation, manipulation, computation, falls within this definition; a montage in depth of the plate (layers) and a morphing in length of its duration (vectors). This can be observed in any current media production from advertising, apps, reality, gaming, documentary and to the remains of fiction itself: It is a 'Volume Image' (Meldgaard 2013: 172–83), since it goes back to Space-Time volume of the brain as the screen of screens and it is informational in its ever increasing production of new visual strata as a plasmatic substitute for a new terrain. The Plasmatic Image is a landscaping or gardening of two distinct traits: layers in depths, morphing in lengths, while relying on the absolute 'Out of Field', that which is not cinema, that which could not occur as 'image only'.

The topology of the 'Before and After'

In the fall issue of *Theory, Society & Culture*, Lury et al. (2012: 3–35) argue that culture itself has taken a topological turn. Not only are its various functions, economies, schemes and operations now governed by topologically driven informatics and data-mining, but the very *Gestalt*, i.e. the way society creates itself, has become topological. It could be argued that we are living in a new form of continuity, endlessly connecting through our gadgets and their combined *informata* (i.e. informational strata), creating a novel and unprecedented *Lifeworld*, prone to new and only as yet to be seen laws of combination, alignment and transversality. In *Architectures of Time* Sanford Kwinter (2001: 120–21) notoriously abandons design for a lengthy discussion of the work of writer Franz Kafka, and the 'becoming topological of prose':

> It is in Kafka then that one may begin to speak not only of a new narrative order of space-time, but of a new topographical mode of writing. Problems of transmissibility and non-transmissibility, affiliation and separation, and of the complex relations of physical parts to (metaphysical) wholes now replace the traditional literary meditation of interiority: meaning, psychology, truth.

In this respect topology plays an important part, both as reflective agent and as a way of operating within this 'New Nature' (Abraham 2009). Topology operates with a set of dimensions wherein certain properties remain or are kept intact, in terms of their relation, through different temporal and morphological changes. In this sense a property of a certain artistic material can be said to create a transversal, when it is allowed to operate and inform diverse layers, configurations and regions of a work of art.

In the pragmatic and concrete work within artistic production, both in architecture and cinema, two topological parameters seem paramount, the 'Out of Field', i.e. that which is defined by being outside the space of the frame, and the 'Before and After', i.e. that which is defined by being outside the timeframe. Ultimately this might lead to an aesthetics, which could be said to be sequential in the sense that it operates as a mathematical function within a given set. A banal example of this would be how the square root of the number 2 operates as a sequence in the group of natural numbers, while creating the relational aesthetics of the standard DIN A format, regardless of their size (A0, A1, A2, A3, A4....). Stemming from this idea we have tried to conceive of the sequence shot and its relation to its context (Troiani and Campbell 2015: 7–16) as a *dark precursor* for a much more radical aesthetics of irrational sequences working in diverse media and creating intensive environments.

In our attempts to unfold these ideas, which question both transcendent and relational aesthetics by applying the idea of a sequential aesthetics, we have tried through our engagement with film to work with a small sequence containing three different stratifications at the same time (Figure 1). We basically set up three screens projecting the same image with a slight dilution of time, which meant that we, in an analytical sense, could 'unfold' or 'spatialize' travelings and sequence shots like the opening of Godard's *Weekend* (1969) or Tarkovsky's pool sequence from *Stalker* (1979). This produced a video-loop that contained three different manifestations of what film people call the 'Out of Field', i.e. the context of the image that in many ways define the content. These three 'Out of Fields' can easily be aligned to an architectural practice and help to describe or determine current architectural phenomena or fields of problems. They consist of the Inside/Outside relation of the frame, the Behind/In front of the Mask and the Before and After of time-based movement. They create a spatio-temporal situation where you can never be sure where exactly the viewer or viewed are placed, in which time or in which version. This creates an n-dimensional image-space, which could be described non-progressively as point, screen, time, space, time, movement (in time), hence a Plasmatic space.

Conclusion: Issues of methodology

In his famous film *Stalker*, director Andrei Tarkovsky (1979) lets his protagonist find his way in 'the Zone' by throwing a bolt tied with a white piece of cloth. This well-known 'throw' of the skilled practitioner and the connotations of 'the Zone' have been seen as a model for creativity, but we might also look at it as a method where all other methods or systematics fail in their rationality. For anyone involved in the processes and production of art, it is evident that such a thing as a method cannot be conceived, since art relies on singular expressions that cannot be arrived at by repeatable means or re-enactments of formulae (Bertram 2010). Art is not a product, which derives from a method, but is the product of an event of which it is in itself an inseparable element. Methods tend to reproduce what is already known by a limitation of possibilities while the production of art aims at producing that which is only virtually a possibility, the emergence of the truly 'New' (Deleuze 2002: 96–97).

Hence the teaching of art, and the research into artistic image production faces some radical methodological issues. How do you actually produce the 'New', and,

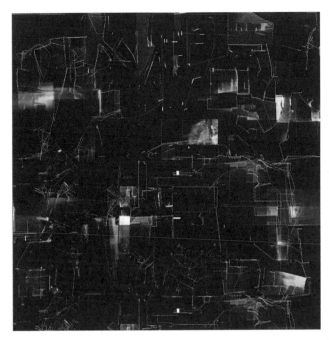

Figure 2: The overall aim of the 'Time crystal' workshop was to create a new relation between drawing, writing and time-based media, a new overflooding of the relation between 'the sayable and the seeable', as Deleuze described it in his book on Foucault. Final Workshop drawing #2 (2000 × 2000 mm) © students involved in the workshop entitled 'How to produce a Time Crystal' taught by Cort Ross Dinesen, Morten Meldgaard, Anders Michelsen and Frederik Thygstrup, 2015.

perhaps much more poignant to teachers and researchers of architecture alike, how do you recognize it when it does happen?

In the well-known text *Der Essay als Form,* Theodor W. Adorno describes the literary form of an essay as specific *'Erkenntnis'*, i.e. knowledge where the issue of morphology of the textual matter itself arises, as intertwined between content and form. Adorno describes how a text can be written, which is not only reproducing thoughts, but which is actually in the process of thinking them. He describes this as a 'carpet of thought operations which creates its own critical density' (Adorno 1998: 107), a process of differentiation that the text tries to open up rather than hide. This is the process or practice that most artists will recognize, not as a method, but as a form of practice: the production through a series of discrete operations of density in a given material, which in turn opens up for a variety of transversals and concrete fault lines that give the final work its vibration and depth (Meldgaard 2013). Godard (1972: 240) said this plainly when referring to his work on *2 ou 3 choses que je sais d'elle* (*Two or Three Things*

I Know about Her) (1967): 'If Cinema = Life, then 1+2+3=4'. In addition to the known (and repeatable) methods of rationality '1+2=3', we must find new modes of counting, 1, 2, 3, 4..., new ways and practices of forcing us by ourselves to think and produce the 'New'.

Acknowledgements

The *Time Crystal Workshop* was held in February 2015 and included students from the Royal Danish Academy School of Architecture programme for *Architecture, Space & Time* and The National Danish Film school *Department of Multicamera Direction*. It was taught by Cort Ross Dinesen, Anders Michelsen and Morten Meldgaard. The image accompanying this text was done by Marie Limkilde and Barbara Bohr, while the drawing was done by a collective of students.

REFERENCES

Abraham, A. (2009), *A New Nature*, Copenhagen: Royal Danish Academy, School of Architecture Publishers.

Adorno, T. (1998), "Essayet som form' (orig. German 'Der Essay als Form' [1958]', in *Noten zur Literatur* Gesammelte Schriften, Band 11, Frankfurt/M: Suhrkamp, 2003, pp. 9–33), *Passage*, 28-29:1, Århus, Århus Universitet, pp. 100–14.

Barthes, R. (1981), *Camera Lucida*, New York: Hill and Wang.

Bergson, H. (2005), *Matter and Memory*, New York, Zone Books.

Bertram, P. (2010), *Intuitiv metode*, København: Arkitektskolens forlag.

Bogue, R. (2003), *Deleuze on Cinema*, New York and Paris: Routledge.

Deleuze, G. (2002), *Bergsonism*, New York, Zone Books.

Deleuze, G. ([1985] 1989), *Cinema 2: The Time-Image* (trans. H. Tomlinson and R. Galeta), Minneapolis, MN: University of Minnesota Press.

—— (2004), *Foucault*, Frederiksberg: det lille forlag.

——([1983] 2005), *Cinema 1: The Movement Image*, (trans. H. Tomlinson and B. Habberjam), London and New York: Continuum and Athlone.

Deleuze, G. and Guattari, F. ([1980] 2005), *Tusind plateauer*, København: Press Edition.

Flaxman, G. (ed.) (2000), *The Brain is the Screen*, Minneapolis, MN: University of Minnesota Press.

Godard, J. ([1967] 1972), 'My approach in four movements', in T. Milne (ed.), *Godard on Godard*, New York and London: Da Capo, pp. 239–40.

Kracauer, S. (2004), *From Caligari to Hitler: A Psychological History of the German Film*, Princeton, NJ: Princeton University Press.

Kristensen, T., Michelsen A. and Wiegand, F. (eds) (2015a), *Transvisuality: The Cultural Dimension of Visuality, Volume II: Visual Organizations*, Liverpool: Liverpool University Press.

—— (2015b), 'Introduction', in T. Kristensen, A. Michelsen and F. Wiegand (eds), *Transvisuality: The Cultural Dimension of Visuality, Volume II: Visual Organizations*, Liverpool: Liverpool University Press, pp. 12–52.

Kwinter, S. (2001), *Architectures of Time*, Cambridge, MA: The MIT Press.

Lash, S. (2010), *Intensive Culture – Social Theory, Religion and Contemporary Capitalism*, London: SAGE Publications.

Lundemo, T. (2004), 'The index and erasure: Godard's approach to film history', in M. Temple, J. Williams, and M. Witt (eds), *For Ever Godard*, London: Black Dog, p. 380.

Lury, C. (2014), 'Surfaces of visualization: The 'awareness' of a topological society', in Hydra Dialogue 5, *Morphology, Topology, and Artifice*, Copenhagen, Denmark, 22–23 May, Copenhagen: Royal Danish Academy of the Fine Arts School of Architecture.

Lury, C., Parisi, L. and Terranova, T. (2012), 'Introduction: The becoming topological of culture', *Theory, Culture and Society*, 29:4-5, pp. 3–35.

Meldgaard, M. (2013), 'Dimensions of the Out of Field', in Kristensen et al. (eds), *Transvisuality: The Cultural Dimension of Visuality, Volume 1*, Liverpool: Liverpool University Press, pp. 173–81.

Merleau-Ponty, M. (1969), *The Visible and the Invisible*, Evanstone, IL: Northwerstern University Press.

Pisters, P. (2003), *The Matrix of Visual Culture – Working with Deleuze in Film Theory*, Stanford, CA: Stanford University.

Troiani, I. and Campbell, H. (2015), 'Orchestrating spatial continuity in the urban realm', *Architecture and Culture*, 3:1, pp. 7–16.

PART IV

MISCELLANEOUS MIXED MODES AND NEW MEDIA

Figure 4 (from Introduction): *Jelloslice* Oil on prepared board. © Michael Webb © Archigram Archive.

You are looking at part of a solidified cone of vision enclosing the landscape of the Henley regatta. Most of the left hand part of the image has been obliterated by cropping; furthermore the cone is truncated horizontally yielding a hyperbolic top surface. I was the beholder representing what I saw, but I moved my easel as it were; it matters not where. And as I did so voids began opening up behind the objects comprising the landscape.

The conic truncation means that these voids will erupt through the hyperbolic top surface. For example, the void created by the large weeping willow tree (centre right) near to the beholder, when it erupts through the surface, will reproduce at larger scale the outline of the tree's hanging tendrils. A second willow further from the beholder will reproduce an outline where the increase in scale is less.

It is assumed that the particulate matter in the air is at such a high level that the cone can be removed from the overall landscape and examined independently. (Webb, unpublished)

19

Visual agency: Participatory painting as a method for spatial negotiation

Agnieszka Mlicka, Visual Facilitator

Imagining a work that behaves like architecture

'Is it possible to imagine a work which behaves like architecture, without 'looking' like architecture?' (Allen 1995: 62) This question was the driving force behind this practice-led research project, which explored how painting can engage a diverse group of stakeholders – from spatial experts to marginalized voices – in the architectural design process. In the works of contemporary painters like Julie Mehretu, Franz Ackermann and Frank Creber, I observed that painting offers medium-specific qualities to visualize the complexity of urban space. Architecture is just one element within the social, economic and political networks of urban space. Qualities such as layering and colour, but in particular the merging of abstract and figurative form, create narratives that speak of possibilities. Through the development of my own art practice, however, I realized that a painting's impact is limited. If it was to become useful within the field of architecture, I would have to engage others in the making of the work. The outcome might not even be physical, but something that emerges from the interaction with people, aligned with the goals of social or dialogic art (Kester 2004) and spatial agency (Awan et al. 2011). Hence, the aim of my research praxis is to develop a method of visualization that can be used for negotiating space as opposed to merely representing space. In this chapter, I set out how and why the method of participatory painting can inspire architects (at an early stage in their education) to engage others in the design process.

The idea that architecture is contingent, thus dependent on various actors, factors and time, poses a challenge to the way that architectural ideas are visualized (Till 2009). Jeremy Till argues that

VISUAL AGENCY

> [t]he reliance on the sketch as the initiator of so much architectural production inexorably leads to a fixation on form and type, as manifested in a product, as opposed to a consideration of use and time, as might be developed in a process.
>
> (2009: 109)

Yet, Stan Allen proposes that abstract painting has an analogous effect to architecture, because 'concepts proliferate in and through the physicality of the work, not as something other than the work' (1995: 61). It replaces the conventional affinity between architecture and sculpture, because while sculpture might look like architecture on grounds of similar material properties, it can never function like architecture. Rather than focusing on similarities such as space, material and tectonics, Allen proposes painting as a new affiliation with architecture based on an analogous effect of surface, event and time. To explain this analogy, he uses the concept of conditional abstraction that 'does not see itself as definitive, but proposes an exact fit between event and structure, between change and duration, between execution and idea' (Allen 1995: 60). Thus, conditional abstraction is a diagram of possibilities rather than the visualization of order to make sense of a disordered world.

The painters that Allen discusses, however, do not in any way engage with space beyond the painting's surface. Whereas it is predominantly 'time' and 'event' that are so particular to the 'behaviour' of architecture, Allen's analysis of paintings by David Reed, Lydia Dona and Jessica Stockholder does not move beyond a discussion of the painting's surface. If contingency cannot be painted, in the same way that a still image cannot contain time, can painting *anticipate* contingency? This would require an interpretation of painting as primarily a process that remains incomplete, open to change and accessible to all. My research imagines a work in continuous progress that incorporates various people's perspective and experience of the city, a work that refers simultaneously to the past, the present and the future of a place. In order to engage multiple voices, participation in this process should not be solution-oriented, but speculative and focused on sense-making – a social process of sharing, acknowledging, interpreting and shaping people's views through practical conversation (Forester 1985: 16–19). The painting functions as a democratic, transparent and creative platform where new relationships are produced, reverberating the idea of painting as a stage on which space is performed rather than represented (Donszelmann 2009: 6). This requires a shift from the conventional view of painting as a vertical window upon the world (or a mirror of society) to a horizontal field of connections and encounters.

301

Offering a platform for negotiating space

To investigate the concept of participatory painting in practice, I facilitated 26 workshops with architects, students of architecture and a diversity of professionals interested in spatial change. Amongst others the group included artists, an engineer, a councillor, a property developer, Ph.D. researchers, psychologists, a handyman, a public media worker, a solicitor, a hospital manager and a pastor. Here, I will focus in particular on the sessions with architecture students (Table 1, Sessions 16–25) in order to draw pedagogical insights, while also referring to the sessions with architects (Table 1, Sessions 10, 11, 13, 26) in order to expose ingrained habits within the profession. The workshops ranged from two to six participants and took circa two hours, during which we discussed a particular project that the students were working on for their studies. I recorded the sessions through audio, video and photography of the painting and, aside of in-session reflection on the process, the participants were asked for feedback through an online questionnaire afterwards. This feedback, in combination with my own reflection on the sessions, was subsequently used in the analysis of the practice.

The research methodology is based on symbolic constructivism, 'a qualitative research approach which uses artlike, non-routine portrayal (e.g., sculpture, photographs, drawing, dramatization, etc.) to elicit, challenge, and shift existing sensemaking frameworks' (Barry 1996: 411). The 26 workshops have gone through several iterations as I experimented with various additional materials and modes of interaction in response to the feedback. Aside from practical changes, most of the adjustments made the workshops more relevant for the participants. It has been argued that participation can only thrive if attention is paid to attitude, relevance and responsibility (Miessen 2010; Till 2011). These three concepts were guiding my questions for the students, for example asking 'why' instead of 'how' they were undertaking a project. I considered 'relevance' in two ways: to what extent the workshop was relevant for the students, which required finding the right balance between my goals and those of the students; and the relevance of their projects that stems from the engagement of multiple voices of insiders (Till 2011: 165). In all sessions, I discussed with the students to what extent they are considering these other voices. It follows Till's suggestion that dealing with contingency is about being open to situated knowledge, understood as the knowledge, hopes and needs of others (2009: 58–61). Within the framework of the sessions with students, my aim was threefold: to think beyond architectural form by considering the wider spatial context; to create a more collaborative platform for imagining space together; and to improve the collaboration through critical reflection on the working process itself.

Session	Participant(s)	Topic
1–9, 12, 14, 15	Diversity of professionals	Various
10	Andrea (architect)	The design of his house (under construction)
11	Ming, Monita (architect, hospital manager)	The design of their imaginary future home
13	Mauro (architect)	The design of his church (finished)
16	Benedetta, Tomas (students)	The development of a natural site outside Florence
17	Paola, Maria (students)	As above
18	Emanuele, Giovanni (students)	The design of a museum for Roosevelt Island in Manhattan, New York
19	Anna, Caterina, Ilaria (students)	The design of a building and redevelopment of a neighbourhood in East London
20	Giada, Mark (students)	As above
21	Ylenia, Mario (students)	As above
22	Edoardo, Marcus (students)	The development of the Olympic legacy in East London
23	Emanuele, Giovanni, Micol (students)	The design of a museum for Roosevelt Island in Manhattan, New York
24	Edoardo, Marcus, Valerio (students)	The development of the Olympic legacy in East London
25	Giulia, Sara, Alessandro, Marco, Grace, Luisa (five students from different design groups and their teacher)	The repurposing of the Sant' Orsola complex, a large building in the centre of Florence
26	Luigi, Federico, Tommaso, Letizia, Antonio (participants in a conference on public space)	The creation of public space in regards to the Social Street movement in Bologna

Table 1: Overview of the workshops.

In the workshops, I encouraged spatial negotiation through the simultaneous use of verbal and visual communication. This approach is related to graphic facilitation, a method of visual communication that was developed in relation to management and organizational studies. It is concerned with questions of effectiveness, productivity and service quality. Drawing conversations during various types of meetings has four positive outcomes: first, it provides clarification of goal and direction (seeing the bigger picture); second, it offers participants insight into multiple perspectives; third, it can give a sense of ownership over the process through increased engagement; and fourth, it becomes possible to share the discussed issues with others (Qvist-Sørensen 2012). To achieve this, graphic facilitation had developed its own visual 'grammar' that is used to organize information and clarify points of view (Sibbet 2008). As such, it is closely aligned with verbal communication, in terms of the way that nouns, verbs and adjectives each have their corresponding symbols. Graphic facilitation is, however, more a recording and summarizing of the conversation rather than an act of visual thinking itself. Instead of a rigid visual language, which would be inaccessible to the untrained hand, I chose to follow a more intuitive mark-making approach in the workshops. This approach is based on three aspects of participatory painting that emerged from the analysis of the practice: unfamiliarity, plasticity and ambiguity. The following sections explain these three concepts through examples from the workshops.

Facing an unfamiliar method

The introduction of an unfamiliar visualization method in the architectural design process has as goal to improve the collaboration between participants. I observed

Figure 1: Video still from Session 26. Whereas the video exposed the difficulties of dialogue between different spatial experts, the painting captured the relationships between institutions, individuals and concepts in the form of a diagram. Video documentation taken by Agnieszka Mlicka on 26 June 2014.

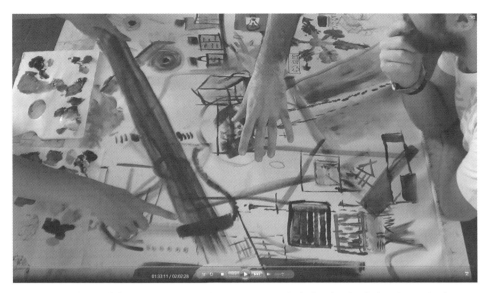

Figure 2: Video still from Session 24. The painting included individual sketches, which were subsequently merged into a design concept that transcended the students' own imaginative capabilities. Video documentation taken by Agnieszka Mlicka on 20 May 2014.

how students' excitement with architectural visualization could result in skipping important stages in the design process, often neglecting the collaborative effort. In Session 19, the students were working on a project consisting of three stages, of which they had just finished the first stage. Before we started the session, one of the students showed me her design of the final building for the third stage of the project: an elevation, cross section and perspective drawing on translucent sheets. While it was an impressive visual presentation, there was no justification for her spatial decisions, the building appeared separated from the urban context, and most importantly, she had not involved the rest of the group in the design of the building. This problem continues beyond architectural education, when architects are confronted with 'others'. Jeremy Till (2005: 23) argues that such community engagement can result in pseudo-participation, for example when public consultations merely serve as platforms to vote on already finished design drawings brought in by the architect. Till (2005: 4) explains that, 'participation remains dominated by the experts who initiate the communication on their own terms, circumscribing the process through professionally coded drawings and language'. The idea of bringing in an unfamiliar method is to prevent this kind of hierarchical superiority through use of professional visual jargon. The simultaneous use of verbal and visual communication limits the possibility of jargon because of the instant act of translation from open conversation. The aim is for experts and non-experts to develop a shared language in the hope of balancing unequal power relationships. The example of Session 26 (Figure 1), held as part of an international conference on public space with a diversity of spatial and local experts, revealed how difficult it is to generate discussion when each individual brings in jargon from their own field of practice. In my in-depth analysis of this workshop, I argue that there has to be the willingness on everyone's part to develop such a shared visual language (Mlicka 2017). Developing the right attitude to work collaboratively, when confronted with varying abilities in a team, should be taught as part of architectural education. In Sessions 22 and 24 (Figure 2), Marcus was more fluent in painting than Edoardo because his architectural training in Brazil had included this type of visual expression. Marcus' designs were prioritized in the group because he was able to visualize his ideas clearly. For Edoardo, it was difficult to contribute as he felt to be less fluent in visualization:

> I must admit that I don't feel at ease painting, I'm not used to that form of expression, but I liked what Agnieszka and Marcus painted, the use of bright colors and the juxtaposition of colors used as symbols and as the representation of reality.
>
> (Session 22)

During the two sessions, we managed to discuss their concerns with the collaborative process and found ways in which they could merge their ideas visually. After the second session, Marcus wrote in his feedback:

> Both sessions have been very useful in regards to the negotiation within the group. Before the session I did not understand many of the ideas of the other guys, luckily the sessions helped me to realize that I had imposed a lot of things that not everyone liked. I think that after the painting we got to a point where the final design appealed and had a bit of each member of the group.
>
> (Session 24)

Previously the students had used an A4 notebook, which did not enable them to work simultaneously. Painting on a large sheet, on the contrary, turned out to be helpful for many students. As Marcus noted, '[t]he size of the painting has helped a lot, because we could represent all that we had in mind' (Session 24). The students' feedback reveals an initial uneasiness with this technique, because of their unfamiliarity with it. Yet their comments also demonstrated their awareness that this group painting process provides collaborative opportunities. Contrary to the expectation that painting requires skills, for most students it proved to be an intuitive process. One student wrote:

It was the first time we used the painting to communicate architecture, so we were inexperienced. Probably our sheet wasn't clear enough, because we should have taken some decisions first. Painting is more emotional and free. It offers more ways to communicate not just the form of our architecture, but even our intents.

(Session 16, Figure 3)

Another noted: 'I think that the use of colours is very important to define an idea or more. Even if you are not a professional painter you can immediately visualize what you're thinking about, and then change it as you prefer' (Session 17), and on the style of visualization commented that the method was a: 'Very free expression using a simple but effective level of communication' (Session 19).

A familiarity with painting, however, does not always imply that there is a participatory mindset. In Sessions 10 and 13 architects Andrea and Mauro respectively were familiar with watercolour painting, which is more like colouring-in drawings. Mauro's sketches were confident and automatic but also identical to his previous paintings of the church he designed (Figure 4). Hence, his contribution was limited to renderings of architectural form rather than interacting with my inquisitive brush strokes to test how the church relates to its surroundings.

Figure 3: Video still from Session 16. The painting consisted of three layers: a map of the site, a diagram of the connections between landmarks and infrastructure, and a symbolic representation of (potential) users of the space – an attempt to expand the teacher's brief to make the project more engaging for the students. Video documentation taken by Agnieszka Mlicka on 15 April 2014.

A painting that remains within established parameters, in terms of line, colour and style of representation, does not accommodate the space for unexpected opportunities. Furthermore, it does not provide scope for a visual collaboration. Mauro painted only on his side of the sheet – sitting down frustrates collaborative work – and the conversation resembled an interview. In the session with Andrea, he expressed dissatisfaction with our approach to mapping out the space because it did not keep to the conventions of architectural drawings, such as the floor plan, the section and the elevation. In his own watercolour paintings, he had developed a particular interest in the elevation, which emphasized the smooth horizontal lines of his buildings in the landscape. Such details were lost in our painting, which became an amalgamation of various perspectives of the building. Andrea suggested using the axonometric in order to make the painting more legible, even though we did not create the work for an audience. Through my visual research practice with architects, it became clear how their spatial thinking is structured through the embodied conventions of architectural rendering. At play in these sessions were, furthermore, other factors that affected the conversation and subsequently the painting process. Factors such as unequal power relationships – resulting for example from age and gender differences – and cultural attitudes at different architecture schools and countries (most of the workshops referred to in this

Figure 4: Video still from Session 13. The architect's tendency to focus on the physicality of architecture made it difficult to move the conversation towards a more critical reflection on the project. The painting shows a clear schism between the two approaches. Video documentation taken by Agnieszka Mlicka on 1 March 2014.

chapter took place at an Italian university). Such influences had undoubtedly an impact on the extent to which the painting process became collaborative.

Exploring the possibilities of plasticity

The paintings from the sessions are a layering of maps, diagrams, perspectives, brainstorms and poetic reflections, revealing the complexity of a place. The possibility of diverse styles of visual expression makes the medium of painting a very 'plastic' medium. Using this plasticity helped students to explore alternative approaches to their projects. In Session 20 with Giada and Mark (Figure 5), the students showed little contextual understanding of the site for which they were designing, even though they had visited the area. The consequence was a tendency to create a utopian masterplan for the area, because there were no boundaries limiting their decision-making. The term 'masterplan' indicates a hierarchical authoritative value – from the students' perspective, they were creating something out of nothing. This is a clear-cut example of what Till (2009: 7–26) refers to as the deluded detachment of the architectural discipline, a state of autonomy that is

Figure 5: Video still from Session 20. The students used the Italian piazza (the oval in the painting) as inspiration for a new public space in East London, sparking a discussion about the (dis)advantages of translating one culture into another, while demonstrating the potential problems of limited situated knowledge. Video documentation taken by Agnieszka Mlicka on 16 April 2014.

first expressed in architectural education. Hence, the challenge in this workshop was to define clear limits for the students' project by making the place come to life through a brainstorm on what is already there. For instance, I suggested they consider the various communities in the area and represent them symbolically in the painting. In the feedback, the students felt that the session helped them to 'tackle design issues from a more "down to earth" point of view [because] as architects, we often forget who we're actually building for and how greatly certain choices can affect communities' (Session 20). The concept of plasticity also refers to the method being flexible and responsive, allowing for various kinds of conversations to take place. In Session 25, for example, the students used a diverse range of visual metaphors to share their stories of the space they were working on (Figure 6). In contrast to Giada and Mark, this group was working locally and knew the place well. They shared stories of their experience of this neighbourhood, their hopes for its redevelopment, as well as theoretical concepts relevant to this project. Although they worked on the same project, the five students were from different design studio groups. This session helped them to exchange insider information and insights from their visits. As a result, the painting speaks of much more than the physical space.

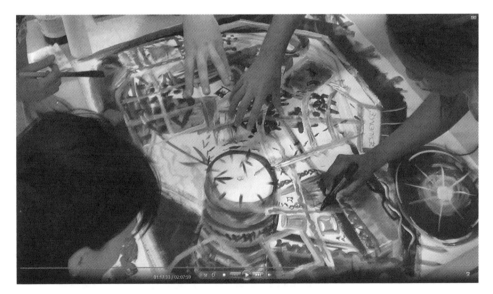

Figure 6: Video still from Session 25. Visual metaphors in this painting speak of the students' experience of, and hopes for, the building: the multi-coloured shadows of the clock indicate the building's previous functions; a mouth swallowing money represents the lack of investment in the building; and the lines refer to the need for resilient solutions for the building. Video documentation taken by Agnieszka Mlicka on 28 May 2014.

It is not always immediately clear from the outset what students struggle with in their design practice, and what the focus of a workshop to respond to this should be. The most productive approach emerges from the interaction of participants and the paintings themselves. Each of the sessions tackled a different type of problem, such as finding better ways of working together, brainstorming on alternative solutions or dealing with a too restrictive brief. The plasticity of a method indicates to what extent switching between various forms of engagement is possible in order to be most relevant for the participants. In co-design, it has been suggested that a 'sensitivity to the coherence of making, telling and enacting in design participation provides sufficient grounding for designers (and non-designers) to make the tools and techniques relevant for whatever participatory action they are involved in' (Brandt et al. 2012: 147). The question that arises when evaluating painting's plasticity is to what extent other tools and materials can be used. In the field of co-design, the concept of the toolkit refrains from predetermining tools and techniques, each with their corresponding mode of interaction. In their definition of the toolkit, Sanders and Stappers (2014: 9) note that its goal is to give non-designers a means of participation in the design process. Indeed, participants in my workshops who were not architecturally trained commented that bringing in other tools such as (coloured) pencils allowed them to express themselves more easily. In some of the early workshops, we added additional materials to the painting such as a string to express movement, a piece of a used palette to show urban density and a transparent sheet to create a new layer. In the workshops with students, however, I decided to keep to acrylic paint only in order to explore the medium on its own. Whereas a toolkit might be advantageous when working with non-experts, I observed in the sessions with architecture students that the sole use of painting tools helped them to steer away from architectural form and, as a result, to think outside of the box.

Embracing painting's ambiguity

The third characteristic of participatory painting that emerged from the practice is that of ambiguity. Painting together is accompanied by uncertainty, because you are never fully sure if you understand the other person's brush strokes. Narratives are built up slowly through layering, symbols and colour, and through the process of asking questions and explaining visual metaphors. Yet, ambiguity and slow communication – the opposite of the efficiency of digital rendering – have the positive effect of stimulating a deeper engagement with the values of others. In this sense, the role of the painting is similar to that of the artefact in co-design:

Taken in isolation, the artefact may say very little or remain highly ambiguous. In fact, this ambiguity is intentional, as it generates opportunities for creativity, expression and discussion. The meaning of the artefact is revealed through the stories told about it and the scenes in which it plays a role.

(Sanders and Stappers 2014: 7)

Yet a painting's ambiguous nature stems from the participants' own creativity, contribution and interaction with each other (visually as well as verbally). In Session 18 with Emanuele and Giovanni (Figure 7), the act of painting revealed intentions which were not clearly expressed through the verbal communication. For some students, like Giovanni, visualizing is a more intuitive way of communicating ideas than talking. His painting style was poetic and independent, and this revealed that his understanding of architecture was similarly about the designing of a masterpiece – a contradiction to what he was saying. Emanuele's painting style was much more influenced by conventional architectural rendering of space, and while he was interested in alternative approaches, he struggled to find adequate ways to express these ideas. By challenging their ideas visually – painting over someone's image can be very confrontational – I questioned their conflicting approaches and helped the students to become more self-critical. This meant that

Figure 7: Video still from Session 18. The painting reveals two divergent approaches to designing: the student on the left follows a more conventional mode of rendering in order to map out the place, whereas the student on the right uses a poetic form of expression to explain his ideas for the project. Video documentation taken by Agnieszka Mlicka on 15 April 2014.

Figure 8: Video still from Session 11. In this challenging session, conflicting needs and contrasting approaches to imagining space had to be reconciled. As a result, the painting was a dense layering of floor plans and symbols to negotiate both the physical and affective features of the shared future home. Video documentation taken by Agnieszka Mlicka on 28 December 2013.

Giovanni had to face the contradictions between his ideas and visualizations, and that Emanuele reflected on the limitations of his studies. The students were keen to return for another session to continue this process of spatial negotiation, together with the third member of their team. In that workshop (Session 23), they painted much more together. Moreover, Emanuele told me that as a result of the sessions he had become more aware of how his approach to architecture differs from the school of thought advocated by his university. He asked for an additional tutorial to discuss how to proceed with his Master's thesis. As he was deeply motivated to work with people, we also considered possible career trajectories after his studies.

Ambiguity appears, at first sight, to hinder the communication, but asking questions is key to showing interest and developing empathy. In Session 11 (Figure 8) with Ming and Monita (a married couple who are an architect and a hospital manager respectively), asking questions started the process of making sense of each other's experience of everyday life at home. Monita's intuitive painting style (for example, a sun in the living room would symbolize a warm atmosphere at home) forced Ming to see other ways of experiencing space. This shifted the dynamic within the session and gave Monita more confidence to contribute to the imagining of their future house. She might not have been able to contribute if we had used conventional architectural drawing methods, because Ming might have taken over the designing process. In fact, after the session, Ming took a sharp pencil and a piece of paper to demonstrate his plan for his ideal house, unambiguously and without having to acknowledge the needs of others. It was a quick sketch of the cross section, accompanied by the comment that this is how it is done. Embracing ambiguity is a slow process of opening up people's minds to alternative ways of doing architecture – a process that could be embedded early on in architectural education. As suggested by Till: 'Where order and certainty close things down into fixed ways of doing things, contingency and uncertainty open up liberating possibilities for action' (2009: 55).

Gaining visual agency

Through the three concepts of unfamiliarity, plasticity and ambiguity, I have tried to define what a participatory painting can achieve: not only recognition of the contingent nature of architecture, but also a way of incorporating it. From the students' feedback, four main effects of painting collaboratively can be extracted. First, the sessions were helpful in understanding and considering others' point of view, both those within the group and the (imagined) stakeholders of the spatial project. Second, the method enabled the students to better communicate and collaborate with each other. Third, it facilitated a creative, analytical and (self) critical thinking process. Finally, participants commented that the painting process was liberating, enjoyable, stimulating and fun – this was also the case in the sessions where I observed that the students lacked enthusiasm for their project and felt restricted by the given brief. These four effects were almost equally present in all sessions, yet there were differences in the extent to which they were acted upon. This brings me to suggest that there is a further potential; that of a transformative learning process, when bringing participatory painting as a pedagogical method into architectural education. David Barry (1996: 417) suggests that '[m]etaphoric portrayal and discussion can allow otherwise hard-to-discuss subjects to be broached as well as being powerful devices for facilitating transformation'. He outlines three types of enquiry – eliciting, revealing and transforming – that are useful to explain the varying levels of engagement (Barry 1996: 422–42). At one end of the spectrum, students appeared to gain new insights, even if they were still unsure as to whether the method was applicable to their project. Eliciting indicates here the process of sense-making that takes place through practical conversations. At this stage, participants become aware of the urban context that they are working with, through the sharing of observations and experiences that are mapped out through painting. The next stage is that of revealing one's own and others' intentions through the process of confronting one another, enquiring further and negotiating different approaches. Here, new meaning is created through the interaction and juxtaposition of viewpoints. Transforming, a final stage that builds upon the previous ones, is triggered by the participants' proactive critical reflection on their own role as a spatial expert. As a result of this, new creative trajectories can be explored that are contingent on the context one is working within. Participation is transformed into collaboration through an embodied understanding of one's responsibility towards others, and one's intentions are aligned with or adjusted to the limitations offered by the context. To gain a deeper understanding of how students can advance through these three stages of enquiry would require working with a group over a longer period of time. Based on this research project, I would like to suggest that alternative approaches to visualization can help students to explore other ways of doing architecture. I call this gaining visual agency: the ability to use a participatory visualization process with the intent to empower others whose voices would otherwise be neglected, thereby subverting the standard modes of image production. One such method, as I have set out, is participatory painting. As a process – the paintings are discarded after each session – it might not be the kind of 'work' that Stan Allen had in mind. As a pedagogical method towards gaining visual agency, however, it might have a longer lasting impact on the discipline of architecture.

REFERENCES

Allen, S. (1995), 'Painting and architecture: Conditional abstractions', *Journal of Philosophy and the Visual Arts*, 5, pp. 60–71.

Awan, N., Schneider, T. and Till, J. (2011), *Spatial Agency: Other Ways of Doing Architecture*, London: Routledge.

Barry, D. (1996), 'Artful inquiry: A symbolic constructivist approach to social science research', *Qualitative Inquiry*, 2, pp. 411–38.

Brandt, E., Binder, T. and Sanders, E. B.-N. (2012), 'Tools and techniques: Ways to engage telling, making and enacting', in J. Simonsen and T. Robertson (eds), *Routledge International Handbook of Participatory Design*, London: Routledge, pp. 145–81.

Donszelmann, B. (2009), 'Proposal for a materialist arena: painted space', in University of Brighton, *Occupation: Negotiations with Constructed Space*, 2–4 July 2009, Brighton: University of Brighton, School of Architecture and Design.

Forester, J. (1985), 'Designing: Making sense together in practical conversations', *Journal of Architectural Education*, 38, pp. 14–20.

Kester, G. (2004), *Conversation Pieces: Community and Communication in Modern Art*, Berkeley, CA: University of California Press.

Miessen, M. (2010), *The Nightmare of Participation (Crossbench Praxis as a Mode of Criticality)*, Berlin: Sternberg Press.

Mlicka, A. (2017), 'Facilitating spatial negotiation: A pragmatic approach to understanding public space', *The Journal of Public Space*, 2, pp. 27–36.

Qvist-Sørensen, O. (2012), 'Draw more, together', *TEDxCopenhagen*, 18 September, http://www.biggerpicture.dk. Accessed 2 February 2018.

Sanders, E. B.-N. and Stappers, P. J. (2014), 'Probes, toolkits and prototypes: Three approaches to making in codesigning', *CoDesign*, 10, pp. 5–14.

Sibbet, D. (2008), 'Visual intelligence: Using the deep patterns of visual language to build cognitive skills', *Theory into Practice*, 47, pp. 118–27.

Till, J. (2005), 'The negotiation of hope', in J. Till, D. Petrescu, and P. Blundell Jones (eds), *Architecture and Participation*, New York: Routledge, pp. 25–44.

—— (2009), *Architecture Depends*, Cambridge, MA: The MIT Press.

—— (2011), 'The King Is Dead! Long Live the Queen!', in M. Miessen and N. V. Kolowratnik (eds), *Waking Up from the Nightmare of Participation*, Utrecht: Expodium, pp. 163–167.

20

'just painting': Performative painting as visual discourse

Tonia Carless, University of the West of England

Introduction: Performative painting as research

Figures 1 and 2 (left to right): Postage stamp prints, archive sample. Anonymous painters. 2015.

Performative painting is a collaborative spatial research that takes representation outside of the specialist worlds of the architecture studio (Figures 1 and 2). It is both visual and spatial, because it is produced in the space between the painter and the sites. It is sociotemporal embracing the historical materialist conception that lived space can only emerge through historical action. The activist element reclaims space in relation to historical action and struggle.

Architectural production is overwhelmingly visual, so research must work through this media to develop and comprehend new forms of knowledge. The project discussed here develops discursive space around visual production and the space of capital investment (often defined through the architectural profession as *regeneration*.) It is a critique of the re-configuration of space that is interdisciplinary. It researches how that re-configured space is read under consumer capitalism and examines local spatial politics, taking Henri Lefebvre's assertion (1974, 1991) that the manifestations of capitalism are not merely happening within space but that they are *about* space.

The visual work (both paintings and the archive) is a critique of the notion that the aesthetic within architecture is a realm distinct and separated from the social or economic. Visual production is an analytical tool that recognizes the shifts in the visual within cultural production – from mechanical to digital – as being co-complicit in the neo-liberal re-configuration of space. It seeks out collaborative potential, and the manual process of corporeally making/performing space on site, an essential part of creative production, allows for both a real and conceptual spatial extension beyond the architectural studio.

Space appropriated by performative painters is a model for the transformation of social and political space because of its ability to explore Lefebvre's notion (1974, 1991) of the confrontation between abstract space and the space of use values. The research methodology used for this project contributes to architectural knowledge by constructing unseen knowledge through a discursive, shared, non-hierarchically formed practice between architect, performance artist, amateur landscape painters and users of space. The practice, whilst activist in nature, posits the painting itself as the site of architectural discourse, recognizing that architectural representation is key in the process of both spatial control and resistance to it.

The research is *en plein-air* in the tradition of nineteenth-century impressionist painting. Its focus is upon the outdoors and follows the French translation of *peinture sur le motif* (painting on the ground). It creates space on the ground, through the experiential medium of performative painting. Here, it is also part of a collaborative exchange as a painting group workshop. It considers public space at the point of change, attempting to paint something lost in the process of redevelopment.

The projects illustrated here include: The Clifton Suspension Bridge, Bristol restoration works (Figures 3 and 4); The former industrial space around Filton Airfield, Bristol (Figures 5 and 6); Birmingham Central Library, designed by John Madin, built in 1974 and demolished in 2015 (Figure 9); and a group of coastal pine trees, adjacent to the public pleasure gardens of the seaside town of Lyme Regis, proposed to be felled as part of a dense residential re-development (Figures 1 and 10). Whilst apparently disparate, each of the four sites demonstrates space being removed when it is not structurally, programmatically or even aesthetically inadequate. As a consequence the sites have become victims of the increasing capitalization of space. The painting constructs images counter to those of the developer and complicit architectural professions. The performative painting constructs new forms of knowledge around architectural space, through the crafting of embedded, site-specific, collaborative visual work, and through the accrued knowledge of the developing archive. The project is about which possible spaces of resistance might be constructed and offered up. Furthermore, performative painting creates a medium through which to investigate the spectacle of architectural image construction. It provides a contribution to urban theory and practice and visual culture, with a focus on spatial politics. The painting projects articulate discursive space around regeneration through this visual methodology. Painting here locates points of ideological stress as a re-conception of the juncture between art and architecture through cooperative collaboration and the social construct of performative painting on the particular sites. It is the spatial connection made between these differing sites, the space represented within the paintings themselves and the space of the surface of the paintings across which the research knowledge is constructed. It is also the space of the archive that currently resides at The Old Shoe Factory, Clifton, Bristol.

The chapter aims to examine the discursive possibilities of performative painting as architectural research method and to posit this as a vital mode of re-configuring the architectural profession's conception of *on site* towards one which might be defined as *in site, in sight* or even *incite* as active participation.

A series of 'paint-in' group workshops developed around different sites (and sights) as an open-source educational forum that develops an archive. Formed out of a collaborative spatial practice, initially with the Bristol-based performance artist Annabel Other, the group consists of amateur painters observing the social life of architecture and landscape through the act of landscape painting. The amateur artists are tourists in the landscape, looking at architectural objects of reinvention and the temporal nature of space at the moment of transition. According to Frow and Schulunke (2008: 59) the position of these visual methodologies within academic research in relation to the archive is important because:

> For academic historians the archival document, corroborated by other forms of 'hard evidence', is the privileged source of historical truth. For such historians, realist historical fictions not only get the facts 'wrong', they involve Manichean structures of empathy and moral allegiance that undermine the complex truths of the written record.

Empathy and value analysis are embraced through painting. What is being painted is the ideological construction of the space through specific terms defined by local users and other spatial analysts. Because the painting is collaborative and happens in an atmosphere of immersive humility there is a further discourse to be painted in. Value analysis is the subjective assessment criteria more usually associated with fine art practice than with architectural design. Value analysis might, for example, constitute questions of beauty, of class or gender and how these might be framed in the context of a historical perspective, or experiential readings of space. Empathy is located as central to architectural understanding, positing architectural practice as a social construct. More recent attempts by the profession to renew its social contract through, for example, 'live projects' may continue to develop the hierarchically formed position of professional/architect/enabler. The amateur artist central to this research project attempts to challenge the established order. The amateur artist and their group form an interruption to the economic flows of capital across the space because they rupture the vindicating ethic of growth that the professional architect is all too readily bound within.

Performative painting embraces the concept of empathy. Occupying the site with local inhabitants allows for an exchange that might enhance empathy through placing one's self in another's position, literally, even if for a brief moment in time. Some paintings are collaborative overworkings (Figure 1) produced by more than one painter. These types of paintings generate a discourse across the surface of the painting, through the fluid medium of the paint itself. The collected works form an archive of the research project.

The paint-in group occupies the space and paints in an otherwise overwhelmingly and increasingly consumerist public sphere. Site occupation is conceived of as an experimental intervention, counter to the concept of experiencing space through a digital viewfinder, or another mediated process that is once corporeally detached from the scene. The group paint-in is also understood to question the current and future functions of the spaces. The intended result of each session is not a design or a painting as the end product but rather a transformation through collective action. The understanding of painting as a critically engaged research emphasizes what painting can do (as an active condition) rather than what it is. It is also restorative of the space rather than destructive. Still, it embraces lines of thinking where the painting works at 'realizing rather than solving problems' (Matta-Clark 1974: 118).

The performative painting has the capacity to construct the unseen. Its value is its realness as a medium. Its capacity to construct a discourse about a space and across the space of the paper itself is a craft production enacted through a fluid medium. It is oppositional to the majority of what constitutes architectural research production, which happens precisely through what Karl Marx (1844, 1978) defined as alienated labour estranged from humanity. Painting is also able to form a direct response to the artists' impressions that prefigure the changing spaces of redevelopment, to develop proximity and to deflect away from the perceived approximation of representation often postulated through the notion of a cultural or technological ideal.

The agency of the research is informed by Michel Foucault's ([1969] 1972) archaeology of the human sciences that demonstrates precisely how 'norms' construct discursive fields. Foucault's concerns with power relations and the social construction of forms of knowledge and identity are key to a discourse analysis. According to cultural geographer Gillian Rose (2007: 175–76) discourse analysis 'concentrates most on the sites of production and audiencing in their social modality'. Audiencing here is that of the group of performative painters and the wider public sphere on site and the subsequent access to the archive.

The work is a process of what Walter Benjamin ([1936] 2008) describes as immanent analysis within the medium of its own formation. Rather than the aestheticization of politics, performative painting aligns with Benjamin's revolutionary praxis of the politicization of aesthetics as antidote. In performative painting there are no exclusions. Looking and seeing manifest in a variety of responses other than the painting response recorded across the surface of the painting. The archive of paintings draws in other public discussions about the sites and their significance.

The research has emerged from spatial practice that reads and critiques existing space through its critical gaze upon global corporate capital and heightened practices of commodification. It originates from theories presented in *The Production of Space* (Lefebvre 1991) and examines what David Harvey ([1984] 1991: 431) refers to as 'the production of space, that was binding together the global and the local in new and quite unfamiliar ways'. It has been developed from spatial theory to pursue 'a more acute way of seeing how space hides its social consequences from us' (Soja 1989: 61) and it proposes painting as a critical spatial practice as part of a spatial agency (Awan et al. 2011).

Painting as research operates here at different levels. First, painting as a research practice allows slowly and carefully looking at, or regarding and imagining existing and future space. It is, second, a discursive practice between the painters and paintings and beyond, where the paintings are exhibited or reproduced as miniature prints, as postage stamps. The digital archive of paintings has the potential to develop the social activist practice of uploading paintings onto, for example, planning portal sites, so the paintings can become part of a shifting design discourse at the planning stages of architectural production.

To actively paint space in this public forum develops a critique of spatial and sociocultural value. The research practice occupies space, imagines it and has the potential to activate it in the wider public imagination. It is proposed

Figure 3: Clifton Suspension Bridge, Bristol. Anonymous painters. 2015.

Figure 4: Clifton Suspension Bridge. Photograph © Tonia Carless, 2015.

as a more effective architectural research than both visual studio production and traditional forms of site analysis because at its centre is an engagement that allows for a spatio-social temporal practice that is about looking at the space. The qualitative research can be evaluated and audited through the archive to assess its credibility with the ethnographic subjects. There are also aspects of technical and historical, quantitative data that will form the origins of the qualitative research methodology. It traverses ethnographic research because the observation of participants becomes more discursive through the productive act of collaborative painting. While the social reality remains un-natural and mediated by the participants, the engagement is shared and equitable within the real social space on the ground. A clear example of this can be seen through the performative painting group attempting to navigate increasingly privatized space[1] during the *en plein air* activities. Painting and its tools, as spatial substance, allow for changing the social relations of research production as an act of improvised transformation.

Painting everyday sights en plein-air

The history of painting *en plein-air* shows concern with the everyday, striving for closer connection to the subject (Dudley Barrett 2010). The sites for this research correspond with the everyday and are peripheral and mostly provincial. A full list of the spaces painted as part of the research forms the developing catalogue for the modern archive and a map for the changing world.

All of the output is concerned with spatial representation. Diversity may be simulated, so it is not intended as a form of replication or recreation/imitation. It seeks out the real rather than that which might be simulated. *En plein-air*

Figure 5: Filton Airfield Bristol. Anonymous painters, 2015.

Figure 6: Concorde Paint-in. Photograph © Tonia Carless, 2015.

painting has the capacity to represent that which first moved the onlooker (Dudley Barrett 2010), as a kind of gut reaction. Early *en plein-air* also prioritized the performative as the 'fascination with the process of painting en plein-air was not only captured in photographs, but also reproduced as postcards and became the subject of many paintings themselves, painters painting painters, painting outdoors' (Dudley Barrett 2010: 32).

The paintings develop a visual methodology for social memory with the recognition of the vulnerability of new media archiving and a larger crisis for cultural memory running across all digital representation. Ippolito and Rinehart (2014) cite Climo and Cattell (2002: 4) highlighting types of collective memories formed through 'social, economic, and political circumstances; by beliefs and values; by opposition and resistance. They involve cultural norms and issues of authenticity, identity and power. They are implicated in ideologies'.

The paintings are visual research that recognizes that architectural design and production operate contextually at a point between continuity and change. The painting of the sites is a historical archaeology, not a nostalgic reconstruction of value, but rather a possible utopian future projection that interrupts the visual flow of global redevelopment space as an 'interpretive framework' (Climo and Cattell 2002: 4) and recognizes that 'to establish genuine cultural pluralism requires concerted socialist action' (Eagleton 2000: 122). The significance of breaking down social memory into formal and informal categories (Ippolito and Rinehart 2014: 16) is useful analysis here when considering what mode of visual architectural research this constitutes. The archive collects information in the physical form of the institution and embraces exchanges across the lived everyday, *en plein-air* experience as a transformative process of collective remembering. For architectural understanding and visual methodology it is an orientating activity that asks what the representations of space will encounter in the future.

'just painting' as activist research

'just painting' is the title of the research project and is a process of architectural and spatial research as cultural negotiation. The term has been taken from the analysis of a postcolonial Aboriginal painting process written about in *The Politics of Just Painting: Engagement and Encounter in the Art of The East Kimberley* (Skerrit 2015). In it, Skerrit argues that the Aboriginal or 'Gija painting might have moved beyond a position of a claim upon authenticity of originating occupation of space, towards a description "divested from the dialogic burden" in favour of a border aesthetic based on cultural negotiation'. Skerrit identifies this position through the Gija artist, Paddy Bedford who is quoted in the preface to *The Museum of Contemporary Art* exhibition catalogue *Storer* (Oliver 2006: 9) as saying that 'he had painted all of his mother's country and all of his father's country and now was "just painting"'. While this analysis relates to a landscape and painting outside of the locational space under investigation here, it is still able to draw in a discussion about ideas of people and their claims upon, and histories of, the land. Painting becomes representative of the 'idea that history is never resolved or complete, but constantly replayed and extended' (Skerrit 2015: 1), expanding upon the belief that there is historical flux within such painting and that 'the border is also a lively, lucid space, where there is scope for a renewed agency and performativity in the handling of culture' (Skerrit 2015: 1).

'just painting' recognizes the cultural imperialism of current urban renewal programmes in the reclaiming of space as valued commodity. The methodology might open a space of change and propose a discourse with outsiders. The research offers possibilities of amateur painting as protest beyond the reach of the law as it interacts with capitalist and global frameworks by, for example, uploading paintings to the planning portal as public comment. The paintings construct new power relations as well as poetic relations. While each paint-in generates specific analyses and discourses, reading across the archive offers a 'performative site of connectivity: a version of world picturing based on our shared contemporary experience of cross-cultural negotiation' (Skerrit 2015: 1).

For this research, 'just painting' could be understood as rectifying an injustice and of making a value analysis through painting. Another suggestion also made through the reading of the Aboriginal artist's use of 'just painting' might be a refusal to accept categorization within academic verbal and textual analysis, recognizing this as merely another form of colonization and institutionalization. The political flows and intensities of the painting actions foreground this as the amateur painting groups enter the contested territories (dis-)armed with brushes and sketch books. The painting also emerges as part of historical action embedded within the histories of architectural representation and the wider public discourse on architecture.

Painting as architectural research

The research takes inspiration from the 1954 public viewing of the discovery of the temple of Mithras under London's Mansion House (Figure 7). The Roman remains were uncovered during rebuilding after the Second World War with a momentary halt in the building to allow for a public viewing of this uncovered and previous space. Over 100,000 members of the public went to the site and it captured the public imagination and fuelled a powerful interest in the history of the space. At a time, before mass camera use, the space was recorded through watercolour paintings *en plein-air* (Figure 7), evidenced by the photographs of queuing 'people with watercolour sketch books' (Jackson 2014). The forensic archaeology and record of the space at the time, together with its circulation within a wider public frame, proved to be a controversial catalyst for resistance to the site's redevelopment. Both

Figure 7: Public viewing of the Temple of Mithras, London. Watercolour painting © H. B. Lambert, 1954.

of these frames of investigation – the detailed study and the public exposure and interaction – are proposed here in this research through the watercolour studies and exhibitions. For this architectural research project it becomes a question of constructing the value of a public space. The research considers corporate claims upon space and the associated process of erasure of spaces and attempts through 'just painting' to re-position contemporary, or more recent historical formations, buildings and locations of everyday life as culturally significant. There are shared interests between archaeology and this painting practice as architectural research as they are both trying to see the unseen or forgotten.

Contemporary artists have more recently returned to the medium of painting, such as the Chinese artist Liu Xiaodong (Figure 8) whose in-situ painting is associated with both performance and immanence and is described as: 'a kind of history painting for the emerging world' (Anon 2015). Xiaodong's work shows action and interaction of the landscape subject and painter.

'just painting' becomes activist research as the figures of the groups of watercolour painters attempt to traverse un-walked landscapes, such as Filton's half-manicured/half-rubble grassy edge between shopping mall and disused runway. This is activist initially because the act of 'just painting' is outside of the framework of the drive-thru landscape of retail commodity. The painters observe

Figure 8: Getting-out-of-Beichuan, Painting © Liu Xiaodong 2010.

this through their painting and with passers-by. One paint-in of a public library and polling station in Sea Mills, Bristol serendipitously observed the 'community payback scheme' of neo-liberal punishment, where offenders are made to serve the community as a form of punishment by painting the railings of the library building. This marketization of prison alternatives is a keen example of Foucault's ([1976] 2009) notion of incarceration being diffused through the entire social body. Perhaps the suggestion here is that through the activist research there is another form of 'community payback'. If, as is contested by this research, public space has become a carcerally generated dystopia of fences, surveillance and checkpoints then it is argued that its opposite might be to navigate these terrains as a discursive practice.

An archive: Painting with watercolour

Watercolour is fast, portable, cheap, fluid and has associations with women's painting, the English landscape tradition and the amateur. It offers the possibilities of non-perspectival and non-orthographic, liquid rendering, as well as multi-layering to encompass the duration of the process of looking. In this project, while the successive layers of paint dry, the group discourse on the history and appearance of the site develops and this is painted in and the process remains visible.

The medium has a history of use for amateur painting of sites by architects and surveyors, from the eighteenth century, like the paintings of Thomas Sandsby, the draughtsman and military surveyor to the Duke of Cumberland who made 'the prosaic tradition of topography – the portrait of a place' (V&A 2016: 1). This tradition continued during the nineteenth century through Architects such as George Gilbert Scott and then early pioneer modernists like Voysey and Rennie Mackintosh, through to more contemporary programmatic architecture, like the 1980s *Narrative Architecture* of Nigel Coates (Jamieison 2013).

Subject matter and medium are deeply interconnected. In painting, solid and void space may be rendered equally palpable so as to have purchase upon the intangible. The painting research process is understood as a fluid state of craft production with the realness of painting being important on many levels. This includes the possibility of retaining the disappearing context of digital archive space, painting's status as a form of non-alienated labour and knowledge production and also that the painting has the capacity to consider the fourth dimension of time and occupied space. The painting of the space and the surface of the painting itself, with its layered build-up of watery coloured deposits, are envisaged (and designed) as sites for the consecutive gathering of significance, memory and place and a process of finding the site of architecture.

Painting as architectural research has the capacity to forge connections between visual representation and the practice of architecture. It is critical of conventional architectural representation that has been reduced 'into a work of art separated from its initial function' (Mlicka [2007] 2014: 4). To counter this Mlicka's study goes on to examine the possibility of the process of negotiating space *through* painting. It differs from this research, in that the researcher is the one who processes these thoughts whereas performative painting collects and potentially proposes new space. Unlike Mlicka this research is amateur, non-specialist and non-hierarchical production. Processing is collective at the paint-in session and beyond through the archive.

The paintings have been made for the purpose of understanding redevelopment and the planning and brief formulation of architecture but there are clear lines and possibilities to material design and spatial detail. So, while the usual notion of painting as architectural representation is about visualization of the end product, this painting is a communication medium and a visual research process. The research intersects spatial and architectural production, developing spatial practice and by doing so re-defines the practice of architecture. It is a critical practice, positioning itself between drawing and building (representational and real) to develop new forms of architectural and spatial knowledge. In *Employing Social Art Practice* (Bojorquez and Garcia 2014: 197) the assertion is that such an approach allows for the development of new knowledge and that 'By inserting social art practice into ethnographic methodology researchers can engage in an alternative immersion into place and a community, allowing for a participatory knowledge construction'.

A demonstration of the paint-in as an act of remembering are the paintings from the *Wake for Birmingham Central Library* (Clawley 2015), held in January 2015, ahead of the proposed demolition of the library. The event was a culmination of a lengthy conflict and protest by *The Friends of The Central Library* to save and reuse the building and its public space. A paint-in took place as part of the wake, alongside a spontaneous public procession of paintings (Figure 9).

This event clearly constructed the performative painting. It also demonstrated how history and memory might be painted back into the present and future construction of the space. The paintings brought to the wake as part of a totemic procession and display of cultural value also reconstructed the same place as a new event. This new event space could be maintained and discursively developed further through the archive. Birmingham Central library held, as part of its collection, a visual picture library that has now been lost as both a public space and an archive. The 'just painting' archive of the library is an attempt to counter this. The research investigates the possibilities of performative painting as a key visual research methodology for architecture because it is direct and unmediated.

Figure 9: Wake for Birmingham Central Library January © Tonia Carless, 2015.

It is argued that this form of discursive painting, as a mode of architectural communication, might allow us to see the relation between material and cultural factors in specific historical transitions. Foucault's perspective is also paramount in 'just painting' whereby the painting serves as an immersive text to speak the unspoken.

Performing the planning process: Painting on water

Other themes investigated considered the wider concept of place, such as a paint-in of a group of trees that form a significant part of the coastal headland landscape of the town of Lyme Regis (Figures 1 and 10). The trees extend out from historic public landscape gardens and were proposed for felling in 2014, as part of the site clearance for alterations of an existing listed building. The new proposal entailed part demolition of a listed building and its redevelopment to form 23 new housing units. The paintings posit the trees as highly significant in the costal landscape of Lyme Regis. The views are constructed from a paint-in boat trip, *en plein-air* position. The trip was to view the terrain and town from the sea, its best vantage position. It allowed the extension of knowledge and discourse with the skipper, the

Figure 10: Lyme Regis view from the sea. Anonymous painters, 11 May 2015.

boat owner and others in the harbour to 'paint in' histories. This painting on water was also chosen because the sea was described in the planning documentation as 'the source of dominant noise' (Redwood 2014: 1). The consultation documents on acoustic noise claim the sound of the waves breaking on the shore exceed that of the proposed commercial extractor, air conditioning and refrigeration units. The sound of the sea is constructed as noise (Redwood 2014) rather than an aspect of its coastal and social condition as a seaside town. The paintings are intended as part of a spatial reappraisal of this assessment. The film of the boat trip and paintings are for exhibition as an upload onto the live planning portal. Here the painting constructs a utopian study through a social or historical archaeology.

Conclusion: Rendering public space

Increasing land values and commodification continue to reframe the economies of their own construction, whilst simultaneously transmitting a uniform and regulated architectural ideal by their images. The performative paintings discussed here offer histories, determined by knowledge and conceptions of space outside of this frame. They have been selected for their knowledge of state withdrawal from the support of industrial manufacturing as a potential source of social provision, employment, training or education (Filton Airport and British Airways Corporation, Figures 5 and 6), public education and civic space (Birmingham Central library, Figure 9) and recreational public facilities (coastal and other bathing pools and landscape gardens, Figures 1, 2 and 10). While at one level 'just painting' as a research method provides an oral-visual-social history project, its primary intention is the reclaiming of space and spatially sited social memory for alternative, imaginative possibilities. This utopian aspect is its primary ambition or research aim.

The collaborative structure of the paint-in critiques singular research practice. The emphasis is upon the performative aspect rather than marketable output. It is worth noting that this is an increasingly marginal position for academic or other quantifiable research to take up, because the output is deliberately intangible, discursive, ephemeral and fleeting. This research makes every effort to reject the singular conception of growth through development and capital accumulation embedded in the neo-liberal framework of academic research. It rejects competitive academic research by its non-hierarchical, non-specialist workshops and discursive, performative painting where all participants are bearers of cultural knowledge, experience and memory (Foucault's contingent practices) across different sites. It engages with the material reality of the spatial construction, or the politics of 'the real'. The performative painters enter the site as productive, non-capitalizing figures.

The research confronts a form of arrested development, in its anthropological or archaeological definition, to negate the technological plateau of redevelopment space where connections between capital and social consequences become erased. It allows for a close inspection of the process of capital accumulation and commodification on the ground, outside of technological dysfunction, or through analysis of the process of capital domination (Foucault 1980). The painting also has an archaeological fascination and attempts a disambiguation that, like the discovery of the Temple of Mithras, might rekindle an imaginative conception to both resist and re-imagine.

'just painting' envisages an interruption to the capitalization of space through a process of performing painterly renderings. To render here is to show the attributes of the space that already exist and potentially which may be re-imagined. To render may also be understood in terms of converting waste material and space into value-added materials and space as a process of extracting what might be of value. Alternatively, it could be considered through its other definition as a form of helpful service.

Acknowledgements

I would like to acknowledge the assistance and support of Dr Igea Troiani who invited me to present my paper 'Visual discourse and spatial extension' that formed the first iteration of this chapter as part of a panel at the AIRG (The All Ireland Architecture Research Group) (2015), Fourth Annual Meeting: 'Redefining Architectural Scholarship through Visual Methodologies', 30–31 January, University College Dublin, Ireland, and again for her suggestion of developing the proposal for the lecture and workshop 'Just painting: Design research as cultural negotiation' as part of the MArchD Research Methods for Design module she developed and led at Oxford Brookes University School of Architecture in October 2015 and 2016.

I would also like to acknowledge the collaborative generosity of the Bristol-based artist Annabel Other, founder member of 'just painting', and the numerous amateur painters who have been willing to share their experience and develop the archive.

REFERENCES

Awan, N., Schneider, T. and Till, J. (2011), *Spatial Agency: Other Ways of Doing Architecture*, Oxford: Routledge.

Benjamin, W. ([1936] 2008), *The Work of Art in the Age of Mechanical Reproduction*, London: Penguin.

Bojorquez, A. and Garcia, M. (2014), 'Employing social art practice', in P. Mortenbock and H. Mooshammer (eds), *Space (Re)Solutions: Intervention and Research in Visual Culture*, Bielefeld: Transcript Verlag, p. 197.

Clawley, A. (2015), 'Death notice and wake', http://keeptheziggurat.tumblr.com/. Accessed 6 January 2015.

Climo, J. and Cattell, M. (eds) (2002), *Social Memory and History: Anthropological Perspectives*, Walnut Creek, CA: Altamira Press.

Dudley Barrett, B. (2010), *Artists on the Edge: The Rise of Coastal Artist's colonies, 1880–1920*, Amsterdam: University of Amsterdam Press.

Eagleton, T. (2000), *The Idea of Culture*, Oxford: Blackwell.

Foucault, M. ([1969] 1972), *The Archaeology of Knowledge*, London: Tavistock Publications.

—— (1980), *Power/Knowledge* (ed. C. Gordon), New York: Pantheon Book.

—— ([1976] 2009), 'Alternatives to the prison: Dissemination or decline of social control?', *Theory, Culture and Society*, 26:6, pp. 12–24.

Frow, J. and Schlunke, K. (2008), 'History experiments: Historical fiction and allegorical truth', in F. Collins (ed.), *Cultural Studies Review*, 14:1, Melbourne: Melbourne University Publishing, p. 59.

Harvey, D. ([1984] 1991), *The Production of Space* (ed. H. Lefebvre, trans. D. Nicholson-Smith), Oxford: Blackwell, p. 431.

Ippolito, J. and Rinehart, R. (2014), *Re-collection: Art, New Media and Social Memory*, Cambridge, MA: The MIT Press.

Jackson, S. (Archaeologist for the London Museum of Archaeology) (22 September 2014), on Angus, Jamie (ed.), 'When The Temple of Mithras was unearthed in London', *Today Programme*, BBC Radio 4.

Jamieson, C. (2013), 'Disturbing architecture catalogue essay', in Nils Jean (ed.), *Disruption RCA research biennial* January, pp. 58–65.

Lefebvre, H. (1969), *Explosions: Marxism and the French Revolution*, New York: Monthly Review Press.

——— (1991), *The Production of Space* (trans. D. Nicholson), Oxford: Wiley-Blackwell.

Marx, K. (1978), '1844 economic and philosophical manuscripts', in R. C. Tucker (ed.), *The Marx-Engels Reader*, New York: W.W. Norton & Company.

Matta-Clark, G. (1974), 'Ant arcotecture, proposal for anarchitecture', in *Laurie Anderson, Trisha Brown, Gordon Matta-Clark: Pioneers of The Downtown Scene New York*, A Barbican Exhibition Catalogue, London: Prestel, p. 118.

Mlicka, A. ([2007] 2014), 'Painting architecture: Towards a practice-led research methodology', in *Studies in Material Thinking*, February 10, Auckland, New Zealand: Faculty of Design and Creative Technologies Auckland University of Technology, pp. 1–19, https://www.materialthinking.org/sites/default/files/papers/SMT_V10_03_Agnieszka%20Mlicka_0.pdf. Accessed 1 September 2015.

Oetterman, S. (1997), *The Panorama: History of a Mass Medium* (trans. D. L. Schneider), New York: Zone Books.

Oliver, T. (2006), Preface to *The Museum of Contemporary Art*, in P. Bedford (ed.), *Exhibition Catalogue*, Sydney: Museum of Contemporary Art Publication, p. 9, http://www.aboriginal-art.de/EN/Literatur_Info_MCA_2006_578.htm#Kla. Accessed 23 November 2015.

Redwood, R. (2014), *Report Noise Survey at The Three Cups Site Lyme Regis Assessment and Supporting documents to Planning application*, http://wam.westdorset-dc.gov.uk/WAM/doc/Planning.pdf?extension=.pdf&contentType=application/pdf&id=1146454. Accessed November 2014.

Rinehart, R. and Ippolito, J. (2014), *Re-Collection Art, New Media and Social Memory*, London: The MIT Press.

Rose, G. (2007), *Visual Methodologies: An Introduction to the Interpretation of Visual Materials*, 2nd ed., London: SAGE Publications pp. 174–76.

Skerrit, H. F. (2015), 'The politics of just painting: Engagement and encounter in the art of the East Kimberley', *Seismopolite: Journal of Art and Politics*, http://www.seismopolite.com/the-politics-of-just-painting-engagement-and-encounter-in-the-art-of-the-east-kimberley. Accessed 23 November 2015.

Soja, E. W. (1989), *Postmodern Geographies: The Reassertion of Space in Critical Social Theory*, London and New York: Verso, p. 61.

Tiroche De Leon Collection Website (2015), *Artist Spotlight: Liu Xiaodong*, 4 January, http://www.tirochedeleon.com/news/artist-spotlight-liu-xiaodong/. Accessed June 2016.

Victoria and Albert Museum (2016), 'British watercolours 1750–1900: The landscape genre', http://www.vam.ac.uk/content/articles/b/british-watercolours-landscape-genre/. Accessed 1 June 2016.

NOTE

1. One such activity involved the attempted paint-in at the Victoria and Albert Museum exhibition of 'Botticelli Re-imagined' in May 2016, where the paints of one of the group were confiscated by the museum security. See also subsequent section 'just painting as Activist Research' the amateur painting groups enter the contested territories (dis-)armed* with brushes and sketch books.

21

Visual heuristics for colour design

Fiona McLachlan, University of Edinburgh

Introduction

This chapter considers the particular role of paint and painting in the development of visual methodologies for architectural research. It will draw on ongoing research by the author together with art historians at the Haus der Farbe, Zurich, specifically relating to colour in twentieth-century and contemporary architectural design. It will reflect on the emergent visual methods developed, placing them in relation to our understanding of visual images more generally in humanities research.

Colour theory has developed, and was communicated historically, through a wide range of visual methods. The two-dimensional colour wheel by Johann Wolfgang von Goethe (Goethe 1809) and three-dimensional 'solids' of Philipp Otto Runge's, 'Farbenkugel' (Runge 1810: 24) are examples of numerous similar devices produced in the search for natural laws to explain and communicate observed phenomena. Often paint was the most readily available medium for illustration, and its immediate connection to colour made it an obvious choice for such research. The above abstractions to diagrammatic, geometrical forms are clearly simplistic, yet such models continue to be used in contemporary literature as a means to illustrate observed relationships between hues, and as tools for the navigation of colour systems. These visual representations clearly fail to communicate the complex metaphysical sensation of colour, experienced as a combination of physio-psychological experience, and individually nuanced by social and cultural values. As a product of light, colour is also ethereal, illusory and ambiguous. Although colour theory is readily available to architects, it does not appear to have had much traction in practice and is largely absent in the formal curriculum architectural education (Jasper 2014). The purpose of the author's continuing research is therefore to consider how architects might develop a more informed use of colour, by offering a critical analysis of existing design practices and through investigation of specific buildings. The production of abstracted painted images as an integral part of the research methodology is suggested as a form of visual heuristic device. It will be argued that the paintings provide the site for a discursive and designerly analysis, the incubation of knowledge and a synthesis between disciplines. The development of visual methodologies plays a productive part in the constructed interpretation of the findings, and as also a means through which research findings can be disseminated to a range of audiences. Three distinctive types of painting have been established, and are used to structure the analysis, namely: visual indexes, two-dimensional building portraits and three-dimensional visualizations.

Visual indexes

The extraordinary hand-painted grids in Boogert's *Traité des couleurs servant à la peinture à l'eau* (1692) represent his detailed investigation of watercolour as a medium, and serve as one of the earliest known diagrammatic portrayals of colour research. The method used was a regular grid and a systematic graphic documentation of modulated tones. We are accustomed to equating colour choice with small swatches or colour chips presented in grid form. The artist Gerhard Richter has played on this familiarity through his series of colour chart paintings started in the mid-1960s (McLachlan 2012: 147). Le Corbusier's 'Claviers de Couleur' for the Salubra wall paper company (1931 and 1959) had a different purpose (Rüegg 1988). His aim was to define and present a range of wallpaper colours collated into themes. The customer would have a heightened sense of security by using a deliberately restricted set of factory-produced colours. A framing device adds to the idea of utility in the catalogue. Although this was essentially a commercial product, it drew on his previous research on a range of colours defined as 'constructive' through his studies with Amedée Ozenfant and from his own paintings. Although he painted throughout his life, he kept a distance between the subject matter of his paintings and his architecture. The canvas gave him space to experiment in colour and form (Gans 2003).

In early stages of the author's research, a triptych painting *Investigations in the Professional Palette* (McLachlan 2008) (Figure 1) was used as an agent to reflect on, and gain a better understanding of, the use of colour within architectural design practice. At one level this device served to record and index colours specified by the author's architectural practice over a sustained period of nearly thirty years and, as such, aimed to reveal the tacit knowledge of the researcher. The use of an abstract grid equalized the extent of the colours, removed them from context, material and surface texture in an attempt to consider the colour palette of the practice's work.

Yet this gridded abstraction is not arbitrary, it was composed as an object in its own right, as well as a visual representation of a raw data collection exercise. It also provides a tool whereby the colours – the results of an investigation through a series of decoration schedules embedded in the practice's job files – are displayed collectively, and in an immediately accessible manner.

Figure 1: McLachlan, F. *Investigations in the Professional Palette*, 2008. Satinwood paint on plywood. [Photo credit: Rachel Travers, University of Edinburgh]

Additionally, the painting acts as an instrument to consider the semiotics of colour. Further layers of meaning were developed during its design and production, and because of its physical presence, it became a device for self-reflection and analysis when subjected to a prolonged and acute gaze. It was designed through an iterative process, and ordered chronologically from left to right. It revealed responses to typology within the practice's architecture, and, in the painting itself, the interaction of strong or muted boundaries between colours. A similarly grid-based installation *Shoulder to Shoulder* (Figure 2), made specifically for an exhibition of a completed research project in Edinburgh (*Colour Strategies in Architecture* 2015), was intended to provide an immersive, sensory experience, inviting the audience to participate by drawing their own conclusions, connections and observations on the interaction and juxtaposition of colour. Here the medium of the painting was very immediate and directly accessible. Gregory Stanczak (2007: 3) suggested that images are 'no longer appendages to the research' or a means through which to communicate findings, but rather that they can be integral to the generation of the research itself. The author's 'index' paintings are therefore *both* the research *and* the visual device through which the research is disseminated.

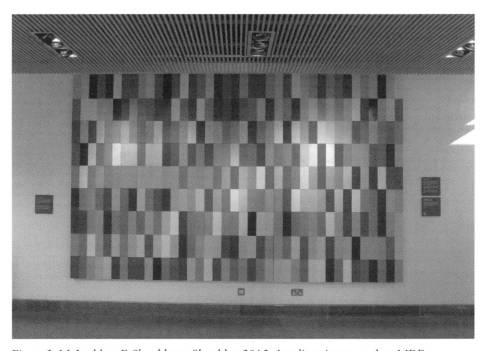

Figure 2: McLachlan, F. *Shoulder to Shoulder*, 2015. Acrylic paint on card on MDF.

Transactions in production – Observation, analysis and synthesis

Researchers at the Haus der Farbe have developed a predominantly visual methodology to document and analyse colour in the built environment. In one project, the research team 'captured' the external façade colour of over 40,000 buildings in Zurich, by visual comparison of the observed colour on site to samples from a range of colour systems (e.g. RAL, NCS). The research team then hand-mixed acrylic paint in the studio to create the equivalent of a data set of large swatches (Rehsteiner et al. 2010). There are a range of digital apps and scientific measuring tools that could do this task and produce a digital palette in seconds, so what did the paint and painting process offer that is not true of other more easily replicated and 'clean' media? The method is essentially experiential and wholly qualitative. It relies on a group of individuals making a judgement on the overall sensation of colour on each building on a given day, time of year and weather condition. Hence the use of the 'seeing eye' is present from the earliest stages of the research. This technique is open to the vagaries of lived experience, because there are many variables at play, not least in the physiology of the observer, and the specific quality of light, shadow and material reflectance. But methods of measurement appropriate to a laboratory are not experiential (at least, not overtly) and cannot replicate the contingent nature of colour perception in the 'real world', which this method aims to expose.

The process of hand-mixing the medium itself requires the researcher to be analytical. Each colour has to be considered and generated through an empirical method, reviewed, and adjusted by eye in relation to the source. The physical process of making gives time to inquire, to think and to develop a deeper understanding of tonal variations that are only apparent through the action of mixing the paint. New knowledge, for example subtle nuances in the overall palette, emerges through this physical action. As colour is always contingent on light and material surface, there can never be complete certainty in any reproduction. This is equally true of digital or printed images, but this experiential method of recording colour by observation and hand mixing may offer a more appropriate and explanatory means through which such research is conducted and communicated.

> In considering what it is to 'make' a painting within the context of research, there are different perspectives to ponder. The study of painting as an inquiry process takes into account more than the physical and formal practices of creating images on surfaces. Not only is the artist involved in a 'doing' performance, but this also results in an image that is a site for further interpretation by viewers and an object that is part of visual culture
>
> (Sullivan in Knowles and Cole 2008: 240)

The same observational and forensic method of data collection was used in a later collaborative and interdisciplinary project leading to a book, *Colour Strategies in Architecture* (McLachlan et al. 2015). In this case, the research team (based in Berlin, Edinburgh and Zurich) included art historians, a colour designer and an architect. This research drew on these established visual methods, and developed new techniques to analyse and present the findings, which are considered below in more detail.

Composite images – Building portraits

While swatches derived from building facades and interiors provide raw data, they give no information on the specific situation – the extent, juxtaposition and location of each observed colour as evidenced on the buildings themselves. In this case, the researchers' aim was to develop a means through which these relationships could be explored and presented. The development of visual, heuristic devices has been proposed as an effective methodology in support of a transactional relationship between academic research and architectural practice (McLachlan and McLachlan 2014: 255). In this case, the collaged 'building portraits' simultaneously depict a presentation of the original data, and a constructed interpretation of research findings, designed to disseminate the new knowledge to a range of audiences.

A collage technique is commonly used to juxtapose remotely sourced images, textures and media to convey meaning, for example in Richard Hamilton's 'Just what is it that makes today's homes so different, so appealing' (1956). The technique itself offers a mode of inquiry and a 'conceptualising approach' (Butler-Kisber in Knowles and Cole 2008: 270) to help develop a response to a research question through drafts and re-drafts in a similar honing to the production of text. In the case of the Colour Strategies project, an abstract portrait of each building was assembled using the painted swatches, and is therefore similarly rich in data. Each coded colour contains information about the original building from which it was sourced. The collage affords an immediate representation of this assembly, with each element layered to denote hierarchy, proportional extent and location (Figure 3). The collage method also enabled the interdisciplinary research team to explore the overall characteristics of the palette and various relationships within it, and so incorporated a layering of tacit knowledge (regarding colour use, geographical and cultural differences, for example) in the research findings. Josef Albers' seminal publication, *Interaction of Color,* used a predominantly visual methodology to introduce the viewer to contingency and doubt. Through the exercises, colour is plainly observed as an unreliable, plastic sensation,

Figure 3: Hand-painted colour portrait based on building study of Hans Scharoun's Reading room, Staatsbibliotheque, Berlin. Collage, acrylic paint on card. Copyright: Haus der Farbe, Fiona McLachlan and Marcella Wenger-di Gabrielle. [Photo by Urs Sigenthaler]

wholly relative to its context. His preferred medium was to collage coloured paper, which was considered as a more reliable tool for students than paint (Albers [1963] 2006: 6, 7).

Visualizations – Spatial painting

The third method for discussion here (following the two-dimensional indexes and building portraits) proved to be the most challenging. The aim was to develop a means through which to investigate and communicate the strategic role of colour within architectural space.

There are a number of examples of contemporary architects who use painted images as part of a practice-based design development as a means of analysis, synthesis and in presentation. Will Alsop used painting as a form of retreat to allow a free flow of consciousness without the necessity of reason or justification and found the very fluidity of the medium is liberating (Porter 2011). Early paintings by Zaha Hadid in *Planetary Architecture Two*, for example, can be seen as exploratory, experimental and designerly investigations. In the accompanying commentary, Alvin Boyarski (in Hadid and Frampton 1983) suggests '... your drawings and paintings seem to transcend the subject matter. They appear to be some form of research'. Hadid's paintings in contrast to those by Alsop, and indeed Le Corbusier's, were always directly related to the projection of the project itself (Hadid and Margolius 2003: 17). The power of the paintings resides not only in the skill of their execution, but also in the use of constructed images, made possible through the medium of painting. The paintings provide extreme viewpoints, depicting anti-gravitational, floating shapes in compositions that could not be achieved in model form, especially before widespread computer usage. The use of strong visual images was clearly influenced by the practices of her tutors and contemporaries – most notably the paintings of two of the women founders of OMA: Zoe Zenghelis and Madelon Vriesendorp, where Hadid later worked. Vriesendorp's paintings became 'the thought diagrams' for *Delirious New York* (Koolhaas 1978), even though some preceded the text (Jencks 2008: 19). The directness, humour and surreal juxtapositions of the images made them highly memorable. They became a powerful iconography – emblematic for the work of their emerging practice. The paintings are an expression of a 'free-floating imagination' (Koolhaas et al. 2008: 262). The visual methodology therefore became critical in communicating provocative and multi-layered meaning.

Hadid's use of colour was often highly intuitive and abstract, using red, blue and yellow backgrounds with turquoise and terracotta planes – studies wrought through consideration of Kasimir Malevich's 'Tektoniks'. Hadid's paintings, some executed by a team, explore, experiment and test design ideas, and can be considered to have contributed to the generation of new knowledge and ultimately to the production of new types of fluid architectural space. By this definition, the paintings can be seen as evidence of a visual design research methodology. Some have a clear narrative, while others remain exploratory. There is also an artistic quality, in that the paintings were not entirely planned in a methodological manner, and the final effect was not necessarily predicted. Hadid (Boyarski and Hadid 1983) notes that the paintings changed the way they thought about the architecture in terms of materials and colour. Within art there is a discourse that would suggest the relationship between painter and painting is at times conversational, and that the painting begins to dictate – to fight back in some way (Mooney 2015: 10). Hadid's paintings defined the design research problem and acted to synthesize a range of factors. The paintings are discursive, providing a means of articulating ideas to interdisciplinary audiences, as well as being tools through which a self-reflexive practice was developed. In this respect, they appear to combine research and artistic production. But to what extent can these activities be considered as examples of visual methodology within practice-based design research? According to Boradkar, a professor of industrial design (2011: 166):

VISUAL HEURISTICS FOR COLOUR DESIGN

> Visual Research in design can [...] serve two roles – it can help us in making sense of the material world in which we live and also help us in understanding the creative process of design thinking.

In the *Colour Strategies in Architecture* research, swatches of observed and researched colour were assembled into a collaged and composite 'visualization', based on the work of the architects studied. The composition of each image was the result of an interdisciplinary discursive process that centred on the production

Figure 4: Hushed Tonalities. Hand-painted collaged visualization based on studies of buildings by Reiach & Hall Architects, Edinburgh, 2014. Light, shadow, soft tones and the influence of landscape are the key elements of this strategy. Copyright: Haus der Farbe, Fiona McLachlan and Marcella Wenger-di Gabrielle. [Photo by Urs Sigenthaler]

and development of a three-dimensional visual representation of the strategic use of colour, demonstrated in an imagined space. The aim was to convey meaning through the choice of spatial configuration and the projection. Taking one particular case, 'Hushed Tonalities', the projection used is part-perspective, part elevation (Figure 4). The colour of the paint in the image not only represents the actual documented data of the observed colours from the building sites, it was used in the constructed visualization to try to understand a particular phenomenon of how these colours are experienced by the body moving through space. Both image and meaning were developed through discussion, the initial study drawings providing the opportunity to tease out previously unseen characteristics and relationships both in colour and architectural form. In terms of research method, the initial drawings were diagnostic and analytical. They could also be considered as evidence of an immersive process that involved diverse methods, including looking, reflecting and adjusting, and undertaken in parallel with the development of a written text. The psychologist Clark Moustakas considers a heuristic methodology to have validity, provided that the researchers constantly seek to appraise and verify the significance of the experience or phenomenon under investigation. Thus an individual experience, drawing on and revealing tacit knowledge, can be reasonably extrapolated to one that may be considered as more widely felt (Moustakas 1990: 33). The visualization can be considered as design research, in that it is situated in a built example. It offers a systematic and critical analysis of how specific spaces work on an experiential level, and provides new insights into the original design process of the architect.

Dissemination and the site of the audience

Gillian Rose, a cultural geographer, counselled on the limitations of such constructional interpretation in relation to critical visual methodology, namely that 'visual images do not exist in a vacuum' (Rose 2001: 37). One must therefore be aware of the method of production and the social norms through which images will be viewed and understood. Rose (2001: 16) suggests that three 'sites' have been accepted at which the meanings of visual images are made, namely: site of production (including the artist and technology), the site of the image itself, and the site of the audience. So, how can painting as a medium contribute to the communication and dissemination of architectural research?

An image is controlled by the position of the viewer and the viewpoint. It is composed through the disposition of its content, by adjacencies and relationships of the objects or directly in the case of a painting, through fields of colour. In addition, because an image can never be 'innocent', it communicates at a subconscious level through 'socially constructed codes of recognition' (Rose 2001: 32). As a means of communicating a visual analysis of an architectural composition, a painting may, in some respects, be more readily accessible than an architectural drawing. The social expectations present in observing an artistic composition may evoke a more direct response than the codified information inherent in an architect's drawing. Additionally, Kress and van Leeuwen (1990: 224) argue that conventional architectural line drawings, drawn for other purposes such as construction, make it 'harder to put the semiotic in the foreground'.

If this logic is followed, then paintings may have the capacity to convey meaning in a form with which audiences are more readily willing to engage, because they tap into certain conventions expected of art. Any composition will be selective in what is chosen to foreground to the audience, and what is omitted. In the visualization illustrated, based on buildings in central Scotland by Reiach and Hall Architects, the aim was to communicate a colour strategy that is largely material based, deliberately subdued in tone and enlivened by the play of light, shadow and the colour of the landscape (Figure 4). Although at first the painting may appear literally descriptive, it is abstracted and is not representative of a specific space. To elicit a feeling of spaciousness, a high perspectival viewpoint was taken to give the impression of suspension in space. The white upper wall wraps across the top of the painting to further suggest a large open space, and a feeling of low northern light and shadow was introduced within the composition by tonal shifts on the floor. The placing of each colour in this instance was intended to convey a restful, calm space, with a passive viewer. Conventions of painting composition, vector lines, figure and ground can therefore be applied to such a visualization to aid in the intended communication.

A second example, based on buildings in Zurich by Knapkiewicz and Fickert, uses a plan projection to place visual emphasis on the façade surface onto which colour has been applied – as a form of mask in support of an illusion to reduce the apparent scale of the building. The visualization presented a means through which the analysis of the strategic role of colour could be determined through an expansive discussion within the research team. Once established, the choice of projection evolved, through a series of studies, from perspective to isometric. The final plan projection was selected in order to emphasize that the role of the colour in this strategy is as a second layer or surface application, which inscribes the building with an additional layer of meaning – in this case a deceptive one (Figure 5).

The use of colour within a painting can provide meaning by cultural association and the provenance of specific hues, and also by characteristics afforded by the specific technique, for example, to add light and shadow, or imply depth through tonal value, or intensity through the level of saturation. Unlike the free choice of colour as a mode of representation in art, these visualizations are highly restricted, as the only colours permissible in the research method are those found on the

Figure 5: 'Second Layer' visualization, based on studies of the buildings of Knapkiewicz and Fickert. Hand-painted collage, acrylic paint on card. Copyright: Haus der Farbe, Fiona McLachlan and Marcellla Wenger-di Gabrielle. Photo: Urs Sigenthaler.

buildings themselves. The meaning of the composition is not therefore to convey the meaning of colour by societal association within the painting itself but rather to communicate the researchers' constructed interpretation of the meaning of the colour within the original architectural projects.

The medium of the production of an analogue painting is counter to the now ubiquitous photo-realistic computer-generated visualizations of contemporary practice. It is clearly hand crafted, and carries with it the tacit knowledge and subjective, social construction of the authors. We can further consider the effect of the material production as an essential part of the making and communication of meaning. For example, Kress and van Leeuwen (1990: 215) discuss the extent to which brush strokes convey the hand of the human making the image. They suggest that the *inscription* of the surface is more focussed in abstract art and colour field painting, whereas *representation* is more significant in conventionally pictorial paintings. In our case, there was an awareness that this level of detail would be important. As a part of establishing a repeatable methodology, the three research teams studios in Berlin, Zurich and Edinburgh used exactly the same type of brush, the same make of paint and the same technique of rolling the paint on the surface, followed by vertical brush strokes. The expression of these fine brush strokes was consciously ordered in the subsequent collages – vertically on the abstract 'building portraits' and horizontally on conceptual spatial 'visualizations'. Only in the case of the portraits of three Berlin underground stations was a horizontal brush stroke employed to signify the way in which the colour is experienced from a moving train. This fine-grained semiotic expression is lost in the reproduction of the paintings in book form (just as is the case in any artwork), and so can be considered as secondary to the research methodology but nevertheless stands as evidence of the handcrafted mode of production and is clearly evident in the exhibited original paintings.

Multiple readings in painting – Doubt, uncertainty, ambiguity

Philosopher Alejandro A. Vallega (2013: 470) considers Paul Klee's specific interest in 'polyphonic seeing' in paintings. He suggests that the viewer is presented with layers of information, multiple readings of space within the painting, through colour, transparency and threaded forms. In architecture, colour and light yield similarly multiple readings, experienced as a dynamic shift in colour temperature as the angle of light changes in a temporal cycle. The movement of the body through space in the three-dimensional realm of architecture is inherently experiential and is challenging to present in a two-dimensional mode. Recent research on colour is beginning to establish post-positivist theoretical positions (O'Connor 2010). The sensory perception of the space is seen as wholly contingent, not only on physio-psychological factors, but also complex social and cultural meanings that may be unique to each individual at a given time and place. Mary Jo Hatch and Dvora Yanow, organizational ethnographers and interpretative methodologists, have drawn comparison between methodological models in painting and counterparts in theory. They suggest that figurative painting is 'objective-realist', and informed by the logic of positivism. Gestural painting, by comparison, is, they suggest, 'a constructivist–interpretive position informed by late 19th to mid-20th century phenomenological, hermeneutic, pragmatist, symbolic interactionist, ethno-methodological and (some) critical theoretical philosophies and theories, along with their later elaborations' (Hatch and Yarrow 2008: 29). Thus the specific form of visual representation chosen should be carefully considered alongside the research methodology. Using their analysis, the ontology of our collages lies somewhere between 'critical realism' and 'constructivism'. Paintings as visual research are epistemologically 'subjectivist' and the methodology used to produce them is a hybrid of post-positivism and hermeneutics. While another research topic might demand a different methodology this is appropriate to the intrinsically contingent, relative and metaphysical nature of colour.

The exploratory nature of architectural design development tends, by its iterative process, to produce many drawings that are temporal, overlaid and cast aside as the design is tested and evaluated through each drawing. Hadid's paintings were a device through which she diagnosed the questions and began to develop conceptual solutions. They were also used as tools in communication of the ideas and to anchor the essence of the proposal during later stages of development. Architects less frequently use paint for this purpose – perhaps because it is more time consuming than a sketch.

Although colour is often used in diagrams and analytical drawings to clarify conceptual components or codify elements, if the aim is to suggest contingency, then a painting also has the potential to be deliberately vague and open to interpretation. For example, Enric Miralles (1994) collaged leaves and twigs in the original competition entry for the Scottish Parliament so as to exploit the 'ambiguity of an ink blot'. Unlike other entries, which went out of their way to represent a clear 'built' proposal, the audience – a jury, half of whom were non-architects – were invited to transpose their own interpretation onto the enigmatic forms, stirred by powerfully symbolic statements of the importance of the land to the Scottish people. Miralles evidently understood the potential of the collage to communicate meaning very differently than the office's exquisite and precise technical drawings. Although a photograph may be presented to an audience as 'truth', Stanczak (2007: 79), a sociologist, argues that 'every image is manipulated, thus no image represents reality'. By comparison with photography, painting is immediately understood to be transparently subjective. Normally in the work of one author it is expected that a painting will be composed to stress one aspect over another, to guide the eye of the viewer across the surface, to suggest depth through tone and highlight, and to generate meaning. Similar to drawing, painting can act as an agent to facilitate dialogue during the analytical stages of research. In the *Colour Strategies in Architecture* project, the visual methodology also provided a means for discussion and an inductive and inter-disciplinary synthesis of the documented palettes in combination with other text-based sources and photographic images. Close observation of the painted swatches laid out adjacent to one another allowed a consideration of overall tone, the influence of the period, and allowed an interpretation of the architects' strategy to emerge. The visual research method facilitated ordering and reordering, teasing out the role of the colour. Numerous iterations of the base drawings were required to be made in a designerly process while trying to understand, then to interpret, a particular phenomenon. Australian artist, author and theorist Graeme Sullivan offers a metaphor to explain the braided nature of visual systems in research, particularly relating to art practice through which design research can be unravelled and expanded into distinct threads. Where not relevant to the argument, the threads can be trimmed or traced through and subsequently rewoven into new knowledge that will contain the rich data in each original thread (Sullivan 2010: 103). The production of images is therefore a key stage in the way in which discoveries can be made and solutions to research problems emerge.

Conclusion

The increased acceptance of visual methods in academic research can provide a new territory for architectural scholarship as a means of inquiry, documentation, critical thinking, analysis and dissemination in support of a transactional relationship between academic research and architectural practice. These heuristic devices offer a new way of reading architecture through a hermeneutic process. As an example, the author's research in colour has provided the basis of the discussion of the particular affordances of painting as a medium. Three distinctive outputs have been established and were used to structure the analysis:

- Abstracted index – used to document findings directly and to demonstrate relationships and interactions, remote from context, scale, surface and typology
- Two-dimensional 'building portraits' – used to evaluate relationships between colours situated relative to their location on the building, the proportional extent of colour elements and the character of the palette
- Three-dimensional visualizations – semi-pictorial, using various painterly devices of composition and viewpoint to bring the viewer into the frame, to indicate sensory experience and the strategy employed

Thus the development of appropriate visual methodologies becomes a direct and productive method seeking to establish new knowledge and to disseminate it back into architectural design practice and to diverse audiences. While the representations may be recognizable to the architects concerned, the aim of the visualizations was to find a method through which the strategic use of colour could be documented and be transferable to other future projects by other architects. Heuristic research as a method allows a form of inquiry, which is immersive, open ended and is essentially a process of self-reflection. If the act of painting is a conversation with oneself, then the potential is to unlock and synthesize tacit knowledge in an intuitive manner. This can be particularly appropriate to elucidate the nature of the particular experience or phenomena under investigation.

As a form of visual research, the chapter has argued that painting provides a space for free-flowing investigation and a basis for collective interpretation of the results. The abstraction from reality has been a significant element in the work discussed. For practice-based research, while drawings and digital renders project visualizations of unbuilt reality as closely as possible, painting can allow a retreat into a more ambiguous, less precise and contingent place to explore critical questions. Painting as a means of communicating architectural research has been shown to have the capacity to convey multiple layers of meaning with an audience in a way that can connect directly in a thought-provoking manner – through the detailed characteristics of the medium of production, through the composition of the image itself and through established cultural understandings of paintings. It has been argued that painting carries with it certain conventions and social expectations, which may make the research more accessible to a wider, untrained audience than the codified language of architectural drawing. The images therefore provide an interpretive space to invite a dialogue between the researcher, the painting and the audience.

The physical presence of a painting as a tangible product of research provides a lasting site for future reflection. In the case of the architectural research discussed, there is a direct correlation between the methodological use of paint as the mode of production, and the subject of the research – namely the experience of colour within architecture. The sensation of colour is immediate, both in the painting, and in the real-life examples under analysis. The hand-painted collages offer an innovative and sensorial way of reading and studying architecture, to place the viewer in direct dialogue with the colour and its strategic role. The process through which the painting emerges has in our case been hybrid, inductive and inter-subjective. It has provided a site for interaction and to make sense of design practices that may otherwise remain tacit. With regard to the particular visual methodologies employed, parallels can be drawn between the research method and consideration of the type of painting appropriate to each aspect of the research. They can be considered as constructivist and interpretivist visual modes of representation and are integral both to the research method and to its dissemination.

REFERENCES

Albers, J. ([1963] 2006), *Interaction of Color*, New Haven, CT and London: Yale University Press.

——— (2013) *Interaction of Color* (digital app), New Haven, CT: Yale University Press, http://yupnet.org/interactionofcolor/. Accessed 7 Aug 2019.

Boogert, A. (1692), *Traite des couleurs servant à la peinture à l'eau*, in the collection at Manuscrits de la Bibliothèque Méjanes, Aix-en-Provence, France, http://www.e-corpus.org/notices/102464/gallery/. Accessed 17 November 2015.

Boradkar, P. (2011), 'Visual research methods in the design process', in E. Margolis and L. Pauwels (eds), *The Sage Handbook of Visual Research Methods*, London: SAGE Publications.

Boyarski, A. and Hadid, Z. (1983), 'Alvin Boyarski interviews Zaha Hadid', in Z. Hadid, K. Frampton and Architectural Association, *Planetary Architecture two* (folio), London: Architectural Association.

Gans, D. (2003), 'Still life after all: Paintings of Le Corbusier', *Architectural Design*, 73:3, pp. 24–30.

Goethe, J. W. (1809), *Farbenkreis zur Symbolisierung des menschlichen Geistesund Seelenlebens*, Frankfurt a. M.: Freies Deutsches Hochstift, Frankfurter Goethe-Museum.

Gray, C. and Malins, J. (2004), *Visualising Research: A Guide to the Research Process in Art and Design*, Farnham, Surrey: Ashgate.

Hadid, Z. and Margolius, I. (2003), 'Paintings as architectural storyboards', *Architectural Design*, 73:3, pp. 14–23.

Hatch, M. J. and Yanow, D. (2008), 'Methodology by metaphor: Ways of seeing in painting and research', *Organization Studies*, 29:01, pp. 23–44.

Jasper, A. (2014), 'Colour theory', *Architectural Theory Review*, 19:2, pp. 119–23.

Jencks, C. (2008), 'Madelon seeing through objects', in S. Basar and S. Trüby (eds), *The World of Madelon Vriesendorp: Paintings / Postcards / Objects / Games*, London: AA Publications, pp. 16–24.

Knowles, J. G. and Cole, A. L. (eds) (2008), *Handbook of the Arts in Qualitative Research Perspectives, Methodologies, Examples, and Issues*, Thousand Oaks, CA: SAGE Publications.

Koolhaas, R. (1978), *Delirious New York: A Retroactive Manifesto for Manhattan*, New York: Monacelli Press.

Koolhaas, R. with Basar, S. and Trüby, S. (2008), 'Worrying kindness and ultimate wisdom', in S. Basar and S. Trüby (eds), *The World of Madelon Vriesendorp: Paintings / Postcards / Objects / Games*, London: AA Publications

Kress, G. and van Leeuwen, T. (1990), *Reading Images*, Geelong, Victoria: Deakin University Press.

McLachlan, E. and McLachlan, F. (2014), 'Colour and contingency: Theory into practice', *Architectural Theory Review*, 19, pp. 243–58.

McLachlan, F. (2012), *Architectural Colour in the Professional Palette*, Oxon/New York: Routledge.

McLachlan, F., Neser, A. M., Sibillano, L., Wenger-Di Gabriele, M. and Wettstein, S. (2015), *Colour Strategies in Architecture*, Basel: Schwabe Verlag A.G.

Miralles, E. (1994), quoted from lecture given at the Royal Incorporation of Architects of Scotland convention, Edinburgh, May 1994.

Mooney, J. (2015), *Simply Painting*, exhibition catalogue, Inverness: Inverness Museum and Art Gallery.

Moustakas, C. (1990), *Heuristic Research Design Methodology and Applications*, Thousand Oaks, CA: SAGE Publications.

O'Connor, Z. (2010), 'Black-listed: Why colour theory has a bad name in 21st century design education', *Proceedings of ConnectED 2010 2nd International Conference on Design Education*, Sydney.

Porter, T. (2011), *Will Alsop: The Noise*, Oxon: Routledge.

Rehsteiner, J., Sibillano, L. and Wettstein, S. (2010), *Farbraum Stadt: Box ZRH*, Zurich: Kontrast Verlag.

Rose, G. (2001), *Visual Methodologies: An Introduction to the Interpretation of Visual Materials*, London: SAGE Publications.

Rüegg, A. (ed.) (1988), *Polychromie architecturale: les claviers de couleurs de Le Corbusier de 1931 et de 1959*, Basel: Birkhäuser (later edition 2006).

Runge, P. (1810), *Farben-Kugel: Oder, Construction des Verhältnisses aller Mischungen der Farben zu einander, und ihrer vollständigen Affinität, mit angehängtem Versuch einer Ableitung der Harmonie in den Zusammenstellungen der Farben; nebst einer Abhandlung über die Bedeutung der Farben in der Natur*. Hamburg: Friedrich Perthes.

Stanczak, G. C. (2007), *Visual Research Methods: Image, Society, and Representation*, Thousand Oaks, CA: SAGE Publications.

Sullivan, G., (2010), *Art Practice as Research: Inquiry in Visual Arts*, Thousand Oaks, CA: SAGE Publications.

Vallega, A. A. (2013), 'Paul Klee's originary painting', *Research in Phenomenology*, 43, pp. 462–74.

22

Digitally stitching stereoscopic vision

George Themistokleous, De Montfort University

Introduction

This chapter is part of a wider research that re-considers the changing role of bodily vision in space and time in relation to digital media and visual technologies. As media and technologies become increasingly more complex and are further integrated within the corporeal visual body, they induce a rethinking of the body itself. Digital technologies allow for older visual devices – in this case the stereoscope – to be thought anew. The interaction between digital media and the stereoscope can offer a contemporary understanding of the body's perception in time and space.

My research is developed through two combined methods: an experimental design practice that involves the making and testing of custom-made optical devices and multimedia installations, and an interdisciplinary theoretical investigation that considers the role of the body in key instances from art, art history, philosophy, cognitive science, digital media and film studies. Theory and practice mutually interact and interrogate each other to generate, address and answer questions, only to raise new questions. The experimental practice informs the theory and vice versa in a continuous loop where visual perception and the thinking of visual perception converge in an often-conflicting dialogue. This generates a constant critique of each other; the production of the work lies at this intersection.

The project entitled *Diplorasis* is a custom-made optical device of my own making. It incorporates established media (stereoscope and montage) and re-configures these through digital programming (image processing, wireless reception, motion control), in order to experiment with contemporary understandings of the body and its visual projections. The *Diplorasis* appropriates and combines readings on embodied and disembodied vision in order to produce a contemporary understanding of vision and its ensuing time. In particular, the work attempts to re-think how a stereoscopic vision and a cinematic vision might be re-configured and synthesized through the use of digital technologies. The embodied perceptual duration assumed by the stereoscope – a device by which two photographs of the same object taken at slightly different angles are viewed together, creating an impression of depth and solidity – offers an important tool to re-consider the disembodied duration of the camera and the technique of montage, as defined by Gilles Deleuze in *Cinema 1: The Movement-Image* (1983). The hybrid techniques that are developed in the *Diplorasis* construct a new articulation of how time is perceived by the cognitive body. This is important today because vision, and hence the body, is increasingly embedded within media environments. The self is multiplied within virtual domains that in turn affect the actual space of the corporeal body. In this respect, it is crucial to think how time-based media represent our spatial environments and how this virtuality shifts the locus of the body.

The making of the *Diplorasis* was triggered by an urge to re-think the relationship between my own physiological visual experience, theoretical writings on vision and other practices that explore visual processes. This chapter will begin by outlining my own visual perception and then will move on to explain the operation of the *Diplorasis*. The device investigates two overlapping intervals: between the body and its projected image, and the time interval between the perceiving body and the stereoscopic and cinematic time that are incorporated in the *Diplorasis*. The first interval – between the body and its projected image – explores bodily vision through the works of Maurice Merleau-Ponty, Drew Leder and an optical experiment by George M. Stratton. This provides an account of bodily vision through the use of the stereoscope and its divergent interpretations by Merleau-Ponty and Jonathan Crary: as bodily vision becomes increasingly intertwined with the stereoscope it alters the thinking of vision and its relation to time. The cinematic eye as explored through montage in the writings of Gilles Deleuze instead begins to introduce the idea of a disembodied visual perception.

The *Diplorasis* mediates, appropriates and re-configures particular aspects of stereoscopy and cinematic montage through the use of digital media. What emerges from this interaction is a new visual practice that generates a new way to think the visual and vice versa. The intersection between bodily and machinic

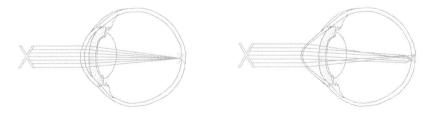

Figure 1: George Themistokleous, diagram of normal eye (left) and keratoconus eye (right).

vision, implicating the body as both subject and image, and mediating between the time of the body in relation to stereoscopy and to montage, begins to trace a new understanding of an 'architecture of sight'.

My vision

The initial concern of the *Diplorasis* was to question how embodied perception was associated with the tools of representation. This apprehension arose due to my own visual misalignment: I have a degenerative eye disorder, keratoconus, in one eye. This produces two concurrent visual perceptions, that of the degenerative and that of the normal eye, which result in a split of the visual image. The Greek word keratoconus is translated as horn-shaped cornea even though the form of the cornea most closely resembles an elongated nipple. Because one of my corneas is rounded and the other is shaped like an elongated nipple, the projection on each retina and their subsequent merging create an image that diverges and whose degree of divergence varies. Within the degenerative eye, light bounces unevenly on the surface of the retina, which causes the image to explode and streak (Figure 1). Even when the cornea is somewhat contained, with the application of a prickly hard corrective lens that holds the cornea in place, there is always a misalignment with the other eye. This misalignment creates a split between each monocular vision. The variation and indeterminacy of the split, with or without a corrective lens, reproduces a doubled and unresolved image. The split of the eyes' monocular functioning and dysfunctioning produces binocular combinations that allow for a re-thinking of visual perception. This situation presents itself as a useful comparison with the representational medium that best corresponds to my visual perceptual state, the stereoscope.

The Diplorasis and its Operation

Diplorasis derives from the Greek words *diplo* and *orasi*, translated as double vision. *Orasi* – the act of seeing – denotes in this case that the eye is an active transmitter of images. *Diplo* or double is used to literally describe the dual operation of the monocular eyes acting both separately and together, and also refers to the two overlapping durations that the device synthesizes.

The *Diplorasis* is a custom-made media installation of my own making that incorporates an optical device within its setup. The technical operation of the *Diplorasis* is not separated from the conceptual understanding of visuality

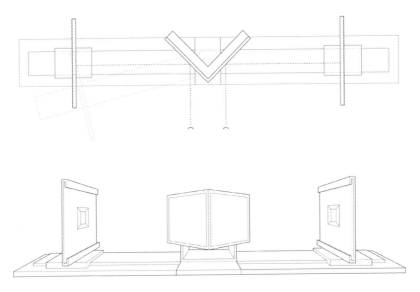

Figure 2: George Themistokleous, drawing of Wheatstone stereoscope (plan and perspectival view). Visual material for *Diplorasis* by George Themistokleous. Software engineering for the *Diplorasis* developed by Savvas Socratous.

that it generates. The *Diplorasis* appropriates the setup of the Wheatstone stereoscope, yet the device extends its operation through the application of a range of media including cameras, controlled motors, LCD screens, Arduino micro-controllers, Raspberry Pi micro-computers and ultrasonic sensors. Sir Charles Wheatstone invented the stereoscope in the 1830s. The Wheatstone stereoscope uses mirrors to create a simulated illusion of three-dimensional space, through the projection of two-dimensional images (Figure 2). These images consist of a photographic pair of two slightly dissimilar photographs; in other words the framed object is photographed from diverging angles. These images are then projected onto the two mirrors. The mirrors are placed at ninety degrees from each other. When viewed from above they form a V-shape. This means that each eye faces one mirrored plane reflecting each image placed on either side. The eyes are framed so that peripheral vision is restricted and each eye focuses directly on the mirror in front of it. The two [monocular] eyes receive the two projected images separately and their coalescence forms the stereoscopic image. The *Diplorasis* aims to further extend the possibility of the stereoscopic overlapping between a diverging and converging image by projecting not one image on either side but instead a sequence of images that are placed on a metal drum (Figures 3 and 4).

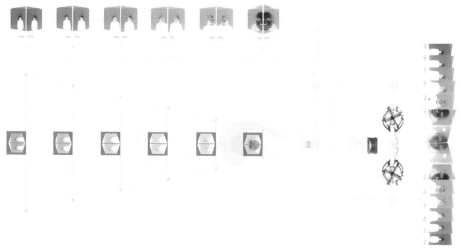

Figure 3: George Themistokleous, diagram of *Diplorasis* operation, plan view.

The digitally controlled drums simultaneously rotate in order for the screens that are fixed to the drums to align. The eyes receive one pair of images for a specified time and then the two drums revolve sequentially for the next pair to align and so on.

This digital stereoscope is placed at the far end of a dark corridor. The device is placed behind a translucent block of vertical acrylic sheets with the form of the human head being carved out from this block (Figures 5 and 6). This cavity, an inverse of a human bust has peephole openings that face the mirrors of the machine behind the screen. As the viewer enters the corridor s/he will observe the screen light emitting from these peepholes. Whilst approaching the light source, s/he is unaware that s/he is being photographed by a DSLR camera (Figure 7). Attached to the camera is a stereoscopic lens, which produces a stereoscopic paired image that is split and then sent to LCD screens placed inside the drum via wireless transmission through the Raspberry Pi (Figure 3). Each screen on either side of the mirrors projects one of the two dissimilar images (Figure 7). The images projected through this stereoscopic setup are of the observer's own body digitally stitched and looped backwards. In other words, one perceives oneself in three-dimensions and walking backwards in the corridor, the same route that s/he traversed moments before. The actual progression of the simulated machine operation projects a rewinding. As the projected body stills revolve, they become digitally misaligned and manipulated. As a consequence the digital stitching of the body is tampered with. This reduplicated and projected self, three-dimensionally simulated, begins to question the inter-relation between the self as object and the self as image (Figure 8).

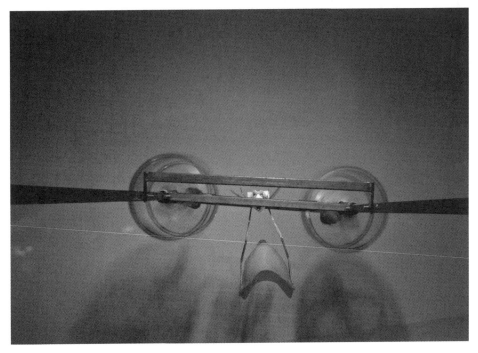

Figure 4: George Themistokleous, photograph of *Diplorasis*, phase b. Testing of drum rotations.

For the duration of the visual experience the bodily viewer confronts and constructs (through the stereoscopic operation) himself/herself as image.

The device therefore brings to the fore two different types of intervals that are inter-related. One interval occurs between the body of the viewer and the viewer's projected image. The other interval, of time, is implicated within the re-configured technologies of the stereoscope and montage. The durational split is thus extended from the stereoscopic apparatus to the space that the body inhabits in 'real' and virtual time. At this point it is important to define the role of duration in the stereoscope by starting from bodily vision.

Bodily vision: The interval of the body and its image

In *The Phenomenology of Perception*, Merleau-Ponty outlines how the 'experience of phenomena is the making explicit or bringing to light of the prescientific life of consciousness' (2009: 68). His critique centres on the notion of self from the Cartesian 'cogito' where the body, considered as a geometric unit, lacks a distinction amongst other objects. For Merleau-Ponty the sensory experience of the body-subject and its interwoven link to the world is the primary zone for our understanding of the world. In Merleau-Ponty's text, the phenomenal body is developed using examples mainly from the visual field. These examples include optical devices, c.g. the stereoscope, eye deficiencies, e.g. diplopia, and optical illusions and experiments such as those conducted by neuropsychologists and cognitive scientists. His critique is directed not only towards the epistemology of the body as a source of deterministic knowledge that leads to a reductive representation of the body rather than an understanding of the body's phenomena, but also towards philosophy and the limitations that it encounters when it confronts the bodily visual field.

One of the examples discussed in *Phenomenology of Perception* is the work by George M. Stratton, a psychologist who conducted optical experiments at the end of the nineteenth century. Merleau-Ponty refers to Stratton's inverted goggle experiment where prisms are used to rotate the perceived image by 180 degrees, making everything appear upside down. Cognitively the body will progressively adjust to the inverted image after about one week. In Merleau-Ponty's description of Stratton's experiment, there are two 'irreconcilable representations of the body' (2009: 286). The dissonance occurs between the inverted visual perception and the tactile sensations that are not inverted. In the course of the experiment the tactile body adjusts to the inverted 'virtual' image. According to Merleau-Ponty, 'everything throws us back to the organic relations between subject and space, to that gearing of the subject onto his world, which is the origin of space' (2009: 293). Here however it might be worth to consider this experiment not as a 'gearing of the subject onto his world' but as the ungearing of the subject from itself. In Stratton's experience of the device, he claims: 'I had the feeling that I was mentally outside my own body' (Gregory 1966: 205). As such, the object may be considered in a different manner, the technical object actively affects the self and produces the dissonance between the cognition of the body and its visual self-projection. In this case the visual device might be re-considered as an active agent that affects the behaviour of the subject.

In another interpretation of the phenomenal body Drew Leder claims that 'the body is not a point but an organized field in which certain organs and abilities come to prominence while others recede' (1990: 24). Here again it becomes important to re-consider how the technical object's relation to the body increasingly affects the bodily schema. Leder, in a similar tone to Merleau-Ponty, calls attention to 'the self effacement of bodily organs when they form the focal origin of a perceptual or actional field, an example of this is the invisibility of the eye within the visual field it generates' (1990: 26). This understanding of the very effacement of the source of vision being both 'origin and terminus' is challenged in the *Diplorasis*. The technical operation of the device thus tries to operate within the bodily visual limitations, calling attention to the interval between the experiencing body and the body as self-projected image.

In this sense the operation of the device refers to Marcel Duchamp's diorama *Étant donnés* (1946–66) and to art critic Rosalind Krauss's interpretation of this work. The installation is arranged behind wooden doors that have two peepholes. Through them the viewer sees a reclining naked female body lying within the landscape, her legs are spread open and the viewer faces her crotch. With one arm she holds a gas lamp. A pierced brick wall frames the overall scene. In this setup the linear perspectival system becomes ironically tangible. The vanishing point and the viewing point become the vagina and the pierced brick wall (picture plane) respectively. Duchamp stages and invites a corporeal relationship with the image. The framed openings suggest binocular vision – yet the projected image is not stereoscopic. As the viewer is 'peeping' into this scene s/he becomes trapped in an optical psychological machine, and s/he becomes voyeur, making the space for viewing and by extension the room of the exhibit part of the setup. In a similar way to *Étant donnés*, the viewer becomes entrapped within the *Diplorasis*; however, when viewing the projections they are made to construct their self-image in the latter. In the *Diplorasis* there is an emphasis on the limits of the Wheatstone stereoscopic functioning: the actual space and the actual viewer become the view, introducing the unexpected interval between the body and its projected image.

Figure 5: George Themistokleous, photograph of *Diplorasis*, view with drums in motion.

The nuanced relationship between bodily vision and its extended visual technologies developed through the *Diplorasis* begins to frame the approach towards the body in the stereoscope.

The stereoscope incorporates the physiological operation of the eyes into its technical construct. Whilst the separated eyes focus on two non-identical reflected images, the optical binocular functioning simulates an illusion of three-dimensional depth. The duration of normal binocular convergence is prolonged in the stereoscope. And once the disparate images converge, this simulated image somewhat 'floats'. One is aware that the synthesis is ready to disintegrate back into shifting planar projections. Merleau-Ponty articulates this merging of the two images as:

> The unity of binocular vision, and with it the depth without which it cannot come about is, therefore, there from the very moment at which the monocular images are presented as 'disparate'. When I look into the stereoscope a totality presents itself in which already the possible order takes shape and the situation is foreshadowed.
>
> (2009: 305)

Whilst the two monocular images converge in binocular vision to create the impression of a single image, we are constantly aware that this convergence is composed of a synthetic duration. Merleau-Ponty emphasizes the monocular functioning of images in normal perception when he writes:

> Monocular images float vaguely in front of things, having no real place in the world; then suddenly they fall back towards a certain location in the world and are swallowed up in it, as ghosts at daybreak, repair to the rift in the earth which let them forth. The binocular object, in which the synthesis occurs, absorbs the monocular images, which in this new light finally recognize themselves as appearances of that object.
>
> (2009: 271)

The totality that Merleau-Ponty refers to is the momentary alignment. The stereoscope is considered here through both the alignment and its non-alignments. And beyond the consideration of the phenomenon of the stereoscopic eye(s) it is important to briefly trace part of the stereoscope's history. This will help clarify the relation between the viewing subject and the stereoscope at the time of its inception.

Art critic and historian, Jonathan Crary offers a different account of the stereoscope in his *Techniques of the Observer*. The operation of the stereoscopic device is explored in relation to scientific discoveries and experiments with the

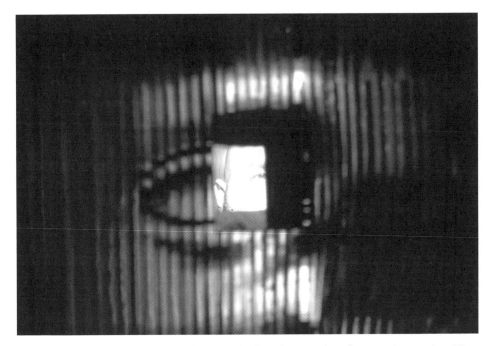

Figure 6: George Themistokleous, photograph of *Diplorasis*, phase b – experimentation. View through eye hole.

eyes themselves. The apprehension of the monocular pair and its functioning prior to the appearance of the observed object became possible in the 1830s, when scientists were able to 'quantify precisely the angular differential of the optical axis of each eye, and to specify the physiological basis for disparity' (Crary 1990: 119).

Within the construct of the stereoscope the eyes' dual operation, monocular and binocular, unfolds. The stereoscopic construct formulated a new relation between the observer and the image in the nineteenth century. Whilst the stereoscope and other optical devices of the first half of the nineteenth century paralleled experiments and scientific discoveries, the understanding of the visual image simultaneously marked a paradigmatic shift that moved away from the ideal eye of the camera obscura and increasingly veered towards the physiology of the human eyes (Crary 1990). This is evident in the stereoscope, whose very structure operates in relation to the discoveries of the optical axes (Crary 1990: 122). As a consequence the stereoscope reflected a wider preoccupation with the physiological functioning and experimentation of the eyes. As the primary area of investigation shifted to the corporeal eyes, the body of the viewer in the stereoscope was made immobile, fixed, the eyes framed, and the projected images would bear no relation to the actual space of the stereoscope. As Crary notes, 'The Wheatstone model made clear the disjunction between experience and its cause [...]' and '[...] the stereoscope also required the corporeal adjacency and immobility of the observer' (1990: 129). All of this staging corresponds to the movement of convergence of the optical axes and their subsequent fusion in the optical chiasma. Ironically, in order for the stereoscopic image to come into being, it is necessary that the physical body, including its peripheral vision be effaced. And when looking at the stereoscopic image itself, Crary writes:

> We perceive individual elements as flat, *cutout forms* arrayed either nearer or further from us [...] there is a vertiginous uncertainty about the distance separating forms. [...] the absolutely airless space surrounding them has a disturbing palpability [...] the stereoscope discloses a fundamentally disunified and aggregate field of disjunct elements.
>
> (1990: 129)

Like translucent planar surfaces, the image integrates and disintegrates due to binocular rivalry and the movements of the eye/s. Surfaces become planar outlines and when the points from each image are mostly aligned, a hallucinatory illusion of three-dimensionality emerges, one that is ready to disintegrate back into its planar projections. The precise framing apparatus of the stereoscope simulates the un-framing of the object itself. And whilst this framing and focusing of the eyes

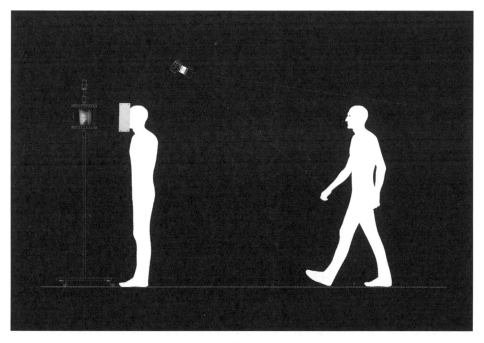

Figure 7: George Themistokleous, diagram of *Diplorasis*, side elevation.

presupposes the effacement of the body within the Wheatstone stereoscope, in the *Diplorasis* the body is reinstated because the observer perceives their own body as image. This paradoxical folding of visuality on itself emphasizes the interval between body and image, and is suggestive of how media increasingly alter the phenomenal understanding of the self-effacing body. The boundary between bodily cognition and the body's virtual projections in space is thus re-configured by our media environments. In this respect one is reminded of Krauss's observation on Duchamp's *Étant donnés*, which places 'the moment of visuality right at that fold between body and world where each seems to occlude the other' (1994: 111).

Machinic vision: The time interval

In his writing on the stereoscope and other optical devices of the nineteenth century, Crary claims that these visual constructions have mostly been cast as precursors to the cinema, and appropriated as earlier models in the evolution of cinema. Crary states that, 'such an approach often ignores the conceptual and historical singularities of each device' (Crary 1990: 110). Within the many examples that are 'in the service of a history of cinema' is Gilles Deleuze's *Cinema 1: The Movement Image* (1983). What is of particular interest here is the visual overlap between Crary and Deleuze's writings on the stereoscope and montage respectively.

In the stereoscope, the image explodes into shifting planes that have no clear association with one another. This disintegration of the image reveals the durational interval and becomes an important harbinger of the conceptual understanding of time that was introduced by the cinematic technique of montage almost a century later. In his seminal publication *Cinema 1*, Deleuze (1983) assigns primary importance to montage, as it is what distinguishes the cinematic eye of the camera from subjective human perception. In his account of the cine-eye there is no reference to the stereoscope (although he briefly refers to the stereoscope in his earlier work *Difference and Repetition* 2014: 64); however, there are various references to the human eye when defining the 'perception-image'. The human eye is considered reductive, it frames a particular point of view as opposed to the cine-eye that offers the opportunity to mediate between subjective and objective poles. Essentially the human eye simply functions as a subjective frame; in other words, it cannot take into account the objective, the 'image in matter', as opposed to the cine-eye. To illustrate this point Deleuze uses as a primary example Dziga Vertov's film *Man with a Movie Camera* (1929).

Montage allows for the superimposition of the moving image, the possibility of, at least, a double durational trajectory implicating the sense of the interval in relation to the standard frame-by-frame scene (Themistokleous 2015). Montage is a cinematic technique that makes evident the conceptualization of time. The various techniques of montage in the early history of the cinema suggest different approaches to the filmic narrative structures in relation to time. The interval in montage is defined as a 'variable present that reveals the immensity of future and past' (Deleuze 2005: 41). Vertov's *Man with a Movie Camera*, a documentary without narrative or actors, utilizes many early experiments with the camera and makes them explicit in the film.

For example, the camera in the first scene is placed atop another camera, and we usually see the camera filming other cameras and machines, or referring back to itself through the lens. There are shots that suggest or celebrate the camera's potential to move beyond the confinements of the human body, e.g. the shot beneath the train tracks or the aerial shots. The movement of the camera already foresees the move away from a human sensory perception. This is revealed more effectively with Vertov's montage, as it became possible to superimpose these 'superhuman' frames of the camera and thus to synthesize disparate distances and speeds. In this sense, Vertov creates a perception that is in *matter* and that expands the perception of time by 'correlating two images which are distant and incommensurable from the viewpoint of our human perception' (Deleuze 2005: 84).

On the other hand, by contrasting the human eye to Vertov's cine-eye, Deleuze relegates the human eye to only one of its functions. The eye as an organ is considered only as a mechanism for contracting. The reverse of an efficiently operating eye, in the mechanical sense, i.e. a degenerative eye, might be more revealing as a machinic assemblage rather than a mechanical system. Deleuze contrasts the machine and the mechanical. The notion of mechanism here is developed from Henri Bergson's *Creative Evolution*. Deleuze writes; '[...] mechanism involves closed systems, actions of contact, immobile instantaneous sections. This is not mechanism, it is machinism. The material universe, the plane of immanence, is the machine assemblage of movement-images. It is the universe as cinema in itself, a metacinema' (2005: 61).

The time interval of the cine-eye is already revealed in the stereoscope. The duration of matter may be experienced when producing two overlapping images that converge and diverge. The reception of the images, in the stereoscope for example, creates an embodied montage as the two divergent monocular images include divergent durations that are superimposed via the binocular operation of the eyes (Themistokleous 2015). The body cognitively experiences these separate and superimposed visual durations. The interval explored here defines the operation of both the stereoscopic and the cinematic image; the unfolding of the interval is what brings the conception of a non-chronological time to the fore.

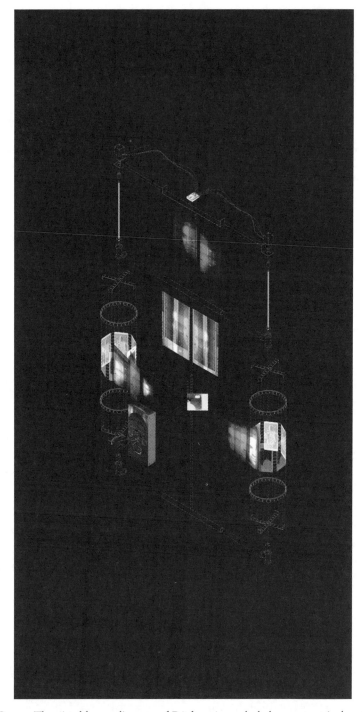

Figure 8: George Themistokleous, diagram of *Diplorasis*, exploded axonometric drawing.

An important difference between the experience of this interval – and hence of duration – through the stereoscope and cinematic montage has to do with the proximity of the eyes to the image. If we take the stereoscope and its reliance on images *near* the viewer, at a specified distance where the optical axis of the eyes will align, the simulated perception is of a directly immediate experience with the image and its ensuing duration. The stereoscope is thus reliant on human visual framing. Yet as the eyes' perception intersect with their prosthetic mechanism, the induced spectral image moves beyond the biological confinements of the eyes. In stereoscopy the illusory intensive image is produced by a careful framing/un-framing of the eyes in relation to a prosthetic instrument. The montage of the cinema allows for a different relationship with the image. Removed from the physiological closeness of the stereoscopic viewer, it scans and is able to synthesize disparate durational vectors. It is able to capture the duration of matter, from all points of view as opposed to the stereoscope. But unlike the stereoscope, it cannot simulate the intensive depth of the image in relation to a viewer. This difference is due to the proximity of reception. The stereoscope gets closer and simulates tangibility but does not have the flexibility of the cine-eye. Both however conceptually reveal the durational interval of the image.

In the volumes on the *Cinema* whilst Deleuze articulates the exceptional conception of cinematic time, it seems that this notion of time remains not only removed from human vision but also confined to the space of cinema. The projection of the moving image onto a vertical screen for fixed observers has already been superseded by newer technologies (most recently the VR head-mounted displays). But this idea of a cine-eye or machinic vision produces a contemporary understanding of a visuality that in turn affects human visual perception. It becomes pertinent to re-think the Deleuzian cinematic eye in terms of digital technologies that allow for this superhuman perception to become incorporated within the bodily schema. The route from the out of body experience in Stratton's experiment to the stereoscopic cut-out array of disjunct surfaces and finally to the machinic perception of time in montage is synthesized in the operation of the *Diplorasis*.

Conclusion

The *Diplorasis* attempts to explore the interval between the duration of montage and the duration of the stereoscope. It does this by simulating a space between the stereoscopic expansive close-up and the cinematic potential for extensity and durational superimposition. This is possible through the application of new digital media, programming languages and microprocessors that are able to control the

VISUAL RESEARCH METHODS IN ARCHITECTURE

projection of images within a stereoscopic framework. The *Diplorasis* research questions both the atopic nature of the viewer and of the resulting image in the stereoscope and the disjunction between the viewer's bodily experience and their projected image. Using playback, the projected images, far from projecting a neutral scene of something 'out there', look back at the viewer. When approaching the device, the viewer is unaware that they will see themselves projected and moving backwards. The interval between the digital and analogue media multiplies the splitting and stitching, from the eyes to the machine to the body. This reproduces a synthetic duration of real-time and playback, digital projections and actual perception.

Of particular interest is not the Deleuzian cine-eye in montage or stereoscopic perception but how these might be mediated through digital media to produce a new understanding of bodily perceptual space. The embodied vision of the stereoscope operates in relation to the disembodied view of the camera. Stereoscopic projection and cinematic montage are combined only through a third technological interface, digital media, which allows for the interval between the two to be re-configured in order to produce a new assemblage. In spite of the importance assigned to a disembodied perception, the *Diplorasis* always returns its projection(s) to the subjective perception of the bodily viewer looking through the device. While the views are dismantled, divided, subdivided and re-configured, they are then re-configured for and by the body that is seeing the display. The process of seeing and its shifting trajectories however propose a new visuality. This new visuality is already embedded within the corporeal, technical and perceptual assemblage of bodies in contemporary media environments.

REFERENCES

Bergson, H. ([1896] 1990), *Matter and Memory* (trans. N. M. Paul and W. S. Palmer), New York: Zone Books.

Crary, J. (1990), *Techniques of the Observer: On Vision and Modernity in the Nineteenth Century*, Cambridge, MA: The MIT Press.

Deleuze, G. ([1966] 1991), *Bergsonism* (trans. H. Tomlinson and B. Habberjam), New York: Zone Books.

—— ([1983] 2005), *Cinema 1: The Movement Image* (trans. H. Tomlinson and B. Habberjam), London: Continuum.

—— ([1968] 2014), *Difference and Repetition* (trans. P. Patton), London: Bloomsbury Academic.

Gregory, L. R. ([1966] 1997), *Eye and Brain: The Psychology of Seeing*, 5th ed., Oxford: Oxford University Press.

Krauss, R. (1994), *The Optical Unconscious*, Cambridge, MA: The MIT Press.

Leder, D. (1990), *The Absent Body*, Chicago, IL: The University of Chicago Press.

Merleau-Ponty, M. ([1945] 2009), *Phenomenology of Perception* (trans. C. Smith), London: Routledge & Kegan Paul.

Themistokleous, G. (2015), 'Folding and doubling: Re-visiting Freud's screen memories', *Lo Squaderno*, 37, pp. 39–43.

Vertov, D. (1929), *Man with a Movie Camera*. Kiev: VUFKU [Vse-Ukrains'ke Foto Kino Upravlinnia].

23

Audio-visual instruments and multi-dimensional architecture

Mathew Emmett, University of Plymouth

Introduction

By exploring multi-dimensional architecture as an extended repertoire for design, the role of perception becomes an integral aspect for architectural thought. This model of design foregrounds the performative relationship of space and its mediation with particular focus on the affective phenomena or 'triggers' that shapes the experiential qualities of an immersive act. However, these considerations require the need for a more sensitive range of tools that can record perceptual data, whilst anticipate new forms of spatial content. Thus by deploying multi-layered sensor technologies together with computational resources borrowed from cognitive science, architecture can evolve a higher-dimensional system for experimentation and testing. Multi-dimensional architecture can therefore transform the architect's role to that of a progenitor of causal effect, and by the origination of an enactive tool set, multi-dimensional considerations put the perceptual, cognitive and associative response at the centre of the discipline.

Multimodal interaction represents an opportunity for better understanding these potentials, and as perception implies interaction with the physical and virtual environment, situationally reflexive instruments must support and present navigational guidance in the recognition of the temporal and contextual cues. This allows for a 'fused' interpretation of visual, audio, haptic and kinaesthetic characteristics. It is not only a design problem to synthesize these instruments, but mappings between communication medium and content need attention to support the management of this data-rich environment.

The research set out within this chapter focuses on the integration of an audio-visual approach whereby the user's interaction enables communication between percipient and the environment. This exchange produces computational abilities derived from site-specific dialogue-driven fusion of an agent interfacing with an external environment. Using this hybrid multi-level design tool set, the integration of perceptual modalities is distributed amongst the various recording or sensor technologies and are merged to create a hyper-vigilant spatial practice.

These instruments originate from a system-theoretic perspective and functioning as a supportive framework to extend the understanding of multimodal perception. The instruments are designed to operate both as a mode for hyper-vigilant sensing but also act as the conveyance medium for affecting perception through biasing and attention transference. Thus I argue for a greater level of human-environment cogency, whilst offering an architectural interpretation of situated cognition (Wilson and Clark 2009: 55) that merges the theory of multimodal fusion with strategies for design.

My research promotes an increased awareness of the causal and synergistic relationships of site-responsive stimuli. This in turn leads to increased granularity of spatial awareness – which I classify as spatio-sensory amplification. Spatio-sensory amplification is the tendency to perceive one's environment as being relatively intense and of a visceral nature, for example the inclusion of latent traces of historical affordance. These cognitive processes tend to indicate a spatial awareness characteristic of a long-latency, and are explored as phenomenologically driven data sets. The epistemological position here follows the mantle of 'practitioner as researcher' (Gray and Malins 2004: 21), whilst the purpose of the research is primed to evolve expert spatial practitioners including architects, spatial designers, composers and wayfinding specialists.

This enquiry opens up the domain of situated cognition as a performative framework for repositioning spatial practice comprised of affect-field feedback values that locate, inter-relate and make malleable, a non-Euclidian space. The research advocates a compositional role for multimodal perception by extending the psychophysical dimension of architectural space so as to yield the 'extra-existents' (Deleuze 1990: 42) for design. Situated cognition considers perception as active and predictive (Noë 2004; O'Regan and Noë 2001) that is, we predict or anticipate the future sensory consequences of potential actions, thereby identifying the contents of perception in terms of our expectations and in terms of profiles of interaction. Therefore cognition cannot be seen as separate from the external environment; rather, knowledge is co-determined by the individual and the context. This position follows the enactive argument for cognition that arises through the dynamic interaction between agent and environment.

This theoretical stance intentionally makes problematic the mind-matter division of Cartesian dualism, by evolving an enactive model of situated cognition as a co-determined construct, mutually formed within the dependencies of feedback loops. Such an architectural model of space necessitates the need for specialized instruments that not only serve to record, measure and interpret this information, but also recognizes and anticipates the speculative question of a design methodology explicitly modifying the processes of cognitive extension.

Gilles Deleuze (1993: 187) contextualizes these mind-body dualisms as a sensation-affect contingent on modes of relationality and writes; 'I become in sensation, and something happens through sensation, one through the other and one in the other'.

Expanding on this thesis my research focuses on the negotiation of space through the mediation and deformation of *becomings*, to use a Deleuzian term, and infers compositional understanding of the perceptual processes that generate multiverse experiences as 'phenomic environments' (Cassidy 1997: 23). These instruments are therefore calibrated to penetrate the 'dualism of bodies or states and effects or incorporeal events' (Deleuze 1990: 9) by propagating the zones and intersections of agent-environment co-determinism whilst developing a transactional dialogue for propagating these inherent qualities – making perception open for experimentation and manipulation.

These theories expand the spatial territory of Neil Spiller's (2002: 5) 'hybrid sites' by questioning perception as an emergent subspace of architectural geometry, insofar as considering situated cognition as a territory that is constructed through prediction and experience. By exploring Deleuze's dualism as a 'site of ecologies' (Spiller 2002: 5) comprised of a dipole environment, charged between agent and environmental conditions, I evolve a hyper-vigilant praxis for amplifying and sustaining these reflexive continuums that lie 'between the effects of the "structure Other" of the perceptual field and the effects of its absence' (Deleuze 1990: 348).

These concerns operate in contrast to the style propelled, object-based, externally driven static forms of architecture commonly found today. In contrast, this research into multimodal perception explores the visceral dimension of space as an extension of three-dimensional space that is both fragile and non-linear and situated within an intense field of causation feedbacks. In doing so it bridges the gap between cognitive science and art practice. This approach appeals to the senses and is part of the spatial experience. The work functions as a strategy to unlock the visceral dimension as an affective multi-dimensional experience, evolving an architectural grammar for spatial agency. Further, the research establishes an inference forecasting model for predictive design, by establishing an audio and visual methodology more attuned to the 'mutual causal connectedness' (Harries-Jones 1995: 37) of agent-environment affordances. This mode of operational practice speculates on the ability to manipulate the inter-relationships within these conditions and advances an extended, extra-dimensional realm of spatiality by means of inter-modulation tweaking, by manner of affective amplification, whereby situated cognition is re-sequenced to an enhanced state of 'spatial intelligence' (Schaik 2008).

Spatial apparatus

Central to the research is the enquiry into the nature of spatial perception and the understanding of whether human emotional states have a measurable effect on our environments. The research seeks to determine methods to record and navigate these ephemeral qualities on the basis of affect, memory and anticipation. The spatial instruments made are designed to amplify these readings in the form of audio-visual feedback, whereby the various instruments are calibrated to externalize the point of exchange between the human-environment interface. In a state of animated affect and akin to forensic profiling, the audio-visual instruments record perceptual friction by calibrating the performative values of multimodal behaviour, including expression accent, physiological instinct, behavioural intuition, cognitive attention and experiential dynamics. These readings, entitled Cognitive-tope data, record where each value is configured between reality and a virtual experience. The premise for the research is to originate a new spatial language made up from the analysis of situated cognition that is formed by the constant breaching of boundaries between physical and virtual space in the realm of the audio and visual. The instruments thus interpret these agencies to determine the dimensional qualities between the 'felt reality of reality' (Massumi 2002: 16) and the external site effectors.

The instruments are made up of a series of organized interacting elements used for recording and triggering perceptional experience, namely audio-visual sensor technologies. These new corporeal technologies including Eye tracking devices; Bio-feedback systems; Cognitive-tope mapping; Arduino components and Human Computer Interfaces; Pure Data programming environments for audio, video and graphical processing; and Trigger projections.

Operating as an intelligent extension to our multimodal bodies, these devices are designed for collecting and receiving data, as well as transmitting perceptually sensitive information as audio-visual information in a live and reflexive manner using real-time processing. Multimodal perception recognizes the integration of the different sense modalities that combine to reveal meaningful perceptual experiences. Here, the technology is used to chart and record the systems of human-environment communication that conveys both a message signal and amplitude reading that measures the force of signal. Thus the spatial apparatus combines data from multiple readings, triangulating the input to inform a more critical methodology. The primary objective here is to design a system of sensors that respond to a variety of stimuli felt by the occupants' experience of the environment at any isolated point in space.

For example the eye tracking system is able to record eye movement of a subject negotiating the changing physical and ambient states of their location. The technology is used to analyse user behaviour by recording visual fixations. The head-mounted kit

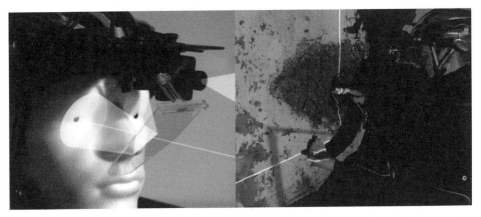

Figure 1: Mathew Emmett with PerceptionLab (Germany). Eye tracking, Roman Baths, Bath.

(Figure 1) is video-based and records the order and number of visual fixations, which are documented by the image processing software. The subject wears a helmet, on which two cameras are mounted; one records the pupil movement, whilst the other records the subject's field of view. Both cameras are calibrated, making it possible to manually plot the subject's eye movements in relation to the viewed scene. This system uses mobile technology (iViewX™ HED by SMI) that allows free movement in space whilst tracking the movements of the pupil relative to the head and field of vision. Simultaneously the software presents a documentary video comprising a scene made up of fixations and saccades, creating a scan path to show loci, duration and salience of visual stimulus. The system tracks iris-pupil contrast, and, rather than calculating statistical representations for the aggregate analysis of the subjects spatial experience, I used the live eye-tracking data to parametrically drive an audio-visual installation called Vection Builder (2010) installed at the Roman Baths, Bath as part of an artist in Residency.

Another sensor technology used is the biofeedback apparatus that measures physiological and biometrical data. This device enables the measurement of temperature and conductance of the skin, respiratory frequency and volume, heart frequency and rhythm and muscle tension. These tools can be used to measure the complex physiological impact of microclimates at particular points in a space over time at a specific length of time. A participant has the sensors attached to their body and carries a mobile device to record the physiological and biometrical impact of the space. That data is recorded by means of a graph line showing the relation between variables over time. When using many participants from the combination of long-term observations, a general pattern of biofeedback responses can be determined, whereabouts a predetermined 'mark' in time creates a series of anchor points, enabling comparison of data.

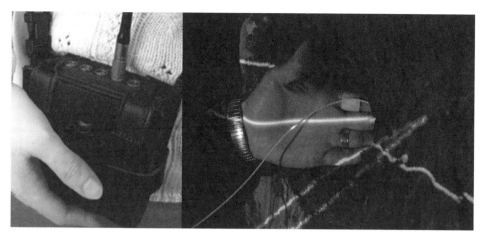

Figure 2: Mathew Emmett with PerceptionLab (Germany). Biofeedback sensor, Roman Baths, Bath.

Each biofeedback response creates a line or gradient tracing the excitation (and inhibition) fluctuations of the participant's central nervous system in direct response to the experiential qualities of any given space. This builds up a profile for understanding the 'strength of stimuli' in correlation to the external environment. These tracings are marked with time units to create graphical images with deformation values that comprise amplitudes per time unit. These readings can reveal reflexive behaviours in space perception, for example when interpreting temperature changes in biofeedback analysis, a temperature rise indicates relaxation, while a temperature drop relates to the activation of tension or stress. The body's temperature drops as a result of the blood being directed away from the subjects' extremities – straight to the vital organs – to facilitate a raised level of arousal. This is known as the 'fight or flight' response, whereby blood flow is increased to the brain and muscle groups to facilitate engaged action. To reach a better understanding of these results, the subjects can be asked to complete a self-reporting feedback task to collect a more interpretivist validity of the findings.

As well as digital sensors, more traditional, self-reporting maps and questionnaires are used to explore a more reflective examination of a site study. These are called Cognitive-tope maps, which are tasked to sequester perceptual-specific data together with qualitative information. Also designed from the perspective of multimodal perception, these graph(ic) representations record the nature and location of situated cognition affects. It was also imperative to ensure that these maps were designed to be as usable as possible. Moreover, within cartography, there is a general rule to not have more than seven different variables to decipher, as it is acknowledged through cartographic research and practice, that more than this creates recall problems for the user – and thus increased difficulty completing the graphic.

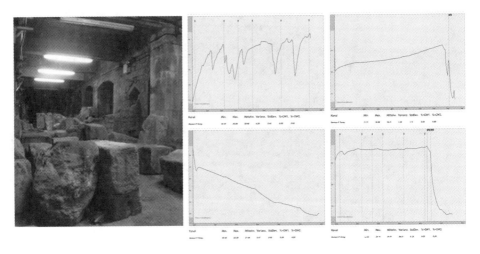

Figure 3: Mathew Emmett, Biofeedback graphs.

There are numerous individual tools and techniques for recording our response to single physical or psychological stimuli in the environment, but what options are available and effective for recording numerous responses at once? There did not seem to be anything that was practical or simple to implement. As such, the Cognitive-tope map was conceived to provide a recording of both physical and psychological responses within the built environment. The basic concept of the tool is that of a graph with the participant or recorder placed at its centre. In order to be reflective of our 3D world, the graph needed to have a way of recording stimuli in all planes. As such it represents a 360° view with graphic codes employed to represent attributes such as location, elevation and signal. A form of graph was devised as it had a basis in familiarity for a potential user, and also enabled quick-and-easy recording of mark-making.

The design of elements in the graphs refers to human form. Vision occupies an appropriate *field* of coverage at the top of the graph (heads-up and forward looking). Sound has 360° coverage, as does smell and touch, although in ever diminishing extents to reflect the distance at which they are normally detected. The manner of representing a user's response is again chosen to reflect some of the norms in the respective fields. For example, a wave-form is used to signify sound recordings, with a greater magnitude for louder sounds. Throughout the design processes, a balance is sought between recording numerous (sometimes simultaneous) stimuli in a clear graphic form that is also relatively simple for the user to undertake.

Recordings were conducted in a serial fashion such that at regular intervals new recordings were made. This would then help construct a response image of a larger site at a particular moment in time; in essence, re-examination of the completed graphs should help re-construct the site.

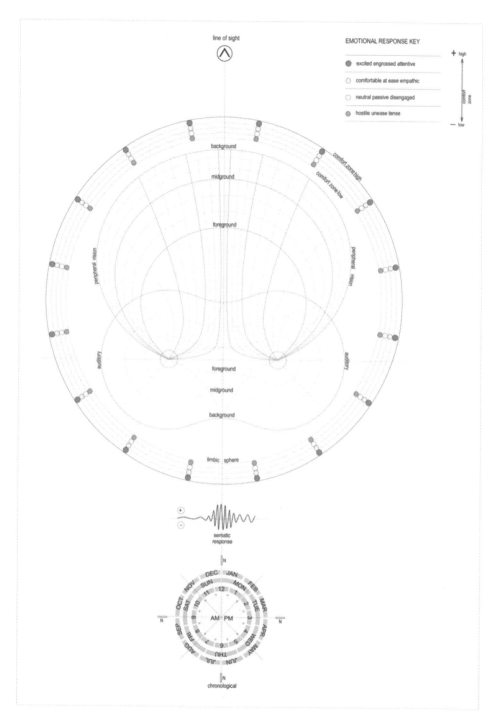

Figure 4: Mathew Emmett, Cognitive-tope map.

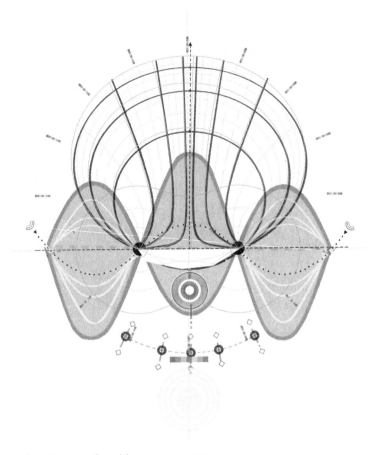

Figure 5: Mathew Emmett, Cognitive-tope prototype.

By placing the researcher at the centre of the inquiry, the method forms an 'integrative observation' (Schwalbach 2009: 17). As identified by sociologist of biomedical science and technologies Adele E. Clarke (2005: 85) in *Situational Analysis*, the researcher carrying out the task is considered the 'research instrument'. Clarke puts forward three helpful modes of situational analysis. First, doing situational mapping does not inform a 'final analytic product' (Clarke 2005: 85), rather it establishes a rigorous strategy for interrogating the data. Second, situational analysis uses visual codes and abstracted diagrams to convey meaning and aid comparison and communication. Third, the process of situational analysis positions the researcher directly within the investigation whereby the experience becomes tacit. Clarke (2005: 84) argues that 'Situational maps and analysis can be used as analytic exercises simply to get the researcher moving into and then around in the data'.

Figure 6: Mathew Emmett, Cognitive-tope pilot.

The Cognitive-tope map integrates Clarke's transactional approach to situational analysis by considering mapping as an 'auxiliary apparatus'[1] (Freud 1963: 208). It provides the spatial practitioner with a specific fieldwork tool to

VISUAL RESEARCH METHODS IN ARCHITECTURE

directly investigate the 'spatial qualities and atmospheric impressions' (Schwalbach 2009: 34). The design of the map exploits a series of visual abstraction processes to circumnavigate problematical linguistic representations of perceptual space, and by constructing a series of radial vertices projected into a plan arrangement, the cognitive-tope mapping system generates a set of overlapping metrical layers that deconstructs perception into concentric fields that are graphically distributed on the page to represent the phenomenal self mimetically.

The metrical layers or field domains consist of a visual field, auditory field, somatic field, limbic field and chronological dial. Each domain has a field view of 360° that converges on two nodal points equidistant from the concentric rings of radial geometry. Each nodal point corresponds to the percipients' left eye/ear and right eye/ear, thereby establishing the bipolar loci of vision and hearing. The cognitive-tope mapping system operates as a form of 'Homuncular or systemic decomposition' (Robbins and Aydede 2009: 107).

Visual, auditory, somatic and limbic fields and chronological dial

The visual field has a bipolar coordinate for locating the left and right eye, with a centreline that runs through the entire spherical field to help establish the direction of the percipient's visual direction. The visual domain is designed to record the user's spatial orientation and visual point of view or POV[2] identified by three hyperbolic curves denoting foreground, mid-ground and background. The visual domain also identifies the user's fovea and peripheral vision. The organizational framework for the visual field evolves from the interpretation of Vieth-Müller's *diagram of visual geometry* in *The Geometry of Visual Space* (Wagner 2006: 33). This model, however, was further developed by the addition of Blain Brown's (2002: 42, 9) 'rule of thirds' that divides the field reference frames into thirds, enabling the domain to be broken down into clearer 'building blocks of scenes'. This framing device establishes a strategy for decomposing the visual scene into tonal blocks that articulate the 'visual forces' (Brown 2002: 37) of the visual field. This enables the user to simplify the range of visual perception and concentrate on evaluating the local tones. This allows for assessing the relationship between form and space, whereby the qualities of the visual scene are abstracted and extended through the interplay of contrast, proportion, intensity, distribution and direction. Three-dimensionality arises from the viewer's use of the fore/mid/background zones, with depth being noted through the overlapping of compositional elements and relative size. By reducing the visual scene into basic tonal elements, the process puts greater emphasis onto the forces of visual composition, rather than scenic detail.

380

The auditory field is acoustically sectioned into three zones of 360° concentric graphs, centred on the bipolar loci of the left and right ear. The participant uses the auditory map to graphically visualize the spatial appearance of the explicit sound event. The auditory field interprets Canadian music composer and environmentalist R. Murray Schafer's (1977: 129) sound envelope topology to visualize the sonic 'attack, body, transient and decay'. By adding a locational component, the user can chart the directional content of the sound, enriching the aesthetic quality of the sonic study with a three-dimensional locator that charts the movement and durational content of the auditory environment.

The somatic field relates directly to body position and movement within the space surrounding the body (Laban). This domain was specifically designed to map the sense of balance, reducing the complexity of accelerometer data into a single section of body awareness, namely the sense of motion, acceleration and balance. The user can chart their somatic awareness on a graph denoting the intensity of body position, marked by the level of joint and muscle tension, together with the ability to maintain a postural equilibrium or balance. The somatic field enables the user to calibrate the body's position adjacent to the environment in a three-dimensional manner.

Limbic derives from neurological science and relates to the brain structures associated with emotion, behaviour and memory (Levitan and Kaczmarek 2002). The term stems from the Latin word 'limbus' that refers to 'border', neatly corresponding to a boundary condition. The limbic field uses a Likert scale to chart the participant's psychological response to capture a value of intensity on a visual analogue scale consisting of radial lines. The limbic field uses a bipolar scaling method to record a hyper-vigilant response to psychological stimuli in conjunction to a positive or negative relationship towards the enveloping environment. The scale operates as a psychometric scale with the addition of a locational component, thus making it possible to site the incidence of cognitive dissonance relative to the participant's origin. The limbic field has a four-point scale with interval levels, which are colour coded to aid legibility. The scale enables the user to reflect on and chart the performativity of the emotive response establishing a form of mapping that charts the psychological inter-relationship of the spatially explicit environment.

Lastly, the chronological dial enables the user to note the time, date and orientation relative to the north point, allowing a temporal and directional framework to be established for sequential mapping and accurate retrieval of data. The cognitive-tope map serves to amplify the perception of space by magnifying the affective stimuli together with charting the locational trigger as a perceived point in space. These maps help build the dynamic values and behaviour of how we perceive, through the use of a visual interface that is designed to visualize the

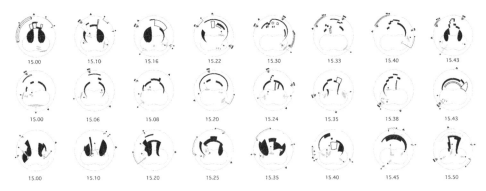

Figure 7: Mathew Emmett, Perception notation matrix.

perception of space with greater granularity of situational depth and temporal awareness. These maps, whilst revealing the forces and sets of attention, can also evoke patterns of signature agent-environment reflexive behaviours leading to a greater understanding of the impact of architectural space on human occupation.

Microcontrollers, sound generation and software

The software used for this research includes Pure Data with custom-made programmes and Arduino components that enable real-time processing capabilities. Because the research involves the study of perception through the movement and interaction of space the software is conceived as a processing vehicle allowing participants to engage and trigger audio-visual responses through the use of sensor technologies and depth/movement sensors. The software enables system–system communication, creating a live, interactive and immersive experience that

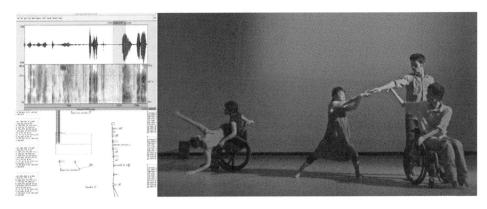

Figure 8: Mathew Emmett with Adam Benjamin. Pure Data patch, *Open State*, Japan.

concomitantly triggers and responds to participatory interaction. Essentially the software creates a live processing engine that drives the research, giving rise to a heightened sense of interaction condition, called 'coaction field' (Tiffin and Terashima 2001). When coupled with sound, the software helps generate data-specific numerical forms that can be translated into sound outputs in a live and reflexive manner.

The audio within my work is designed to telescope the immersive qualities of the spatial setting. Tending to use site- or data-specific sounds, I use Pure Data – a visual programming language similar to MaxMSP, created by Miller Puckette – to generate sounds from live data streaming generated from the various sensors and/or for generating sounds and interactive multimedia works by synthesizing audio effects from earlier profiling experiments. Simply listening to an environment can trigger a greater consciousness for a space; the sound portrays its three-dimensional volume, materiality, layout and function. These features can be transcribed into a form of notation, that when reverse engineered and charged with sonic output, creates a sound world characteristic of situated cognition. These audio investigations respond to the phenomenological experiences of occupying an environment without the sense of light.

The tool set for this research includes affective cueing. The audio-visual instruments include the design and projection of visual 'triggers'. These use a simple abstracted language designed for biasing attentional pickup through the use of visual cues that have a high visual impact value, designed to modify behaviour.

Figure 9: Mathew Emmett with Adam Benjamin. *The Birth of Memory*, sound-dance collaboration.

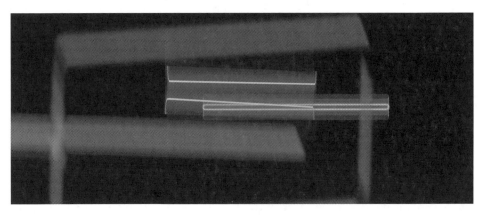

Figure 10: Mathew Emmett, Trigger frame sequence.

The trigger events consist of tilting verticals known as the Coriolis illusion in flying. They create conflict between vision and balance, the simultaneous expansion and contraction of overlapping frames create a 'trombone' (Morris 2007: 61) moment and pitching with acceleration. This emphasizes the sense of gravitational pull to the observer. These visual illusions attract the participant's eye to a series of attentional cues and aim to trigger a shift in perception and bodily recognition of spatial occupancy.

As well as to positively prime an observer's attention, they can also be used to elicit modes of body-space conflict. These trigger events are designed to function as an 'anti-environment' (McLuhan 1970: 30) device. These visual projections play with the notion that when the environment fails to meet our expectations, these aspects are suddenly in the forefront of our perceptual experience. It is proposed that visual cues can be designed to lead participants to have certain expectations. This can thereby influence their perceptual experience – as used in cinematography to instruct a particular emotive response. Known as 'phi phenomenon' (Corrigan and White 2009: 524) visual cues give rise to the psychophysical illusion of movement through, and within, architectural space.

Conclusion

This research advances the understanding of hyper-vigilant spatial analysis. It enhances knowledge into and the application of audio-visual instruments for site analysis and experimental architectural practice. This work argues for a greater awareness of spatial perception together with environmental cogency through the design and calibration of these instruments. It promotes an increased awareness of the causal and synergistic relationship of site-responsive stimuli leading to somatosensory amplification of affective site readings, latent traces and affordance triggers. The audio-visual devices explored here are attuned to record, reveal and amplify these design contingencies, and by synthesizing an operant tool set the participants' spatial consciousness is elevated to a higher level of spatial acuity, pulling the percipient into a more immersive mode of hyper-vigilant attention. These instruments engage the body with the site in a more fundamental manner. The body comes to know itself more as a relational mode of interchange whereby the audio-visual instruments actively promote an interactionist methodology, repositioning architectural practice to that of an 'effector system' (Robbins and Ayded 2009: 7). By advocating perception as an effective structure for design consideration, these audio-visual instruments penetrate the inner essence of perceptual space to provide a greater in-depth understanding of the reception of and effect on architectural space.

REFERENCES

Brown, B. (2002), *Cinematography, Theory and Practice, Image Making for Cinematographers, Directors, and Videographers*, Boston, MA: Focal Press.

Cassidy, T. (1997), *Environmental Psychology: Behaviour and Experience in Context*, East Sussex: Psychology Press Ltd.

Clark, A. (1998), *Being There, Putting Brain, Body, and World Together Again*, Cambridge, MA: The MIT Press.

Clarke, A. E. (2005), *Situational Analysis, Grounded Theory After the Postmodern Turn*, Thousand Oaks, CA: SAGE Publications.

Corrigan, T. and White, P. (2009), *The Film Experience: An Introduction*, Boston, MA: Bedford/ St. Martin's.

Csillag, A. (2005), *Atlas of the Sensory Organs: Functional and Clinical Anatomy*, New Jersey: Humana Press Inc.

Deleuze, G. (1990), *The Logic of Sense*, London: The Athlone Press.

Gray, C. and Malins, J. (2004), *Visualizing Research: A Guide to the Research Process in Art and Design*, Farnham, Surrey: Ashgate.

Harries-Jones, P. (1995), *A Recursive Vision: Ecological Understanding and Gregory Bateson*, Toronto, Buffalo and London: University of Toronto Press.

Levitan Irwin, B. and Kaczmarek, L. K. (2002), *The Neuron Cell and Molecular Biology*, Oxford: Oxford University Press.

Massumi, B. (2002), *Parables for the Virtual, Movement, Affect, Sensation*, Durham, NC: Duke University Press.

Morris, N. (2007), *The Cinema of Steven Spielberg, Empire of Light*, London: Wallflower Press.

McLuhan, M. (1970), *Counterblast*, London: Rapp & Whiting Ltd.

Noë, A. (2004), *Action in Perception*, Cambridge, MA: The MIT Press.

O'Regan, J. K. and Noe, A. (2001), *A Sensorimotor Account of Vision and Visual Consciousness*: *Behavioral and Brain Sciences*, 24:05, pp. 939–73.

Robbins, P. and Aydede, M. (2009), *The Cambridge Handbook of Situated Cognition*, Cambridge: Cambridge University Press.

Schafer, M. (1994), *Soundscape: Our Sonic Environment and the Tuning of the World*, Rochester, Vermont: Destiny Books.

Schaik, L. (2008), *Spatial Intelligence: New Futures for Architecture*, Chichester: John Wiley & Sons.

Schwalbach, G. (2009), *Basics, Urban Analysis,* Basel: Birkhäuser Verlag AG.

Spiller, N. (2002), *Reflexive Architecture*, Chichester: John Wiley & Sons Ltd.

Tiffin, J. and Terashima, N. (2001), *HyperReality, Paradigm for the Third Millennium*, London: Routledge.

Wagner, M. (2006), *The Metric of Visual Space*, Berlin: Springer-Verlag.

Wilson, R. and Clark, A. (2009), 'How to situate cognition, letting nature take its course', in P. Robbins and M. Aydede (eds), *The Cambridge Handbook of Situated Cognition*, Cambridge: Cambridge University Press, pp. 55–77.

NOTES

1. First published in 1925, Sigmund Freud's essay *The Mystic Writing Pad* offers writing as a tool to bring together modes of sensations, both conscious and subconscious within a recording framework to make the data available for later recollection.

2. In film-making the visual point of view is abbreviated to 'POV' and can assume objective and subjective associations according to the location of the camera in relation to the performer's perspective.

24

Kaleidoscopic drawings: Sights and sites in the drawing of the city

Sophia Banou, University of West of England

Extended visions and limited perceptions

A new perception of space as a kinetic condition emerged with the experience of the modern metropolis as well as the perceptive explorations of modernist scientists and pictorial artists. Nineteenth-century developments in the field of optics led to the popularization of a series of visual devices that either imitated or expanded the capabilities of human vision. The increasing mobility of everyday life through the mechanization of not only vision, but also production and locomotion, contributed to the cultivation of a visual culture that was radically informed by these physical *exosomatic* re-configurations of seeing, that is, modes of seeing that were derived from the cyborg intertwining of an 'artificial body' or device and the human being's own 'natural equipment' (Innis 2002: 131–32). Yet, despite these extensions, this emerging visual culture was certainly still laden with strongly prevailing remnants of pre-existing scopic regimes (Metz 1982: 61). The manipulation of the corporeal subjectivity of the observer that this visual culture entailed uncovered the limitations of human perception, and revealed a discrepancy between the visually perceived and the materially present, with implications for spatial representation.

Nevertheless, in architectural representation the panoptic simultaneous gaze of the ichnographic plan, foreshadowed in the divine elevated viewpoints of the bird's eye view, emerged as the dominant paradigm. The plan overcame some of the limitations and spatial distortions that the single point-of-view perspective created and offered a 'scientific' exactitude, in agreement with the rationalist tendencies of functionalist architecture. However, the image of the city that it created, relying on conventions established as early as the fifteenth century, was partly in opposition to the shifting experience of the modern city. The totalizing view of the plan matched the newly conquered view of aerial mobility and, in its abstraction, liberated the impression of the static observer of the bird's eye view, conferring upon the observer/reader a free movement across the spaces of the city that are revealed there with equal accuracy. Nevertheless, the city itself is rendered as absolutely static. The plan presents the viewer with a selective image, avoiding embrace of the complex interactions of movement at the essence of the modern experience of the city.

Is this discrepancy between the static representation and the kinetic perception a representational or a scopic issue? Representational criteria in normative architectural drawing are traditionally submitted to the criteria of materiality as expressed through a duration, which is masked by constancy in the process of visual perception. And indeed, the representational is inevitably visual due to its involving an act of reading. But does the represented need to be respectively scopic? How are the symbolic and semiotic actions of the drawing as looking at, and as being looked at, informed by the collective voyeurism that regulates the image of the city? Is there any room left in the city's utopia for the secondary scopic regimes emerging from a 'visual-specificity'?

Matters of modernity

At the heart of modernity, Henri Bergson was also concerned with the conjunction of matter and movement, of physical material presence and mental construct within the workings of human perception. He oddly addressed this by introducing the image as a hinge between the physical and the mental: 'half-way between the "thing" and the "representation"' (Bergson 1896: xiii). By discussing perception and matter through the image, Bergson's approach may also appear to suggest a primacy of the visual. However, he does not limit the image to the visual nor the imaginary. Instead of a visual manifestation of matter, what Bergson asserted through the image is the participation of the human agency in 'pure perception' (matter) and in the multiplicity of conscious perception (memory). Consciousness is then regarded as the degree of difference between matter and memory. Such an understanding of the image proposes an idea of multiplicity, of both the actual and the virtual as an accumulation of images, a kind of montage that is always the result of a movement: a transference that represents duration. This process of translation from the real to the representation and, conversely, from the representation to the real constitutes a continuity, constantly negotiated by the human body as a 'privileged image' (Bergson 1896: 6).

To return thus to the image of the city as a movement from matter to memory is to return to an image of knowledge of the city as a recollection enriched by both the conscious and the unconscious. The suturing of the two that is entailed in human perception is what Bergson has paralleled to an internal 'cinematograph': a mechanism that does not translate, but projects the heterogeneous continuity of duration on discrete spatialized instances only to mentally produce a new continuity out of them. 'Such is the contrivance of the cinematograph. And such is also that of our knowledge', wrote Bergson (1911: 306). But this is only an abstraction that seeks to rationalize our understanding of the multiplicity of presence, by rendering the kinetic process visible as a static object:

> Each of our acts aims at a certain insertion of our will into the reality. There is, between our body and other bodies, an arrangement like that of the pieces of glass that compose a kaleidoscopic picture. Our activity [...] each time no doubt giving the kaleidoscope a new shake, but not interesting [sic] itself in the shake, and seeing only the new picture. [...] the cinematographical character of our knowledge of things is due to the kaleidoscopic character of our adaptation to them.
>
> (Bergson 1911: 305)

The newly conquered comprehension of modernity, of a vision and space in motion, that Bergson's theory of duration foreshadowed, was realized by cinema and its derivative media (Beller 2002) and has since continued to expand in parallel to practices of spatial representation such as digital modes of visualization. However, on assimilating perception and producing 'consciousness' (Beller 2002: 69) what the idea of space and perception as kinetic conditions challenges and negates is the role of architectural representation as a visual language free of presuppositions and thus able to both look and speculate, rather than simply to simulate. Normative architectural representations have traditionally proposed a 'material' criterion for the visual and, in return, a visual criterion for the material. It is this material bias that has largely defined the establishment of presence within, and consequently without, representation. Yet, what is commonly excluded is not merely the unseen as the 'not-constant', but also the unseen as the inter-subjective gaze that will constitute representation as a collective terrain of consciousness rather than a ready-made virtuality: a kind of 'visual-specificity' that may not be 'material', yet is visually materialized through representation.

The encounter with the city is often considered an affair of the eye and the image of the city indeed takes shape at the intersection of a multiplicity of visual regimes. Nevertheless, the agency of this image does not rely on the primacy of a hegemonic universal vision but rather on the malleability of visual perception. As much as eyes somewhat cunningly 'reorder' in order to cognitively conquer, they are in turn 'ordered' by the gaze and the scopic exchanges that the gaze entails.

Within this field of congested visualities, architectural drawing can be considered itself as a device for *looking*: a visual device that is capable of offering a unified field of inter-textual visibility in lieu of a universal vision. Despite the distinct conventions that have structured and predetermined the 'field of view' of architectural representation from time to time, drawing can be considered itself as a kind of visual prosthesis, as an exosomatic device that brings things into visibility by overcoming the limitations of our visual perception and proposing alternate spatializations.

Rules of (visual) engagement

The concept of the scopic regime does not regard the possible configurations of the physiological aspect of seeing but the ideological dimensions that permeate the understanding of its translation from the physiological to the psychological, that is to say, the structuring of the exchanges of meaning that take place between visual perception and knowledge (Jay 1993: 7). As Martin Jay (1988) notes, there is never a universal and dominant vision, but a number of scopic regimes that coexist and often compete with each other. This condition of overlapping, and particularly competing, regimes seems to become more prominent throughout modernity and its derivative visual cultures.

As opposed to ocular-centrism, which alludes to the workings of the eye, the concept of the scopic regime regards visuality as 'sight as a social fact' (Foster 1988: ix). The distinction between vision and visuality does not point to an opposition between the nature and culture of vision, but to a distinction between the eye as subject and as object. The scopic equally involves the modalities of looking and representing. At the same time, a regime, or a set of rules, suggests indeed a hegemonic intention in relation to vision and its related practices. It is these regimes then, rather than vision itself, that are capable of regulating and perhaps even dominating our knowledge of the real through the image, thus raising issues of ideology and intentionality with regards to the politics of observation and representation. The play between vision and visuality, as socially guided ideology, becomes central for the understanding of the city, as eye and city are staged in a dialectic opposition between conditions of observation and representation.

The often antagonistic coexistence of multiple scopic regimes has been historically made manifest in the representation of cities. The shadow of the Ptolemaic distinction, between mathematical abstraction and qualitative resemblance, has historically marked the understanding of the city through varying instrumentalizations of vision. The positioning of the 'looking eye' has defined the development of representational regimes through scopic attitudes that define not only the observation of their subject, but also the reception of the image presented. The instrumentalization of the view is evident in the use of vantage points for conceptual construction, but also primarily for the associative validation of, and immersion in, urban representations, as seen in Francesco Rosselli's 'View with a Chain' of Florence (ca. 1485), or 'The Merian Map' of Paris (1615). The depiction of the artist at work in the former, or of an envisioning citizenry in the latter, establishes a 'reality' (Marin 1988: 178–179) of the image by embedding the body of the receiving viewer into the representation. This attachment to land as a kind of natural prosthesis to the observing body was primarily present in oblique and multiple view representations, as the connecting point between an institutional, meaning-laden visuality and an individual experience of situated perception.

Visual specificities

The numerous visual devices that emerged in the nineteenth century evoked a fascination with the visual and the possibilities of its extension while having a direct affect upon the development of a wider understanding of spatiality. This is reflected in the common use of such devices as models for the mechanism of human perception. Yet, it is also equally revealing of the devising of vision at the interplay of both perception and representation. Bergson's reference to the cinematograph is only one of many. However, it is perhaps its juxtaposition with the analogy of the kaleidoscope that becomes more critical. The kaleidoscope models the complexity of visual perception as taking place through the synergetic interaction between multiplicity and order, between the randomness of the event and the addition of the structural geometric order of its mirrors. As an act of observation where scopic and representational regimes become fused, architectural drawing constitutes itself as a 'shake', and a looking through from one space to another, from the space of the city to the space of architectural representation.

The concept of a kaleidoscopic knowledge of the city through its image was examined in the installed drawing 'Kaleidoscopic City' (2013) (Figure 1).[1] This drawing of the city of Edinburgh examined urban representation, putting pressure on the historical constitution of its visual codes by addressing the ways our visual perception has been extended and transformed under the influence of modernity. Taking the form of a sited installation, the drawing considered the ways in which visual relations and modes of perception come to play in the process of reading (and consequently writing) both the city and the drawing. Kaleidoscopic City considered how, in architectural thinking, representational systems and their semiotic function become tangled with institutional, collective, as well as individual scopic regimes. Ideological effects of power, knowledge and desire, which can be conscious and unconscious, universal and site-specific, are embedded in the ways in which what is considered as present in the object of representation is *made* present within architectural drawing.

Figure 1: General view of the Kaleidoscopic City installation, Inspace Gallery, Edinburgh. Image by Sophia Banou, October 2013.

This installation/drawing proposed a mapping of the city that engaged with previously established images already pertaining to the site. It considered the ways in which notions of specificity might expand from the idea of a physical context, or site-specificity, into notions of 'visual specificity'. It is these specificities that emerged from the past and present of the city that were anticipated not as unique conditions but as instances of a different kind of mobility entailed in architectural and, particularly, in urban representation.

Distinct modes of representation were introduced into the space of the drawing through the tracing of the actions of six corresponding characters (Figure 2). As each of these visual 'orders' were equally considered in the writing of the drawing as script, it became relevant that each one was also involved in its

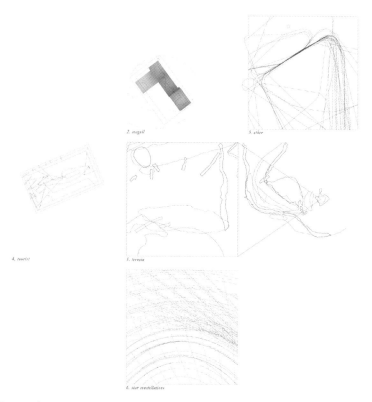

Figure 2: The six characters comprised of (1) a photographic camera, which was embedded in the recording of the survey; (2) a seagull; (3) the ether of the city as configured by the passing planes; (4) a tourist; (5) the volcanic bedrock of the city's terrain and (6) the star constellations crossing the sky above the site. These corresponded to the following representational regimes respectively: (1) the panorama; (2) the bird's eye view; (3) the aerial view; (4) the postcard; (5) the geological map and (6) the sky map. Created by Sophia Banou.

respective reading. Scopic regimes and the respective modes of representation then emerged not only as modes of sight, but also as 'sites' that interacted with the representation of the city as the actual site. Six sites that acted as viewing devices for the city were recognized in (1) Calton Hill, (2) Edinburgh Castle, (3) the Camera Obscura Tower, (4) The Royal Observatory, (5) the National Museum of Scotland and Edinburgh Castle and (6) the hilly mass of Arthur's Seat (Figure 3). Each representational regime and its corresponding scopic modes were transposed into the drawing through the surveying of their corresponding character. Their scopic attitudes were also enacted into the observation of the drawing, in an exchange of sites and sights between the drawing and the city (Figure 4).

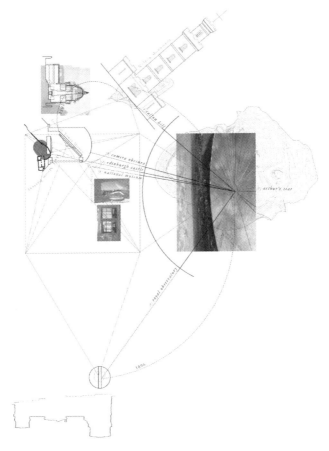

Figure 3: Site plan. The general site was punctuated and eventually represented by means of six urban sites that related to the representational and scopic regimes. Created by Sophia Banou.

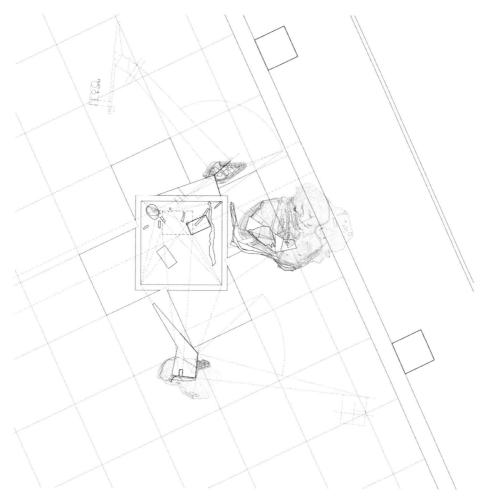

Figure 4: Plan. Kaleidoscopic City situated in the Inspace Gallery, Edinburgh. Created by Sophia Banou.

Trans-scripts, visions and figurations

The subject of patent controversy between David Brewster in Scotland and Alphonse Giroux in France, the kaleidoscope was described by Giroux as a 'transfigurator' (Didi-Huberman 2000). This definition does not foreground the operation of the kaleidoscope as the application of a geometric narrative of visual constancy, but as a process of decomposition and re-composition of a view or image.

In the essay 'Connaissance par le Kaléidoscope' ('Knowledge through the kaleidoscope') Georges Didi-Huberman (2000) recalls, through Walter Benjamin, Charles Baudelaire's fascination with the kaleidoscope as a 'scientific toy'. Drawing from Baudelaire's 'Philosophy of the toys', Didi-Huberman proposes that the toy, as a 'theory of knowledge', progresses through the operations of disconnection and composition. There is a constant negotiation between the de-construction and the re-composition of an image, the smashing and the re-assembling of the toy, which is carried out through the performance of play, as a process of acquiring and ordering knowledge. The kaleidoscope, a rational 'toy' (Brewster: 163), produces a 'proper' – in Greek καλόν (kalòn) – image of valid knowledge. The disconnection of matter, the removal from context, provides for the composition of a new image; a de-territorialization that signifies the (re)definition and thus the conquering of the toy. Accordingly, Benjamin (1985: 34) posits the kaleidoscope as analogous to a process of history as knowledge. This suggests a process of knowledge as representation, which progresses with the decomposition and re-composition of the origin. Through Benjamin's notion of a 'mirrored order' we can consider the dominant scopic regimes as regimes of representation and knowledge, situated between Brewster's idea of rational ordering and Giroux's concept of transfiguration. The kaleidoscope ultimately represents both the instability of matter considered as physical presence, and the instability of memory as the 'conquering' of matter. Through the 'device' of representation, both images of matter and memory are de-territorialized and thus able to open up the possibility of the production of new meaning.

In Kaleidoscopic City the transcription of the sites into the drawing also delivered five new visual devices: the Mirror, the Observatory, the Cabinet, the Telescope and the Terrain, which doubles by joining Edinburgh Castle and Arthur's Seat (Figures 5–8). These prosthetic devices acted as directed, ordered openings to the installation-drawing, fragmenting, multiplying and re-organizing it as object and offering a range of sightings and, consequently, readings. The wilful and spontaneous inhabitation of the drawing by the viewer, looking through the designated devices as well as through the provisionally allocated traces, in turn re-composed and complemented the drawing's transparency and vertical expansion (Figures 9 and 10). This expansion of the drawing into three-dimensions was an opportunity to peek into the space of drawing and to experience the immersive effects of its kaleidoscopic operation. In this physical manifestation of the negotiations that take place within the representational space of the drawing, hierarchies between the 'ordering' and the 'ordered' became interchangeable, and the primacy of vision over matter was challenged through the materialization of both into the drawing. The elusive matter-image of the city was indeed transfigured by acquiring a new form and materiality.

In urban representation, it can be said that the image of the city has indeed been constructed kaleidoscopically: seeking to acquire a *connaissance* of the city, to produce an image that would be proper according to the occasional scientific

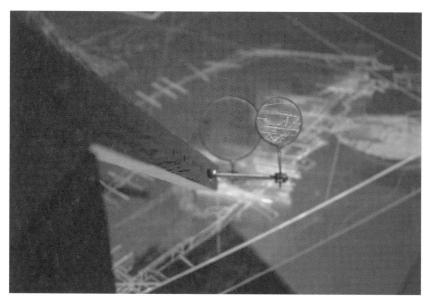

Figure 5: The Telescope, standing for Calton Hill's Nelson Monument, enables the reading of a constellation of inscribed acetates, which juxtapose the planar path of the tourist with delineations of perspectival views. Image by Sophia Banou, 5 October 2013.

Figure 6: The sum of the acetates is stored in The Box: a wooden repository of images, which, containing miniaturized representations of the city, reincarnates in the drawing the National Museum of Scotland. Image by Sophia Banou, 7 October 2013.

Figure 7: A series of solid clay components interrupts the transparency of the installation, partially grounding the drawing by materializing the volcanic bedrock of The Terrain, which encompasses both the Edinburgh Castle Rock and Arthur's Seat. Image by Sophia Banou, 6 October 2013.

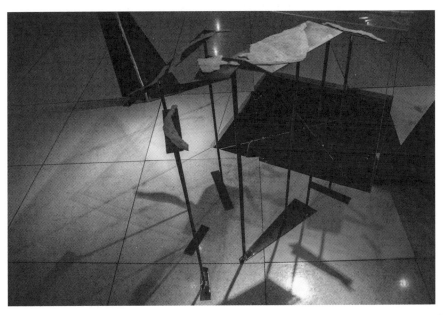

Figure 8: On the side of Arthur's Seat to the East, The Terrain expands the drawing laterally, offering a key for the recognition of the various urban sites that anchor the drawing. Image by Sophia Banou, 7 October 2013.

Figure 9: Looking through The Observatory. A directed upwards view through The Observatory into The Mirror enables the 'aerial' transversal reading of the drawing from above. Image by Sophia Banou, 4 October 2013.

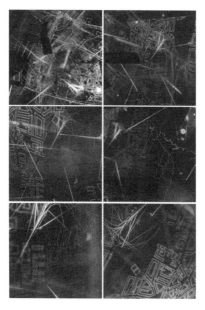

Figure 10: Looking through: 'kaleidoscopic' images emerging from the spontaneous visual fixing of the inscribed traces by means of photography. Image by Sophia Banou, 7 October 2013.

or ideological expediency of the representation. At the same time however these representations have always denied looking at and acknowledging the multiplicity of their object. Among the various 'orders' and 'regimes' that work upon constructing the image(s) of the city, drawing emerges as a visual device, an optical toy of reason, making the world visible through its own selective mirrors. Eventually however, it succumbs to one dominant scopic regime: the gaze of the drawing's reader as the ultimate inhabitant of the inter-subjective and contingent visual territory that is architectural drawing. This reader, often, is not a stranger to the drawing's script: in the process of surveying through drawing the architect takes turns in both writing and reading the drawing (Banou 2015a: 214). The act of looking re-sites and re-introduces the drawing through the reader's inhabitation of sites of sights and alternate visual devices.

For, after all, what would remain of the image of the city without any bias, without any subject? What 'eyes' would the disciplinary architectural drawing gaze through without any convention? Representation emerges in the kaleidoscope as a constitutive act, which in the inter-textually formulated unstable image of the city, takes on multiple forms and is conditioned by multiple operators. What is perhaps limiting in the representation of the city in architecture is not the application of convention as regime, but its acceptance as singular. In this context, the regimes involved can be considered as distinct situations, as staging both city and drawing in specific conditions of observation that are projected onto the collective and individual understanding of the city. In the abundance of constructed visualities that the current cinematic ubiquity and plurality of the image promises (Banou 2016), the hierarchy between the institutional and the individual can be challenged to include a collective inter-subjectivity in architectural representation considered as a kind of visual specificity. Both city and drawing emerge as the terrains of innumerable gazes. Equally approachable and ungraspable, they unfold kaleidoscopically at the conjunction of an in-situ sensory experience and the representation of visions past.

REFERENCES

Banou, S. (2015a), 'Animated gazes: Motion and representation in the kaleidoscopic city', *Drawing On Issue 1: Presents*, http://drawingon.org/issue/01. Accessed 22 January 2018.

——— (2015b), 'Textual cities/working drawings: Rereading the space of drawing', in K. Havik, S. Oliveira, J. Mejia Hernandez, M. Proosten and M. Schafer (eds), *Writingplace: Investigations in Architecture and Literature*, Rotterdam: NAi 010 Publishers, pp. 206–15.

——— (2016), 'Drawing the digital: From "virtual" experience of spaces to "real" drawings', in L. Allen and L. Pearson (eds), *Drawing Futures: Speculations in Contemporary Drawing for Art and Architecture*, London: UCL Press, pp. 20–27.

Beller, J. (2002), 'KINO-I, KINO-WORLD: Notes on the cinematic mode of production', in N. Mirzoeff (ed.), *The Visual Culture Reader: Second Revised Edition*, New York and London: Routledge, pp. 60–85.

Benjamin, W. (1985), 'Central park', *New German Critique*, 34, pp. 32–58.

Bergson, H. ([1896] 1911), *Matter and Memory (Matière et mémoire)* (trans. from French by N. M. Paul and W. S. Palmer) London: George Allen and Unwin.

—— (1911), *Creative Evolution (L'Évolution créatrice)* (trans. from French by A. Mitchell), New York: Henry Holt.

Brewster, D. (1858), *The Kaleidoscope: Its history, theory and construction*, London: John Murray.

Didi-Huberman, G. (2000), 'Connaissance par le Kaléidoscope: Morale du joujou et dialectique de l'image selon Walter Benjamin' ('Knowledge through the kaleidoscope: The philosophy of toys and the dialectical image according to Walter Benjamin'), *Etudes Photographiques*, 7, https://etudesphotographiques.revues.org/204?lang=en. Accessed 10 October 2013.

Foster, H. (1988), *Vision and Visuality*, Seattle: Bay Press.

Innis, R. E. (2002), *Pragmatism and the Forms of Sense: Language, Perception, Technics*, Philadelphia, PA: Pennsylvania University Press.

Jay, M. (1988), 'The scopic regimes of modernity', in H. Foster (ed.), *Vision and Visuality*, Seattle: Bay Press, pp. 3–23.

—— (1993), *Downcast Eyes: The Denigration of Vision in Twentieth-Century French Thought*, Berkeley, CA: University of California Press.

—— (1996), 'Disciplinary prisms: Responding to my critics', *Comparative Studies in Society and History*, 38:2, pp. 388–94.

Marin, L. ([1981] 1988), 'The king and his geometer', in L. Marin, *The Portrait of the King*, Minneapolis, MN: University of Minnesota Press, pp. 168–79.

Metz, C. (1982), 'The passion of perceiving', in C. Metz, *The Imaginary Signifier: Psychoanalysis and Cinema*, Bloomington, IN: Indiana University Press, pp. 58–68.

NOTE

1. This project was produced in the context of the Ph.D. by Design thesis *The Kinematography of a City: Moves into Drawing* (ESALA, 2016), which was supervised by Prof Mark Dorrian and Dr Ella Chmielewska and funded by the Bodossaki Foundation. It was originally installed at the Inspace Gallery in Edinburgh. See Banou (2015a).

Notes on Contributors

Sophia Banou (PhD) is a Lecturer in Architecture at the University of the West of England. She has studied architecture in Athens (Greece) and holds a PhD in Architecture by Design from ESALA (Edinburgh, 2016). She has taught at Newcastle University and The University of Edinburgh while she is a registered architect in the UK (ARB) and in Greece (TEE). Her doctoral research examined issues of architectural representation, considering space as a temporal and ephemeral condition. In this line, Sophia engages with installation as a form of drawing in space, and thus of foregrounding architectural representation as situated spatial practice.

Peter Blundell Jones (1947–2016) was a British architect and architectural historian. He trained as an architect at the Architectural Association School, and held academic positions at the University of Cambridge, London South Bank University and the University of Sheffield. His influential monographs on architects like Asplund, Häring and Scharoun traced an alternative modernist line, deeper and more subtle, to the orthodoxies of modernism, as well as an alternative history: *Modern Architecture through Case Studie*s. Latterly his work and publications focused on participation and the vernacular, in particular through East-West studies.

Hugh Campbell is Professor of Architecture at the School of Architecture, Planning and Environmental Policy, UCD, Dublin. He is editor of *Art and Architecture of Ireland, volume 4, Architecture 1600–2000* (Yale University Press, 2014) and author of *Space Framed: Photography, Architecture and the Social Landscape* (Lund Humphries, 2020).

Tonia Carless (PhD) is a Senior Lecturer in Architecture at the University of the West of England, Bristol. Her research is about spatial politics and everyday life, the production of public space and utopia and panoramas and their contemporary representational relationship with digital technology. She also researches through design, drawing and practice. She is a founder member of the collaborative research group and *Just Painting* archive.

Shelly Cohen is an architect, curator and researcher. Her work focuses on the social and political dimensions of architecture. With various associates, she curated a series of exhibitions, which critically explored the ways in which planning and design shape everyday life in spaces of defence, housing and consumption in Israel. From January 2017, Cohen is a postdoctoral fellow at the Technion (Israel Institute of Technology, Faculty of Architecture and Town Planning). Cohen's PhD thesis from Tel Aviv University (Planning for the Environment with Communities— PECLAB, Department of Geography and the Human Environment) addresses the relations between the ethical, social and aesthetic aspects in architecture for marginalized groups in Israel.

Willem de Bruijn (PhD) is a Senior Lecturer in Architecture at the Arts University Bournemouth where he teaches contextual studies and supervises research degrees. He studied architecture at the TU Delft and KTH Stockholm and completed a PhD in History and Theory of Architecture (2010) at The Bartlett School of Architecture. His thesis, an investigation into architecture and alchemy, was nominated for the 2011 RIBA President's Award for Research. Articles relating to the thesis have been published in *The International Journal of the Book* (2005/06; 2007), *Library Trends* (2012) and *Footprint* (2012). His current research revolves around the role of the image and the visual in developing new approaches to teaching history and theory within architecture and the arts. He also practices as an artist and has participated in various exhibitions in the United Kingdom, The Netherlands and Brazil.

Mathew Emmett is a neo-noir architect who disrupts the original use and perception of buildings. Drawing upon intermedia disciplines spanning video, sound and digital performance, he infects architectural spaces with an altered sense of reality. Addressing both destructive and redemptive themes in society today, his work reveals multilayered references to the continual study of the Isenheim Altarpiece. He has collaborated with Kraftwerk co-founder Eberhard Kranemann, Candoco Dance Company founder Adam Benjamin, Node electronics composer Dave Bessell, and architectural theorists Neil Spiller and Charles Jencks. In June 2016, he performed *Sender/Receiver* at the opening of the Blavatnik Building, Tate Modern London. Emmett studied at the Architectural Association, Bartlett School of Architecture, Central St Martins, has a PhD in situated cognition, and in 2007 studied space music under Karlheinz Stockhausen, Kürten.

Suzanne Ewing is an architect, educator and Professor of Architectural Criticism at the Edinburgh School of Architecture and Landscape Architecture (ESALA) at the University of Edinburgh. She co-founded ZONE architects in 2002, and contributes to the practice through invited urban projects and competitions, brief shaping, critical review and project dissemination. Publications include *Saltcity: Cádiz Field + Work* (2008), *Architecture and Field/Work* (2011), *Marseille: Irrigations* (2012), *Spaces of Tolerance* (2021). Since 2013 she has been co-editor of the international award-winning journal *Architecture and Culture*.

Marc Goodwin is an architectural photographer, writer and teacher. His work has been published in five books commissioned by architects as well as a city guide to Barcelona. He has published repeatedly in *Archdaily*, *Wallpaper*, *Domus*, *JA+U*, *The Finnish Architectural Review*, *Sveriges Arkitekter*, *AD*, *Mas Context*, *Wall St Journal*, *Dezeen*, *Dwell* and *Detail*. Marc graduated Summa Cum Laude from UCSD where he studied English and Photography. He received an MA in Image and Communication from Goldsmiths University, London and a Doctorate from Aalto University, Helsinki. His recently published doctoral thesis 'Architecture's Discursive Space, Photography' opposes conventional architectural photography to one that focusses on a system of atmospheres. He is currently working on an atlas of architectural studios around the world.

Valeria Guzman-Verri is a researcher and Senior Lecturer at the School of Architecture and at the Society and Culture PhD Programme at the University of Costa Rica. She holds a PhD in Histories and Theories of Architecture from the Architectural Association School of Architecture (2010). She specializes in visual culture of modern and contemporary architectural and graphic design and the relations between form, knowledge and power. She has published in *Jefferson Journal of Science and Culture* (University of Virginia), *Annals of the Institute of Aesthetic Research* (UNAM, Mexico), *Revistarquis* (University of Costa Rica), *Bitácora* (UNAM), *Dearq* (Universidad de Los Andes, Colombia), amongst others.

Popi Iacovou is a Lecturer in Architecture at the University of Cyprus. She received her PhD from The Bartlett School of Architecture, University College London, funded by the A.G. Leventis Foundation and the FfWG (UK). She holds an MPhil in *Architecture and the Moving Image* from the University of Cambridge and a Diploma in Architecture from Aristotle University of Thessaloniki. Her research focuses on the intersection between architecture, performance and the moving image. She has previously taught at Central Saint Martins College of Art and Design, University of Cyprus, University of Nicosia and Neapolis University Pafos. She has published internationally and her films and architectural design work has been shown in various film festivals and architectural exhibitions.

David Jones (PhD) is an academic and strategic planner with the Wadawurrung Traditional Owners Aboriginal Corporation, Ballarat/Geelong, Australia.

A graduate of the universities of Melbourne and Pennsylvania, his teachings and research explore and chart new culturally rich nuances of place. He is the author of *Adelaide Park Lands & Squares Cultural Landscape Assessment Study* (2007), which underpins the successful nomination of the Adelaide Park Lands to the Australian National Heritage Register.

Gavin Keeney (PhD) is Creative Director of Agence 'X', an artists' and architects' re-representational bureau founded in New York, USA, in 2007. His most recent books include: *Knowledge, Spirit, Law: Book 1, Radical Scholarship* (2015); and *Knowledge, Spirit, Law: Book 2, The Anti-capitalist Sublime* (2017).

Aglaia Konrad is an Austrian, self-taught as an artist, lives in Brussels and teaches at the LUCA School of Arts. Since the early 1990s she has developed a strong interest in urban space, architecture, sculptural architecture and their various mixtures. In 1992 she discovered the Egyptian (new built cities) 'Desert Cities' and became intrigued by the vast scale of this development such that she began a long-term project (2004–08). Her work appears in various media including film, video, photography and installations and she has participated in many international exhibitions. Publications: *Elasticity* (2002); *Iconocity* (2005); *Desert Cities* (2008); *Carrara* (2011); *Zweimal Belichtet* (2013); *Aglaia Konrad: From A to K* and *SCHAUBUCH: Skulptur* (2017); *Japan Works* (2020).

Ruxandra Kyriazopoulos-Berinde is an architect and researcher based in Romania with practice experience in Scandinavia and the United Kingdom. Her focus areas are heritage, phenomenology and film. In 2016 she completed an AHRC-funded PhD at the School of Architecture, University of Sheffield, exploring the filmic spaces of Andrei Tarkovsky's and Ingmar Bergman's works. She was also a research associate in the AHRC project 'The Cinematic Musée Imaginaire of Spatial Cultural Differences' project based at University of Cambridge, Department of Architecture.

Lesley Lokko is Dean of The Bernard & Anne Spitzer School of Architecture at The College of New York. She was the founder and director of the Graduate School of Architecture at the University of Johannesburg from 2014–2019 and is also the author of eleven best-selling novels. She received her BSc (Arch) and MArch from the Bartlett School of Architecture, University College London, and her PhD in architecture from the University of London. She has taught at schools of architecture in the United States, the United Kingdom, as well as South Africa, where she was Visiting African Scholar at the University of Cape Town. She is the editor of *White Papers, Black Marks: Race, Culture, Architecture* (University of Minnesota Press, 2000) and has been an ongoing contributor to discourses around identity, 'race', African urbanism and the speculative nature of African architectural space for over twenty years.

Ray Lucas is Reader in Architecture and Director of Humanities at the Manchester Metropolitan University, part of Manchester School of Architecture. Past work includes a PhD in Social Anthropology on drawing and notations as examples of creative practices that allow thinking by doing; MPhil by research in Architecture on the discipline's relationship with film's structural concepts such as montage, spectatorship and narrative; and research projects on sensory experience in the city. Recent and forthcoming publications include *Research Methods for Architecture* for Laurence King (2016); *Drawing Parallels: Knowledge Production in Axonometric, Isometric and Oblique Drawings* for Routledge (2019) and *Anthropology for Architects: Social Relations and the Built Environment* (2020) for Bloomsbury. Lucas is currently working on *A Graphic Anthropology of Sanja Matsuri*, a legacy of the ERC-funded project 'Knowing from the Inside' led by Tim Ingold at the University of Aberdeen.

Povilas Marozas is a landscape architect and a researcher. He studied architecture at Vilnius Geriminas' Technical University and architectural history at the Bartlett School of Architecture, UCL. Since 2012 Marozas has been working as landscape architect in London where he is currently part of Periscope Landscape and Architecture Studio. Povilas has a continuous interest in the complex relationship between architecture and photography and his research centres on examining the role of photography in architectural historical and theoretical discourse.

Fiona McLachlan is Professor of Architectural Practice at the University of Edinburgh and is an architect and educator. She teaches architectural design and professional practice and is a past Head of the Edinburgh School of Architecture and Landscape Architecture (ESALA). She is the author of *Architectural Colour in the Professional Palette* (2012), and a co-author of *Colour Strategies in Architecture* (2015). Her architectural practice, E & F McLachlan Architects, which was included in *New Architects: A Guide to Britain's Best Young Architectural Practices* (1998) specialized in social housing including dwellings for wheelchair users and housing for frail elderly.

Morten Meldgaard (PhD) is Associate Professor at the Royal Danish Academy of Arts, School of Architecture, Institute for Building, Landscape & Planning. He has a PhD in film and architecture and is furthermore trained as a film director at the National Danish Film School and as an architect at the Royal Danish Academy.

He teaches at the Royal Academy School of Architecture, as head of the BA programme 'complexity and practice' and at the National Danish Film school, where he was also head of research (2013–14). He published the feature-length documentary 'KIM' (2009) and a Double CD entitled 'Soundtrack_Remix' (2010). His thesis 'Clocks for Seeing' was accepted in 2009. He has written articles and papers for a variety of magazines and conferences. In 2018 he co-authored the installation CHERISH, in the Copenhagen monumental Marblechurch, consisting of 16,000 pink handmade paperflowers, heralding a holistic outlook and the cherishing of Mother Earth.

Agnieszka Mlicka is an artist, researcher and visual facilitator based in Copenhagen. She founded Visual Agency to facilitate workshops and courses using the method of collaborative visual thinking, in order to stimulate curiosity, creativity and collaboration in various types of meetings (visualagency.org). This method emerged from her interdisciplinary, practice-led PhD research at Central Saint Martins, University of the Arts London, which investigated painting as a way of facilitating spatial negotiation in urban planning. Agnieszka holds a BFA in Fine Art from the University of Oxford and an MA in Painting from the University of the Arts London. Having widely exhibited, with artworks in private and public collections, her current social art practice focuses on community building, circular economies to reduce, reuse and upcycle, and dancing outdoors to inspire alternative uses of public space (agnieszkamlicka.com).

Miguel Paredes Maldonado (PhD) is a Lecturer at the University of Edinburgh, a chartered architect and a partner in Cuartoymitad Architecture & Landscape, an award-winning research and design studio with an internationally published and exhibited body of work. He taught at the Universidad Politécnica de Madrid (ES) before relocating to Edinburgh in 2013. He has also acted as visiting faculty at the Karlsruhe Institute of Technology (DE), Università degli studi di Cagliari (IT), the Frank Lloyd Wright School of Architecture (USA) and the Technische Universität Graz (AT). His research is articulated through writing, but also speculative design and architectural practice, dealing primarily with ephemerality and the development of the public commons. He has written extensively about the influence of new materialism in contemporary spatial practices, with an emphasis on the affordances and challenges of pervasive digitalization. His current research focuses on the intersection of digital technologies, urban public space and contemporary design theory.

Susanna Pisciella is a researcher at IUAV University of Venice in the field of Architectural Design and Theory. She has collaborated in both research and teaching with the UAQ-ANAHUAC Querétaro, PUC de Santiago de Chile, HCU

Hamburg and UNIPR Parma. She completed her PhD at IUAV in 2011 with a thesis on Peter Eisenman's theory work published with the title *Peter Eisenman Gher-Ghar,* Mimesis Edizione (2018). Recent publications written with R. Rizzi include *John Hejduk. Bronx,* Mimesis Edizione (2020), *Architettura. I pregiudicati,* Mimesis Edizione (2016), *Il Cosmo della Bildung,* Mimesis Edizione (2016).

George Themistokleous (BA, MA, MArch, PhD) is an architect, media artist, lecturer in Architecture at De Montfort University and visiting lecturer at the University of the Arts Helsinki (Live Art and Performance Studies). He is the director of para-sight (www.para-sight.org), an interdisciplinary spatial practice. His research explores the changing role of the body via assemblages of older and emerging visual media, including custom-made devices and multimedia installations. His design research has been published in edited books, academic and design journals, and selected/exhibited in various platforms including: *Acadia: Posthuman Frontiers* (2016), Venice Architecture Biennale (2018), ACM Siggraph (2018), Future Architecture Platform (2019), Leonardo LABS database (2019) and Ars Electronica Festival (2020). He is co-editor of *This Thing Called Theory* (Routledge).

Tariq Toffa is an educator, writer and architect, and convenes history and theory of architecture at the University of Johannesburg. He coedited the multidisciplinary volume on critical pedagogy *Standing Items: Critical Pedagogies in South African Art, Design and Architecture* (2020). His research interests include the histories and contemporalities of colonialism/apartheid, contemporary urbanisms, and critical thinking around space, education and society. He was manager of the South African chapter of the Dallant Networks/Ford Foundation project 'Urban Impact' or URB.im, an inter-Global South platform for which he wrote regularly on social and urban issues in the South African city, and was also manager of the Social Housing Focus Trust (SHiFT), an NGO that provided expertise on the role and design of housing/human settlements in transforming the built environment.

Igea Troiani (PhD) Subject Head of Architecture and Professor of Architecture at the University of Plymouth, UK. She was formerly the Dean of International Affairs and Professor of Architecture at Xi'an Jiaotong-Liverpool University (XJTLU) in China. She has taught and/or practiced architecture in the UK (Oxford), China (Suzhou), Germany (Münster) and Australia (Brisbane and Melbourne). Her research traverses the fields of architecture, urbanism, ecology, sociology, politics, economics, and visual culture focusing in three areas: 1) the social production of architecture; 2) architecture and media (focusing on filmmaking) and; 3) architectural labour, neoliberalism and sustainable ecologies. Igea's other books include *The Politics of Making* (2007), *Transdisciplinary Urbanism and Culture* (2017); *Architecture Filmmaking* (2019) and *Spaces of Tolerance* (2021). She was recipient of a Research Excellence Award in 2017 and is founder and editor-in-chief of the interdisciplinary, award-winning journal *Architecture and Culture* that publishes exploratory research that is purposively imaginative, rigorously speculative, visually and verbally stimulating.

Niek Turner (PhD) is a Lecturer in Architecture at the School of Natural and Built Environment at Queen's University Belfast. He is a fully qualified architect with over 10 years' experience in practice throughout the United Kingdom and Ireland working on several award-winning projects of varying scales. He has an ongoing academic interest in architecture and media that has spawned previous architectural research into varied subjects including contemporary electronic music and alchemy. He recently completed an AHRC-funded PhD at the Centre for Architecture and the Visual Arts at the University of Liverpool, which expanded on this interest by utilizing computer visualization techniques to explore the use of space in the early films of Soviet Avant-Garde film director, and one-time architecture student, Sergei Eisenstein.

Haim Yacobi (Bartlett Development Planning Unit, UCL) is an architect and professor who specializes in critical urban studies. His academic work focuses on (post)colonial architecture, planning and development in Israel/Palestine, the Middle East and Africa. Spatial justice and urban health, contested urbanism, transnational migration and informality are in the core of his research and consultancy work, teaching and activism.

Index

Note: Illustrations are denoted by the use of *italics*. Notes are shown as page followed by note and number, e.g. 42n2.

A

Abbott, Berenice, 129
Aboriginal painting process, 324
abstract painting, 300, 301
Accra, Ghana, 279–84
Ackermann, Franz, 300
Acropolis, Athens, 242–3
acrylic paint, 339
Action! (mapping exercise), 282–5
activist research, 'just painting' as, 324
Adorno, Theodor W., *Der Essay als Form*, 19, 71, 294
aerial photography, 75n9, 282, 388
aerial view, *393*
Africa, 19, *62*, 74–5n3, 276–85
Age of Reason (Enlightenment), 49, 50, 227, 284
aggregates, online, 151
aggregates, paratactic, 148
Airey, Janie, 157n9
Albers, Josef, *Interaction of Color*, 340–1
Alberti, Leon Battista, 203, *203*, 204–6
Aldo Rossi: An Exhibition of Drawing (1976 exhibition), 43
Aleksandr Nevskiy (Alexander Nevsky) (Eisenstein), 234, 237
Alexander, Christopher, 148

alignment, momentary, 361
Allen, Stan, 22, 301, 315
AlSayyad, Nezar, *Cinematic Urbanism: A History of the Modern From Reel to Real*, 235
Alsop, Will, 22, 341, 342
ambiguity, painting's, 311–14
American Prospects (Sternfeld), 135
American Society of Landscape Architects (ASLA), 221
analogy, use of, 6, 43–56, 91
analysing output, *242*
Anatomical Theatre (engraving), 47, *47*
Andrea (participatory painting workshop), 307, *308*
Andrey Rublyov (Andrei Rublev) (Tarkovsky), 247, 252
Anelli, Marco, *Portraits in the Presence of Marina Abramović*, 271
anexact geometries, 8, 118, 119, *121*, 122
animating points of view (filmic process), 268, 272
animation, 262
Annunciation, The (Savinio), 268
anthropology, 26, 77, 83–9, 87–8, 273
'anti-environment', 384
anti-intellectualism, 227

'An unexpected juncture' (Eisenstein), 233

apartheid colonialism, 74–5n3, 276

Apparecchio alla morte (Apparatus for Death) (Saint'Alfonso de Liguori), 56

Arab neighbourhoods, 176–7, 179, 183, 184–5

archaeology, 80

arches, Roman, *203*, 204–6

Archigram (avant-garde architectural group), 21, *298*

architect-performer concept, 266, 269, 273–4

Architects' Journal, The (AJ), 40, 41

architectural phenomenography, through film, 247–58

architectural photography books, 141

Architectural Review, The (journal), 40

Architecture in the Age of Divided Representation (Vesely), 266

Archizines, 152, 155n2

Arduino micro-controllers, 356, 382

Arendt, Hannah, 225

argumentation, pictorial, 202–3

Aristoteles, *Etica Nicomachea*, 50

Arnheim, Rudolf, 148

'Arrival City' project, 64, 75n5

Arsuf, Israel, 180, *181*

Art and Agency (Gell), 76

Artaud, Antonin, 270

art history, 7, 13–14, 26, 150, 201–2

Arthur's Seat, Edinburgh, 394, 396, *398*

Artificial Intelligence (AI), 21

'Art in the age of mechanical reproduction' (Benjamin), 231

Artists is Present, The (Abramović), 271

ArtStor Digital Library, 210

Astruc, Alexandre, 17, 223, 252

asymptomatic ellipses, 222–4

Atta-Mills, John, 283

audience, site of, 344–7

audio-visuality

Emmett and, 24–5

instruments, 370–85

recordings, 267, 272

auditory field, 381

Australia, 17

Avedon, Richard, 148

axonometric projections, 35, 83, *84*, 86, *88*, 93n5, 308, *366*

B

Baan, Iwan, 130, 157n9

Bachelard, Gaston, 257

Badger, Gerry, *The Photobook: A History*, 132–3

Baldasso, Renzo, 103–4

Bal, Mieke, *Travelling Concepts in the Humanities*, 27

Banham, Reyner, 16

Banou, Sophie, *Kaleidoscopic City*, 25, 387–400, *392–5*, *397–9*, 401n1

Barak, Yair, *180–1*, *182–3*

Barbican Centre, London, 38, 42n2, 152

Barry, David, 314

Barthes, Roland, *Camera Lucida*, 28, 129, 180, 193, 285, 289

Bataille, Georges, 7

Batteux, Charles, *Les beaux arts réduits à un même principe*, 219

Baudelaire, Charles, 'Philosophy of the toys' 395–6

Bauen in Frankreich (Giedion), *126*

Bayer, Herbert, 10

Beaux-Arts, 37, 270

beaux arts réduits à un même principe, Les (Batteux), 219

Becher, Berndt and Hilla, 148, 179

Bedford, Paddy, 324

Beer-Sheva, Israel, 180, *181*, 183

'Before and After', topology of the, 292–3

INDEX

Behne, Adolf, 37

being, drawing as, 76–92

being in the world, mode of, 76, 79–80

being, perception as, 81–3

Belting, Hans, 67–8, 75n9, 82

Benjamin, Adam, *382, 383*

Benjamin, Walter
  and 'experience', 95
  immanent analysis, 321
  on the kaleidoscope, 395–6
  on Neurath's pictograms, 110n1
  Turner and, 17
  'untidy child', 99
  'Art in the age of mechanical reproduction'
    231
  Illuminations, 225–6
  'modes of perception', 232

Berger, John, 201

Bergson, Henri, 76, 119, 289, 388–9, 391
  Creative Evolution, 365

Berinde, Ruxandra Kyriazopoulos- 17–18,
  247–58

'Beyond the shot' (Eisenstein), 233–4

Bilderatlas Mnemosyne (Warburg), 14,
  201–12, *204, 206*

Bilderreihen (*Image-series*) (Warburg), 202

Binet, Hélène, 157n9

Bing Image Search, 208

binocular vision, 38, 360, 361

biofeedback apparatus/graphs, 374–5,
  375–6

biography, 251

bird's eye view, 388, 391, *393*

Birmingham Central Library, 328, *329,* 331

Birth of Memory, The (sound-dance
  collaboration), *383*

black, projecting on (filmic process), 269–70

Blessed Givers Church, Accra, 283–4, *284*

Blossfeldt, Karl, 148

blot-reading game, 101

blue images, 144–5

Blundell Jones, Peter, 5–6, 8–9, 35–41

bodily vision in space and time, 353–68

body and image, interval of the, 358–64

body, space and, 39

Boeri, Stefano, 279

Bogdanovich, Vitaly, 13, 192, 194, 195

Bohr, Barbara, *288*

Bojorquez, April, 328

Boogert, A., *Traité des couleurs servant à la
  peinture à l'eau*, 336

Boradkar, Prasad, 342–3

Bordwell, David
  The Cinema of Eisenstein, 233
  Film Art: An Introduction, 240–1

Born, Ernest, 37

'Botticelli Re-imagined' (016 V&A exhibition),
  334

bottom-up practices, 113, 123n2

Bourbonnais, Sébastien, 117

Bourdieu, Pierre, 7, 11, 77–9, 128

Box (image repository), *397*

Boyarski, Alvin, 342

Brecht, Bertolt, 270

Brewster, David, 395, 396

Bristol, 318

British Airways Corporation, 323, 331

Broken Manual (Soth), *137, 138*

Bronenosets Potemkin (*Battleship Potemkin*)
  (Eisenstein), 17, 232, 233, 234, 236, 237,
  238–40, 243

Brown, Blain, 380

Brueghel, Pieter the Elder, *The Conversion
  of Saint Paul*, 101, 135

Brunelleschi, Filippo, 203

Builder, The (journal), 40

Building Design magazine, 35, 40

building portraits, 270–4, *273,* 340–1, *341,* 349

Bulgakowa, Oksana, *Sergei Eisenstein: A
  Biography*, 233

Burckhardt, Jacob, 203
Burden of Representation, The (Tagg), 150
Burgin, Victor, 13, 192–4, 196, 197
  Thinking Photography, 192
  'Looking at photographs', 193
  'Photographic practice and art theory', 192–3
  'Photography, phantasy, function', 193
Burke, Edmund, *A Philosophical Enquiry into the Origin of Our Ideas of the Sublime and Beautiful*, 222

C
Cabinet (visual device), 396
Cache, Bernard, 8, 115
Cagliari, Sardinia, *114–16*, 116, 119–20, *120*
Cairo-Alexandria Desert Road, 158, *160–75*
Callahan, Harry, 130
calligraphy, 251
Calton Hill, Edinburgh, 394, *397*
Calvino, Italo, 50
Camera Lucida (Barthes), 129
Camera Obscura Tower, Edinburgh, 394
Campany, David, 129
Campbell, Hugh, 11, 127–38
Cape Town, University of, 58–9, 60, *60*, 276
capitalism
  consumer, 318
  neoliberal, 64, 121, 225, 227
Caravaggio, Michelangelo Merisi da, *Narcissus*, 269
Carless, Tonia, 23, 25, 317–31, *322–3*
Cartesian space, 120
Cartier-Bresson, Daniel, *The Decisive Moment*, 130–1, 132
cartography, 375
Casa Malaparte, Capri, 260–74, *263*
  list of spaces, 261–2
Casa Malaparte (Talamona), 260–1
cathedrals, Italian, 204–6

Cattell, Maria, 323
Cemetery of Pleasures, Lisbon, 52, *52*, 55
'Cento' (poetry form), 237
Central Park, New York City, 225
Certosa of Pavia, 53, *53*
Cervantes, Miguel de, *Don Quixote*, 278
Česonis, Gintaras, *Raktai Į Lietuvos miestus*, 13, 192, 194, 196
Cézanne, Paul, 67–8, 134
Chevrier, Jean-François, 271, 273
children
  drawing and, 97, 98
  games and, 48, 95, 100, 101
  visualization and, 101
Chiupachenko, Vasilij, 13, 191, *191*, 192, 194, 195
Choisy, Auguste, *Histoire de l'Architecture*, 243, 244
Christianity, 49, *62*
chronological dial, 381
churches, 280, 282–4
ciné-cento, 236–42, *236*
cinema, 288–9, 364
Cinema, 1: The Movement-Image (Deleuze), 354, 364, 367
Cinema of Eisenstein, The (Bordwell), 233
cinematic architectural experience
  categories, 255–6, *256*
cinematic space, 39
Cinematic Urbanism: A History of the Modern From Reel to Real (AlSayyad), 235
cinemetrics, 241, 243
Cine-Scapes: Cinematic Spaces in Architecture and Cities (Koeck), 244
circularity, 47
cities, 14–16, 43–56, 387–400
  African, 19
  desert, 12, 158, *160–75*
  nature of, 279
  visual events in, 231

INDEX

Cities, Architecture and Society (Venice Architecture Biennale, 2006), 105
citizenship, an education in, 104–6
Clancy, Alice, 128
Clarke, Adele E., *Situational Analysis*, 378–9
Clawley, Alan, 328
Clément, Gilles, 17, 219–20
client preference/rejection, 142, *143–4*, 149, 156n3
Cliff of Punta Massulo, Capri, 262, *263*, 268, 269
Clifton Suspension Bridge, Bristol, *322*
Climb of Mount Carmelo (San Juan de la Cruz), 54, *54*
Climo, Jacob, 323
CNC code, 119
Coates, Nigel, *Narrative Architecture*, 327
cognition, situated, 371–2
'cognitive dissonance' (definition), 71
cognitive processes, 81
Cognitive-tope maps, 25, 375–6, *377*, 379–82
Cognitive-tope prototype/pilot, *378–9*
Cohen, Shelly, 176–85
collage
  architectural, 209–11
  digital, 269, 272
  mnemonic, 202–3, 207
  natural, 348
  technique, 340, *341*, *343*, 346, 347, 350
  in texts, 201
Collage Workshop (UEL), 209–10
collecting (filmic process), 267
Colomina, Beatriz, *Privacy and Publicity: Modern Architecture as Mass Media*, 244
colonialism, apartheid, *60*, 74–5n3, 276
colour
  charts/systems, 22, 335

design, 335–50
photography and, 142–5
theory, 335
three-dimensionality, 335
use of, 23–4, 93n5, 342, 345
Colour Strategies in Architecture (McLachlan), 340
Colour Strategies in Architecture project, 338, 340, 343–4, 348
commercial photography, 11–12, 142–3, *143–4*, 152, 195–6
communication, 22, 96, 103, 311
community payback scheme, 327
composing sounds (filmic process), 268–9
composite images, 340–1
computer technology
  audio-visual sensor, 373
  drawing, 35, 38–9, 83
  film, 17, 228, 232–3, 235–7, 243
  photography, 151
  Raspberry Pi, 356, 357
  software, 21
  usage, 342
  visualizations, 346
Concise Townscape, The (Cullen), 244
Concorde Paint-in, *323*, 331
confinement, spatiality of, 284–5
conic truncation, 20, 298
'Connaissance par le Kaléidoscope' ('Knowledge through the kaleidoscope') (Didi-Huberman), 395
consciousness
  Bergson on, 388–9
  eye, 96
  gestures, 270
  phenomena and, 358
  'popular preconscious', 196
  visual, 8, 105, 106
  writing and, 386n1
constructed scene photography, 132

415

Constructing the View (2013 symposium), 140n1

Constructing Worlds – Photography and Architecture in the Modern Age (2014 exhibition), 127–8, 152

Construction site of the first school of Visaginas (Chiupachenko), 191–2, *191*

constructivism, symbolic (definition), 302

'contextual' visual positions, 13

Conversion of Saint Paul, The (Brueghel), 101

Coriolis illusion (perception), *384*

Corner, James, 68

'corporeality' (design process methodology), 70

Cosmographia (Ptolemy), 104

'Couture's Glorious Excess' (Lindbergh, *Vogue)*, 224

Crary, Jonathan, 24, 354
  Techniques of the Observer, 361–2, 363, 364

Creber, Frank, 300

Crewdson, Gregory, 132

crisis and self-analysis, 226–8

criticality, 196, 197

'critical visuality', 1–3, 3, 6, 28

Cruz, Teddy, 72

Cullen, Gordon, *The Concise Townscape*, 244

cultural geography, 14, 19

cultural theory, 197, 202

'Cushicle' project (Webb), 21

D

Daichendt, G. James, 28

D'Alembert, Jean le Rond, *Encyclopédie*, 49

dance/movement, 91, *382–3*

dancing maenad, *206*, 207, 208

Dante Alighieri, 54

data-based urban drawing, 112–22, *114–16*

data collection, 116, 241, 250, 337, 340

Daumal, René, *Le Mont Analogue*, 6, 53

David's Island Strategic Plot Drawing (Kulper), *4, 5, 34*

Deakin University, Australia, 222

Dean, Tacita, 17, 222, 223

death analogy, 43, 48, 56

de Bruijn, Willem, 14, 201–12

de Certeau, Michel, 89

decipherment, 100, 193, 375

Decisive Moment, The (Cartier-Bresson), 130–1

decolonization, 7, 13, 19, 58, 277–8

Deep Play (video installation), 105–6

Degas, Edgar, 81

de Landa, Manuel, 113, 122, 123n1

Deleuze, Gilles, 287–9
  De Landa on, 113
  on Foucault, 290, *294*
  'journeyman', 119
  on mechanism, 365
  mind-body dualisms, 372
  Cinema, 1: The Movement-Image, 354, 364, 367
  Difference and Repetition, 364

Delirious New York (Koolhaas), 342

Denver project, Johannesburg, 69, 75n11

Der Himmel über Berlin (*Wings of Desire*) (film), 39

Derrida, Jacques, 118, 278–9

desert cities, 158–9, *160–75*

Desert Cities project (Konrad), 12

"Design for and with Local Communities" projects, 64, 75n4

design process methodology, 70, 78

design-research process, 69–70, *70*, 71–2, 260–74

design-research projects, 59, 65, 69, *70*, 75n6

deterritorialization, 13

Dictionnaire Raisonné de l'architecture Française du XI au XVI Siècle (Rational Dictionary of French Architecture from the XI to the XVI Century) (Viollet-le-Duc), 36

Diderot, Denis, *Encyclopédie*, 49

Didi-Huberman, Georges, 'Connaissance par le Kaléidoscope' 95, 96, 395–6

Difference and Repetition (Deleuze), 364

digital editing, 289

digital media, 353–68

digital technologies, 19, 21–4, 105, 228, 232

Diplorasis (etymology), 355

Diplorasis project, 353–68, 356–8, 360, 362–3, 366

Diplorasis (Themistokleous), 24

Dirlik, Arif, 6–7, 59

disciplinarity, 71–2

Disciplinary Frame, The (Tagg), 149

discursive spaces, 60

dissemination and the site of audience, 344–7

documentary photography, 128, 130, 150

Doing Sensory Ethnography (Pink), 26

Doing Visual Ethnography (Pink), 26

Dona, Lydia, 301

Don Quixote (Cervantes), 278

'double event', 271

drawing

  as being, 76–92

  Bristol board, 93n5

  children's, 97, 98

  computer technology in, 35, 38–9, 83

  conversations, 303–4

  data-based urban, 112–22, 114–16

  digital, 262

  by hand, 6, 7

  imagination and, 8

  kaleidoscopic, 387–400

  line, 40, 80, 267–8, 272, 345

machine, 117, *117*

medium of, *4, 5–9*

as perception, 80–1

robotic environment, 116, 119

drums, digitally controlled, 356–7, *358*

DSLR camera, 357

dualism, 227, 371, 372

Duchamp, Marcel, *Étant donnés*, 360, 364

Dujardin, Filip, 157n9

Duomo di Milano, 51–2, *51, 55*

Durand, J. N. L. 50

duration, 119–22

'duration' (definition), 119

Dürer, Albrecht, 202

Dusseldorf School, 130, 132

Dusseldorf School of Photography (Gronert), 130

dwelling, in the world, 82

E

Eames, Charles and Ray, 16

East London, University of, 209–10

Eclectic Atlases, The (research project), 19, 279

ecological systems theory, 226–7

Ecological Urbanism, 227

economic collapse, African, 282–3

Economic Scheme (Isotype project), 99–100, *100*

Eco, Umberto, 193

'ecstatic truth' 138

Edinburgh, 391–400, *392–5, 397–9*

Edinburgh Castle, 394, 396

Edinburgh Castle Rock, *398*

Edoardo (participatory painting workshop), 306

education

  architectural, 58–72, 201–12

  buildings, *191*

  in citizenship, 104–6

film art, 240–1
visual, 95–6, 101
visual scholarship and, 276–85
Eggleston, William, 132
Egypt, 158
Egyptian tomb murals, 101
Eisenman, Peter, *Houses of Memory: The Texts of Analogy*, 43, 48, 91
Eisenstein at Work (Leyda and Voynow), 234
Eisenstein, Mikhail, 232
Eisenstein, Sergei, 231–45
  Godard on, 291
  the individual shot, 236
  Aleksandr Nevskiy (Alexander Nevsky), 234, 237
  'Beyond the shot', 233–4
  Bronenosets Potemkin, 17, 232, 233, 234, 236, 237, *238–40*, 243
  'Laocoön', 237
  'Montage and architecture' 86, 232, 234, 242–3, 245
  'Piranesi or the flux of form', 232, 234
  Stachka (The Strike), 236, 240
  Staroye i Novoye (The Old and the New), 232
  Towards a New Architecture, 243
  Towards a Theory of Montage, 234, 236
  'An unexpected juncture', 233
  'Yermolova', 234
Elements (Euclid), 123n3
elevations, 35, 37, 83, *84*, 93n5
eliciting enquiry, 314
Elkins, James, 129
ellipses, asymptomatic, 222–4
Emanuele (participatory painting workshop), 312–13, *312*
embodied knowledge production, 13, 91, 196–7
Emmett, Mathew, 24–5, 26, 370–85, *374–9*

empathy, 319–20
Employing Social Art Practice, 328
Encyclopédie (Diderot and D'Alambert), 49
Engberg, Siri, 138
Enlightenment (Age of Reason), 49, 50, 227, 284
en plein-air painting, 23, 318, 322–3
enquiry, types of (participatory painting), 314–15
Enrich, Victor, 157n9
environment, perception in the, 76, 116
epistemic inferiority, 61
epistemic privilege, 61, 72
Epstein, Mitch, 132
'*Erkenntnis*' (definition), 294
Ernst, Max, *La femme, 100 têtes*, 104
Eros, 223
Étant donnés (Duchamp), 360, 364
ethnography, 26, 179, 250, 322, 328
Etica Nicomachea (Aristoteles), 50
Euclidean space/geometry, 120, 123n3–4
Euclid, *Elements*, 123n3
Evans, Walker, 129, 130
exact geometries, 118
exchange practices, 79–80
existentialism, 89, 223
exteriors, 142, 144, 205, 207, *207*, 260
eyes
  consciousness, 96
  diagrams of, *354*, *355*
  eye holes, *362*
  keratoconus (disorder), *354*, *355*
  'looking eye', 390–1
  tracking system, 373, 374, *374*

F
'Farbenkugel' (colour sphere) (Runge), 335
Farnell, Brenda, 94n6
Farocki, Harun, 8, 17, 111n15, 222, 223
  Deep Play, 105–6

INDEX

fashion industry, 224–5
fear and space, 183–4
fear, sense of, 183–4
feedback, student, 306–7, 310
femme, 100 têtes, La (Ernst), 104
Feyerabend, Paul, 148
Fickert, Axel, 345, *346*
fiction-reality, 53
fiction, writing and, 278
field/land textures, *103*
figurations, 395–400, *397–9*
figurative painting, 300, 347
film, 15–20, *15*, 39, 86, *216*
   architectural phenomenography through, 247–58
   art and, 240–1, 252
   composing sounds, 268–9
   computer technology in, 17, 228, 232–3, 235–7, 243
   criticism, 226
   design-research, 260–74
   essays, 17, 20, 217–29, *222–3*
   'freezing', 252
   mapping, *242*
   mass, 240
   montage methods, 17, 231, 237, 274, 364–5
   negatives, 228–9, 289
   photography, 182
   positives, 228
   process, 266–9, 272
   projecting on black, 269–70
   shoot preparation, *15, 216*
   space of, 231–45, *238–40*
   stills, 241, 252–4, *253–4*, 262–5, *264–6*, *288*
   techniques, 20
Film Art: An Introduction (Bordwell and Thompson), 240–1
filmmakers, 20

Film Style and Technology: History and Analysis (Salt), 241
filters, online, 151
Filton Airfield, Bristol, *323*, 326, 331
fine-art photography, 128
Fine Arts, 219, 221
'*Fine Line, A*' (2006 Mapping project), 280–2
Fischli, Peter, 16
Fisher, Jean, 59
'Flâneur Forever' (Hermès ad campaign), 224
flâneurie ('wandering aimlessly'), 224–5, 237
flat space, *239*
Flaxman, Gregory, 290
Fletcher, Banister, *A History of Architecture on the Comparative Method*, 40
'flow' forms, data, 113–14, *115*, 117, 119
focalization, 26–7
Forbidden City, China, 37
'forced route' (*parcours obligé*), 98
fore/middle/background space' *238*
Foster, Hal, 25
Foucault, Michel, 149–50, 282–3
   Deleuze on, 290, *294*
   Flaxman on, 290
   on incarceration, 327
   on 'norms' 321
   plans, 6, 38
   Discipline and Punish: The Birth of the Prison, 284
Frampton, Kenneth, 48
Frankfurt School, 225, 226
'freezing' film, 252
Freud, Sigmund, *The Mystic Writing Pad*, 386n1
Fried, Michael, 129
From Hieroglyphics to Isotype: A Visual Autobiography (Neurath), 7–8, 95–106, *97*, *103*, 111n10

419

From Naples to Capri (Iacovou), *263, 264,* 272

Frow, J. 319

G

game/lesson (Neurath), 96–8, *97*

game of the goose (board game), 47, 48, *48*

Gandy, Joseph, 22

Garcia, Matthew, 328

Gatlinburg, Tennessee, 134

Gell, Alfred, *Art and Agency,* 76, 94n6

General Psychopathology (Jaspers), 248

geography, 251

geo-localized data points, *114–16,* 116, *120*

geological map, *393*

geometry

anexact, 8, 119, *121,* 122

Euclidean, 120, 123n3–4

space and, *239*

structure, 83–5

types of, 118

Geron, Amit, 179–80, *180–1,* 182

Geschwindt, Tim, *60*

Gesetzmässigkeit im Gesellschaftsleben, statistische Studien, Die (Mayr), *102*

gest (theatrical technique), 270

gestural painting, 347–8

gestures, 270–1

Getting-out-of-Beichuan (Xiaodong), *325,* 326

Ghana, 279–84

Ghirri, Luigi, 49

Giada (participatory painting workshop), 309, *309*

Gibson, James, 76, 80, 81

Giedion, Sigfried, *Space, Time and Architecture,* 3, *9,* 10–11, 12, 14, *126*

gift-giving practices, 79–80

Gija painting, 324

Giovanni (participatory painting workshop), 312–13, *312*

Giroux, Alphonse, 395

GIS/ space data, 21

globalization, 6–7, 19, 58–9

glossolalia (speaking in tongues) (definition), 285

Godard, Jean-Luc, 17, 222, 223, 291

Le Mépris, 18

2 ou, 3 choses que je sais d'elle, 294–5

Weekend, 293

Goiris, Geert, 157n9

Goodwin, Marc, 11–12, 141–53, *143–4, 146–7*

Google Image Search, 14, 41, 206–8, *207–8,* 210

Google Streetview, 129

GPS-tracking smartphone apps, 116, *116,* 118

Graham, Dan, *Homes for America,* 148

graphein, 251, 252

Graphic Anthropology of Namdaemun Market, A (case study), 77, 83–9, *84–8, 90*

graphs, statistical, 105–6

-graphy (etymology), 251

Grey, Brendan, 75n4

grey-scale images, 144–5

grids

abstract, 336–7

perspective and, 142–8

technology and, 151–2

Griffith, D. W. 291

Gronert, Stefan, *Dusseldorf School of Photography,* 130

Grosfoguel, Ramón, 61

Grospierre, Nicolas, 13, 192, 194, *194,* 195–6

grounded theory, 250

grounding, literal, 5–6

INDEX

Gruyaert, Harry, 224
Guattari, Félix, 113, 119, 121, 122
Gursky, Andreas, 132
Guzmán-Verri, Valeria, 7–8, 9, 95–106

H
Habermas, Jürgen, 104
habitus, 7, 11, 76, 77–80, 89, 91
habitus (definition), 78, 128
Habraken, John, 65
Hadid, Zaha, 22, 348
  Planetary Architecture Two, 341–2
Haifa, Israel, 180, *181*, 182
Hälfte des Lebens (Hölderlin), 49
Hamilton, Richard, 340
hand drawing, 6, 7
Haraway, *Situated Knowledges: The Science
  Question in Feminism and the Privilege
  of Partial Perspective*, 3, 13, 196–7
Harbusch, Gregor, 10
Harrison, Charles, 69
Harvard Project on the City (Koolhaas
  et al), 282
Harvey, David, 321
Hatch, Mary Jo, 347–8
Haus der Farbe, Zurich, 24, 335, 339
Hays, K. Michael, 141
Heidegger, Martin, 7, 76, 82
Hejduk, John, *The Silent Witnesses*, 48,
  201
Henley Regatta, *20*, 298, 298–9, *298*
Hermès (fashion house), 224
Herzog, Werner, 138
'heterotopias' concept, 283
heuristics, visual (colour design), 335–50
Heydenreich, Ludwig H *203*, *209*
hieroglyphics, 101, 234
Hilbert, David, *Grundlagen der Geometrie*,
  123n3
Hillbrow, Johannesburg, 66–7

Himeno, Tomohiro, *Gradation with Multi-
  Layer*, *210*
Hip, Lance Ho, *70*
Hiroshima Projection (Wodiczko), 270–1
*History of Architecture on the Comparative
  Method, A* (Fletcher), 40
history of art photography, 228
Hofer, Candida, 129, 132
Hölderlin, Friedrich, *Hälfte des Lebens*, 49
Holl, Steven, 22
horizon diagram, *263*
Horn, Walter, 37
Ho, Stephanie, 'Point Henry', Dream Line,
  218–19, 222
Hotel Aukštaitija, Visaginas, *198*, 199
Hotel Visaginas project (Grospierre), 192,
  194, 195–6, 197, *198*
House in Jaffa, A (2015 exhibition), 185
Houses of Memory: The Texts of Analogy
  (Eisenman), 43
housing
  Certosa of Pavia, 53, *53*
  developments, 148, 158, 188–90, *189*, 329
  projects, 182, 185
'How to produce a Time Crystal' (2015
  workshop), *288*, *294*
Humphrey, Nicholas, 134
Hunt, John Dixon, 221
'Hushed Tonalities' (*Colour Strategies in
  Architecture* project), 343–4, *343*, 345
Husserl, Edmund, 'The origin of geometry',
  118

I
Iacovou, Popi, 18, 260–74, *263–6*
identity, perception and, 82
Ignalina Nuclear Power Station, Lithuania,
  189–90, 195
Iles, Chrissie, 271
Illuminance (Kawauchi), *131*, *133*, *135*

Illuminations (Benjamin), 225–6

Illuminists, 50

image content, *288*

Image Music Text (Barthes), 28

imaginary landscapes, 268

imagination, 6–7, 58–72

  drawing and, 8

  playful, 98–100

  projective, 91

  Rossi and, 44, 48

imaging, and writing, 208, 209–10

immanent analysis, 321

immigrants, 177, 180, 183, 184, 221

indexes

  abstracted, 349

  photography, 152, 180

  visual, 13, 24, 196, 336–8, *337–8*

  web-page, 207

individual shot, space of, 236

industrialization, 99, 220

inexact geometries, 118

'Informal settlement', 69–70, 75n10

information age, 104

information society, 104

infoscapes, 8, 105–6

Ingold, Tim, 7, 76, 77, 80–2, 91

insanity-sanity tension, 284–5

inscription, 251–2, 347, *399*

inscriptive practices, 76–92

Inspace Gallery, Edinburgh, *392, 395*

Institute for Architecture and Urban Studies
  (IAUS), 48

'intensive culture', 19

Interaction of Color (Albers), 340–1

interior-exterior aspect, 45–6, *45–6*

interiors, 144–5, *146*, 195–6, 199, 205, 260

interviews (data collection), 250, 270–1

intimacy (reading/drawing), 278

intimate space, *240*

'introduction' (design process methodology),
  70

inverted goggle experiment, 359

Investigations in the Professional Palette
  (McLachlan), 336, *337*

Invisible Cities (Calvino), 50

Ippolito, Jon, 323

I Quattro Libri dell' Architettura (*The*
  Four Books of Architecture) (Palladio),
  37

Ise Grand Shrine, Japan, 55–6

Islamic culture, 67

isometric projections, 35

Isotype project (Neurath), 96, *97*, 98–100,
  100, 103, 104–5, 110n3

Israel, 179–80, *180–1, 182–5*

Italy, 49, 391

Ivanovo detstvo (*Ivan's Childhood*)
  (Tarkovsky), 247, 252

Izenour, Steven, 16

J

Jabel Mukaber, Jerusalem, 176–7

Jaffa, Israel, 180, *181*, 185

Jansen, Win, 105

jardin en mouvement, Le (film), 219

Jaspers, Karl, *General Psychopathology*,
  248

Jay, Martin, 390

Jelloslice (Webb), *20*, 298–9, *298*

Jerusalem, 176–85, 180, *181*

'Jerusalem Stone', 176–7

Jewish neighbourhoods, 176–7, 179, 180,
  182–4

Jisr az-Zarka-Caesarea, Israel, 179, *180*,
  182, 185

Johannesburg, University of, 58–9, 61, 64,
  65, 75n4, 279

Jones, David, 17, 217–29

Joselit, David, 'On aggregators', 151

journals, 40, 41, 151–2, 155n2, 292

junkspace, 220, 221

'just painting', 317–31

INDEX

K

Kafka, Franz, 287, 292

kaleidoscopes, 395–6

Kaleidoscopic City, 25, 391–400, *392–5*, *397–9*

kaleidoscopic drawings, 387–400, *399*

Kawauchi, Rinko, 132–4
  photographer, 11, 136, 138
  Illuminance series, *131*, *133*, *135*
  Utatane, 132–3, *134*

Keeney, Gavin, 17, 217–29

Kentridge, William, 91

keratoconus eye (disorder), *354*, *355*

Klee, Paul, 347

Knapkiewicz, Kaschka, 345, *346*

knotting, 78

knowing, ways of, 76

Koeck, Richard, *Cine-Scapes: Cinematic Spaces in Architecture and Cities*, 244

Konrad, Aglaia, 12, 158, *160–75*

Koolhaas, Rem, 220, 221, 279, 282
  Delirious New York, 342

Krauss, Rosalind, 26, 360, 364

Kress, Gunther, 345, 347

Krivý, Maros, 123n1

Kuleshov, Lev, 236

Kulper, Perry, David's Island Strategic Plot Drawing, 3, 4–5, *4*, 8, 21, 34, *34*

Küchler, Suzanne, 78

Kwinter, Sanford, *Architectures of Time*, 287, 292

Kyriazopoulos-Berinde, Ruxandra *see* Berinde, Ruxandra Kyriazopoulos-

L

'la belle nature', 219

labelling, types of, 254, *254*

Lagos, Nigeria, 282

Lambert, H. B., Temple of Mithras, London, *325*

landscape architecture, 17, 219–29

'Landscape Narrating & Meaning' (2014 Deakin University seminar), 222

'Laocoön' (eisenstein), 237

La production de l'espace (*The Production of Space*) (Lefebvre), 226, 321

Lash, Scott, 19

Las Vegas, 15–16, *15*, 147–8, *216*

Las Vegas Electric (video), 16

layering, gradation and, *210*

LCD screens, 356, 357

Learning from Las Vegas (LLV) studio, 16

Learning from Las Vegas (Venturi, Scott Brown and Izenour), 15, 147–8, 216

Le Corbusier, 35, 40, 232, 243, 342
  'Claviers de Couleur' 336

Leder, Drew, 354, 359

Lefebvre, Henri, *La production de l'espace*, 6, 23, 38, 226, 318, 321

Le Mépris (*Contempt*) (Godard), 18, 260

Le Mont Analogue (*Mount Analogue*) (Daumal), 53

lesson/game (Neurath), 96–8, *97*

Leyda, Jay, *Eisenstein at Work*, 234

Libera, Adalberto, 260–1

life analogy, 43

light and space, *210*

light reflection, 180

Liguori, Saint'Alfonso de, *Apparecchio alla morte*, 56

limbic field, 381

Limkilde, Marie, *288*

Lindbergh, Charles, 135–6

Lindbergh, Peter, 'Couture's Glorious Excess' (*Vogue*), 224

line drawings, 40, 80, 267–8, 272, 345

line, the authority of the, 101–4, *102–3*

linguistic analysis, of photographs, 193–5

'l'instant decisif', 130–1

literary criticism, 226

Lithuania, 13

lived space, 247–8

'Living Space'(1998 exhibition), 180

localism, 58–9

Local series exhibitions, 184–5

Lod-Pardes-Snir, Israel, 179, *180*

Lokko, Lesley, 19, 276–85, *281*

'Looking at photographs' (Burgin), 193

'Loop' (Limkilde and Bohr), *288*

Los Angeles, 16

Lucas, Ray, 7, 9, 12, 76–92, *84–8, 90*

Lyme Regis, Dorset, *317*, 330–1, *330,*
331

Lynn, Greg, 118

M

McHarg, Ian, 221

Machine in the Garden: Technology and the
Pastoral Ideal, The (Marx), 220, 227

machinic vision, 364–7

Mackintosh, Rennie, 327

McLachlan, Fiona, 23–4, 26, 335–50

Madejska, Agata, 157n9

madness, 282, 284–5

maenad, dancing, *206*, 207, 208

magazines, 35, 40, 151

Malanggan (wooden carving), 78

Malatesta, Sigismondo Pandolfo, 204

Malevich, Kasimir, 'Tektoniks' 342

Manovich, Lev, 17, 235, 237, 243
  Language of New Media, 232–3
  Software Studies Initiative, 232
  Visualising Vertov, 241

Man with a Movie Camera (Vertov), 364–5

mapping projects, 280–5

'mapping the film' (Turner), *242*

maps, 25, 38, 99, 375–6, *377, 393*

maps, statistical, 105

Marcus (participatory painting workshop),
  305, 306

Marker, Chris, 17, 222, 223

marketplace, agency matrix of, 85–6, *86*

markets, 77, 83–9, *84–8*, 280

mark-making approach, 304

Mark (participatory painting workshop),
  309, *309*

Marozas, Povilas, 13, 188–99, *189, 198*

Marton, Ference, 249

Marx, Karl, 320

Marx, Leo, *The Machine in the Garden:*
  Technology and the Pastoral Ideal, 220,
  226, 227

mass media, 231, 240, 244

'masterplan' (definition), 309

Mauro (participatory painting workshop),
  307, 308, *308*

Mauss, Marcel, 80

Maxwele, Chumani, 58–9

Mayr, Georg von, *Die Gesetzmässigkeit im*
  Gesellschaftsleben, statistische Studien,
  102

Mbembe, Achille, 278

mechanosphere, 121

medium-content exchange, 24–5

Mehretu, Julie, 300

Meldgaard, Morten, 19, 287–95

memory, role of
  Bergson on, 388
  habitus and, 79
  home and, 17–18
  images and, 28
  questions of, 6
  recalling, 55
  Rossi and, 43, 45
  social and cultural, 323

Merian map of Paris, 391

Merleau-Ponty, Maurice
  bodily vision, 24, 354
  on Cézanne, 134
  chiasm, 289
  perception, 80, 81

INDEX

The Phenomenology of Perception, 358–9, 361

metamorphic compositions, 45, 50–1

meta-photography, 228

'methodological' reflexivity, 69

methodologies, visual, 1

metric measure (definition), 123n3

Michaud, Philippe-Alain, 205

Milan, 51, *51*

Ming and Monita (participatory painting workshop), 313–14, *313*

Miralles, Enric, 348

mirrors, use of, *356*

Mirror (visual device), 396, *399*

mise-en-scène, 238, 252

Misrach, Richard, 132

Mississippi, USA 135–7

Mitchell, W. J. T., *Picture Theory*, 27–8

mixed media, 20–6, 262, 356
  animation, 261–2, 268, 269–70, 271, 272

Mlicka, Agnieszka, 22–3, 25, 300–15, *304–5, 307–10, 312–13,* 328

mnemonic collage, 202–3, 207

mobile technology, 374

models, 3D 267

modern art, 67–8

Modernism, 7–8, 10–11, 48, 225

modernity, matters of, 388–90

modernization, 11, 89, 220

Modern Man in the Making (Isotype project), *100*

Modern Movement, 7–8, 37, 44, 48

Modi'in-Maccabim-Re'ut, Israel, 180, *181*

Moholy-Nagy, László, 10

Mokrzycka, Olga, *194*, 195

monastic life, 36, *36, 56*

Moneo, Rafael, 48

monocular images, 361, 365

'Montage and architecture' (Eisenstein), 232, 234–5, 242–3, 245

montage methods
  film, 17, 231, 237, 274, 364–5
  Godard on, 291
  photography, 11

montage/visual, as a new language for research, 233–5

Morris, Errol, 153

Morrison, Lester B. 137

Morris, Rosalind C. 91

Mosquera, Gerardo, *59*

motifs, 14, 78, 136, 201, 204–5

Moustakas, Clark, 344

movement/dance, 91, *206, 207, 208, 382–3*

Moving Israel's Coastal Highway (2010 exhibition), 185

Muller, Johan, 72

multi-dimensional architecture, 370–85

multimedia installations, 353–68

multi-modality, 62–3

Munsell, Albert H. 22

Murray, Martin, 64

Mutations (Koolhaas et al), 282

Mystic Writing Pad, The (Freud), 386n1

N

Nabian, Nashid, 105

Namdaemun Market, Seoul, 77, 83–9, *84–8, 90*

Nancy, Jean-Kuc, *The Pleasure of Drawing*, 81

Narcissus (Caravaggio), 269

Narrative Architecture (Coates), 327

narrative structure, 242

National Museum of Scotland, Edinburgh, 394, *397*

Nature morte (2015 exhibition), 228–9

negatives (film), 228–9, 289

'Negatives' ('Photograms and Negatives'), 228

425

Negev, Israel, 180, *181*
Nemeth, Elisabeth, 100
Neurath, Otto, *From Hieroglyphics to Isotype: A Visual Autobiography*, 7–8, 95–106, *97, 103*, 111n10
'New Topographics' (1972 exhibition), 131
New Topographics (Salvesen), 130
Niagara Falls, 137
Nigeria, 282
non-discursive image, 224–6
Nostalghia (Tarkovsky), 247, 252, *253*
novel (definition), 278

O

Observatory (visual device), 396, *399*
October magazine, 151
offices, 37–8
Offret (The Sacrifice) (Tarkovsky), 247, 252, *253*
oil painting, *20, 21*
Old Glory (Raban), 140n2
Old Shoe Factory, Clifton, Bristol, 319
Olmsted, Frederick Law, 225
OMA (Office for Metropolitan Architecture), 342
Ong, Walter, 91
online aggregates, 151
online image-atlas, 14, 41, 206–8, *207*, 210
On Photography (Sontag), 129
'open game' (*jeu ouvert*), 98
Open State, Japan, *382*
Oppositions Book Series, 48
optical
  custom-made devices, 353–68
  illusions/experiments, 359, *384*
  theory, 67
optics, 24
Oratorio di San Bernardino, Perugia, 205

Ordnance Survey (OS), 38, 42n3
Other, Annabel, 319
'other', 'self' and, 69
'Out of Field' 19, 292, *293*
  projects, 19, *288*
Ozenfant, Amedée, 336

P

Padenie dinastii Romanovykh (*The Fall of the Romanov Dynasty*) (Shub), 237
paganism, 206
painting, 20–4
  Aboriginal process, 324
  abstract, 300, *301*
  acrylic, 339
  as architectural research, 325–7
  en plein-air, 23, 318, 322–3
  figurative, 300, 347
  gestural, 347–8
  'just painting' 317–31
  oil, *20, 21, 298*
  'paint-in' group workshops, 319, 320, 334
  participatory, 300–15
  peinture sur le motif, 318
  performative, 23, 317–31
  spatial, 341–4
  on water, 329–30
  watercolour, 49, 307–8, 325–9, *325–6, 330,* 336
'paint-in' group workshops, 319, 320, 334
Palestinian neighbourhoods, 176–7, 182, 185
Palladio, Andrea, *I Quattro Libri dell' Architettura*, 37
Pallasmaa, Juhani, 28
panopticon, 149, 150
panoramic images, 145, *146–7*
Papua New Guinea, 78
parallelism (definition), 123n3
paratactic aggregates, 148

INDEX

Pardo, Alona, 127
Paredes Maldonado, Miguel, 8, 9, 112–22, *114–17, 120–1*
Parikka, Jussi, 121
Paris, 391
parks, 225
Parr, Martin, *The Photobook: A History*, 132–3
patents, 395–6
Pattern Language, A (Alexander et al), 148
peinture sur le motif (painting on the ground), 318
Peirce, Charles Sanders, 180
perception
  being as, 81–3
  drawing as, 80–1
  environmental, 76, 116
  limited, 387–8
  modes of, 232, 373, 388
  notation matrix, *381*
  sensory, 80–1, 347, 376
PerceptionLab (Germany), 374, *374–5*
performative
  approaches, 1, 13
  painting, 23, 317–31
  practices, 22, 27, 278
  research, 18
Performing Casa Malaparte (Iacovou), 262–74
  'On the Boat', *264*
  'Raining Windows', *264*, 268
  'Salon', *265*, 268
  'T-Corridor', *266*
Perniola, Mario, 104
Perry, Ted, 234
perspective, 67–8, *68*, 75n9, 142–8, *238*
Pevsner, Nikolaus, 202
Phaidon Atlas of Contemporary World Architecture, 144–5, 156n4

phenomenography, 17–18
  categories, 255–6, *256*
  versus phenomenology, 248–51, *250*
  phenomenon+graphein, 251–2
  reclaiming, 252–4
  through film, 247–58
phenomenology, 24, 80–1, 134
Phenomenology of Perception, The (Merleau-Ponty), 358–9, 361
phenomenology versus phenomenography, 248–51, *250*
phenomenon (etymology), 252
Philosophical Enquiry into the Origin of Our Ideas of the Sublime and Beautiful, A (Burke), 222
philosophy, 76, 115, 131, 148, 359, 396
Photobook: A History, The (Badger and Parr), 132–3
'Photograms and Negatives' series (2015), 228
Photographer's Eye, The (Szarkowski), 129
Photographic Architecture in the Twentieth Century (Zimmerman), 127–8
'Photographic practice and art theory' (Burgin), 192–3
photographies journal, 151–2
photography, 9–14
  aerial, 75n9, 282, 388
  and architecture's discursive space, 141–53
  art and, 128, 228
  Bergson on, 289
  Blundell Jones on, 38–9
  colour and, 142–5
  commercial, 11–12, 142–3, *143–4*, 152, 195–6
  computer technology in, 151
  constructed scene, 132
  differentiating, 91
  documentary, 128, 130, 150
  equipment, 130, 131, 133
  film, 182

indexes, 152, 180

linguistic analysis, 193–5

meta-, 228

montage methods, 228

Namdaemun Market, Seoul, 83

photo development, 290

Pont Transbordeur, *9*

source, *90*

still-life, 228–9

street, 130

and thinking about architecture, 127–38

weather conditions and, 143, 146, 156n4

wondrous moment, 132

'Photography, phantasy, function' (Burgin), 193

photorealistic representations, 269–70

pictograms, Isotype, 99–100, *100*, 104, 110n1

pictorial argumentation, 14, 202–3

Picture Theory (Mitchell), 27–8

Pieterse, Edgar, 64, 278

Pifferer, J. F., *48*

Pink, Sarah, *Doing Visual Ethnography* and *Doing Sensory Ethnography*, 26, 179

'Piranesi or the flux of form' (Eisenstein), 232, 234–5

Pisciella, Susanna, 6, 9, 43–56, *51–2*

Pisters, Patricia, 289

Planck, Max, *Planck Constant*, 54, 55

plane, image, 234–5

Planetary Architecture Two (Hadid), 341–2

plans/planning

by hand, 6, 7

handling, 35–41

and sections, 35, 38, 39, 40

site, *394–5*

urban, 244

plants, still-life photography, 228–9

plasmatic image, 287–95

plasticity, possibilities of, 309–11

playful agencements, 98–101, 110n4

playing, with signs, 98

Pleasure of Drawing, The (Nancy), 81

poetical document, 273

poetry, 237, 273

'Point Henry', Dream Line (Ho), *218–19*, 222

point of view (POV), 265, 268, 272, 364, 380, 386n2

politics, displaying, 184–5

Politics of Just Painting: Engagement and Encounter in the Art of The East Kimberley, The (Skerrit), 324

'polyphonic seeing' 347

Pont Transbordeur, Marseille, *9*, *126*

'popular preconscious' 196

portraits, building, 270–4, 273, 340–1, *341*, 349

Portraits in the Presence of Marina Abramović (Anelli), 271

portraiture, 18, 136, 271

positives (film), 228

postcard view, *393*

post-industrial landscape, 17, 227

Po Valley, Italy, 49

power relationships, unequal, 308–9

Powers of Ten (film), 16

practice-based methods, 1–2

Praia, Cabo Verde, 279

preconscious, popular, 196

preparation, film shoot, *15*, *216*

Princen, Bas, 157n9

Privacy and Publicity: Modern Architecture as Mass Media (Colomina), 244

Probst, Barbara, 157n9

process philosophy, 148

production

mode of, 13, 115, 347, 350

transactions in, 339–40

production of space, 321

INDEX

projecting on black (filmic process), 269–70

projections, 93n5

protests, 60, *60*, 276, 286n1

pseudo-objective practices, 227

psychoanalytic theory, 192, 193

psychogeography, and the 'film essay' 217–29

Ptlolemy, *Cosmographia*, 104

public spaces, 63, 330–1

'Public space | Spaces of publics' project, 67, 75n8

Pugin, Augustus, 22, 35

punishment, 327

Pure Data, 382, *382*, 383

Q

qualitative methodological strategies, 1, 322

R

Raban, Jonathan, *Old Glory*, 140n2

racialization, 64

Raktai J Lietuvos miestus (*Keys to the Cities of Lithuania*) (Česonis), 192

Ramla, Israel, 179, *180*, 183

Raspberry Pi micro-computers, 356, 357

readings, multiple (painting), 347–9

'real space' 118

redevelopment, 318–19, 321, 323, 325

Redstone, Elias, 127, 152

Reed, David, 301

reflection, 180, 269

reflexivity, 68–71

regeneration, 318

regularity

  discursive, 149–50

  and repetition, 55, 141, 146–7, 148, 152–3

Reiach & Hall Architects, Edinburgh, *343*, 345

relays, information, 117–22, *117*

reliefs, sculpted, 205

Renaissance, European, 67, 201–12, 284

Rencontres Photography Festival, 148

repetition

  element, 51

  regularity and, 55, 141, 146–7, 148, 152–3

representation, 347

revealing enquiry, 314–15

Reyner Banham Loves Los Angeles (film), 16

Rhodes, Cecil John, 58–9, *59*, 276

Richter, Gerhard, 336

Rickard, Doug, 129

Rinehart, Richard, 323

risk-taking, conceptual, 5

rituality

  Bourdieu and, 79

  Rossi and, 45, 50, 55–6

rivers, pictorial images of, 140n2

Robbins, Rev Royal, *The World Displayed*, 46

Robinson, Prudence, 105

robotic drawing environment, 116, 119

Rogoff, Irit, 13, 196, 197

Rohe, Mies van der, 127, 130

Roman Baths, Bath, 374, *374–6*

Romanticism, 227

Roös, Phillip B., 221

Rose, Gillian, *Visual Methodologies*, 1, 24, 26, 321, 344–5

Rosselli, Francesco, 'View with a Chain' 391

Rossi, Aldo

  Le distanze invisibili, 55–6

  A Scientific Autobiography, 6, 43–56, *44*

Royal Observatory, Edinburgh, 394, 396

Rubenstein, Daniel, 151–2

Ruff, Thomas, 228

'rule of thirds', 380

Runge, Philipp Otto, 'Farbenkugel', 335

Ruscha, Ed, 16
Russia, 232

S
St Gall monastery, 5, 35–6, *36*
Saint-Martin, Fernande, 143
Salm, Frank van der, 157n9
Salt, Barry, 241, 243
Salvesen, Britt, *New Topographics*, 130
San Carlone (statue), *45*, 46, 47
Sanders, Elizabeth, 311, 312
Sandsby, Thomas, 327
sanity-insanity tension, 284–5
San Juan de la Cruz, *Climb of Mount Carmelo*, 54, *54*
Sansi, Roger, 80
Savinio, Alberto, *The Annunciation*, 268, 275n1
Schafer, R. Murray, 381
Scharoun, Hans, 39, *341*
scholarship and education, architectural, 201–12, 276–85
Schulunke, K. 319
Schulz, Josef, 157n9
Scientific Autobiography, A (Rossi), 6, 43–56, *44*
Scotland, 348
Scott Brown, Denise, 3, 15–16, 148, 216
Scott, George Gilbert, 327
script, pictorial, 208, *209*, 233–4
sculpture, *45*, 78, 205, 301
Sea Mills, Bristol, 327
'Second Layer' visualization, *346*
section, plan and, 35, 38, 39, 40
sections, 83, *85*, 86
seeing, experiences of, 95, 278–9
see, learning to, 95–106
self-analysis, crisis and, 226–8
'self' and 'other', 69
semiotic theory, 180, 192–5

Sennett, Richard, 71
SenseAble City Lab (MIT), 105, 113
sensitivity, reflexivity and, 69
sensors, 356, 382
sensory perception, 80–1, 347, 376
Separation (2005 exhibition), 12–13, 178–85, *180–1*
separation wall, Jerusalem, 13, 176–85
Sergei Eisenstein: A Biography (Bulgakowa), 233
shadows, 101
shopping, 280, 282
Shore, Stephen, *The Nature of Photographs*, 11, 129
Shoulder to Shoulder (McLachlan), 338, *338*
Shub, Esfir, *Padenie dinastii Romanovykh (The Fall of the Romanov Dynasty)*, 237
Sieyès, Abbé, 219–20
silent films, 240
Silent Witnesses, The (Hejduk), 201
silhouettes, 101
Siman-Tov, Orit, 179–80, *180–1*, 182, 183
Simondon, Gilbert, 8, 116, 117, 119
Simone, AbdouMaliq, 278
Singapore, 220
site-responsive stimuli, 371
siting/surfacing, 63, 270, 344–7
Situated Knowledges: The Science Question in Feminism and the Privilege of Partial Perspective (Haraway), 196–7
Situational Analysis (Clarke), 378–9
Situationism, 224
Six Memos for the Next Millennium (Calvino), 50
Skerrit, Henry F., *The Politics of Just Painting: Engagement and Encounter in the Art of The East Kimberley*, 324
sky map, *393*
Sleeping by the Mississippi (Soth), 135, *136–7*
Smart Cities, 112–14, 121

INDEX

'smartness', 113, 121
Soane, John, 22
social
  analysis, 68–9
  memory, 323
  power relations, 7
  science, 14
  separation, 13
  theories, 61
'sociological reflexivity', 7
Socratous, Savvas, *356*
Software Studies Initiative (website), 235
Solyaris (*Solaris*) (Tarkovsky), 247, 252
somatic field, 381
Sonnemann, Ulrich, 18, 248–9
Sontag, Susan, *On Photography*, 129
Sorkin, Michael, 155n2
Soth, Alec, 11, 132, 134, 135–8, *136–7*
  Broken Manual, *137*, 138
  The Last Days of W, 137–8
  Sleeping by the Mississippi, 135, *136–7*
sound composition, 268–9
sound-dance collaboration, *383*
South Africa, 19, 58–67, 72, 276–9, 285
space and light, *210*
'Space framed – Photography and the human
  habitat' (UCD Architecture module),
  128–30, 140n1
space, in a frame, 145–6, 148
space negotiation (workshops), 302–15,
  303, *304–5*, *307–10*, *312–13*
space, of individual shot, 236
spaces of publics, 63–5, *65*
Space, Time and Architecture (Giedion),
  10–11, *126*
spatial
  apparatus, 373–80
  awareness, 371
  change, 302–15, *303–5*, *307–10*, *312–13*
  discourses, 60

intelligence, 372
interpretation, 183–4
negotiation, 300–15
painting, 341–4
-related disciplines, 71–2
separation, 13, 179–85, *180–1*
shot, 241, 242
turn, 66
spatiality
  of confinement, 284–5
  de Certeau, 89
  territory and, 67
spatio-sensory amplification (definition),
  371
Speaking in Tongues (Lokko), 276, 284–5
Spiller, Neil, 372
Spintex Road, Accra, 279–84, *281*
spirituality, 62
Stachka (*The Strike*) (Eisenstein), 236, 240
Stadler, Hilar, 16
Stalker (Tarkovsky), 247, 252, 293
stamp prints, postage, *317*, 331
Stanczak, Gregory, 338, 348
Stappers, Pieter, 311, 312
Staroye i Novoye (*The Old and the New*)
  (Eisenstein), 232
State Library, Berlin, 39, *341*
statues, *45*
stereoscopes, Wheatstone, 24, *356*, 362, 364
stereoscopic vision, digitally stitching,
  353–68
Sternfeld, Joel, *American Prospects*, 134
Stierli, Martino, 16, 216
still-life photography, 228–9
stills
  film, 241, 252–4, *253–4*, *262–5*, *264–6*, *288*
  video, *218–19*, 262, *304–5*, *307–10*, *312–13*
Stirling, James, 35
stitching, digital (stereoscopic vision),
  353–68

Stockholder, Jessica, 301
Stone Town, Zanzibar, 279
Stratton, George M. 354, 359
street photography, 130
'structures' (design process methodology),
  70, 78
Struth, Thomas, 129, 132
students, 15–16, 58–9, 61–5, 67, 69–70, 72,
  216
subconsciousness, 270, 344–5, 386n1
'substantive' reflexivity, 69
Sullivan, Graeme, 339, 349
surfacing/siting, 63
Surrealism, 224, 268, 273
swatches, colour, 24, 336, 339, 340, 349
Sykes, Krista, 141
syntax diagrams, *87*
Szarkowski, John, *The Photographer's Eye*,
  11, 129

T
Tafuri, Manfredo, 48
Tagg, John, 142
  The Burden of Representation, 150
  The Disciplinary Frame, 149
taking position/taking sides, *95*
Talamona, Marida, *Casa Malaparte*, 260–1
Tamari, Yuval, 183
Tarkovsky, Andrei, 18, 247–8, 252–4, 293
taxation, 283
'technical ensemble' 116–22
'technical ensemble' (definition), 116, *117*
Techniques of the Observer (Crary), 361–2, 363
technologies, digital, 19, 21–4, 221
technology, and grids, 151–2
'Tektoniks' (Malevich), 342
Telescope (visual device), 396, *397*
Tema, Ghana, 280
Tempio Malatestiano, Rimini, 204–6, *204,*
  206–7

Temple of Mithras, London (Lambert), *325,*
  331
temporal space, 270
Ten Gazes from Jaffa (2009 exhibition), 185
Terrain (visual device), 396, *398*
'territorialized strata', 123n1
territory, 66–7, *66*, 75n7
testimonies, 2
textures, field/land, *103*
Thanatos, 223
The Last Days of W (Soth), 137–8
The Machine in the Garden: Technology and
    the Pastoral Ideal (Marx), 220
Themistokleous, George, 24, 26, 353–68,
    354, 356–8, 360, 362–3, 366
Theory, Society & Culture (journal), 292
Therapontos, Nasia, 268–9
Thinking Photography (Burgin), 192
Third Estate, 219–20
Third Landscape, 219–22
thirds, rule of, 380
Thompson, Kristen, *Film Art: An*
    Introduction, 240–1
Thoreau, Henry David, *Walden*, 227
thought-image (*Denkbild*), 226
three-dimensionality, 267, 335, 349, 376,
  380, 396
Till, Jeremy, 23, 300–1, 302, 305, 314
time and space, bodily vision in, 353–68
'Time crystal' (2015 workshop), *288, 294*
time interval (machinic vision), 364–7
time, passing of, 119
Toffa, Tariq, 6–7, 9, 58–72, *59*
Tolia-Kelly, Divya, 26
top-down practices, 8, 113, 113–15, 123n2
topography, 327
topology, 292–3, 381
Touch of Evil, A (film), 39
Towards a New Architecture (Eisenstein),
  243

432

INDEX

Towards a Theory of Montage (Eisenstein), 234, 236

Traité des couleurs servant à la peinture à l'eau (Boogert), 336

transactions in production, 339–40

transcripts (data collection), 250

transforming enquiry, 314–15

trans-scripts, 395–400, 397–9

'Trans-Vertovian' (definition), 291

transvisuality, 19, 289–91

travel, 231

Travelling Concepts in the Humanities (Bal), 27

trigger frame sequence, *384*

Trojan Horse, 46, *46*, 47

Tsivian, Yuri, 241

Tughendhat House, Czech Republic, 127

Turner, Niek, 17, 231–45, *236*, *238–40*, *242*

2 ou 3 choses que je sais d'elle (*Two or Three Things I Know about Her*) (Godard), 294–5

two-dimensionality, 234–5, 349

typologies, 50, 66, 129, 179–80, 338

U

ubuntu ('humanity'), *62*

UJ_Unit2: Architecture and Agency (experimental design-research studio), 65, *65*, 75n6

unconsciousness, 79, 91, 193, 223, 268, 389

unequal power relationships, 308–9

unfamiliar space, *239*

unfamiliar visualization method, 304–9

universities, 286n1

urban
data-based drawing, 112–22, *114–16*
mapping flows, 113, *114–16*, 119
planning, 244
rural–urban tensions, 61, 74–5n3
space, 64

urbanization, 12, 23, 43, 66, 158, 221

urgent imagination, testing techniques of, 58–72

V

'vague conception', 28

Vallega, Alejandro A., 347

value analysis, 319–20

van Eck, Caroline, 202

van Leeuwen, Theo, 345, 347

Vaux, Calvert, 225

Vection Builder (audio-visual installation), 374

Venice Architecture Biennale (2006), 105

Venturi, Robert, *Learning from Las Vegas*, 16, 147–8

'Vertical Montage', (Eisenstein), 234

Vertov, Dziga, *Man with a Movie Camera*, 235, 364–5

Vesely, Dalibor, *Architecture in the Age of Divided Representation*, 266, 272

video
loop, 292
recording, 16, 83, 250, 251, 281–4
stills, *218–19*, 262, *304–5*, *307–10*, *312–13*
walk-through, 39

Vidler, Anthony, *Warped Space*, 233

Vienna Circle, 110n8

Vieth-Müller diagram, 380

View from the Road, The (film), 15, 216

'View with a Chain' (Rosselli), 391

Viollet-le-Duc, Eugène, *Dictionnaire Raisonné de l'architecture Française du XI au XVI Siècle*, 5, 36

Virtual Reality (VR), 21, 367

virtual reconstructions, 39–40

Visaginas, Lithuania, 188–99, *189*

vision, embodiment of, 196–7

visions, 387–8, 395–400, *397–9*

433

visual
  agency, 314–15
  communication, 22, 96, 103
  consciousness, 8, 105, 106
  culture, 26–9, 201
  discourse, 317–31
  education, 95–6, 101, 201, 210
  field, 380
  indexes, 13, 24, 196, 336–8, *337–8*
  language, 233–5, 243, 270–1
  mapping, 241
  media, 3
  practice, 2–3, 115, 354–5
  rules of engagement, 390–1
  and spatial interpretation, 183–4
  specificities, 391–5
  technology, 353–68
  theory, 67
Visualising Vertov (Manovich), 241
visuality (definition), 25
visualization
  children and, 105
  of information, 105
  spatial painting, 341–4
  three-dimensional, 349
  unfamiliar method, 304–9, *304–5*, *307–9*
Visual Methodologies (Rose), 1
Viva Las Vegas (film), 16
vocabulary, architectural, 279
Vogue, 224
'voicing', 61–2, *62*
'Volume Image', 291
Voynow, Zina, *Eisenstein at Work*, 234
Voysey, C.F.A, 327
Vriesendorp, Madelon, 22, 342

W
Walden (Thoreau), 227
wallpaper, 336
Warburg, Aby, *Bilderatlas Mnemosyne*, 14,
  201–12, *204*, *206*

Warped Space (Vidler), 233
watercolour, painting with, 49, 307–8,
  325–9, *325–6*, *330*, 336
water, painting on, 329–30
wave-form, 376
Ways of Seeing (Berger), 201
weather conditions, photography and, 143,
  146, 156n4
Webb, Michael, *Jelloslice*, 3, 20–1, *20*, 25–6,
  298–9, *298*
Weekend (Godard), 293
Welles, Orson, 39
Wenders, Wim, 39
West Africa, 280–5
'What Is the Third Estate?' (Sieyès),
  219–20
Wheatstone, Sir Charles, 24, 356
Wheatstone stereoscope, 356, *356*, 362,
  364
Whitehead, Alfred North, 148
Wiener Methode der Bildstatistik (Neurath
  project), 96
Wigley, Mark, 142
Wikipedia, 41
Winckelmann, Johann Joachim, 203
Winogrand, Garry, 131
Wittkower, Rudolf, *Architectural Principles
  in the Age of Humanism*, 202
Wodiczko, Krzysztof, *Hiroshima Projection*,
  270–1
Wölfflin, Heinrich, 10
Wolf, Michael, 129, 157n9, 220, 221
wondrous moment photography, 132
World Architecture News (website), 40
World Cup (2006), 105–6
World Displayed, The (Robbins), 46
writing
  academic skills, 209–11
  consciousness and, 386n1
  fiction and, 278
  and imaging, 208, 209–10

INDEX

learning to write, 91
of phenomena, 251–2
as a tool, 386n1

X

Xiaodong, Liu, Getting-out-of-Beichuan, 326, *326*

Y

Yacobi, Haim, 176–85
Yanow, Dvora, 347–8
Yen, Yuehping, 91

'Yermolova' (Eisenstein), 234–5
Young, Michael, 72
Yuri Tsivian (website), 241

Z

Zenghelis, Zoe, 342
Zerkalo (*Mirror*) (Tarkovsky), 247, 252, *253*
Zimmerman, Claire, *Photographic Architecture in the Twentieth Century*, 127–8
'the Zone', 293
Zurich, 24, 335, 339, 345